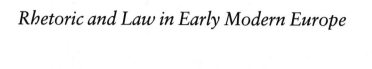

Rhetoric and Law in Early Modern Europe

EDITED BY VICTORIA KAHN
AND LORNA HUTSON

Rhetoric and Law
in Early Modern
Europe

Yale University Press
New Haven/London

Set in Sabon type by Keystone Typesetting, Inc.
Printed in the United States of America.

Library of Congress Cataloging-in-Publication Data
Rhetoric and law in early modern Europe / edited by Victoria Kahn and
Lorna Hutson.
    p. cm.
  Includes index.
  ISBN 0-300-08485-4 (cloth)
    1. Law — Europe — Language — History.   2. Law — Europe — Methodology —
History.   3. Rhetoric — Europe — History.   4. Forensic oratory — History.
I. Kahn, Victoria Ann.   II. Hutson, Lorna.
KJC408 .R48 2001
808'.06634 — dc21   00-043770

A catalogue record for this book is available from the British Library.

The paper in this book meets the guidelines for permanence and durability of the
Committee on Production Guidelines for Book Longevity of the Council on
Library Resources.

10 9 8 7 6 5 4 3 2 1

Contents

List of Contributors

KATHY EDEN is Mark Van Doren Professor of Humanities at Columbia University and author of *Poetic and Legal Fiction in the Aristotelian Tradition* (Princeton, 1986) and *Hermeneutics and the Rhetorical Tradition: Chapters in the Ancient Legacy and Its Humanist Reception* (New Haven, 1994).

CARLA FRECCERO is professor of literature at the University of California, Santa Cruz. She is the author of *Father Figures: Genealogy and Narrative Structure in Rabelais* (Ithaca, 1991) and *Popular Culture: An Introduction* (New York, 1999), and coeditor with Louise Fradenburg of *Premodern Sexualities* (New York, 1995).

PETER GOODRICH is Corporation of London Professor of Law, Birkbeck College, University of London, and professor of law, Cardozo Law School (New York). His recent works include *Oedipus Lex: Psychoanalysis, History, Law* (Berkeley, 1995), *Law in the Courts of Love: Literature and Other Minor Jurisprudences* (London, 1996), and *Law and the Unconscious* (London, 1998). His current work is in the form of a treatise on the history of women's courts.

LORNA HUTSON is professor of English at the University of California, Berkeley. She is the author of *Thomas Nashe in Context* (Oxford, 1989) and *The Usurer's Daughter* (London, 1994) and the editor of *Ben Jonson: Volpone and Other Plays* (London, 1998) and *Feminism and Renaissance Studies* (Oxford, 1999). She is currently working on a study of law, rhetoric, and gender in early modern England.

CONSTANCE JORDAN is the author of *Renaissance Feminism: Literary Texts and Political Models* (Ithaca, 1990) and *Shakespeare's Monarchies: Ruler and Subject in the Romances* (Ithaca, 1997) and a coeditor of *The Longman Anthology of British Literature* (London, 1998). Her current scholarship focuses on the literary representation of property in early modern England and its American colonies.

VICTORIA KAHN is professor of rhetoric and comparative literature at the University of California, Berkeley. She is the author of *Rhetoric, Prudence, and Skepticism in the Renaissance* (Ithaca, 1985) and *Machiavellian Rhetoric: From the Counter-Reformation to Milton* (Princeton, 1994), and coeditor of *Machiavelli and the Discourse of Literature* (Ithaca, 1993).

JANE O. NEWMAN is professor of comparative literature at the University of California, Irvine. The author of *Pastoral Conventions* (Baltimore, 1990) and *The Intervention of Philology* (Chapel Hill, 2000), she has also written articles on feminist theory and on the historiography, political theory, and literary and material cultures of early modern Central Europe. Her new project is entitled "Recentering Europe: Genealogies and Counter-Genealogies of Renaissance and Early Modern Studies, 1860 to 1989."

ANNABEL PATTERSON is the Karl Young Professor of English at Yale University. Her most recent books are *Early Modern Liberalism* (Cambridge, 1997) and *Andrew Marvell: The Writer in Public Life* (London, 2000). She is currently editor-in-chief for the Yale edition of the prose works of Andrew Marvell.

DAVID HARRIS SACKS, professor of history and the humanities at Reed College, is the author of *The Widening Gate: Bristol and the Atlantic Economy, 1450–1700* (Berkeley, 1991) and *Trade, Society, and Politics in Bristol, 1500–1640* (New York, 1985) and coeditor with Donald Kelley of *The Historical Imagination in Early Modern Britain: History, Rhetoric, and Fiction, 1500–1800* (New York, 1997). At present he is completing a book on the language and culture of liberty in sixteenth- and seventeenth-century England.

BARBARA J. SHAPIRO is professor in the Department of Rhetoric at the University of California, Berkeley. She is the author of *John Wilkins, 1614–72:*

An Intellectual Biography (Berkeley, 1969), *Probability and Certainty in Seventeenth-Century England* (Princeton, 1983), *Beyond Reasonable Doubt and Probable Cause: Historical Perspectives on the Anglo-American Law of Evidence* (Berkeley, 1991), and *A Culture of Fact: England, 1500–1720* (Ithaca, 2000).

JOHANN P. SOMMERVILLE is professor of history at the University of Wisconsin, Madison. His writings include *Politics and Ideology in England, 1603–1640* (London, 1986), *Royalists and Patriots: Politics and Ideology in England, 1603–1640* (London, 1999), and *Thomas Hobbes: Political Ideas in Historical Context* (New York, 1992).

ALAN STEWART is a lecturer in late medieval and Renaissance English at Birkbeck College, University of London. He is the author of *Close Readers: Humanism and Sodomy in Early Modern England* (Princeton, 1997), *Hostage to Fortune: The Troubled Life of Francis Bacon* (with Lisa Jardine as co-author, London, 1998); and *Philip Sidney: A Double Life* (London, 2000). He is currently editing a new edition of Bacon's *Correspondence*.

LUKE WILSON is associate professor of English at the Ohio State University. He has written articles on Renaissance literature, medicine, and law, and *Theaters of Intention: Drama and the Law in Early Modern England* (Stanford, 2000). His current project is a history of early modern anonymity.

Introduction

LORNA HUTSON

VICTORIA KAHN

It is hardly surprising to find rhetoric and law conjoined in a collection of essays on early modern Europe. The humanistic revival of ancient eloquence, though frequently evoked in contrast to the "barbarity" of legal studies, was just as frequently proposed as the means for their salvation. Rhetoric and law as a topic in early modern studies has tended, then, to be identified as the investigation of the impact of humanistic rhetoric on the study and practice of civil and national law. For Italy and France, Donald R. Kelley's magisterial *Foundations of Modern Historical Scholarship* traced the origins of modern historicism to the philological approaches that Guillaume Budé, Andrea Alciato, and others took to the texts of Roman law.[1] For England, studies by W. Prest of the Inns of Court, and articles by D. S. Bland, R. M. Fisher, and R. J. Schoeck have been devoted to assessing the extent to which the study of the common law in the sixteenth century was actually affected by the humanists' ambition that "the pleadyng and reasonyng of the lawe" should be, in Sir Thomas Elyot's words, "brought to the auncient fourme of noble oratours."[2] For legal studies, research into the origins of the Anglo-American law of evidence has uncovered its relation to classical concepts of proof, partly mediated through a Europe-wide topico-rhetorical tradition.[3] And recently English legal historians have challenged F. W. Maitland's thesis — which was once something of an impediment to the pairing of rhetoric and English law — about the resistance of English common law to the intellectual energies of the Continental legal Renaissance. In two related and wide-ranging essays on the subject, J. H. Baker has dispelled Maitland's image of a "crepuscular common law" on the point of collapse in "those dark days of Tudor despotism."[4] Continental legal humanism (as Kelley showed) was largely academic in its impact, and the English courts of common law were hardly losing business for lack of it; moreover, law reporting, which Maitland also thought to be in decline, continued in manuscript reports of which nineteenth-century scholars were ignorant.[5] More significant than the chimerical "continuity" of sixteenth-century English law, it now appears, are the momentous changes and developments the law underwent, some of which have rhetorical connections insofar as they reflect the impetus of humanist education.[6] All this and more could fairly be said to define a field of study in rhetoric and law in early modern Europe.

The story of what brings this collection together, however, does not simply end there. To Richard Schoeck's complaint, made in 1983, that "the vital question of the relation of rhetoric and law . . . remains pretty much where I left it in 1953," the response might be made that the conceptualization of this "vital question" has been completely transformed by developments in the disciplines of literary, historical, and legal studies from the 1960s onward. Schoeck's 1983 article ends with a plea that we endeavor to recover, from commonplace books and other records, a sense of legal humanists at work: "We move," he concludes, "towards a glimpse of them in the great halls of the Inns in a moot or reading and we begin to understand them at work in the candlelight, with a Quintilian or Cicero open on the table before them."[7] Although recent scholarly interest in the materiality of the book, and in the sociology and history of reading, has in fact cast light on the way in which classical texts were read by sixteenth-century humanists,[8] the point of the present collection on rhetoric and law is less the recovery of the historical personality of the individual lawyer reading or writing rhetorical texts than the investigation of the relations between rhetorical or literary production and legal practice as these discursive fields conceptualized, or produced accounts of, human agency and subjectivity in the early modern period.

New questions have been made possible by the theoretical and critical movements — structuralism and poststructuralism, feminism, new historicism, cultural materialism, and lesbian and gay studies — which have redefined the object of study in literary, historical, and legal disciplines. For literary studies in the early modern period, the effect of "new historicism" has been, in the words of Louis Montrose, "a refiguring of the socio-cultural field within which canonical Renaissance literary and dramatic works were originally produced." Work has been done to resituate such works, "not only in relation to other genres and modes of discourse, but also in relation to contemporaneous social institutions and nondiscursive practices."[9] This redefinition of the object of literary study has emphasized the literary text's contribution to the constitution of subjectivity and agency in the past and has to some extent opened up a dialogue with social historians — in particular, perhaps, with the feminist social historians and historians of homosexuality, for whom legal records are vital sources of evidence. The work of Alan Bray on English prosecutions for sodomy, and of Natalie Zemon Davis on Jean de Coras's text of the trial of Martin Guerre and on French pardon tales, has been exemplary in this respect and has elicited responses from literary critics investigating the representation of same-sex desire, the relation between legal imposture and the impostures of fiction, or the literary and dramatic "voices" of women as these might relate to the voices of women in court records of defamation proceedings.[10] Social historians, in their turn, have turned in their interpretations of legal depositions to theories of the poetics of narrative; Natalie Davis appeals to sixteenth-century oratorical theory and twentieth-century narratology to justify attending to the "fictive" quality of sixteenth-century letters of remission for crime.[11] More generally, of course, new historicism's concern with the contribution of the literary text to the formation of subjectivity in the past has been profoundly influenced by the Michel Foucault of *Discipline and Punish* and *The History of Sexuality* — in particular, by Foucault's interest in the regulation of the subject by extrajuridical forms of power, which has inspired the drawing of speculative (and not always entirely convincing) parallels between such institutions as the Renaissance theater and the Counter-Reformation confessional.[12]

At the same time, the idea of the law as an autonomous discipline has, in the same period, undergone transformation by Derridean models of deconstructive reading and Foucauldian notions of institutional power. "As against the dominant view of legal language as a discrete and unitary genre of written authorities constituting a written code, which, if correctly . . . interpreted, forms a series of necessary truths," writes Peter Goodrich, "a critically adequate reading of the law should take account of the various levels of law as a social discourse, as a series of institutional functions and rhetorical effects, a project which requires reading within the legal text precisely those facets or meanings of legal regulation and discipline which its self-protective doctrines of unity, coherence and univocality have traditionally sought to exclude."[13] Thus, for example, Goodrich's work on sixteenth- and early seventeenth-century common law controversially reads its claims to unity and coherence as the repression of its spiritual counterpart, or rather, the repression of a recognition that as secular law the common law was "simply one of numerous legal jurisdictions, a pluralism of laws which reflected the hierarchy and diversity of the sources of knowledge and representations of truth."[14] Different kinds of questions thus become possible topics of a legal history reconceived as "a critical reading of the law." To questions concerning the emergence of doctrines and forms of legal action that have traditionally preoccupied legal historians can be added questions about change in the social and psychic functions performed by certain legal institutions, and the differences that changes in jurisdiction—such as the wholesale transference of legal actions involving breach of faith in contracts from the spiritual courts to the courts of common law—might have had on the boundaries of selfhood in the past.

Such questions converge with questions that critics working in early modern studies (historical and literary) are posing in the wake of deconstruction and the new historicism. Thus, for example, Ian Maclean, in a critique of the argument that French and Italian humanists anticipated post-Saussurean theories of language and meaning, turned to law for evidence of concern with establishing intention in determining the actionability of language (in slander cases, for example).[15] Although Maclean's argument rather surprisingly takes no account of sexual difference in the distinction between actions for slander in temporal and in ecclesiastical law, his turning to law as a site in which problems of language and meaning emerge in social, rather than abstract, contexts is nevertheless significant.[16] From another angle, Luke Wilson has proceeded with his work in English literature by turning to sixteenth-century legal discourses of intention and liability in homicide cases in order to raise questions about the dramatic and poetic representation of intentional action, questions hitherto precluded by the new historicist focus on the formation of subjects through relations of power and signification.[17] Like Maclean's, Wilson's investigations into the ways in which intention is conceptualized in legal reports and treatises touch on the sixteenth-century elaboration of Aristotle's theory of *epieikeia,* or equity, according to which the failure of the positive law to provide in its wording for the contingencies of a particular case should be rectified by "deciding as the lawgiver himself should decide if he were present."[18] The topic of equity was widely diffused in the legal discourse of the sixteenth century, in England through the writings of Christopher St. German, the reports of Plowden and Coke, and treatises by Edward Hake, Sir Thomas Egerton and others.[19] Work on the deliberative basis of dramatic theory and composition in the Renaissance by Marvin Herrick, Kathy Eden, Joel Altman, and Terence Cave has illuminated the close correspondence between Aristotle's theory of what constitutes a "complex" plot (which involves a movement from "error" [*hamartia*] to knowledge through inference from artificial proofs) and Aristotle's conception in the *Nicomachean Ethics* of equity as the corrective of the "error" of the positive law.[20] Sixteenth-century dramatists brought up on humanist editions of classical comedy and on Erasmus' adaptation of classical discussions of "artificial proof" would have been familiar with the notion of a relationship between the dilatory plea of equity as a corrective to the letter of the law, and the dilatory temporal space occupied by the hypotheses and "errors" generated by the dramatic text.[21]

Moving in the other direction, we find in critical legal studies the rejection of a strictly intentionalist hermeneutic in favor of a deconstructive attention to those instances in the text of the law in which its logic is undone by rhetorical undecidability. The deconstructive trend in legal studies is not without relevance to the topics treated in this book. As J. R. Balkin has pointed out, for example, P. S. Atiyah's study of legal and philosophical attempts to account for the binding power of promises is effectively deconstructive of a pervasive assumption in legal and philosophical discourse that it is the *intention* to be bound (particularly when no explicit promise is communicated) that creates an obligation.[22] As Atiyah himself makes clear, however, the operation of such assumptions in legal thought belongs to the period between 1770 and 1870, in which the "classic contract model," with its stress on the importance of freedom of choice as the origin of legal and moral obligation, became dominant. For this to happen, however, elements of earlier legal thinking on actionability of promises had to become opaque, to be reduced, in Atiyah's words, to "a technicality, a curiosity of legal history."[23] Such was the fate of the "doctrine of consideration," according to which the actionability of the informal promise depended on the proving of sufficient "consideration" (defined variously as profit to the defendant, detriment to the plaintiff, or the existence of mutual promises) for it to have been made.[24] That nineteenth- and twentieth-century legal and philosophical discourse can assume the declaration of intention to be the paradigmatic way of creating obligation may be said, then, to be a reversal of the cultural logic of "consideration," a concept that both denies the validity of an intention, except as part of a narrative sequence of material transactions, and imagines the intention so defined to be accessible only by inference from that narrative.

The sixteenth century—the period in which the "consideration" clause came to be standard in pleadings involving breaches of payment—was also that in which the tort of "assumpsit" was coming to replace the old common-law action of debt. In an essay reprinted here, Luke Wilson argues that the increasing use of assumpsit in actions for the recovery of debts on informal contracts in the sixteenth century introduced a new sense of the temporality of contract, and a new emphasis on viewing interiority in terms of intentional action. Whereas the old action of debt conceives of a bargain as an atemporal exchange of goods, the triumph, in the watershed decision of Slade's case (1602), of the idea that "every contract executory imports in itself an assumpsit," has the effect of investing contract with the retrospective temporality of a sequential narrative, involving "the promises, deceits, motivations and considerations according to which action organises itself." Thus, whereas the classic contract model dominant in the nineteenth century involves a metaphysics of presence in imagining the anteriority of the act of will to the communication of the promise, its seventeenth-century antecedent for a while preserved the sense in which the anteriority of the intention is a retrospectively constructed fiction, a probable account of an interior state offered in explanation for a sequence of events. Wilson suggests that, in the culture in which assumpsit prevails, "social actors are forced to assume a habit of constant self-examination, attending to their own consciousness and continually constructing intentional accounts of their actions."[25] And yet a habit of "constant self-examination," had, of course, been encouraged by both the internal and external courts of the Church since the sixth century.[26] The significance of states of intention with regard to a moral obligation to fulfill promises had been discussed in the medieval literature of casuistry; indeed, as A. W. B. Simpson demonstrates, the discussion of what makes promises binding in the second dialogue of Christopher St. German's influential treatise on common law, *Doctor and Student* (1530), derives from two of the most popular fifteenth-century handbooks for confessors.[27] Moreover, as R. H. Helmholz has shown, the rise of assumpsit as a common-law substitute for the old action of debt can be matched, in the sixteenth century, against the decline of the ecclesiastical courts' jurisdiction over sworn promises to pay, known as *causa fidei laesionis seu perjurii* (accusation of breach of faith, or perjury).[28] As Richard Cousin, a sixteenth-century apologist for the jurisdiction of the ecclesiastical courts, reminded his common-law antagonists, the Church had once routinely overseen the performance of contracts: "It was very usuall for men in those dayes, at the making of any contracts . . . for their more securitie, to make faith or othe for performance. . . . Then if the other party failed of performance, he was by proces Ecclesiat. called before the Ordinary, as to answere for an act done afore him, or *pro fidei laesione:* which failing being confessed or proved, the offendor was enioyned grievous penance & compelled by censures to keep his faith or othe, by satisfying of the other partie."[29]

By this means, continued Cousin, "most lay contracts of goods & chattels were . . . drawn into Ecclesiasticall courts."[30] The pleading of a suit of fidei laesionis bore certain similarities to the pleading of assumpsit; the function of the "consideration" for the promise was fulfilled by the canon law *causa promissionis* or lawful, honest, and possible cause. Yet there were also differences between the two: the tort of assumpsit alleged deceit on the part of the defendant and emphasized the material damages resulting to the plaintiff from this deceit, whereas in the spiritual action the emphasis was on the danger in which his broken promise had placed his soul, the remedy for which was (as Cousin says) "grievous penance."[31] An account, then, of the development of the conceptualization of interiority in the literature and law of contract of the early modern period is not unrelated to the histories of the subsumption of the spiritual by the common law, and of the inward displacement of the domain of conscience, even — possibly — of the metamorphosis of "casuistry" into the category of "character" in secular literature.[32] The purpose of a collection drawing on the research and analytical expertise of specialists in legal, literary, and sociohistorical studies of the early modern period is to make possible the development of such interdisciplinary accounts as these.

It requires a convergence of disciplines, for example, to do justice to the material, social, and political transformations masked by the apparent continuity of appeals to natural law within the discourse of positive law. As is well known, appeals to natural law were a crucial part of the early modern rhetoric of law. In the dominant view, derived from Aristotle, Cicero, Seneca, and others, natural law referred to a repository of moral precepts distinct from conventional notions of justice, or to "immutable principles of nature, discoverable by the use of reason."[33] In these works, natural law was deduced from the exercise of our rational capacities of deliberation and was thus identical for all practical purposes with reason. In the Christian reception of Greek and Roman sources, natural law was identified both with divine law or uncorrupted reason and with the relative natural law that was accessible to human reason after the fall. The Church Fathers also equated natural law with conscience or with the law "written on the heart." In the twelfth century, Gratian identified natural and divine law or the revealed law of Scripture in his handbook of canon law, the *Decretum*. In addition, he legitimated custom as a source of law, as long as it did not contradict "truth, reason, Christian faith, or natural law."[34] In the *Summa theologica*, Thomas Aquinas argued that humans participate in divine law by virtue of reason, and that the precepts of natural law are to practical reason what the first principles of demonstration are to speculative reason.[35] Invocations of natural law in this tradition call up a continuity of thought stretching from Aquinas to the seventeenth century; Johann Sommerville, in support of this argument, quotes a Jacobean cleric, William Pemberton, asserting that God has "instamped in man's nature" a rule by which he can "live well."[36]

Contextualizing appeals to natural law within the history of changes in the practical workings of the law, however, can reveal startling discontinuities with regard to the scope of the juridical regulation of the subject. Christopher St. German, who in his *Doctor and Student* derived all human law from the law of reason, or nature, which "is wryten in the herte," though obscured by sin and passion, might seem to be purely Aquinian.[37] St. German was careful at the same time, however, to insist that even that aspect of God's law which has been directly revealed to man is merely human law; the moral law does not include laws "shewed by reuelacion of god for the polyticall rewle of the people." It follows, of course, that "all the lawes Cannon be not lawes of god."[38] The effect of St. German's anticanon law polemic was to displace the dispensation of moral law on matters involving property from the spiritual courts to the inward court of individual conscience. Following St. Augustine's *De libero arbitrio*, St. German argues that it is right that temporal laws leave certain wrongs unpunished, for God's eternal law punishes these in the internal forum of conscience: "As saynt Augustyn sayth in the first boke of fre arbytrement the lawe of man may not punysshe all offences: for yf all offencis shuld be punysshed the comon welth shulde be hurte as it is of contractes/for it can not be auoydyd but that as longe as contractes be sufferyd many offences shall folowe therby & yet they be sufferyd for the common welthe."[39] The offenses encouraged by the toleration of informal contracts are, of course, breaches of faith and nonpayment of debts; St. German contests the right of the church courts to adjudicate these, on the basis that they have no privileged access to the "inward intente of the hert."[40] His argument tends to make the law adjudicating property relations more conscionable without making it, like spiritual jurisdiction, confessional. The enormous influence of *Doctor and Student*, as well as St. German's part in the Henrician reformation, worked to ensure that his arguments took effect in legal practice; here was an instance in which the appeal to an apparently conventional definition of natural law was part of a radically transformative rhetoric, anticipating in practical effect revisions of natural law that took place in the seventeenth century.[41]

In the work of some seventeenth-century writers, natural law not only responded to momentous political, religious, and epistemological changes, it also suffered a sea change of its own. Aiming to provide a nonconfessional basis for social harmony and political order, figures such as Hugo Grotius, Thomas Hobbes, and Samuel Pufendorf proposed a revised doctrine of natural law predicated in part on the minimalist principles of sociability (with the exception of Hobbes), self-interest, and the natural right of self-preservation.[42] This "minima moralia" offered a secular basis for political association to those of different faiths. It was thus, in the first instance, not so much a direct response to skepticism as it was to irrational dogmatism and the religious wars.[43] Yet, to Hobbes and Pufendorf in particular, the appeal to natural right also seemed better able to harness the amoral calculus of passion and interest of some of their contemporaries — a calculus that resembled the power politics of Thucydides or of the sophist Callicles in Plato's *Gorgias* more than it did classical or Christian notions of virtue and vice. Finally, such a minimalist doctrine of natural law was better suited to the new world of experimental science. Whereas older doctrines were predicated on the belief in a natural moral order dictated by God, the doctrines of Hobbes and Pufendorf drew near to "the developing scientific view of the world as totally neutral with respect to value."[44] God was still the creator of the world, but human beings were the proximate creators of value, by virtue of their voluntary social and political arrangements.

Hugo Grotius' *De jure belli ac pacis* (1625) stands on the cusp of this transformation of natural law. On the one hand, in explaining human notions of justice and obligation, Grotius invoked Stoic principles of natural sociability and innate "seeds of virtue" that contemporary readers would have been familiar with from classical and Christian treatises on rhetoric and moral philosophy. On the other hand, Grotius asserted the heuristic divorce of natural law from divine law: "What we have been saying [about the existence of a natural law of justice] would have a degree of validity even if we should concede [*etiamsi daremus*] that which cannot be conceded without the utmost wickedness, that there is no God, or that the affairs of men are of no concern to Him."[45] God is the creator of natural law as an autonomous principle of human agency. It is this autonomy, according to Grotius, that makes politics susceptible to the kind of systematic analysis or scientific "method" that others were applying to the physical world. The relative autonomy of human agency also explains Grotius' interest in and tolerance of the great diversity in positive laws and forms of government among nations. While asserting his preference for monarchy, Grotius argued that all legitimate governments were predicated on individual consent. Such consent, in turn, legitimated resistance in cases where it might be "without disturbance to the commonwealth." According to this argument, God permits the exercise of human discretion and volition, which Grotius, like St. German, explicitly links to the issue of equitable interpretation of the law.[46]

The interpretation of Grotius has been central to the ongoing scholarly debate about whether there was in fact a new approach to natural law in the seventeenth century. Standing in for the problem in synecdochic fashion is the fact that Grotius's controversial phrase "etiamsi daremus" appears in the work of his scholastic predecessors, along with many of his arguments about natural law and natural rights. For some scholars, including Johann Sommerville in Chapter 13, this locates Grotius squarely in the tradition of Aquinas,

Francisco de Vitoria, and Francisco Suárez. For others, Grotius' innovation is, paradoxically, his recourse to humanist rhetoric, his invocation of classical literary and philosophical authorities to make an essentially neoscholastic theory of natural law accessible to a wider reading public.[47] Still others, not disputing the continuity of vocabulary but focusing on the new uses to which traditional concepts such as natural law may be put, have detected a real break with the older tradition.[48] At the very least, it was apparent in the seventeenth century that Grotius could be evoked in support of innovation as well as tradition. Samuel Rutherford, whom Sommerville cites for his opinion that Grotius was a royalist, used Grotius' own views to justify resistance to Charles I. Robert Filmer attributed this argument to Grotius himself, arguing that Grotius' view that "property as it now exists was introduced by human will" produced "divers dangerous and seditious conclusions," including the view that "the moral law depends upon the will of man," and the view that individuals have the right to resist their sovereigns.[49]

Whatever we make of Grotius' relation to the scholastic tradition of natural law, it is clear that Hobbes and Pufendorf saw themselves as departing both from that tradition and from the humanist rhetorical tradition with which it was sometimes allied. Although Hobbes wrote an abstract of Aristotle's *Rhetoric*, in *Leviathan* he famously associated the study of classical rhetoric with sedition and civil war: "By reading of these Greek, and Latine Authors," he complained, "men from their childhood have gotten a habit (under a false-shew of Liberty,) of favouring tumults, and of licentious controlling of their Soveraigns; . . . as I think I may truly say, there was never any thing so deerly bought, as these Western parts have bought the learning of the Greek and Latine tongues."[50] Equally disturbing to the peace were the rhetorical activities of preachers who incited commoners to rebel by instructing them in the interpretation of Scripture.[51] By contrast, Hobbes believed that political conflict could be avoided if the commonwealth could be fashioned according to the method of the natural sciences. Accordingly, natural law was stripped of its moral content and reduced to the right to self-preservation. Although other laws could be rationally deduced from this first principle, they had no normative force in the state of nature, the war of all against all, where individuals feared violent death at the hands of their fellows. The natural right of self-preservation then dictated the setting up of a sovereign with the power to enforce obedience. According to Hobbes, such a minimalist account offered a secure basis for an Erastian government and thus a solution to religious conflict and civil war. But it did so, many of his contemporaries charged, at the price of assimilating natural law and conscience to positive law, and the rational activities of interpretation and persuasion to the sovereign's dictates.[52]

Similarly inspired by scientific method, Pufendorf argued, against Aristotelian ethics, that the moral sciences were capable of scientific certainty.[53] Although the morality of human actions was contingent on free will, that human beings were capable of moral action was the result of divine fiat. In contrast to physical entities, which were morally indifferent objects in the natural world, moral entities were norms, values, obligations, and rights created by human will and intelligence, and authorized by the divine will. As a result, law was defined simply as the decree of a superior (ultimately God), without reference to any independent notion of the good.[54] As in the case of Hobbes, Pufendorf's "command theory" of natural and positive law, simultaneously divorced from and yet modeled on the certainty of the natural sciences, was a far cry from the humanists' conception of a natural law informing the practical activities of rhetoric and politics.[55]

In England, in contrast, the radical potential of natural law remained closely linked to the rhetorical tradition — as Hobbes himself noted when he attributed the civil war to familiarity with the Greek and Latin tongues. In practice, natural law was also frequently assimilated to the "artificial reasoning" of lawyers in ways that had political implications as well. In his *Nomotechnia* of 1631, Henry Finch declared that the law of nature and of reason, or "the law of reason primary and secondary," is the source of positive or common law. In *The English Lawyer* (1631), John Dodderidge, a justice of the Court of the King's Bench from 1612 to 1628, claimed that English laws, like all other laws, "are derived from the Law of Nature, and do concurre in the principles of Nature and Reason." By reason, both Finch and Dodderidge meant the artificial reason of common lawyers, that is, the expert ability to reason dialectically in Aristotelian fashion and "to find out the truth by argument and disputation." Sir Edward Coke, chief justice of the Court of Common Pleas and later of the King's Bench, famously argued that such artificial reasoning was what distinguished the professional expertise of the common lawyer from the mere opinion of the sovereign. Not by chance, Coke was dismissed from the bench by James I in 1616, and later, as a member of Parliament, played an important role in the ongoing struggle concerning the prerogatives of the Crown.[56] He was one of many lawyer-M.P.'s to make common cause with Puritan critics of the king in the 1620s and '30s.

As Coke's activities suggest, in England, as on the continent, law and political theory were closely linked.[57] Both older and newer notions of natural law formed a series of shifting alliances with a native tradition of constitutionalism. The doctrines of an "ancient constitution" and "fundamental liberties," ratified by the Magna Carta, custom, and common law, accorded easily with the notion that the sovereign was constrained by substantive moral principles of natural law.[58] Equally important, and compatible with the ancient constitution, were Continental and English arguments concerning the natural right of self-preservation and the natural-law doctrine of the social contract. In response to these arguments, James I and his supporters began to articulate an increasingly absolutist position. In his legal dictionary *The Interpreter* (London, 1607), the civil lawyer John Cowell defined "king" as "above the Law by his absolute power . . . . And though at his coronation he take an oath not to alter the lawes of the land: Yet this oath notwithstanding, hee may alter or suspend any particular lawe that seemeth hurtfull to the publike estate."[59] James was forced to suppress this volume in response to the outrage of members of Parliament.

The fundamental legal and political liberties of the subject were tested in an important series of constitutional law cases from Bates's case in 1606 to the Shipmoney case in 1638. At stake in all of these cases was the king's prerogative to overrule common law.[60] This controversy implicated the jurisdictional struggle between the common-law courts and Chancery, which decided questions of equity. In finding for the Crown in Bates's case Chief Baron Fleming identified common and civil law, only then to make a crucial distinction between the king's ordinary and absolute power that disabled the objections — and the equitable interpretation — of common lawyers:

> That of the ordinary is for the profit of particular subjects, for the execution of civil justice, the determining of meum . . . and by the civilians is nominated jus privatum and with us common law; and these laws cannot be changed without parliament. . . . The absolute power of the King is not that which is converted or executed to private use, to the benefit of any particular person, but is only that which is applied to the general benefit of the people, and is salus populi; as the people is the body and the King is the head . . . and as the constitution of this body varieth with the time, so varieth this absolute law according to the wisdom of the King, for the common good.[61]

In the decades that followed this controversial decision, common lawyers joined with Puritan and parliamentary critics of the Crown to resist any encroachment on the fundamental liberties of the English people. Political theorists working in the tradition of natural law put forward theories of contractual political obligation that challenged James's and Charles's interpretation of the royal prerogative. During the civil war, politically engaged writers such as John Milton, Henry Parker, and Samuel Rutherford drew on Continental theorists of resistance, Selden, and Grotius to elaborate a powerful defense of parliamentary sovereignty based on native English liberties and a people's natural right to self-preservation.

In his epilogue to these developments, *A Dialogue Between a Philosopher and a Student of the Common Laws of England,* Hobbes traced the civil war in part to the common lawyers' view that "Reason is the life of the Law, nay the Common Law it self is nothing but Reason."[62] As we have already observed and as the "Philosopher" in Hobbes's *Dialogue* makes clear, this view had been championed by Edward Coke, Bacon's antagonist in Slade's case and a formidable defender of the common law against James I's doctrine of royal supremacy. In the *Dialogue* Hobbes took up Bacon's defense of the royal prerogative, though without any of Bacon's optimism about the contribution of rhetoric to law and politics. Instead, Hobbes argued that the common lawyer's identification of authority with reason prompted the exercise of individual judgment and in so doing discouraged political obedience. Like the preacher's invitation to scriptural interpretation, the common lawyer's view that laws are grounded on reason could only give rise to sedition. Hence the necessity of a sovereign maker or interpreter of the law. Hobbes thus subordinated common law to the sovereign, to statute law, and to equity. But equity was not associated with natural law, practical reason, or individual conscience, but with positive law, the court of Chancery, and the royal prerogative.

Frederick Pollock once referred to the law of nature as "an engine of dialectic."[63] By describing natural law in this way, Pollock meant to call attention to its use as a weapon of rhetorical controversy. But in the seventeenth century, natural law was rhetorical and dialectical in another way as well. As we have seen, although in some ways more radically rhetorical (if by this we mean antifoundational) than the older notions of a substantive natural law, the new doctrines of natural law adopted the language of scientific "method" rather than that of humanist rhetoric. According to some scholars, they thus promised a response not only to religious dogmatism but also to the skeptical challenge posed by the nascent historicism of the early modern period — a historicism that was itself fostered by humanist training in rhetoric as well as by contemporary social and political upheaval.[64] But despite the intention of their proponents, the new doctrines did not necessarily guarantee a more secure political order: like older conceptions of natural law, the new minimalism both dictated the subject's obedience to positive law and legitimated resistance in those cases where the sovereign could no longer offer protection to his subjects. Hobbes notoriously conceded this point in *Leviathan:* "The Obligation of Subjects to the Soveraign, is understood to last as long, and no longer, than the power lasteth, by which he is able to protect them. For the right men have by Nature to protect themselves, when none else can protect them, can by no Covenant be relinquished" (21.153). In contrast to older notions of natural law, however, Hobbes's derivation of natural law from natural right all too obviously challenged the belief in an objective moral order and, in so doing, drew near to the skeptical tendencies of sophistic rhetoric.[65] To Leo Strauss, one of Hobbes's most trenchant modern critics, the voluntarism of modern natural-rights theory dealt a death blow to ancient natural law and anticipated the loss of substantive ethical value in the Enlightenment notion of aesthetics and in modern liberalism. Yet, as Strauss's own politically conservative reaction suggests, the appeal to natural right retains a power to challenge established values.[66] From this perspective, then, one legacy of early modern natural law to the modern period might be construed as a rhetorical or immanent critique of foundationalism, a critique associated with some of the approaches that have shaped modern studies of law and rhetoric: the *Ideologiekritik* of the Frankfurt School, deconstruction, feminism, and critical legal studies.

Rhetoric and Law in Early Modern Europe begins with an interpretation of the place of Slade's case in cultural history. In Chapter 1, David Harris Sacks traces changes in the meaning of the legal term "consideration" from its open-ended inclusion of nonworldly reasons for making promises in St. German's *Doctor and Student* (1530) to its being defined in 1624 as "the material cause of a contract." The explanation for this limiting of the word's semantic range lies in the rise of the action of assumpsit and its triumph in the case of *Slade v. Morley* in 1602. As Sacks lucidly identifies it, the issue in Slade's case was whether or not to collapse the distinction between a contract and a promise. The decision that a contract was, as Sacks puts it, "a special class of promise" laid the foundation for the "will theory" of the Scottish Enlightenment, for every contract was henceforth identified as based on an implicit promise. Sacks explains this outcome as arising from the inadequacy of compurgation as a method of proof in the old common-law action of debt. The continuity of St. German's objections to the notion that the canon law could examine "intention" in matters of promissory obligation, along with his objections to the Church's use of the ex officio oath to try heretics, points to what would become, in the course of Elizabeth's reign, a widespread dissatisfaction with compurgation as proof of intention or conscience. Yet, as Sacks concludes, the emergence of "consideration" in its limited, worldly sense as the public test of the likelihood of a promissory intention marks a radical departure from Aristotelian and Scholastic thinking on the moral psychology of promises. The transformation would leave a lasting mark on the Anglo-American legal and philosophical tradition.

Barbara Shapiro has been concerned in her work with changing conceptions of proof in legal and other discourses, of which the gradual rejection of compurgation forms a part. In earlier books, Shapiro has revealed the relationship between legal and scientific senses of the "probable" in the seventeenth century.[67] In Chapter 2 she turns her attention to the sixteenth century, and to the effect that the humanist revival and popularization of classical distinctions between "inartificial' and "artificial" proof in forensic oratory was to have on the ways in which justices of the peace examined their witnesses before trial. Kathy Eden and others have done work on the familiarity shown by Renaissance commentators on drama with the Aristotelian distinction between inartificial and artificial proof.[68] The novelty of Shapiro's research consists in her discovery of fascinating evidence from sixteenth-century justicing handbooks that the very techniques that Cicero and Quintilian and their humanist promulgators offered as strategies for the enhancement of rhetorical performance were being explicitly adapted by justices of the peace in their relatively new roles as examiners of suspects.

Carla Freccero begins Chapter 3 in dialogue with Natalie Davis, who juxtaposes "sixteenth-century legal texts and Renaissance novellas" in *Fiction in the Archives*.[69] Specifically, Freccero starts by questioning the basis of Davis's distinction between tales composed to elicit compassionate judgment from the king in a plea for mercy and stories apparently told for entertainment by the king's sister, Marguerite de Navarre. Canon law recognized consent between contracting parties as sufficient to the formation of a valid marriage. Read in the context of sixteenth-century France's repudiation of that criterion, the *Heptaméron*'s play with truth claims and thematic concern with the status of women as victims of rape and contractors of clandestine marriage can be understood as an indirect comment on the limits and possibilities of women's agency in the new "marital regime." Freccero focuses on parallels between the *Heptaméron*'s story of Rolandine, who promises herself in marriage, against her father's and the queen's will, and archives relating to the conflict of monarchical power over the marriage of Marguerite de Navarre's own daughter, Jeanne D'Albret. Freccero concludes by speculating on the links between Marguerite de Navarre's Protestant sympathies and Rolandine's claim to be justified by God in independently contracting a marriage.

Freccero's chapter points to a link between the French Renaissance novella and the writings of sixteenth-century French lawyers on the threat constituted by female agency in clandestine marriage; Pierre Boiastuau (who edited the first edition of Marguerite de Navarre's stories) was a law student of Jean de Coras, and both he and François de Belleforest (who was present at Coras's sentencing of Arnold du Tilh in the trial of Martin Guerre) consistently elaborated on the tragic consequences of clandestine marriage in their translations into French of the Italian novels of Bandello.[70] For Peter Goodrich, such a consonance between the legal and the literary texts of the French Renaissance written by men is symptomatic of the suppression of an earlier French jurisdiction and literature, one that was concerned neither with the punishments due to lovers who contravened marital law nor with the means of securing wifely obedience and fidelity (common topics in Belleforest and Boiastuau) but with questions of love as a science of erotic relationship. As in his other writing, Goodrich is concerned in Chapter 4 with a history of the law that attends to what has been forgotten or has had to be excluded. The "gay science" of amorous jurisdiction in fourteenth-century Toulouse constitutes just such an object of amnesia and denial, explained by scholars variously as a metaphor for lack or a disguised domination of women. Goodrich suggests that we begin by rejecting the antinomy of law and love that these dismissals imply, and look for the meaning of "gay science" in the critique it offers of the modern legal tradition's failure to to address the domain of intimacy, the space and temporality of "l'entre-deux."

Goodrich suggests that the jurisdiction of the courts of love, concerned as it was with the private life of emotion, the "intimacies of the polis," existed in a space between the secular and the spiritual jurisdictions. Alan Stewart's analysis in Chapter 5 of the intertwining of charges leading to the fall of Lord Chancellor Bacon in England in 1621 focuses rather on what one man's loves and intimacies reveal about the paradoxes of secular and spiritual jurisdiction over sexuality after the Reformation. On the whole, what the common law claimed from the Church courts at the Reformation was jurisdiction over matters involving property; so lay contracts concerning goods and chattels, and slander suits involving material damage to the plaintiff, ceased to be overseen by the Church. Sexual conduct, however, and sexual slander remained the preserve of the ecclesiastical courts, which were becoming, as Richard Wunderli has remarked, "women's court[s]" (which says a lot about the allocation by gender of moral responsibility for sex).[71] The perplexed logic of this transformation emerges in relation to its exception: the sexual sin of sodomy was, in the same historical moment, redefined as a secular crime, a capital offense. Stewart's chapter, starting from the curious interchangeability of charges of bribery and sodomy that becomes apparent in libels against Bacon in the 1620s, pursues the hypothesis that Bacon's sexual practices could not be prosecuted, or appear as crimes, precisely because of their identification with and subsumption under alleged criminal offenses relating to justice and other men's goods. Whereas the irregular sexual conduct of women inevitably dishonors the household, thereby bringing the private into the public realm and requiring public penance and contestation, men's irregular conduct seems to remain (in England at least) a household affair, invisible until invoked as revelatory of other crimes.

Luke Wilson's essay (Chapter 6) has already been mentioned for its innovative thesis about the effect of Slade's case on the temporality of contract. Wilson opens with the proposal made first by Henry Sumner Maine, and more recently by Don Wayne, that the ruling in Slade's case can been seen as crucial to England's transition from a status society to a contract society. Whereas Wayne sees a mercantile notion of contract as encroaching on the common law, Wilson sees, rather, the "invasion of business relations" by habits of thought that derive from the ethical underpinnings of the tort of assumpsit; specifically, by the idea that "you are legally responsible for the states of mind — intentions, motives, and so on — that the law may decide to find" in your casual parole contracts. Ben Jonson, whose writing is nothing if not sensitive to the problems of being made legally liable for imputed intentions (witness the trial of Silius in *Sejanus*) proves a veritable barometer to the changes Wilson describes, as Jonson's "Epistle to Mr Arthur Squib" plays with competing accounts of the time scheme and motive for a loan and its repayment, and his famous play *The Alchemist* "emerges into language *as* a promise."

The greater interdisciplinarity encouraged by the linguistic turn in history and law, and by the new historicism of literary studies, does not preclude the risk that theoretical models may be borrowed from a discipline in which the research on which they were based has been superseded. Lorna Hutson, in Chapter 7, suggests that such may be the case with the "theory of the King's Two Bodies" based on Ernst Kantorowicz's reading of F. W. Maitland's interpretation of a select number of the reports of the Elizabethan jurist, Edmund Plowden. The influence of Kantorowicz's work has been considerable. O. Hood Phillips, in *Shakespeare and the Lawyers* (1972), endorses Kantorowicz's somewhat extreme view that "English jurists not only developed 'a theology of Kingship' but worked out a 'Royal Christology.'"[72] Foucault's indebtedness to Kantorowicz in *Discipline and Punish* has ensured the continuing popularity of the theory among new historicist and poststructuralist critics of Renaissance literature. Hutson's chapter shows that, in his own time at least, Plowden's reports were famous rather for applying to English common law an Aristotelian theory of equity that would enable lawyers to construct their own interpretations of a burgeoning body of statutory legislation by hypothesizing legislative intention. A modified version of late sixteenth-century thought on the "body politic" emerges, with implications for reading the representation of legal, political, and intentional structures in *Richard II* and the two parts of *Henry IV*.

An emphasis on the political dimension of positive law also characterizes Constance Jordan's reading of Montaigne's 1580 "Apologie pour Raimond Sebond" (Chapter 8). Jordan argues that Montaigne articulated the most radical critique of natural law in sixteenth-century France, a critique that was bound up with his politically motivated defense of positive law. Specifically, the "Apologie" addressed a crisis in law and government, brought on by violent religious conflict. Parties on all sides of the conflict appealed to divine and natural law, whether to uphold divine right or to legitimate political resistance. Montaigne was unique in resisting these absolutist epistemological claims, and so unique in delineating a polity with no basis for radical resistance. His conviction that natural law is illegible led him to discover a basis for government in positive law and to propose a purely secular state, in which divine will and religious doctrine are not essential first principles but strategic fictions. Montaigne's skepticism thus underwrites a rhetorical view of political authority: divine and natural law are unknowable because they are outside discourse; hence the necessity of obeying the positive legal discourse of one's country. In the end, however, Montaigne's published critique of natural law runs counter to his supposed quietism: his assertion that he does not choose carves out a space of resistance, despite the illegibility of natural law. *Discours* itself guarantees the possibility of rational critique.

In Chapter 9, Annabel Patterson considers the career and treason trial of Algernon Sidney, whose *Discourses on Government* became a canonical text for a later generation of revolutionaries. At the center of Sidney's theoretical and polemical writings was a devotion to an ideal of law that "no passion can disturb." This ideal of impartiality may strike us now as commonplace, but it conflicted with the regular practices of early modern jurisprudence, according to which both counsel and a copy of the indictment were commonly denied to the defendant. Although Sidney himself had not shunned such practices, his *Discourses* illustrated his obsession with just and unjust tribunals. This obsession cannot be explained by generalized theory of resistance to the illegitimate exercise of power, according to Patterson. In contrast to Locke, who placed natural-law contract theory at the center of his *Two Treatises,* Sidney focused on the particularities of the English legal system, on the ancient constitution and statute law as the grounds for the constitutional contract rather than a consequence of it. For Sidney as for many of his contemporaries, state trials were tests of the power of this legal system against the corrupting forces of passion and interest. Patterson explores the role seventeenth-century records of these trials played in creating "an alternative legal canon" for dissenting political parties or persecuted minorities. Central to this alternative canon were the powerful rhetorical speeches for the defense. In preparing for his own trial in 1683, Sidney himself had studied the treason trial of Sir Nicholas Throckmorton in 1553 for conspiring against Mary Tudor; his own trial, as well as his rhetorical analysis of it in his "Apology," were to become exemplary for a later generation of dissenters.

Law, political theory, and affect are central in a different way to Victoria Kahn's argument in Chapter 10. In the scholarly literature, the natural-law theory of contract is often represented as a set of antinomies involving rationalism and voluntarism. The (usually male) subject of contract must reason according to natural law, but he must also consent to the contract of his own free will. In the seventeenth century, Kahn argues, some theorists of contract tried to address these antinomies by exploring the role of the passions in motivating the subject of political obligation. Passion, a traditional — and typically gendered — subject of classical and early modern manuals of rhetoric, becomes a locus of a materialist rhetoric of obligation, of a Foucauldian disciplining of the early modern legal subject of contract. Kahn explores this process in the work of William Gouge, Thomas Hobbes, and John Milton. Together, these authors illustrate the early modern preoccupation with the necessity of producing certain passions — whether in relation to traditional obligations or natural rights. In so doing, Kahn argues, they help us to understand the emergence of the argument that the production of the right passions constitutes the subject of rights.

This linking of passion and right contrasts with another model of early modern subjectivity — Macpherson's "possessive individualism." According to Macpherson, the early modern sense of self and conception of natural rights were modeled on the right to property. Macpherson traced this preoccupation with property to the nascent capitalism of the seventeenth century. Economic conditions certainly contributed to the rapidly changing social and political relations of the early modern period; yet, as the work of Richard Tuck and others has suggested, the early modern conceptualization of individual rights in terms of ownership or property was in some ways traditional, deriving in part from the notion of dominium in Roman law.[73] It was in opposition to such a notion of property rights, Kathy Eden argues in Chapter 11, that Erasmus articulated his own intellectual project. Eden explores Erasmus' construction of an ideal of intellectual property from the resources of humanist rhetoric. In his *Adages,* a collection of thousands of proverbs with commentary, Erasmus aimed to make the heritage of classical antiquity the common possession of his readers. In contrast to the *res,* the thing or object that was at the center of the Roman law of property or private possession, the proverb is a literary form that "defies ownership." Playing with the Roman legal notion of res as private property only to subvert it, Erasmus offered instead "res literaria," a common literary wealth that could serve as the model of a social and political commonwealth. Thus, at the very moment when his collaborator, the printer Aldus Manutius, was embroiled in several lawsuits concerning intellectual property (privileges to publish and patents on Greek and Latin typefaces),

Erasmus was embarking on an ambitious intellectual project to discourage the idea of copyright in the realm of ideas. At the same time, we might add, in a characteristic move, Erasmus also assiduously advertised his own — his very own — intellectual contributions to this common heritage. The *Adages* thus stands as a vexed emblem of the early modern literary commonwealth: a moving effort to make the riches of antiquity more widely available, a stunning success in marketing the Cliff Notes to Classical Culture, and a monument to Erasmus' own Herculean efforts, the *Adages* dramatizes the tension between a shared heritage and the individual labor of appropriation, between the rhetorical commonplace and the legal conception of property.

The Erasmian rhetorical project and the appeal to natural law are central to Jane Newman's discussion of Grotius. In Chapter 12, Newman counters the contentions in recent work on race in the early modern period: analyzing Grotius' fascination with the Ethiopian church, Newman shows that Grotius was less interested in the Ethiopians' race than in their religious practices, less interested in their putative otherness than in their possible sameness. In an era of religious wars, the Ethiopian church stood as an example of confessional sameness across cultural and political difference. For Newman, Grotius' proto-ethnographic technique — his discovery of consensus and likeness beneath superficial difference — is informed by the principles of humanist philology and Erasmian irenicism. These same principles are at work in Grotius' theological dialogue *Meletius* and his great work of jurisprudence, *De jure belli ac pacis*. In the former, Grotius urged greater toleration of individual religious practices, given the agreement on essential precepts; regarding the latter, he urged toleration of political differences once the objective principles of justice and natural law were accepted. With its voluminous citations from classical literature and moral philosophy, as well as contemporary works, *De jure* stands as a monument to humanist rhetoric and nascent historicism, which in turn helped lay the foundations for religious toleration and international law. In the context of Grotius' irenic project, the Ethiopians are not so much racial others as "defenders of Christian unity" and exemplary "agents of international legal maturity."

Johann Sommerville concludes *Rhetoric and Law in Early Modern Europe* with a bracing contribution contesting the existence of a modern school of natural law (Chapter 13). Sommerville takes issue with Richard Tuck, Knud Haakonssen, and the editors of this book, who have argued that the seventeenth century broke with the Scholastic tradition of natural law represented by Aquinas, Suárez, and others. No such departure took place, Sommerville argues, because no new rhetoric was in evidence: "Shifts in ideas are commonly accompanied by linguistic change," and two of the figures most frequently cited as part of the new school of natural law — Grotius and Selden — demonstrate no such change. The view of natural law they put forward in their works was not conceived as a response to skeptical relativism; it is no more minimalist, individualistic, secular, or radical than the work of earlier, Scholastic writers. In his scrupulous reading of early modern natural law, Sommerville challenges those who have defended the innovations of seventeenth-century legal and political theory. He invites us to make the case in rhetorical terms, by attending to what it might mean to quote authoritative sources in a new context or new way. If the association of rhetoric and law in the early modern period teaches us anything, it is that in some cases "the case is altered."

Notes

1. Donald R. Kelley, *Foundations of Modern Historical Scholarship: Law, Language and History in the Renaissance* (New Haven, 1970).

2. Sir Thomas Elyot, *The Boke named the Governour* [1531] (London, 1907), 66. See Wilfred Prest, *The Inns of Court Under Elizabeth I and the Early Stuarts 1590–1640* (London, 1972); R. J. Schoeck, "Rhetoric and Law in Sixteenth-Century England," *Studies in Philology* 50 (1953): 110–27; D. S. Bland, "Rhetoric and the Law Student in Sixteenth-Century England," *Studies in Philology* 54 (1957): 498–508; Louis Knafla, "The Law Studies of the Elizabethan Student," *Huntington Library Quarterly* 32 (1969): 221–40; R. M. Fisher, "Thomas Cromwell, Humanism and Educational Reform," *Bulletin of the Institute of Historical Research* 50 (1977): 151–63; R. J. Schoeck, "Lawyers and Rhetoric in Sixteenth-Century England," *Renaissance Eloquence*, ed. James J. Murphy (Berkeley, 1983), 274–91.

3. Alessandro Giuliani, "The Influence of Rhetoric on the Law of Evidence and Pleading," *Juridical Review* 7 (1962): 216–51.

4. J. H. Baker, "English Law and the Renaissance," *The Reports of Sir John Spelman*, 2 vols. (London, 1978), 2: 23–51, quotation on p. 23. See also Baker, "English Law and the Renaissance," in *The Legal Profession and the Common Law* (London, 1986), 461–76, and F. W. Maitland, "English Law and the Renaissance," *Selected Historical Essays of F. W. Maitland*, intro. Helen M. Cam (Cambridge, 1957), 135–51.

5. Baker, "English Law and the Renaissance," 26.

6. For example, Baker enumerates the following effects of humanism on the law: 1) attempts to improve the literary form and language of the law, 2) a tendency to explain the law historically, 3) the pursuit of a utilitarian idea of the "commonwealth," 4) an "equitable" approach to a variety of individual cases, and 5) an unprecedented confidence in the use of legislation to regulate society. See "English Law and the Renaissance," 28–46.

7. Schoeck, "Lawyers and Rhetoric," 291. Schoeck's image is derived from Puttenham's anecdote about coming upon Sir Nicholas Bacon "sitting in his gallery alone with the works of Quintillian before him," *The Arte of English Poesie*, ed. G. D. Wilcox and A. Walker (Cambridge, 1936), 140.

8. On the reading practices of sixteenth-century English humanists, see Anthony Grafton and Lisa Jardine, " 'Studied for Action': How Gabriel Harvey read his Livy," *Past and Present* 129 (1990): 30–78.

9. Louis A. Montrose, "Professing the Renaissance: The Poetics and Politics of Culture," *The New Historicism*, ed. H. Aram Veeser (New York and London, 1989), 17.

10. See Alan Bray, *Homosexuality in Renaissance England* (London, 1982); Natalie Zemon Davis, *The Return of Martin Guerre* (Cambridge, Mass., 1983); and Davis, *Fiction in the Archives: Pardon Tales and Their Tellers in Sixteenth-Century France* (Stanford, 1987). For examples of literary criticism and social history in dialogue over legal topics, see Stephen Greenblatt, "Psychoanalysis and Renaissance Culture," *Literary Theory/Renaissance Texts*, ed. Patricia Parker and David Quint (Baltimore, 1986), 210–24; Lisa Jardine, "Why Should He Call Her Whore? Defamation and Desdemona's Case," *Reading Shakespeare Historically* (London, 1996), 19–34; Lynda Boose, "The Priest, the Slanderer, the Historian and the Feminist," *English Literary Renaissance* 25 (1995): 320–40; Alan Stewart, *Close Readers: Humanism and Sodomy in Early Modern England* (Princeton, 1997); and Chap. 3.

11. Davis, *Fictions in the Archives*, 2–3 and notes; see also the discussion of narrative in Laura Gowing, *Domestic Dangers: Women, Words and Sex in Early Modern London* (Oxford, 1996), 41–48.

12. See, for example, Steven Mullaney, "Apprehending Subjects, or the Reformation of the Suburbs," *The Place of the Stage: License, Play and Power in Renaissance England* (Chicago, 1988), 88–115.

13. Peter Goodrich, *Legal Discourse: Studies in Linguistics, Rhetoric and Legal Analysis* (Basingstoke, 1987), 205–6. See also *Critical Legal Studies*, ed. Allan C. Hutchinson (New York, 1989); and Christopher Norris, "Law, Deconstruction and the Resistance to Theory," *Journal of Law and Society* 15 (1988): 166–87. For Derrida on law, see "Force of Law: The 'Mystical Foundations of Authority,' " trans. Mary Quantance, in *Deconstruction and the Possibility of Justice,* ed. D. Cornell, M. Rosenfield, and D. G. Carlson (New York, 1992), 3–67, lucidly discussed by Willy Maley, "Beyond the Law? The Justice of Deconstruction," *Law and Critique* 10 (1999): 49–69.

14. Peter Goodrich, "Salem and Bizance: A Short History of Two Laws," *Law in the Courts of Love* (London, 1996) 10.

15. Ian Maclean, *Interpretation and Meaning in the Renaissance: The Case of Law* (Cambridge, 1992).

16. Maclean's neglect of sexual difference is surprising, because he has written learnedly on Renaissance attitudes toward women. In fact, it seems as though the issue of *intent* to defame, central to Maclean's argument, is not vital in women's actions. See Gowing, *Domestic Dangers*, 72–73. For an example of a legal dispute in 1606 in which sexual innuendo against a woman was denied on the grounds that there was no malicious intent, see Lorna Hutson, "*Ethopoiea*, Source-Study and Legal History: A Post-theoretical Approach to the Question of 'Character' in Shakespearean Drama," *Post-Theory: New Directions in Criticism,* ed. Martin Macquillan, Graeme MacDonald, Robin Purves, and Stephen Thomson (Edinburgh, 1999), 151–52.

17. Luke Wilson, "*Hamlet, Hales v. Petit,* and the Hysteresis of Action," *ELH* 60 (1993): 15–55; Wilson, "*Hamlet:* Equity, Intention, Performance," *Studies in the Literary Imagination* 24 (1991): 91–113.

18. Aristotle, *Nicomachean Ethics,* trans. H. Rackham (Cambridge, Mass., 1932), 5.10.5, pp. 314–17.

19. See Maclean, *Interpretation and Meaning,* 181–85; and Chap. 7. On equity, see also Stuart E. Prall, "The Development of Equity in Tudor England," *American Journal of Legal History* 8 (1964): 1–19.

20. See Marvin T. Herrick, *Comic Theory in the Sixteenth Century* (Urbana, Ill., 1950); Joel B. Altman, *The Tudor Play of Mind: Rhetorical Inquiry and the Development of Elizabethan Drama* (Berkeley, Calif., 1978); Patricia Parker, "Shakepeare and Rhetoric: "Dilation" and "Delation" in *Othello,*" in *Shakespeare and the Question of Theory,* ed. Patricia Parker and Geoffrey Hartman (London, 1985), 54–74; Kathy Eden, *Poetic and Legal Fiction in the Aristotelian Tradition* (Princeton, N.J., 1986); and Terence Cave, *Recognitions: A Study in Poetics* (Oxford, 1988), 28–54.

21. Familiarity is shown, for example, by Shakespeare's *Comedy of Errors,* in which the day of errors is offered to Egeon as the mitigation of a sentence of death by a duke who declares himself "not partial to infringe our laws." The example is noted by Parker, "Shakespeare and Rhetoric," 54; Wilson, "*Hamlet:* Equity, Intention, Performance," 91–113; Altman, *Tudor Play of Mind,* 169–71; and Lorna Hutson, *The Usurer's Daughter* (London, 1994), 196.

22. J. M. Balkin, "Deconstructive Practice and Legal Theory," *Yale Law Journal* 96 (1987): 743–86, esp. 767–72.

23. P. S. Atiyah, *Promises, Morals and Law* (Oxford, 1981), 4.

24. As J. H. Baker observes, "No other doctrine in English law can compete with 'consideration' for greatest diversity and complexity of historical explanation," a fact which itself suggests the extent to which its rationale was obscure after the seventeenth century. See Baker, "Origins of the 'Doctrine' of Consideration, 1535–85," in *On the Laws and Customs of England: Essays in Honour of Samuel E. Thorne,* ed. Morris S. Arnold, Thomas A. Greene, Sally A. Scully and Stephen D. White (Chapel Hill, 1981), 336–58, and 336n for a bibliography of earlier literature.

25. See Chap. 6.

26. T. N. Tentler, *Sin and Confession on the Eve of the Reformation* (Princeton, N.J., 1977), 1–22; Joseph Marcos, *Doors to the Sacred: A Historical Introduction to the Sacraments of the Christian Church* (London, 1981), 328–45.

27. A. W. B. Simpson, *A History of the Common Law of Contract* (Oxford, 1975), 376–96.

28. R. H. Helmholz, "Assumpsit and *Fidei Laesio,*" *Law Quarterly Review* (1975): 406–32.

29. Richard Cousin, *An Apologie of, and for, Sundrie Proceedings by Jurisdiction Ecclesiasticall, of late times by some challenged* (London, 1591), 51. Ibid., 51.

31. Ibid., 52

32. See Goodrich, *Law in the Courts of Love,* 25; Edmund Leites, "Casuistry and Character," in *Conscience and Casuistry in Early Modern Europe,* ed. Edmund Leites (Cambridge, 1988): 119–33; and Chap. 11.

33. Francis Oakley, "Medieval Theories of Natural Law: William of Ockham and the Significance of the Voluntarist Tradition," *Natural Law Forum* 6 (1961), 68. Aristotle distinguished natural and conventional justice in book 5 of the *Nicomachean Ethics;* on

natural law, see also, for example, Aristotle, *Rhetoric* 1373b4; Cicero, *De officiis* 1.31, *De re publica* 3.33, *De legibus* 1.33–36, *De inventione* 2.65, 2.162; Seneca, *Epistulae morales* 90.

34. See the discussion of Gratian in James A. Brundage, *Medieval Canon Law* (London, 1995), chap. 7, esp. 154 and 158.

35. Thomas Aquinas, *Summa Theologica,* first part of second part [1–2], questions 93 and 96.

36. Johann Sommerville, *Politics and Ideology in England, 1603–1640* (London, 1986), 15.

37. Christopher St. German, *Doctor and Student,* ed. T. F. T. Plucknett and J. L. Barton (London, 1974), 14–15. Richard White, *Natural Law in English Renaissance Literature* (Cambridge, 1990) regards St. German on natural law as merely derivative of Aquinas.

38. St. German, *Doctor and Student,* 20–23.

39. Ibid.; St. Augustine, *On the Free Choice of the Will,* trans. Thomas Willams (Indianapolis, Ind., 1993), 10.

40. St. German, *Doctor and Student,* 230; see also 108–109.

41. On St. German's part in the Henrician reformation, see John Guy, *Christopher St. German on Chancery and Statute* (London, 1985). Like rhetorical argument on both sides of a question, natural law has always been a double-edged sword. In the sixteenth century, the belief in a law of reason or a natural moral order underlying the differences of positive law and social custom could be both reassuring and challenging. In response to the religious conflicts of the Reformation, the discovery of the New World, the growth of the modern state, and astonishing developments in natural science, natural law offered a way of intellectually accommodating radical social and political change. It also provided a criterion for judging radically new experiences and for adjudicating the cases of conscience confronting the early modern individual. Thus, humanist treatises on rhetoric, philology, and neostoic philosophy; absolutist works of political theory and monarchomach treatises on political resistance; and the work Spanish Catholic and Protestant jurists and theologians all found occasion to appeal to natural law. Although for many writers of the early modern period natural law in conformity with divine law dictated political obedience, natural law could also inspire a radical critique of positive law. This was particularly true of resistance theorists on the Continent and in England. In his *Du Droit des magistrats* (1574), the Calvinist Theodore Beza declared, "Equity and natural law, on which all human society depends, permit no doubt [that] . . . in all agreements based solely on the consent of the contracting parties, the obligation may be broken by those who have made it for sufficient cause — from which it follows that they who have the power to create a king have the power to depose him." In the 1640s, Henry Parker, John Milton, and their confederates similarly appealed to equity and natural law to justify resistance to Charles I.

42. In *De jure belli ac pacis libri tres,* ed. James Brown Scott, trans. Francis W. Kelsey, with Arthur E. R. Boak, Henry A. Sanders, Jesse S. Reeves, and Herbert F. Wright, 2 vols. (Washington, 1913), Grotius derived the principle of sociability from the Stoics (Prolegomena, section 6). There is considerable scholarly debate about whether early modern notions of natural law depart in any significant ways from classical or medieval notions. See also Knud Haakonssen, *Natural Law and Moral Philosophy* (Cambridge, 1996),

Richard Tuck, *Philosophy and Government, 1572–1651* (Cambridge, 1993), and Ian Shapiro, *The Evolution of Rights in Liberal Theory* (Cambridge, 1986). Scholars emphasizing continuity include Brian Tierney, *The Idea of Natural Rights: Studies on Natural Rights, Natural Law and Church Law, 1150–1625* (Atlanta, 1997), who argues that modern theories of natural right developed in the twelfth century; James Gordley, *The Philosophical Origins of Modern Contract Doctrine* (Oxford, 1991); Johann Sommerville, "From Suárez to Filmer: A Reappraisal," *Historical Journal* 25 (1982): 525–40; and Sommerville, *Politics and Ideology,* e.g., 12–17.

43. That Grotius, Selden, and Hobbes were responding in part to contemporary currents of skepticism is the argument of Richard Tuck in *Philosophy and Government.*

44. J. B. Schneewind, "Pufendorf's Place in the History of Ethics," *Synthèse* 72 (1987), 130.

45. Grotius simultaneously derived the natural law of justice from the necessary maintenance of the social order and from the "direction of a well-tempered judgement" (*De Jure,* "Prolegomena," sections 8–11). On Grotius' distinctive use of the phrase "etiamsi daremus" (Prolegomena, section 11), see Knud Haakonssen, "Hugo Grotius and the History of Political Thought," *Political Theory* 13 (1985): 239–65; and A. P. D'Entrèves, *Natural Law: An Introduction to Legal Philosophy,* 2nd ed. (London, 1970): "Grotius's aim was, to construct a system of laws which would carry conviction in an age in which theological controversy was gradually losing the power to do so" (55). For a contrasting view, see Chap. 13.

46. Grotius, *De jure,* 1.4.7.3–4

47. This is James Gordley's argument about Grotius in *The Philosophical Origins of Modern Contract Doctrine;* see 122–32.

48. See Haakonssen, *Natural Law and Moral Philosophy,* Tuck, *Philosophy and Government,* and Shapiro, *Evolution of Rights.*

49. See Samuel Rutherford, *Lex, Rex* (London, 1644), question 15, esp. p. 110; and Robert Filmer, *The Originall of Government,* in *Patriarcha and Other Writings,* ed. Johann P. Sommerville (Cambridge, 1991), 220–21.

50. Hobbes, *Leviathan,* ed. Richard Tuck (Cambridge, 1991). Chapter is cited first, followed by page number, as here: 21.150.

51. Hobbes, *Brief of Aristotle's Rhetoric,* in *The Rhetorics of Thomas Hobbes and Bernard Lamy,* ed. John T. Harwood (Carbondale, Ill., 1986). For Hobbes's attack on rhetoric, see, for example, *Leviathan,* chaps. 4, 5, and 8 (on metaphor), and chap. 17. For his attack on preachers, see his history of the civil war, *Behemoth, or the Long Parliament,* ed. Ferdinand Tönnies (Chicago, 1990). On Hobbes's attitude towards rhetoric, see Victoria Kahn, *Rhetoric, Prudence, and Skepticism in the Renaissance* (Ithaca, N.Y., 1985), chap. 6; David Johnston, *The Rhetoric of "Leviathan"* (Princeton, N.J., 1986); Victoria Silver, "Hobbes on Rhetoric," in *The Cambridge Companion to Hobbes,* ed. Tom Sorell (Cambridge, 1996), 329–45; Quentin Skinner, *Reason and Rhetoric in the Philosophy of Hobbes* (Cambridge, 1996); and Sorell's earlier "Thomas Hobbes: Rhetoric and the Construction of Morality," *Proceedings of the British Academy* 76 (1991): 1–61; Tom Sorell, "Hobbes's Unaristotelian Political Rhetoric," *Philosophy and Rhetoric* 23 (1990): 96–108, and "Hobbes's Persuasive Civil Science," *Philosophical Quarterly* 40 (1990): 342–51.

52. Paradoxically, given Hobbes's own antipathy to classical rhetoric, some of his critics represented this assimilation as merely a rhetorical tour de force. See, for example, John Eachard, *Mr Hobb's State of Nature Considered* (London, 1672; Liverpool, 1958), 21–22.

53. Samuel Pufendorf, *De jure naturae et gentium libri octo,* trans. C. H. and W. A. Oldfather, 2 vols. (Oxford, 1934), book 1, chap. 2.

54. Ibid., 2.3.20; 4.4.1.

55. Although Pufendorf put forward a command theory of law, it is important to note that he saw himself as taking issue with Hobbes's argument that "justice, as well as ownership, owes its origin in the final analysis to commonwealths" (*De jure,* 1.7.13). Pufendorf always insisted that the ultimate authority for natural and human law was God. For an account that emphasizes Pufendorf's radical voluntarism, see Schneewind, "Pufendorf's Place in the History of Ethics," esp. 127–30.

56. This summary of Finch and Dodderidge is taken from J. W. Tubbs, "Custom, Time, and Reason: Early Seventeenth-Century Conceptions of the Common Law," *History of Political Thought* 19 (1998): 394–96. Henry Finch's *Nomotechnia* was written in law French in 1613 and published in translation as *Law: or, A Discourse Thereof* (London, 1627). Like other scholars, Tubbs points to the fact that "all common lawyers who had read Sir John Fortescue and Christopher St German had been exposed to the Aristotelian tradition in logic and rhetoric, even if they had no formal university training." (397). On Coke, see, among others, J. G. A. Pocock, *The Ancient Constitution and Feudal Law,* rev. ed. (Cambridge, 1987); Charles Gray, "Reason, Authority, and Imagination: The Jurisprudence of Sir Edward Coke," in *Culture and Politics, From Puritanism to the Enlightenment,* ed. Perez Zagorin (Berkeley, Calif., 1980), 25–66; and Richard Helgerson, *Forms of Nationhood* (Chicago, 1993). On the alliance of common lawyers and Puritan critics of the Crown, see John Dykstra Eusden, *Puritans, Lawyers, and Politics in Early Seventeenth- Century England* (New Haven, 1958).

57. In his introduction to Gierke's *Natural Law and the Theory of Society,* Ernest Barker insisted that the formative influence on English political theory was Roman rather than common law (xxii). This may be true in the narrow sense that the idea of the social or political contract derived ultimately from Roman law. However, most scholars of early modern England stress the inextricability of disputes about common law and the development of political thought. See, among others, Eusden, *Puritans, Lawyers, and Politics;* Frederick Pollock, "The History of English Law as a Branch of Politics" in *Jurisprudence and Legal Essays* (New York, 1961), 185–211; Margaret Judson, *The Crisis of the Constitution* (1949; New Brunswick, N.J., 1988); Francis D. Wormuth, *The Royal Prerogative, 1603–1649* (Ithaca, 1939); Louis A. Knafla, *Law and Politics in Jacobean England* (Cambridge, 1977); Johann Sommerville, *Politics and Ideology in England;* W. J. Jones, *Politics and the Bench: The Judges and the Origins of the English Civil War* (New York, 1971); and David Sacks's and Lorna Hutson's essays in this volume.

58. For the classic scholarly treatment of the ancient constitution, see J. G. A. Pocock, *The Ancient Constitution and Feudal Law,* rev. ed. (Cambridge, 1987). Pocock argues that the common law was regularly identified with immemorial custom in the seventeenth century. For a counterargument that identifies two traditions of thinking about common law in this period, see J. W. Tubbs, "Custom, Time, and Reason," 363–406.

59. Sommerville argues that divine-right absolutism was a response primarily to Catholic theories of political contract and only secondarily to domestic political disputes (*Politics and Ideology,* chap. 1). See 121–26 on the controversy over Cowell's *Interpreter.*

60. For discussions of these cases, see Judson, *Crisis of the Constitution;* Wormuth, *The Royal Prerogative;* and Sommerville, *Politics and Ideology.*

61. T. B. and T. J. Howell, ed., *A Complete Collection of State Trials* (London, 1816), vol. 2, col. 389; quoted in Francis Oakley, "Medieval Theories of Natural Law," 76.

62. Thomas Hobbes, *A Dialogue Between a Philosopher and a Student of the Common Laws of England,* ed. Joseph Cropsey (Chicago, 1971), 54. The *Dialogue* was composed between 1662 and 1675 and published posthumously in 1681, two years after Hobbes's death. See the excellent introduction to this edition by Joseph Cropsey.

63. Frederick Pollock, "The History of the Law of Nature," in *Jurisprudence and Legal Essays* 135.

64. On the nascent historicism of the early modern period, see not only Kelley, *History, Law and the Human Sciences,* but also Friedrich Meinecke, *Machiavellism,* trans. Douglas Scott (New Haven, Conn., 1957), and Leo Strauss, *Natural Right and History* (Chicago, 1950). On the link between rhetoric and historicism in the early modern period, see Nancy S. Struever, *The Language of History in the Renaissance* (Princeton, N.J., 1970). For an argument that Hobbes and Grotius were responding to early modern currents of skepticism, see Richard Tuck, *Philosophy and Government.* For an argument that Grotius' method shows a nascent historicism, see Chap. 12 in this volume.

65. On Hobbes's derivation of natural law from natural right, see *Leviathan,* 14.91.

66. Leo Strauss, *The Political Philosophy of Hobbes,* trans. Elsa Sinclair (1936; Chicago, 1963), 161, n. 2. On the association of natural right, historicism, and liberalism, see Strauss, *Natural Right and History.* On the use of the tradition of natural law to support a radical critique of the status quo, see Ernst Bloch, *Natural Law and Human Dignity* (Cambridge, Mass., 1986).

67. Barbara Shapiro, *Probability and Certainty in Seventeenth-Century England* (Princeton, N.J., 1983); *"Beyond Reasonable Doubt" and "Probable Cause"* (Berkeley, Calif., 1991).

68. See note 20.

69. Natalie Z. Davis, *Fiction in the Archives,* viii, 5.

70. See Davis, *Return of Martin Guerre,* 99–103; 104–13; Hutson, *Usurer's Daughter,* 156–57, 186, 192–93.

71. Richard Wunderli, *London Church Courts and Society Before the Reformation* (Cambridge, Mass., 1981), 76; see also Baker, *Reports of Sir John Spelman,* 2:238–42, 255–59.

72. As David Norbrook observes, in "The Emperor's New Body? *Richard II,* Ernst Kantorowicz and the Politics of Shakespeare Criticism," *Textual Practice* 10 (1996), 329–30.

73. C. B. Macpherson, *The Political Theory of Possessive Individualism: Hobbes to Locke* (Oxford, 1962). In *Natural Rights Theories* (Cambridge, 1979), 3, Richard Tuck argues that Macpherson is correct about the possessive quality of seventeenth-century rights talk, but that this notion of possession is apparent much earlier in the language of dominium.

The Promise and the Contract in Early Modern England: Slade's Case in Perspective

DAVID HARRIS SACKS

In contemporary Anglo-American law there is an intimate connection between promises and contracts.[1] Both depend on the performative aspects of language — on the way the utterance of certain forms of words, whether by mouth or in a written instrument, amounts not just to the communication of meaning but also to the execution of action. Promises and contracts both create agreements between persons or groups. So long as the agreement has been intentionally and voluntarily made, and the action resolved upon is not illegal or immoral or impossible to perform, it is commonly understood to have binding moral force. But in the Anglo-American legal tradition, only if there has been the exchange of a valuable consideration is a promise enforceable in law. This doctrine has shaped our views of human agency and rationality, of civil society and the state, of morality and justice. It also colors our understanding of the relationship of language to law. This paper undertakes to examine some of its intellectual and cultural implications as they developed in early modern England.

Consideration

There is probably no more important or more arcane and complicated concept in the English common law than "consideration." It has long been a

familiar, everyday word referring to the act of attentively or carefully thinking about, reflecting on, or contemplating a person, thing, idea, or subject.
In medieval legal contexts, the term "consideration" emphasized the connection of a given agreement to the reasons or motives the party or parties
had in undertaking it. The agreement would be binding if the party had a
reason acceptable in conscience for making it; otherwise not. As such, it was a
term commonly employed in canon-law jurisdictions where the focus was on
the causes, *causae,* that bound the parties to perform the acts to which they
had agreed.

Christopher St. German conveys much this sense in his *Doctor and Student*
(first published in 1530), one of the most influential legal texts of its era. In the
voice of the Doctor, St. German stressed that one who made a vow to God
"vppon a dellyberate mynde entendenge to perfourme yt ys bounde in conscyence to doo yt/ thoughe yt be onely made in the herete withoute pronoun-
synge of wordes." Similarly, a promise made for charitable purposes or in the
"seruyce of god" would be binding "thoughe there be no consyderacyon of
worldly profyte that the graunter hath had or intended to haue for it, so long as
he "that made the promyse intended to be bounde" by it." Only "yf hys
promyse be so naked that there is no maner of consyderacyon why yt shoulde
be made/ than I thynke hym not bounde to perfourme it." Here the public
benefit itself represents a sufficient cause or motive to give the promise its
power. Although the Student responds that all promises lacking any evidence
of a quid pro quo, even those for the honor of God or the welfare of the
community, would have no obligatory force under the common law, nothing
he says challenges the Doctor's open-ended usage of the term "consideration."[2]

In this context, "consideration" carries a broad, generic meaning encompassing all circumstances in which there are good reasons for performing a
promise, whether or not something of tangible value has been or will be
exchanged for it. It refers to a contemplative act, something looked at not just
closely, but inwardly. The use of the term in evaluating the enforcement of
promises and agreements connects the act with the antecedent thought processes in which the reasons for it are weighed.

The connection of a doctrine of quid pro quo with the concept of contractual obligation had itself long been familiar by St. German's time.[3] St. German's Student conveys the central idea in arguing that promises are binding in
common law only if "he to whome the promyse ys made: haue a charge by
reason of the promyse whyche he hathe also perfourmed."[4] The point is that in
these circumstances the party to whom the promise had been made would be
the victim of a "prejudice" if it was not executed.[5] But it was only in the
mid-1530s that the term "consideration" was first employed in common-law

pleadings to convey a similar idea, and only in the 1560s that anything approaching a theory of consideration linking it to the doctrine of quid pro quo began to be articulated.[6] By the later sixteenth century, however, the phrase "in consideration" was used to link supposedly separate undertakings to perform bargains or contracts previously entered into "for" stated sums.[7] These facts themselves reveal, as we shall see, the existence not only of new forms of pleading in the common law of contract, but also of the increasingly complicated kinds of contractual relationships taking hold in the commercial environment of the period.

Despite these developments, the continued use of the word "consideration" in the broad and general sense employed by St. German remained quite stable into the seventeenth century. In 1574, for example, the judges in Calthorpe's case defined the term as "a cause or meritorious occasion, requiring a mutual recompense in fact or law."[8] A similar sense is conveyed in the 1590s in William West's *Symbolaeography*. A "Couenant or agreement which hath a cause," he says, "is termed a Contract, which is nothing els but an agreement with a lawful cause or consideration." Those lacking a "cause" are "bare agreements," or "naturall obligations," such "as recompensing, requiting and other bare promises without lawful consideration."[9] Citing *Doctor and Student*, West defines "cause" as "a business, which being approued by law, maketh the Obligation rise by the contract, & the action vpon the obligation."[10]

By the 1620s, however, the concept of consideration had evolved in the language of the law. The 1624 edition of John and William Rastell's *Les Termes de La Ley*, first published a century before, finally introduces "consideration" as a legal term. It is defines as "the material cause of a contract without the which no contract can binde the party."[11] The concept of "material cause," derived from Aristotelian metaphysics, focuses instead on the thing or things of value exchanged between the contracting parties that distinguished the "consideration" from the human and divine purposes — the first and final causes — for which an action is undertaken, as well as from the efficient causes, namely the actions of exchange performed by the parties. "Contract" itself had long been defined in *Termes de La Ley* as "a bargaine or couenant betweene two parties, where one thing is giuen for another which is called (*Quid pro quo*)."[12]

By 1624 consideration had become equated, in effect, with quid pro quo.[13] The explanation for this change lies in the development of the action on the case in *assumpsit* for breach of promise. The action itself had evolved in a long line of cases on the enforcement of parol agreements that distinguish between the original agreement and the parties' subsequent promise to perform what had been agreed upon. Grounding the case on the assumpsit, as it was called, moved it into the realm of tort law, where more flexibility was available to plaintiffs in pleading and proof.[14] The term "consideration" was first introduced in a few such cases around 1540 initially to accommodate anomalous circumstances where it was not possible to allege directly that the promise in question had been made "in return for" a specific sum. By the end of the sixteenth century, however, "consideration" had almost completely displaced competing formulations as the term of choice in assumpsit cases.[15] According to Sir Matthew Hale, Chief Justice of King's Bench in Charles II's reign, this "multiplication of Actions upon the Case, which were rare formerly," also accounts in large measure for the huge increases in business in the central courts that he describes.[16] Critical to this history is the broad reconceptualization of the law of contract culminating in 1602 in Slade's case, to which we now turn.

The Assumption of Debt

The case of *Slade v. Morley* was first heard in the Devon Assizes in Lent 1595, and afterward in the Queen's Bench in 1596, and then before all the judges in the Exchequer Chamber during Michaelmas 1597. It was subsequently debated in similar circumstances, though sometimes in different locations, in 1598, in 1601, and twice in 1602 before being finally decided in Trinity in 1602. It is a remarkably widely reported case, thanks to numerous manuscripts as well as printed versions in the reports of Moore, Yelverton, and Coke.[17] These facts alone suggest the importance with which the case was viewed at the time. Here are the circumstances as they emerge from the record.

The dispute arose with respect to the sale of wheat and rye sown by John Slade in November 1594 on an enclosed field of eight acres he leased in Halberton, Devon. In May 1595, when the grain "had grown into ears" and while it was still in the field, Humphrey Morley had bargained for and bought it for the sum of sixteen pounds, promising to pay the sum at the Feast of St. John the Baptist next ensuing. The day passed without payment, and later, on the last day of September 1595, Morley, according to Slade, "was oftentimes thereunto required" by the latter "to pay him, or any way to content him." Morley allegedly refused, "whereupon" Slade "saith he is injured, and hath sustained damage to the value of 40l. and thereof bringeth suit."[18]

The language places the case in the realm of trespass. The suit therefore is for damages incurred as a result of Morley's alleged breach of promise, not for the recovery of a debt per se. Morley pleaded "non assumpsit modo et forma," arguing that he had made no separate promise on which the assumpsit would lie, but only had a "simple contract" with Slade.[19]

The exact and somewhat convoluted phrasing in the original declaration is important. In a lengthy and somewhat convoluted narrative, Slade, through his lawyers, insisted that Morley "did assume, and faithfully promised" to pay Slade the sixteen pounds "in consideration" of the fact that Slade had bargained and sold to him the crop then in the field.[20]

The language expressly conveys the sense that the promise for future payment was given as the quid pro quo for the consideration of the crop. This was no *nudum pactum*. Nevertheless, there was neither a "specialty" to record the debt nor an allegation that subsequent to the making of the agreement Morley had ever assumed or promised to pay it. So the central question was whether or not it could be treated as an action for trespass as well as an action for debt.[21]

In Lent 1595 the suit came before a jury at the assize court for Devon held at Exeter Castle, which found that Morley had indeed bought the wheat and rye for sixteen pounds as Slade had alleged, and "that betwixt the said John Slade and the said Humphrey Morley, there was no promise or taking upon him, besides the bargain aforesaid." However the jurors recognized the intrinsic problem with Slade's declaration, namely the absence of a claim that Morley had ever separately undertaken to perform his part of the original bargain, and issued a special verdict leaving it to the judges to determine whether or not Morley did "take upon him in the manner and form alleged." If he had, they agreed to award Slade his sixteen pounds, and an additional twenty shillings for damages. With this special verdict, the case came before the Queen's Bench during Hilary in 1596 and again during Michaelmas when the court decided that Morley "did take upon him" the obligations Slade had declared and ordered that the latter recover the damages and costs found by the jury, and also a further nine pounds "for his charges and costs," amounting in all to twenty-six pounds.[22]

Subsequently, John Dodderidge, appearing for Morley, came before all the judges in the Court of Exchequer Chamber and objected to the outcome on two grounds. First, he averred that the "plaintiff upon his bargain might have ordinary remedy by action of debt and therefore should not have an action on the case, which is an extraordinary."[23] His point was not only that the ordinary action should prevail over the extraordinary one but that the common law system of writs would be threatened if, as J. H. Baker puts it, the "same *cause* of action" could give "rise to two different *forms of action*."[24] Second, Dodderidge objected that maintenance of Slade's action took "away the defendant's benefit of wager of law, and so bereaves him of the benefit which the law gives him, which is his birthright. For peradventure the defendant has paid or satisfied the plaintiff in private betwixt them, of which payment he has no witness, and therefore it would be mischievous if he should not wage his law."[25]

We learn from Coke's report that the courts of Queen's Bench and Common Pleas were divided on these objections: the justices of the Queen's Bench held for Slade, but those of Common Pleas the contrary. Hence, "for the honour of the law, and for the quiet of the subject in the appeasing of such diversity of opinions" the case proceeded to further arguments "before all the Justices of England, and Barons of the Exchequer . . . and after many conferences between the justices and barons, it was resolved that the action was maintainable, and that the plaintiff should have judgement."[26]

According to Coke, the justices explicitly decided "that every contract executory imports in itself an *assumpsit*, for when one agrees to pay so much money, or to deliver any thing, thereby he assumes or promises to pay, or deliver it, and therefore when one sells any goods to another, and agrees to pay so much money at such a day, in that case both parties may have an action of debt, or an action on the case on *assumpsit*, for the mutual executory agreement of both parties imports in itself reciprocal actions on the case, as well as actions of debt."[27] In other words, the judges settled two matters. They agreed first that the making of a simple contract was simultaneously the making of a promise. In consequence, they also agreed that where there were executory agreements, that is, agreements requiring the future performance of their terms, the aggrieved party was able to chose whether to bring an action of debt or action on the case, suing "at his election" either for what he was owed or for damages incurred from the failure to perform the agreement.[28]

Regarding any claim of mischief to the defendant should he not be able to wage his law, where he might have paid "in secret," the justices answered, according to Coke, "that it should be accounted" the defendant's "folly that he did not take sufficient witnesses with him to prove the payment made: but the mischief would be rather on the other party, for now experience proves men's consciences grow so large that the respect of their private advantage rather induces men (and chiefly those of declining estates) to perjury; for *jurare in propria causa . . . est saepenumero hoc seculo praecipitium diaboli ad detrudendas miserorum animas ad infernum*; and therefore in debt, or other action where wager of law is admitted by the law, the Judges without good admonition and due examination of the party do not admit him to it."[29] According to the epigram, anyone who would swear an oath in his own cause risks falling headlong down to the devil and thrusting his soul into Hell.

The foregoing contains many complex technical issues, but for the present only "wager of law" need detain us.[30] The ancient law of debt on a contract permitted this procedure where there were parol agreements whose terms or their satisfaction could not be attested by witnesses or a sealed instrument. Basing the matter on Morley's putative assumpsit thereby shifted it into the realm of actions on the case, where disputes were tried by juries and commonly depended on the sworn testimony of witnesses. Although such jury trials did not yet operate according to the modern law of evidence, the jurors, independently selected from among men of the neighborhood unrelated to the parties, were triers of fact. In wager of law, the compurgators or oath helpers — typically eleven in number[31] — swore to their belief in the veracity of the oath-taker, who normally would have been a friend or neighbor.[32]

Although in a purely technical sense this was an "ancillary" matter, it is clear, as Baker has argued, that "the replacement of debt by the action on the case was principally motivated, from the plaintiff's point of view, by the desire to avoid wager of law."[33] Coke, in his *Commentary on Littleton,* makes the same point a bit more sharply: "The law presumeth that no man will forsweare himselfe for any worldly thing; but men's consciences doe grow so large . . . as they choose rather to bring an action upon the case upon his promise, where in (because it is *trespasse sur le case*) hee cannot wage his law, than an action of debt."[34]

In acting for Morley, Francis Bacon had centered his discussion against the ouster of the defendant from "his law," on the difficulties in making proof where the contract was privately negotiated and the contractual obligations were technical and complex. He argued especially that it prevented the defendant from being "surprised in his proof." Bargains and contracts, he said, "are often made in secret and it would be most inconvenient that on every private bargain between men they were compelled to call unto them a notary or witnesses to prove the bargain." Because of these often informal circumstances in which contracts were made and the requirement of unanimity in jury verdicts, "private contracts are difficult to be tried by juries." Even where "the contract be made in the presence of witnesses, yet the proof of it is very dangerous and uncertain, when the wresting or mistaking of a word may alter the whole substance of the contract."[35]

Against the argument that "wager of law is an occasion of great perjury," Bacon took the view that the danger of uttering falsehoods under oath was the greater where the courts relied on juries and witnesses. "For where by wager of law the defendant himself may be perjured, the trial of such secret matters by inquest gives occasion to twelve jurors and also to several witnesses to be forsworn." In Bacon's view, justice was served not only by the sanctity of the oath, which placed the soul of the oath-taker in jeopardy before God, but also by the need to enlist the aid of a body of supports, similarly willing to place their souls in jeopardy.[36]

In the proper circumstances wager of law was a just and effective instrument of proof. However, it was not only the widespread belief in God's certain punishment of perjury that gave it its power. The procedure depended on the defendant's ability first to find sufficient pledges for his appearance to perform the oath. Then it was necessary for his eleven compurgators to swear with him, putting their own souls and credit at risk with his.[37] Within the framework of local markets and regimes of credit discipline, where a trader's good name, personal honor, and reputation for performing his obligations were his principal assets, the risks attendant on false swearing were material as well as spiritual. A tradesman who acquired a reputation for failure to pay debts or for false dealing of any sort would soon find that his credit was naught, or nearly so. Credit transactions were ubiquitous at all levels of late medieval and early modern society. As more and more people came to depend on market exchange for food, drink, clothing, and other consumer goods, or for their incomes or livelihoods, credit was increasingly important as one of the principal binding forces in society. Few among the English, even the very wealthy, had large sums of money at hand for very long; instead they commonly were borrowers and lenders at the same time, taking in sums from their own debtors and paying them out again to creditors.[38]

Since virtually all market exchange depended on credit in one form or another, the risk of perjury to the trademan's material welfare gave immediacy and reinforcement to the spiritual danger into which his soul would fall. This regime worked a good deal less effectively, however, where the parties had only a limited acquaintance with one another or were only intermittently engaged in exchange transactions. If parties were unacquainted or lacked mutual friends, or if the transaction involved unusually large sums, it was common to secure debts with conditional bonds, which when presented in court would prevent defendants from being permitted to wage their law.[39] But with small transactions, even among relative strangers, the inconveniences and added cost of using such sealed instruments outweighed any additional security that might have been gained. Wager of law, therefore, would apply mainly in disputes involving relatively modest sums, where in the ordinary course of affairs bargains and settlements very likely would have been concluded in private.[40]

Given the presuppositions of Christians and the marketplace practices of the early modern English, neither wager of law nor trial by jury was more likely to encourage perjury. Nevertheless, so long as wager of law was available as a defense, plaintiffs would have found themselves at some disadvantage in transactions where sealed instruments had not been used, while defendants who had privately settled their parol agreements enjoyed some protection against the danger of falsely grounded lawsuits. To avoid the prospect of wager of law where parol contracts were in dispute, plaintiffs often brought their business to privileged merchant courts, such as the market courts of corporate towns and chartered boroughs, or, as time went by, to the prerogative courts and courts of equity, where wager of law was not permitted.[41]

By Henry VIII's reign, more and more cases of debt also were finding their way into the common-law courts, driven there because inflation now made many small matters, previously restricted to the local courts, eligible for jurisdiction of the central courts in Westminster.[42] At the same time, the number of small transactions concluded in private were rapidly on the rise in rural as well as urban communities, not only among the growing population of petty tradesmen and dealers in the towns but also among men like John Slade who were engaged in the marketing of agricultural produce.[43] In the sixteenth century, King's Bench was already doing what it could to accommodate their needs, including promotion of assumpsit to ease the burdens of plaintiffs in contract cases. Among other changes, by the end of the century its judges were no longer requiring plaintiffs to allege the existence of a separate promise in such cases. Hence, wager of law rose mainly in disputes on parol contracts brought to Common Pleas, whose main business concerned actions of debt and whose judges strictly upheld the rigors of the register of writs.[44]

Because it was brought on a simple contract, Slade's case represented the perfect test for settling this disagreement between the jurisdictions. Since there was no allegation of subsequent promise by the defendant, it was necessary for Slade's lawyers to collapse together the contract and the promise to perform it, thereby treating the making of a contract as the equivalent of a speech act.[45] Coke, arguing on Slade's behalf, put the point in exactly these terms: "When the plaintiff said 'You shall have my corn' and the other said 'You shall have so much money for your corn' these are express promises. And these words *assumpsit, promisit,* and *agreeavit* are all synonymous and of one signification. Would you have every plain man use the proper words 'I assume' and 'I take upon myself'? It is not necessary. If he says 'I promise' or 'I agree' it is as much as and all one. And if you will deny that there was any promise here, there was no contract either."[46]

Viewed in this light, Slade's case was about the "language game" of contract-making. Bacon and the other lawyers appearing for Morley held that for good and prudent reasons the rules imposed a sharp distinction between a contract and a promise and required that different facts must be alleged to frame a suit on each. "For action on the case must be grounded on deceit or breach of promise," Bacon argued, "but in debt on a contract there is no deceit or breach of promise supposed. For a bargain changes the property of each part, and therefore in action of debt it is alleged that the defendant detains the money or thing demanded as if it was his before; to wit, the plaintiff had the property of it by the contract. And therefore when the plaintiff demands only that which was his before, it cannot be said that he is deceived by the defendant; but that the defendant detains that of which the property was in the plaintiff."[47] According to this analysis, only an expressed promise could be the subject of suit. Coke and the others appearing for Slade saw contracts as a special class of promises—namely promises where there was a sufficient consideration to make them legally binding. They saw promises implied in contracts, even where they were not overtly expressed. This view permitted plaintiffs a free choice whether to bring their suits on the contract itself or on the promise to perform it. The court, in deciding for Slade, accepted the latter interpretation.

Moves and Mentalités

The prevailing judgment of legal historians has been that the court's embracing arguments about "implied promises" represents an insignificant feature of the case—a vehicle for accomplishing what the lawyers and judges were really after—namely, the displacement of the older forms of action in contract with new ones capable of attracting potential plaintiffs to the common-law courts in the sorts of contract dispute that were becoming more and more frequent.[48] In this interpretation, Slade's case was a "move," to adopt J. G. A. Pocock's usage, one of a series of "assertions, and essentially contestable assertions at that, made by identifiable actors in identifiable circumstances for identifiable reasons," not features of *mentalité,* rooted in "a habit of mind bred by education and practice."[49] Moves are highly sensitive to the particularities of the historical setting in which they are made. Mentalités persist despite those same particularities and change by paradigm shifts.

There seems little doubt that the winning argument in Slade's case, and especially the decision as formulated in Coke's report, should have a place in a narrative of moves in the history of the English law. By the beginning of the sixteenth century, common lawyers and judges, especially those connected with King's Bench, felt considerable concern about their loss of business to the equity jurisdictions and prerogative courts—no trivial matter in an era of rapid inflation. It is no surprise, therefore, that during the sixteenth and seventeenth centuries a host of new common-law remedies were invented to help lawyers hold on to cases that threatened to migrate elsewhere. The rise of the action on the case in assumpsit in King's Bench is itself part of this market-driven process.[50]

In one way, of course, the mentality of the common lawyers was itself a mentality of moves—a habit of mind that led them not only to reach into their bag of pleading maneuvers to advance the interests of the clients they represented but also to transform particular results into precedents and then to extend them as far as they could. Coke's report, representing what were mainly "the heads of his own argument" on Slade's behalf as the "resolutions" of the court, is itself an example of this process. It filled the space left by the absence of a definitive statement of the court's reasoning and thereby fixed all future discussions of contracts according to its substance.[51]

Nevertheless, Slade's case also has a place in the history of changing assumptions and habits of mind. Wager of law resides at the heart of the matter, because its rationale was called into question by the shifting frameworks of market exchange, by the increased willingness and capacity of litigants to bring their disputes to courts remote from the localities in which they had originated, and by deepening skepticism about oaths. Wager of law raised two related problems, social and conceptual at the same time.

The first concerned the capacity of oaths to constrain the consciences of those who took them. We have already noted the epigram cited by Coke pointing out the incentive for perjury where oath-takers were defending their own vital interests. The epigram summarizes a conventional argument commonly made by medieval civil and canon lawyers. What had changed, however, was the setting in which the oath might be administered. As already noted, wager of law worked effectively enough in local courts where the defendant was well-known to his oath-helpers and had a reputation to uphold among them. The social and institutional constraints were somewhat diminished when suits were heard in Westminster, far away from the place where the original transactions had occurred.[52] Finding compurgators there would have been difficult had it not been for the fact that by the sixteenth century a professional class of oath-helpers waited at the doors of the courts of common law to perform the service for a fee.[53]

But more than the breakdown of procedure or outright corruption troubled the critics of wager of law. Even where the defendant might have been well known to the compurgators, it was doubtful whether they could genuinely attest to his truthfulness. In its own way, this doubt arose from the very source of skepticism that underpinned the rejection in common law of promises that lacked a quid pro quo. In arguing against the enforcement of promises where only a charitable purpose could be discovered, St. German's Student insists "that no accyon can lye . . . vpon suche promyses/ for yt ys secrete in hys owne consceynce whether he entended for to be bounde or naye. And of the entent inwarde in the herte: mannes law can not Juge/ and that ys one of the causes why the lawe of god ys necessary (that ys to saye) to Juge inwarde thynges."[54]

Seen in this light, wager of law was as intrinsically problematic as a bare promise, even though oath-helpers were merely attesting to the defendant's credibility and not swearing to the factual truth of the defendant's oath or testifying to his intentions. If the conscience of the defendant could not be directly interrogated by anyone but God, oath-helpers were themselves able only to speak to their belief in the defendant's truthfulness, on the basis of his outward behavior in past times, not to his inward state at the moment he swore his oath.[55]

Ancient doubts about the accessibility of the conscience to public scrutiny, traceable to St. Augustine, only deepened in the Reformation era, especially as challenges were mounted to the use of ex officio oaths in ecclesiastical jurisdictions to root out religious dissent.[56] The issue is intimately connected to the law of contract as it had been developing in the sixteenth century. St. German, for example, made criticism of the oath a cause of his own. In his *Treatise concernynge the diuision betwene the spiritualtie and temporaltie* (1532) and in *Salem and Bizance* (1533), he made almost the same case against the oath in matters of heresy as he did against bare promises.[57] "For if it be secrete in" a man's "own breste," he said in the latter work, "none can be iuge but god only, that is the sercher of mans herte." Unless a witness to some overt and public expression of belief could stand as accuser, "no man may after the lawe be detected of heresie."[58] According to this view, the oaths lacked epistemological force, since there would be no independent means to judge the veracity of the oath-taker.

The same issue reemerged at the end of the sixteenth century in connection with ecclesiastical efforts to root out dissent from the Church of England. James Morice, a Middle Temple lawyer active in parliamentary service in the 1580s and early '90s,[59] singled out how such oaths in effect violated fundamental principles of natural justice, potentially forcing them either to denounce or perjure themselves or to accept imprisonment for contempt if they refused to swear. All properly constituted judicial actions, he says, require three distinct persons: an accuser, an accused, and a judge. But the "Iudge, who imposeth the oath, is him selfe . . . the partie accuser, and so both Iudge and Promoter . . . Or else the Deponent must of necessitie susteine two principall partes in judgement, that is to say *Actor & Reus,* Accuser and accused."[60]

Medieval canon lawyers had often complained that the use of the ex officio oath in effect made those administering it judges in their own causes.[61] Morice, in effect, extended the point to the oath-takers as well. By potentially forcing them either to denounce or perjure themselves or to accept imprisonment for contempt if they refused to swear, it placed them in a self-contradictory condition, inherently repugnant to the law of nature. "Know we not that all, or the moste part of men," he said, "will rather hazard their soules then put their bodies to shame and reproach: presume the lawe neuer so much that after fame they should not make scruple to discouer them selues." Against the argument that oath-takers are "not trusted alone," but bring "compurgators, who depose . . . waying his feare of God, and former conuersation," Morice insisted that this procedure only makes them worse. "For what doe those compurgators but by lending their oathes, justifie in effect him to be honest, whom fame and the former deponents" previously had alleged "to be dishonest." Compurgation offered no rational basis for settling such differences.[62]

Since Morice sought to demonstrate the injustice of the ex officio oath under English law, he went to some pains to distinguish it from wager of law, singling out the voluntary character of the latter.[63] However, Coke, in acting for Slade as well as in reporting Slade's case, made similar arguments against wager of law itself. "At this day," he said, "wager of law is too common, and the consciences of men exceeding bad and hasty to commit perjury for profit. And by allowing this action you will lead their souls away from such devilish perils."[64] We have already noted the Latin maxim he quoted on this point in the body of his report. He used the same tag a few years later in offering a declarative opinion to the Privy Council on the ex officio oath. Coke had concluded not just that the risks of perjury were equally great in these two ostensibly different realms but also that the voluntary character of oaths was effectively undermined whenever the material interests of the parties were at stake, whether in ecclesiastical or in lay jurisdiction.[65]

A neo-Augustinian view of conscience provides the link between the two forms of oath. According to William Perkins, conscience is "part of the understanding in al reasonable creatures, determining of their particular actions, either with them or against them." Its "proper end . . . is to determine of things done . . . to take the principles and conclusions of the minde and apply them, and by applying either accuse or excuse."[66] Since "it is placed in the middle betweene man and God . . . vnder God and yet aboue man," it "is known to none, beside himselfe, but to God, and bound only by God's word." On this basis, Perkins accepted the use of oaths, but "never . . . in way of confirmation, but onely in case of meere necessitie. . . . When all other humane proofes do faile," he says, "then it is lawfull to fetch testimonie from heauen, and to make God himselfe our witnes. In this case alone, and neuer else, it is lawfull to vse an Oathe."[67]

This view of conscience, and the intensified awareness of the human proclivity to sin that commonly went with it, created a serious problem of proof in contract law. Given the inaccessibility of the soul to all outside inquiry, even oath-helpers with long-standing personal knowledge of the party on whose behalf they swore were no more qualified than paid professionals in knowing whereof they spoke. If the inner wishes, desires, and intentions of the parties were beyond the capacity of any mortal to know, what was needed was a public test of the existence of the contract.

Since human law could judge only outward signs, of which the most salient in contract cases would be the exchange of money or its equivalent, it was necessary to imagine a two-part process: an inner act of will, made in that same secret sanctuary where conscience resides, and an outward manifestation of that act in the form of "consideration," which depended on facts that could be alleged and inquired into, as the burdens of conscience could not. The consideration showed good reason for believing that the defendant had indeed offered a promise and genuinely intended to be bound by his words.[68]

Consideration made the forming of a contract simultaneously the yielding of a promise to meet the obligations it entailed. It mediated between the will to do a thing and the actions by which that will was accomplished, moving parol agreements from the inner world of the parties' intentions, where conscience alone bound them, to the outward world of enforceable obligations. Focusing on the "material cause" of the contract—something empirically determinable by rational observers—exposed the secret sanctuary of the conscience to public tests, thereby permitting third parties to judge what had been done in the exchange of promises. It also allowed disputes to be treated as trespasses, where decisions rested on the judgments of jurors, grounded in the testimony of witnesses.

Freedom of Contract

According to St. German's Student, the law of contract arises from the law of property, both of them human creations made necessary by the beginnings of civilization. The Student imagines a time when men lived in a presocial state and there was no need for law to govern the distribution or exchange of private property. "For whan all thynges were in comon: yt neded not to haue contractes/ but after property was broughte in: they were ryght expedient to all people/ so that a man myght haue of his neyghbour that he had not of his owne/ & that could not be lawfully but by hys gyfte/ by waye of lendynge/ concord/ or by som lease/ bargeyn/ or sale/ and such bargaynes and sales be called contractes/ & be made by assent of the partyes vppon agreement betweene theym of goodes or of landes for money or for other recompence."[69] Once private property was in place, it "folowed in reason that suche landes and goodes as a man had/ ought not to be taken fro hym but by his assent or by order of lawe."[70]

This principle of assent carried with it a conception of freedom, for assent required a willing concurrence in the agreements reached or the actions performed. It was a commonplace — traceable to Aristotle's idea of justice — that binding consent could not be coerced.[71] Charles Fried has suggested that this view of contract links our notions of individual property rights, protected under law, with our capacity to "dispose of these rights on the terms that seem best to us."[72] It makes us the agents of our own obligations, marking out a realm of human interaction where our duties spring from our own voluntary commitments, rather than from the specific dictates of divine and natural law, such as those set out in the Ten Commandments, or from the moral imperatives imposed on us by our different offices or callings.

Fried's conception is closely connected with what is known as the will theory of contract, since the object of the contractual exchange is understood to be a mutual concurrence of free and independent wills in the benefits of the transaction. In its fully developed form, this view treats obligations as arising on the basis of the purposes or intentions of the parties, not in regard to anything they have done; indeed at the time the contract was agreed nothing may yet have been done at all, save the promising of some future action. The effect is to move the discussion of contract from a framework derived from the Aristotelianism of the scholastics and the canon lawyers, and to anchor it within modern theories of natural rights, political economy, and utilitarianism.[73]

In treating the virtue of justice, Aristotle distinguished between voluntary acts we perform by choice and those we undertake impulsively: "By choice those we do after deliberation, not by choice those we do without previous deliberation."[74] His concept of consent applied in its fullest form only to the former.[75] According to Aristotle, deliberation is concerned only with "things that are in our power and can be done" and "that happen in a certain way for the most part," but where outcome is "obscure" in the particular circumstances or "is indeterminate."[76] His argument focuses on how we connect our actions and choices to our desires and goals.ing. "Every action and choice," he says, "is thought to aim at some good."[77] Deliberation concerns the relation of means to these ends; the latter are determinate and the former are the processes that move us toward them.

"We deliberate," he insists, "not about ends but what contributes to ends . . . Having set the end," or taken it was given, we "consider how and by what means it is to be attained; and if it seems to be produced by several means [we] consider by which it is most easily and best produced, while if it is achieved by one only [we] consider how it will be achieved by this and by what *means* this will be achieved, till [we] come to the first cause, which in the order of discovery is last."[78] We need not deliberate about ultimate ends, for these always relate to the good, but only about the most effective means of achieving them. "The end being what we wish for," he says, "the things contributing to the end

[are] what we deliberate about and choose." Hence, actions concerning the latter must be according to choice and voluntary," since a similar process underpins the exercise of all the virtues, he concludes that virtue "also is in our power, and so too vice."[79]

In an Aristotelian view, therefore, our choices in making promises or reaching agreements are intimately connected with promoting a flourishing life for ourselves and our communities. Freely offering a gift or a charitable donation, with the expectation of no material reward, demonstrates the virtue of liberality, by which virtuous individuals neither spend more than they possess nor hoard their riches, but use them to live well and benefit others. Freely assenting to buy or sell a commodity for an agreed-upon price demonstrates the virtue of commutative justice, by which they fairly acquire an item they need or want in exchange for something of equal value. Together, these two forms of exchange hold society together, making each of us dependent on the rest for the achievement of our individual and collective ends. Translated into the realm of promise-making and promise-keeping, these socially valuable purposes represent the "cause" that motivated us to utter our pledge and that give it its force. They make the promise of a gift and the contract or bargain equally binding in moral terms, although as *Doctor and Student* makes clear, only the latter was enforceable in the common-law courts.[80]

Viewing the "consideration" in a contract as its "material cause" represents a significant break from this Aristotelian manner of thinking. By concentrating primarily on the items given and received in exchange, it points the process of deliberation away from first and final causes and toward purely worldly ones. A proper choice in undertaking a contract or offering a promise now can be made only in calculating whether the agreed-on "price" in goods, services, or money would adequately satisfy us for the value of what we have offered in recompense. The point is clearly articulated in Thomas Hobbes's famous analysis of contract in *Leviathan,* which treats the process of exchange along lines paralleling those developed by the common lawyers in the later sixteenth and early seventeenth centuries.[81]

According to Hobbes, what "men call CONTRACT" is the "mutuall transferring of Right."[82] "Whensoever a man Transferreth his Right, or Renounceth it," Hobbes says, "it is either in consideration of some Right reciprocally transferred to himselfe; or for some other good he hopeth for thereby. For it is a voluntary act; and of the voluntary acts of every man, the object is some *Good to himselfe*."[83] The critical difference from Aristotle concerns how Hobbes understands the idea of "good." For Hobbes, the word itself refers to no more than the object of a individual's "Appetite or Desire." Its point of reference is the person who uses it, "there being nothing simply and absolutely so; nor any rule of Good and Evill, to be taken from the nature of the objects themselves."[84] Good and evil are located among the passions, and are reducible to an individual's sensations of pleasure and pain, which are the "interiour beginnings of voluntary motions." On this model, "reason" is "nothing but *Reckoning* (that is Adding and Subtracting) of the Consequences of the generall names agreed upon, for the *marking* and *signifying*" of these thoughts.[85]

When translated into the realm of promises and contract, Hobbes's views take on the shape of later "will theories." "Words alone," he says, if they be of the time to come, and containe a bare promise, are an insufficient signe of a Free-gift and therefore not obligatory. For if they be of the time to Come . . . they are a signe that I have not given yet, and consequently that my right is not transferred, but remaineth till I transferre it by some other Act." In making this point, Hobbes focuses closely on the concept of "will," and draws an important distinction about the giving of promises. "There is a great difference," he says, "in the signification of these words . . . *I will that this be thine to morrow,* and *I will give it thee to morrow:* For the word I will in the former manner of speech, signifies an act of the will Present; but in the latter, it signifies a promise of an act of will to Come: and therefore the former words, being of the present transferre, a future right; the later, that be of the Future, transferre nothing. But if there be other signes of the Will to transferre a right, besides Wordes; then, though the gift be Free, yet may the Right be understood to passe by words of the future."[86] So long as there has been a "mutuall translation, or change of Right," words can bind whether they are of the present, past, or future. "Therefore he that promiseth onely, because he hath already received the benefit for which he promiseth, is to be understood as if he intended the Right should passe: for unlesse he had been content to have his words so understood, the other would not have performed his part first." Hence "for that cause," Hobbes says, "in buying, and selling, and other acts of Contract, a Promise is equivalent to a Covenant; and therefore obligatory."[87]

In articulating these ideas, Hobbes was restating within his own philosophical system the concept of "consideration" as it had developed in the common law during his lifetime. They demonstrate that for him the form of one's words was critical in turning mere promises into contracts, but also that words alone were insufficient to bind anyone.

The transformation in the law of contract embodied in Slade's case represents both a shift within the structure of *mentalité* and a move in an ongoing argument among interested parties. To have made the move recorded in Slade's case—collapsing contract and promise into one—the lawyers and judges needed to find acceptable, or at least plausible, the moral psychology that emerged from the decision. If it had been conceptually disquieting to see the making of a contract in two intimately linked stages — an inner intention to act, which then produced an outward exchange manifesting the intention — the lawyers would not have been able to mount an effective argument for the view. Their ability to treat the workings of the self in this manner grew out of the intense questioning of the idea of conscience unleashed during the Reformation. Changes in this framework of thought in turn provided the necessary context for the moves they made to promote changes in the law of contract.

Culture — the habits, norms, and practices by which human beings live their collective lives — arguably lies at the conjunction of these two realms and develops through their mutual interaction. In Slade's case we can see the culture of the common law developing as the rhetorical training of the lawyers and judges converged with their assumptions about the world, inculcated through their upbringing, education, and life experiences. The culture of human agency, obligation, and selfhood is similarly grounded, resulting from the union of moves with *mentalités* that connect doctrines and discursive practices with institutions that authorize and forbid particular actions.

The modern law of contract was constructed from a variety of religious and philosophical sources and judicial precedents about which there was no firm consensus until Slade's case. Once Coke presented his own arguments as though they were the court's, his report shaped all future pleadings in the law of contract, molding the way promises and contracts were subsequently made, interpreted, and enforced. The decision in turn reinforced the performative and internalist view of selfhood that underpinned it, and thereby endorsed a view that endowed the self with explicit and enforceable rights and liabilities. The selves we have are what they are because of the actions we can perform, and those actions are defined, in significant measure by the laws, customs, and practices governing the social world in which we live.

Notes

1. See, e.g., P. S. Atiyah, *Promises, Morals, and Law* (Oxford: Clarendon Press, 1981); P. S. Atiyah, "Contracts, Promises, and the Law of Obligations," in P. S. Atiyah, *Essays on Contract,* 2nd ed. (Oxford: Clarendon Press, 1990), pp. 10–56; Charles Fried, *Contract as Promise: A Theory of Contractual Obligation* (Cambridge: Harvard University Press, 1981).

2. Christopher St. German, *Doctor and Student,* ed. T. F. T. Plucknett and J. L. Baron (Selden Society, 91, 1974), p. 229; for the early publishing history of St. German's text, see pp. lxix–lxxvi.

3. A. W. B. Simpson, *A History of the Common Law of Contract: The Rise of the Action of Assumpsit* (Oxford: Clarendon Press, 1987), pp. 153–64, 193–96; J. H Baker,

"Origins of the 'Doctrine' of Consideration, 1535–1585," in J. H. Baker, *The Legal Profession and the Common Law: Historical Essays* (London: Hambledon Press, 1986), pp. 369–91, esp. pp. 387–89.

4. St. German, *Doctor and Student*, p. 230.

5. A. K. Kiralfy, *The Action on the Case: An historical survey of the development of the Action up to the year 1700, in the light of the original plea rolls and other unpublished sources. With an excursus in the doctrine of Consideration and a note on Case in Inferior Courts* (London: Sweet & Maxwell, 1951), pp. 170–71.

6. Ibid., pp. 176–77; Simpson, *Common Law of Contract*, pp. 318–19; John Spelman, *The Reports of Sir John Spelman*, 2 vols., ed. J. H. Baker (Selden Society, 93–94, 1977), 2:287–92; Baker, "Origins of the 'Doctrine of Consideration, 1535–1585," pp. 368–91.

7. Spelman, *Reports*, 2:287–88.

8. Calthorpe's case (1574), Dyer 336b, as cited in Simpson, *Common Law of Contract*, p. 323.

9. William West, *Symbolaeography Which may be termed the Art, Description or Image of Instruments, Extraiudicial, as Couenant, Contracts, Obligations, Feffements, Graunts. Wills, &c Or, The paterne of Praesidents. Or The Notarie or Scrivener*, 2nd ed. (London: 1592, STC 25267a), sig. A4[c]; later editions give *Doctor and Student*, book 2, chap. 24, as the source; see, e.g., *Symbolaeography* (London, 1597; STC 25268.5) sig. A3[a]. In his first edition of 1590, West defines a contract as "a couenant grounded vpon a lawfull cause or consideration, & which bringeth forth an action. For which cause it is said to *be Vltro citroq; obligatio*, as buieng, selling &c., because the buier is bound to yeeld the price agreed vpon, and the seller the thing sold; and so in other contracts, either partie by law is bound to other to do . . . some thing, which is called an obli[g]ation"; William West, *Symbolaiographia. Symbolæographia. Which may be termed the art, description, or image of instruments, couenants, contracts, &c. Or the notarie or scriuener* (London, 1590, STC 25267), sig. ¶¶1v.

10. West, *Symbolaeography*, sig. A4[c]. In *The Interpretor*, first published in 1607, John Cowell, Regius Professor of Civil Law at Cambridge, adheres to the same usage, citing and paraphrasing West; John Cowell, *The Interpretor: Or Booke Containing the Signification of Words* (Cambridge, 1607, STC 5900), sig. S3[a]; see James Gordley, *The Philosophical Origins of Modern Contract Doctrine* (Oxford: Clarendon Press, 1991), pp. 49–57. "Requiting," as West uses the word, equates "naturall obligations" with the ethical duties arising in the ancient gift economy; see Lucius Annaeus Seneca, *The vvoorke of the excellent philosopher Lucius Annaeus Seneca concerning benefyting, that is too say the dooing, receyuing, and requyting of good turnes*, trans. Arthur Golding (London, 1578, STC 22215).

11. [John Rastell and William Rastell], *Les Termes De La Ley: Or, Certaine difficult and obscure Vvords and Termes of the Common Lawes of this Realme expounded. Now newly imprinted, and inlarged and augmented* (London, 1624, STC 20716), f. 91v. After publication of the first edition in 1523 (STC 20701), there were thirty-six further editions down to 1742.

12. [Rastell and Rastell], *Les Termes De La Ley*, f. 97v.

13. For similar reasoning, see, e.g., Brett's case (1600), Cro. Eliz. 755, in A. W. Renton,

M. A. Robertson, and G. Ellis, eds., *The English Reports,* 176 vols. (Edinburgh: W. Green, 1900–1930) [hereafter referred to as *ER*], v. 78, pp. 987–88; Sir Edward Coke, *The First Part of the Institutes of the Laws of England; Or, A Commentary upon Littleton,* 2 vols., ed. Charles Butler (London: J. & W. T. Clarke; Saunders & Benning; A. Maxwell; S. Sweet; H. Butterworth; Stevens & Sons, R. Pheney; and J. Richards, 1832) [hereafter cited as Co. Litt.], 47b: "In every contract there must be a *quid pro quo,* for *contractus est quasi actus contra actum.*" The first edition of Coke's *Commentary on Littleton* dates from 1628 (STC 15784).

14. The literature on this subject is extensive. For general discussion, see C. H. S. Fifoot, *History and Sources of the Common Law: Tort and Contract* (London: Stevens & Sons, 1949), esp. pp. 330–94; Kiralfy, *Action on the Case,* pp. 137–50; Theodore F. T. Plucknett, *A Concise History of the Common Law,* 5th ed. (Boston: Little, Brown, 1956), pp. 628–70; S. F. C. Milsom, *Historical Foundations of the Common Law,* 2nd ed. (Toronto: Butterworths, 1981), pp. 243–360; J. H. Baker, *An Introduction to English Legal History,* 3rd ed. (London: Butterworths, 1990), pp. 360–426; S. J. Stoljar, *A History of Contract at Common Law* (Canberra: Australian National University Press, 1975), pp. 37–88; Simpson, *Common Law of Contract,* pp. 199–315; David Ibbetson, *A Historical Introduction to the Law of Obligations* (Oxford: Oxford University Press, 1999), pp. 126–54.

15. Baker, "Origins of the 'Doctrine' of Consideration," pp. 371–74; see also Simpson, *Common Law of Contract,* pp. 318–19.

16. Sir Mathew Hale, *The History of the Common Law of England,* ed. Charles M. Gray (Chicago: University of Chicago Press, 1971), p. 113. Hale's *History of the Common Law* was first published in 1713.

17. Moo. (K. B.) 433, in *ER,* 80, pp. 677–78; Yelv. 20, in *ER,* 72, p. 15; 4 Co. Rep. 91a–95b, in *ER,* 76, pp. 1072–79; J. H. Baker, "New Light on Slade's Case," in Baker, *Legal Profession and the Common Law,* pp. 395–96.

18. 4 Co. Rep., 91a–b, in *ER,* 76, p. 1072.

19. Ibid. 92b, in *ER,* 76, p. 1074.

20. Ibid., 91a–b, in *ER,* 76, p. 1072.

21. See Baker, "New Light on Slade's Case," p. 414.

22. 4 Co. Rep., 91b–92a, in *ER,* 76, pp. 1073–74.

23. Ibid., 92b, in *ER,* 76, p. 1074.

24. Baker, "New Light on Slade's Case," p. 415; Baker quotes Dodderidge's exact words, p. 398, n. 29; see also Simpson, *Common Law of Contract,* p. 294; cf. A. W. B. Simpson, "The Place of Slade's Case in the History of Contract," *Law Quarterly Review* 74 (1958): p. 382.

25. 4 Co. Rep. 93a, in *ER,* 76, p. 1074; see also Baker, "New Light on Slade's Case," p. 415; Simpson, *Common Law of Contract,* pp. 297–99.

26. 4 Co. Rep. 93a, in *ER,* 76, p. 1075; see also Baker, "New Light on Slade's Case," pp. 411–21; Simpson, *Common Law of Contract,* pp. 295–97.

27. 4 Co. Rep. 94a–b, in *ER,* 76, p. 1077; see also the comment of John Popham, Chief Justice in the Queen's Bench, 9 November 1602, Baker, "New Light on Slade's Case," p. 408. The term "executory" in this context refers to acts or dispositions intended to take or capable of taking full effect only at a future time. Its opposite is "executed," where

the act or disposition has already occurred and the right or property has already been transferred.

28. See 4 Co. Rep. 93a, in *The ER*, 76, p. 1075; the same argument was made by Laurence Tanfield, appearing for Slade, Michaelmas 1598, in Baker, "New Light on Slade's Case," p. 398. On this same point Francis Bacon, appearing for Morley, 13 May 1602, made the opposite case, ibid., p. 402. For context, see ibid, pp. 411–21; David Ibbetson, "Sixteenth Century Contract Law: *Slade's Case* in Context," *Oxford Journal of Legal Studies* 4 (1984): pp. 295–317, esp. pp. 296–307; see also David Ibbetson, "Assumpsit and Debt in the Early Sixteenth Century: The Origins of the Indebitatus Count," *Cambridge Law Journal* 41 (1982): pp. 142–61.

29. 4 Co. Rep. 95a, in *ER*, p. 1078.

30. "Law" in this context traditionally conveyed the sense of "right"; Simpson, *Common Law of Contract*, p. 138.

31. See the remarks of Dodderidge, Michaelmas 1597, and Bacon, 13 May 1602, in Baker, "New Light on Slade's Case," pp. 407–8 and 407, n. 80; see also Co. Litt. 295a; William M. McGovern, Jr., "Contract in Medieval England: Wager of Law and the Effect of Death," *Iowa Law Review* 54 (1968–1969): p. 19; Simpson, *Common Law of Contract*, pp. 137–40; Baker, *Introduction to English Legal History*, pp. 87–88. The number of compurgators required in different jurisdictions could range from two to twelve; see McGovern, "Contract in Medieval England," p. 27; Thomas Powell, *The Attorneys Academy, or The Manner and forme of proceeding practically, vpon any Suite, Plaint, or Action whatsoeuer, in any Court of Record whatsoeuer, within this Kingdom* (London, 1623, STC 20163), p. 132; Sir Frederick Pollock and Frederic William Maitland, *The History of English Law Before the Time of Edward I*, 2 vols. 2nd ed., ed. S. F. C. Milsom (Cambridge: Cambridge University Press, 1968), i, 635; Craig Muldrew, *The Economy of Obligation: The Culture of Credit and Social Relations in Early Modern England* (London: Macmillan, 1998), p. 206.

32. Plucknett, *Concise History*, pp. 115–16; Baker, *Introduction to English Legal History*, pp. 5–7, 87–88.

33. Baker, "New Light on Slade's Case," p. 415.

34. Co. Litt. 295a.

35. Bacon, 13 May 1602, in Baker, "New Light on Slade's Case," pp. 406–7. Bacon goes on to insist that using an oath in these circumstances "is according to the law of God," citing Heb. 6:16; see also Bacon, Michaelmas 1598, in Baker, "New Light on Slade's Case," p. 401.

36. Bacon, 13 May 1602, ibid., p. 407. Bacon's point, Baker says, was that "a fraudulent debtor would more readily buy another man's conscience than endanger his own soul, and would therefore prefer to remain mute and hire witnesses than to swear falsely with the support of wagermen" (ibid., p. 425).

37. Simpson, *Common Law of Contract*, pp. 138–40; see also Baker, *Introduction to English Legal History*, pp. 395–96; Milsom, *Historical Foundations*, pp. 292–93.

38. See David Harris Sacks, *The Widening Gate: Bristol and the Atlantic Economy, 1450–1700* (Berkeley: University of California Press, 1991), pp. 59–84, 357–61; Muldrew, *Economy of Obligation*, pp. 1–11, 121–95, and *passim*; Craig Muldrew, "Interpreting the Market: The Ethics of Credit and Community Relations in Early Modern England," *Social History* 18 (1993): pp. 163–83.

39. See Simpson, *Common Law of Contract,* pp. 88–126; Baker, *Introduction to English Legal History,* pp. 368–69.

40. S. E. Thorne, "Tudor Social Transformation and Legal Change," in S. E. Thorne, *Essays in Legal History* (London: Hambledon Press, 1985), pp. 206–8; Baker, "New Light on Slade's Case," p. 425.

41. David Harris Sacks, *Trade, Society, and Politics in Bristol, 1500–1640,* 2 vols. (New York: Garland Publishing, 1985), 2:156–201; Muldrew, *Economy of Obligation,* pp. 204–13; Craig Muldrew, "Credit and the Courts: Debt Litigation in a Seventeenth-Century Urban Community," *EcHR,* 2nd ser., 46 (1993): pp. 22–38; Plucknett, *Concise History of the Common Law,* pp. 657–70; Baker, *Introduction to English Legal History,* pp. 31–32; J. H. Baker, "The Law Merchant and the Common Law Before 1700," in Baker, *Legal Profession and the Common Law,* pp. 341–68.

42. Milsom, *Historical Foundations,* p. 292; J. S. Beckerman, "The Forty-Shilling Jurisdictional Limit in Medieval English Personal Actions," *Legal History Studies,* 1972, pp. 110–17.

43. See Muldrew, *Economy of Obligation,* pp. 13–119; Alan Everitt, "The Marketing of Agricultural Produce, 1500–1640," in John Chartres, ed., *Agricultural Markets and Trade, 1500–1750* (Cambridge: Cambridge University Press, 1990), pp. 15–156; J. A. Chartres, *Internal Trade in England, 1500–1700* (London: Macmillan, 1977); T. S. Willan, *The Inland Trade: Studies in English Internal Trade in the Sixteenth and Seventeenth Centuries* (Manchester: Manchester University Press, 1976); Joan Thirsk, *Economic Projects and Projects: The Development of Consumer Society in Early Modern England* (Oxford: Clarendon Press, 1978); C. G. A. Clay, *Economic Expansion and Social Change: England, 1500–1700,* 2 vols. (Cambridge: Cambridge University Press, 1984), 1:102–41, 165–213; 2:1–42.

44. Baker, "Law Merchant and the Common Law," pp. 354–59; Spelman, *Reports,* pp. 48, 52; Baker, "New Light on Slade's Case," pp. 411–21; Baker, *Introduction to English Legal History,* pp. 49–59; Milsom, *Historical Foundations,* pp. 297–308, 346; Simpson, *Common Law of Contract,* pp. 199–247, 281–315; Ibbetson, "Sixteenth Century Contract Law," pp. 296–99.

45. See, e.g., Atiyah, *Promises, Morals, and Law,* pp. 99–106.

46. Coke, Michaelmas 1597, in ibid., p. 398, n. 27. Laurence Tanfield put the point in similar terms, Michaelmas 1598, ibid., pp. 397–98.

47. Bacon, 13 May 1602, in Baker, "New Light on Slade's Case," p. 402.

48. See, e.g., ibid., pp. 422, 431; Milsom, *Historical Foundations,* pp. 309–15; Ibbetson, "Sixteenth Century Contract Law," pp. 315–17; see also Spelman, *Reports,* 2:51–63.

49. J. G. A. Pocock, *The Ancient Constitution and the Feudal Law: A Study of English Historical Thought in the Seventeenth Century: A Reissue with a Retrospect* (Cambridge: Cambridge University Press, 1987), pp. 262, 279; see also Pierre Bourdieu, *Outline of a Theory of Practice,* trans. Richard Nice (Cambridge: Cambridge University Press, 1977), pp. 168–69; Clifford Geertz, *The Interpretation of Cultures: Selected Essays* (New York: Basic Books, 1973), pp. 87–125, 193–233.

50. Margaret Blatcher, *The Court of King's Bench, 1450–1550: A Study in Self-Help* (London: Athlone Press, 1978).

51. Baker "New Light on Slade's Case," pp. 426–32; see also Simpson, *Common Law of Contract,* pp. 297–315.

52. See Margaret Blatcher, "Touching the Writ of Latitat: An Act 'Of No Great Moment,' " in S. T. Bindoff, J. Hurstfield, and C. H. Williams, eds., *Elizabethan Government and Society: Essays Presented to Sir John Neale* (London: Athlone Press, 1961), pp. 188–212; Blatcher, *Court of King's Bench*, 15–19, 154–71; C. W. Brooks, *Pettyfoggers and Vipers of the Commonwealth: The 'Lower Branch' of the Legal Profession in Early Modern England* (Cambridge: Cambridge University Press, 1986), pp. 48–111.

53. Powell, *Attorneys Academy*, p. 132; E. S., *The Discouerie of The Knights of the Poste: Or the Knightes of the post, common bayler newly Discried* (London, 1597, STC 21489); Margaret Hastings, *The Court of Common Pleas in Fifteenth Century England: A Study of Legal Administration and Procedure* (Ithaca, N.Y.: Cornell University Press, 1947), pp. 197–99; Baker, "New Light on Slade's Case," pp. 424–25; Baker, *Introduction to English Legal History*, pp. 87–88; Milsom, *Historical Foundations*, pp. 51, 212–13; Simpson, *Common Law of Contract*, p. 298.

54. St. German, *Doctor and Student*, p. 230; see also the discussion, derived from Jean Gerson, of synderesis and conscience, ibid., pp. xxvi–xxviii, 2–4, 78–95, 128, 129, 207–12, 213.

55. See [James Morice], *A briefe treatise of Oathes exacted by Ordinaries and Ecclesiastical Iudges* ([Middelburg, 1590?], STC 18106), p. 21. Levy dates the drafting of this treatise to 1591 or 1592, but argues that it was published abroad only in 1598, with a second printing in 1600: Leonard W. Levy, *Origins of the Fifth Amendment: The Right Against Self-Incrimination*, 2nd ed. (New York: Macmillan, 1986), p. 194. The treatise was, however, expressly answered in Richard Cosin, *An apologie of sundrie proceedings* (London, 1593, STC 5821); see also the first edition of this work: Richard Cosin, *An apologie of, and for, sundrie proceedings* (London, 1591, STC 5820). The common law itself exacted no material penalty. either on defendants or compurgators, for the spiritual offense of perjury and would not permit the ecclesiastical courts to be involved in any way in cases of debt among the laity: Simpson, *Common Law of Contract*, p. 138. The Elizabethan perjury statute was directed only against false witnesses: "Act for the punyshement of suche persones as shall procure or commit any wylfull Perjury," 5 Eliz. I, c. 9 (1563), *Stat. Realm* 4: 436–38; see Plucknett, *Concise History of the Common Law*, pp. 130–43.

56. See R. H. Helmholz, "The Privilege and the *Ius Commune*: The Middle Ages to the Seventeenth Century," in R. H. Helmholz, Charles M. Gray, John H. Langbein, Eben Moglen, Henry E. Smith, and Albert W. Alschuler, *The Privilege Against Self-Incrimination: Its Origins and Development* (Chicago: University of Chicago Press, 1997), pp. 17–46; see also John H. Wigmore, *A Treatise on the Anglo-American System of Evidence in Trials at Common Law*, 3rd ed., 10 vols. (Boston: Little, Brown, 1940), vol. 8 (rev. 1961 by John H. McNaughton), chap. 80: "Privilege against Self-Incrimination," sect. 2250; John H. Wigmore, "Nemo Tenetur Prodere Seipsum," *Harvard Law Review* 5 (1891): pp. 71–88; Levy, *Origins of the Fifth Amendment*, pp. 19–29; Mary Hume Maguire, "Attack of the Common Lawyers on the Oath *Ex Officio* as Administered in the Ecclesiastical Courts in England," in Carl Wittke, ed., *Essays in History and Political Theory in Honor of Charles Howard McIlwain* (Cambridge: Harvard University Press, 1936), pp. 200–209.

57. Christopher St. German, *Treatise concernynge the diuision betwene the spiritualtie*

and temporaltie (London, [1532?], STC 21587), ff. 14v–16v; [Christopher St. Germain], *Salem and Bizance* (London, 1533, STC 21586), ff. 83r–84r; See also Thomas More, *The Complete Works of St. Thomas More*, 15 vols. (New Haven, Conn.: Yale University Press, 1963–1993), vol. 9, *The Apology*, ed. J. B. Trapp, pp. lii, lviii, lx–lxiv, lxxx, 89–90, 130–35, 164, 188–89, 211, 294, 298, 337, 351, 376–79; ibid., vol. 10, *The Debellation of Salem and Bizance*, ed. John Guy, Ralph Keen, Clarence Miller, and Ruth McGugan, pp. xix, lxviii, lxx, lxxx–lxxxv, xcvi, 86–146, 272–73, 355–59, 368, 370; Levy, *Origins of the Fifth Amendment*, pp. 64–66. *Salem and Bizance* was written in response to Sir Thomas More's *Apology*. St. German also was thoroughly familiar with, and possibly a party to, the denunciations of ecclesiastical jurisdictions contained in the draft bill against heresy of 1529 and in the Supplication against the Ordinaries of 1532; More, *Complete Works*, 10:lviii–lxii.

58. [St. German], *Salem and Bizance*, f. 83r–v; More, *Complete Works*, 10:355.

59. For Morice's career see "James Morice," in P. W. Hasler, ed., *The House of Commons, 1558–1603*, 3 vols. (London: History of Parliament Trust, 1981), 3:98–100.

60. [Morice], *A briefe treatise of Oathes*, p. 9; see also [James Morice], "A Remembrance of Certeine Matters concerninge the Clergy and theire Jurisdiccion: Ao Dni 1593," Cambridge University Library MS Mm. 1.52 [Baker MS 40], pp. 105–34; Levy, *Origins of the Fifth Amendment*, pp. 195–200. Sir Edward Coke was speaker of the House in 1593, when Morice raised his doubts and introduced two bills in the Commons to remedy the faults he saw.

61. Helmholz, "Privilege and the *Ius Commune*," pp. 19, 24.

62. Ibid., pp. 23–24; Morice is describing the process of compurgation in ecclesiastical courts by which those brought before them would be permitted to clear their names; see Helmholz, "The Privilege and the *Ius Commune*," p. 33.

63. [Morice], *A briefe treatise of Oathes*, pp. 27–30; Morice's other arguments on the efficacy of wager of law are similar to those made by Bacon in his argument in Slade's case; compare Bacon, 13 May 1602, in Baker, "New Light on Slade's Case," pp. 406–7.

64. Coke, 17 October 1601, in Baker, "New Light on Slade's Case," p. 407, n. 74. At the conclusion of his report, Coke reiterates the same point in his own voice: "I am surprised," he says, "that in these days so little consideration is made of an oath, as I daily observe"; 4 Co. Rep., 95b, in *ER*, p. 1079. He also declares, "Cum jurare per Deum actus religionis sit, quo Deus testis adhibetur tanquam is qui omnium rerum maximus, &c."

65. 12 Co. Rep. 26, in *ER*, 77, p. 1308; Coke here says it is quoted from "a Civilian"; see Charles M. Gray, "Self-Incrimination in Interjurisdictional Law: The Sixteenth and Seventeenth Centuries," in Helmholz et al., *Privilege Against Self-Incrimination*, pp. 61–65; Charles M. Gray, *The Writ of Prohibition: Jurisdiction in Early Modern English Law*, 2 vols. (New York: Oceana Publications, 1994), 2:328–33. In 1607, Nicholas Fuller, in arguing against the ex officio oath in Maunsell and Ladd's case, invoked Coke's Latin tag again, this time quoted directly from Coke's report in Slade's case: [Nicholas Fuller], *The Argument of Master Nicholas Fvller in the Case of Thomas Lad and Richard Mansell, his Clients* (n.p., 1607, STC 11460), p. 11; see Gray, "Self-Incrimination in Interjurisdictional Law," pp. 70–77; Gray, *Writ of Prohibition*, pp. 340–70; see also Levy, *Origins of the Fifth Amendment*, pp. 229–65.

66. William Perkins, *A Discovrse of Conscience. Wherein is set dovvne the nature,*

properties, and differences thereof: as also the way to get and keepe good Conscience, 2nd ed. (Cambridge, 1608), in *The Workes of That Famovs and Vvorthie Minister of Christ, in the Vniversitie of Cambridge, M. William Perkins,* 3 vols. (Cambridge, 1609, STC 19649), 1:510.

67. William Perkins, *The Whole Treatise of the Cases of Conscience* (Cambridge, 1606, STC 19669), pp. 44–45, 380. For St. Augustine, see Charles Taylor, *Sources of the Self: The Making of Modern Identity* (Cambridge: Harvard University Press, 1989), pp. 127–42; Gareth Matthews, *Thought's Ego in Augustine and Descartes* (Ithaca, N.Y.: Cornell University Press, 1992); John M. Rist, *Augustine: Ancient Thought Baptized* (Cambridge: Cambridge University Press, 1994); Christopher Kirwan, *Augustine* (London: Routledge, 1989); Henry Chadwick, *Augustine* (Oxford: Oxford University Press, 1986); and the essays by Frederick J. Crosson, Scott MacDonald, William E. Mann, Simon Harrison, Simo Knuuttila, and Gareth Matthews in Gareth Matthews, ed., *The Augustinian Tradition* (Berkeley: University of California Press, 1999).

68. Simpson, *Common Law of Contract,* p. 407. A more specific theory that "consideration" should be viewed as "evidence" is traceable to Lord Mansfield in *Pillans v. Van Mierop* (1765), but it is was rejected by the courts; see Stoljar, *History of Contract at Common Law,* pp. 102–4; Baker, *Introduction to English Legal History,* pp. 399–400.

69. St. German, *Doctor and Student,* p. 228; see also pp. 133, 197.

70. Ibid, p. 222. For the central importance of mutual assent in contracts, see also West, *Symbolaeographia,* sigs. ¶¶ 1r–2v; West, *Symbolaeography,* 2nd ed., sigs. A3[a]–B3[b]; Gordley, *Modern Contract Doctrine,* pp. 41–45, 82–93; see also Atiyah, *Promises, Morals, and Law,* pp. 177–84.

71. Aristotle, *Nic. Eth.* III.1.1109b30–1111b3, V.8.1135a16–1136a9, in Aristotle, *The Complete Works of Aristotle: The Revised Oxford Edition,* ed. Jonathan Barnes, 2 vols. (Princeton, N.J.: Princeton University Press, 1984), 2:1752–55, 1791–93; see Gordley, *Modern Contract Doctrine,* pp. 7–8, 10–68.

72. Fried, *Contract as Promise,* p. 2. For discussion of the rise of the will theory, see Ibbetson, *Introduction to the Law of Obligations,* pp. 203–44.

73. Atiyah, *Promises, Morals, and Law,* pp. 12–22; P. S. Atiyah, *The Rise and Fall of Freedom of Contract* (Oxford: Clarendon Press, 1979), pp. 36–90, 212–16, 405–19; Gordley, *Modern Contract Doctrine,* pp.7–8, 169–229–48.

74. Aristotle, *Nic. Eth.* V.8,1135b9–11, in *Complete Works,* ii, p. 1792.

75. Gordley, *Modern Contract Doctrine,* pp. 82, 85–89.

76. Aristotle, *Nic. Eth.* III.3.1112a31, 1112b8–10, in *Complete Works,* ii, p. 1756.

77. Ibid., I.1.1094a1–2, 2:1729.

78. Ibid., III.3.1112b11–19, p. 1756.

79. Ibid., III.4.1113a15–5.1115a6, pp. 1757–60; for some guidance, consult C. D. C. Reeve, *Practices of Reason: Aristotle's Nicomachean Ethics* (Oxford: Clarendon Press, 1992), pp. 67–98, esp. pp. 79–84, 87–91; J. O. Urmson, *Aristotle's Ethics* (Oxford: Blackwell, 1988), pp. 38–61; T. H. Irwin, *Aristotle's First Principles* (Oxford: Clarendon Press, 1988), 328–46; David Wiggins, "Deliberation and Practical Wisdom," in Amélie Oksenberg Rorty, ed., *Essays on Aristotle's Ethics* (Berkeley: University of California Press, 1980), pp. 221–40.

80. St. Germain, *Doctor and Student,* pp. lv–lix, 230–33.

81. Atiyah, *Promises, Moral, and Law,* p. 13, 178–79; see also Muldrew, *Economy of Obligation,* pp. 321–25.

82. Thomas Hobbes, *Leviathan,* ed. Richard Tuck (Cambridge: Cambridge University Press, 1991), p. 94.

83. Ibid., p. 93.

84. Ibid. p. 39.

85. Ibid., pp. 32, 37–38, 40.

86. Ibid., p. 95.

87. Ibid.

2

Classical Rhetoric and the English Law of Evidence

BARBARA J. SHAPIRO

Given the long-standing association between law and rhetoric, there has been surprisingly little real study of the impact of rhetoric on the Anglo-American legal tradition. Commentators have alluded to forensic oratory in a general way, noted similarities between the win-lose environment of courts and the forms of debate, and pointed to the lawyer's need for oratorical skill. Some detailed study has been done. R. J. Schoeck has discussed rhetoric and the law in connection with the Renaissance, Alessandro Giuliani has explored the influence of rhetoric on the law of evidence and pleading, and Wilfred Prest and D. S. Bland have drawn connections between rhetoric and the teaching of early modern English law.[1] I propose to take these efforts one step further by focusing on the rhetorical origins of elements in the Anglo-American criminal law of evidence.

I shall attempt to show that the distinction between artificial and inartificial proofs and its elaboration by Roman rhetoricians first influenced the Romano-canon legal tradition and then, in tandem with the Renaissance revival of rhetoric, helped shape important features of English criminal law and procedure. I shall describe how the English legal concepts relating to "suspicion," pretrial examination by justices of the peace, jury evaluation of witness credibility, and "circumstantial evidence" are linked to classical rhetorical sources and to the Romano-canon tradition and show how early modern jurists shaped and reshaped rhetorical materials to serve the needs of a developing legal system.

The first part of the essay outlines the relevant portions of the rhetorical tradition. The second draws attention to their transmission to the developing medieval Romano-canon legal system. In the last and most detailed part shows how these rhetorical concepts became embedded in English legal procedure.

Classical Rhetoric: Artificial and Inartificial Proofs

The ancient philosophers were concerned with certain or demonstrative knowledge; rhetoricians, by contrast, focused on areas of life where only probability obtained. "Probability" was a crucial concept in the kind of everyday decision-making with which the law courts dealt. Probability in the rhetorical context did not refer to particular pieces of evidence in the modern sense but rather to the likelihood, verisimilitude, and persuasiveness of the general account of the case presented to the decision-maker. Emphasis in the rhetorical texts is thus on presenting a successful argument, and not on satisfying particular legal criteria.[2] For Aristotle and his successors, inartificial proofs, which included "witnesses," "tortures," and "contracts," were not furnished by the orator, although they might be reenforced or countered by him. More important were the artificial proofs constructed by the orator's "art" or "artifice." The first the orator simply made use of; the second he "invented."[3]

It was in Roman rhetorical training, which became essential for participation in politics and public life, that the Aristotelian categories were elaborated and extended, primarily in the context of forensic oration. The Roman law of evidence as such was largely undeveloped.[4] The most admired and best-known rhetorician of the Roman era, Cicero, was the author of *De inventione*, a work devoted primarily to the judicial oration and in particular to constructing arguments for and against those accused of crime. Providing an elaborate treatment of what he called "the conjectural issue," sometimes translated as the "issue of fact," Cicero explores those situations and categories especially relating to "inference."

All inferences, according to Cicero, are "based on arguments from the cause of the action, from the character of the person involved, and from the nature of the act." "Cause" was presented under the "heads of impulse and premeditation." "Love, anger, grief, [and] intoxication," were the source of impulse. In addition to these causes, the orator should deal with issues of glory, power, wealth, and enmity in order to show "that no one else had a motive for committing the crime" or that "no one had so strong or sufficient a motive." If others also had reasons for committing the crime at issue, the orator for the prosecution must show that they lacked the power, opportunity or desire to do so.[5]

Inferences were also to be drawn from "persons," especially the accused person. Particularly pertinent attributes were gender, ancestors, kin, age, temperament, and physical constitution.[6] Suspicions were suggested "by a man's way of life when the question is asked how and with whom and by whom he was reared and educated, and with whome he lives, what his plan or purpose in life is, and what his home life is like." Arguments might be developed from the person's "fortune, whether slave or free, wealthy or poor, famous or unknown, successful or a failure, a private citizen or a public official." Such arguments worked for the orator because "habit consists of a complete and abiding constitution of mind or body." Arguments could also be constructed relating to a person's "Interest." The aim was to discredit the accused, for there could be "little foundation for a motive . . . unless . . . suspicion is cast on the character." The orator thus sought to discredit the accused's past life by noting conviction or suspicion of previous criminal acts. "[E]verything that detracts from the defendant's honor and repute" was used to diminish his defense. If his reputation was excellent, the orator must argue that the accused's true character had previously been concealed and that his previous life was not relevant. A "man's fortune, his nature, manner of life, interests, deeds, accidents, speeches, purposes" contributed to the credibility of the charges against him.[7]

Those arguing on behalf of the accused were to turn all these arguments upside-down, emphasizing the accused's upright character, his relation to parents, kin, and friends. If there were discreditable phases in his past life, the orator emphasized the role of envy, backbiting, and false opinion, or perhaps attributed past mistakes to folly, necessity, or youth. One might also argue that the defendant's life, character, and past deeds were irrelevant to the matter now at issue. The orator was to run through this elaborate check list of categories and "twist [them]to the advantage of his own case, making them tell in opposite directions though he follows a similar course of rules." "Suspicion" might also be derived from the act itself. Its time, place, and occasion as well as its "adjuncts" and "consequences" were to be treated. Visible signs, too, were important, of which Cicero provides a list including pallor, blood, or lust before, during, or after the act.[8]

Quintilian's *Institutes of the Orator,* designed as an educational work for young gentlemen, provides a similar treatment for those learning the art of rhetoric. He too distinguishes between inartificial and artificial proofs. He thus shows how tortures, one of the inartificial proofs, might be used positively by the orator as a necessary means of obtaining trust, or denounced as yielding false testimony given only to avoid pain. Witnesses and hearsay could similarly be used pro and con.[9]

Quintilian also outlines arguments associated with signs, tokens, indications, and vestiges that "consist of some certain thing to mean and point out another." Like Cicero, he shows how "circumstances" or signs, or *indicia,* as later Romano-canonist lawyers would call them, might be used in either accusation or defense. Bloodstains might be a sign that murder had been committed or the result of a bloody nose. Quintilian not only suggests that signs may be more or less certain but also indicates, in a passage that would be echoed both in Continental and English law, that some signs might be very powerful in conjunction with other proofs.[10]

The rhetorical treatise *Rhetorica ad Herennium,* for many generations attributed to Cicero, was probably the most direct means of transmission of the Ciceronian approach to later times. It was readily available during the early Middle Ages. Here again, counsel for the prosecution and defense were advised on how to make use of a series of argumentative categories. Echoing Cicero, the author notes under the category of "Probability" that orators consider "motive" and "manner of life." Motivation treated discussion of advantages and the benefits of honor, money, or power. Prosecutors would emphasize and defendant's counsel belittle their importance, the latter arguing that it is "unfair to bring under suspicion of wrongdoing everyone to whom some profit has come from an act." Accusers in discussing "Manner of Life" should draw attention to whether the accused had been previously suspected of a similar crime and, if the crime involved money, show that the defendant had always been covetous. Defenders, on the other hand, should emphasize the person's upright life or turn to arguments dealing with "thoughtlessness, folly, youth, force, or undue influence." "Comparison" arguments could be used by prosecutors showing that no one but the defendant could have committed the act, "or at least not so easily," while the defense would argue that the crime benefited others as well, or that others as well could have done the deed.[11]

The *Rhetorica ad Herennium* also placed considerable emphasis on "signs." These included "the Place, the Point of Time, the Duration of Time, the Occasion, the Hope of Success, the Hope of Escaping Detection," as well as whether the "above mentioned signs coincide." It is then argued that "through Presumptive Proof guilt is demonstrated by means of indications that increase certainty and strengthen suspicion." Such "signs" fell into three periods: that "preceding the crime, contemporaneous with the crime, [and] following the crime." This temporal categorization would reappear in English legal texts. With respect to the first category, one considered:

> where the defendant was, where he was seen, with whom seen, whether he made some preparation, . . . or showed any sign of having confidants, accomplices, or means of assistance; whether he was in a place, or there at a time, at variance with his custom. In respect to the period contemporaneous with the crime we shall seek to learn whether he was seen in the act; whether some noise, outcry, or crash was heard; or, in short whether anything was perceived by one of the senses. . . . In respect to the period following the crime, one will seek to discover whether after the act was completed there was left behind anything indicating that a crime was committed, or by whom it was committed.[12]

One noted whether the body of the deceased was swollen and black and blue, in which case poisoning was indicated. Footprints or blood on the clothes of the accused too were treated as "signs."

Other signs associated with guilt or innocence were also to be noted. Prosecutors would, therefore, if possible, "say that his adversary, when come upon, blushed, paled, faltered, spoke uncertainly, collapsed, or made some offer-signs of a guilty conscience. . . . The defendant's counsel, if his client has shown fear, will say that he was moved . . . by the magnitude of his peril. If the client has not shown fear, counsel will say that he was unmoved because he relied on his innocence."[13] Orators could use similar argumentative devices to support or discredit testimony of witnesses, confessions under torture, presumptive proofs, and rumor or hearsay. The "authority," lifestyle, possible partiality, and consistency of the witnesses are to be invoked by the orator as well as their actual opportunity to observe the events to which they have testified.[14]

The treatment of "presumptive signs" too would reappear in Continental and English law concerning what came to be called presumptive proofs or circumstantial evidence. It was advantageous, the author wrote, to argue that "when there is a concurrence of many circumstantial indications and signs that agree with one another, the result ought to appear as clear fact, not surmise." It could be argued that such signs "deserved more credence than witnesses," who might be "corrupted by bribery, or partiality, or intimidation, or animosity." Arguments against presumptive proofs or "signs" should try to "show that nothing is safe from attack by suspicion" and that the signs in question applied to other persons as well. Speakers might argue that it was "a shameful outrage to consider suspicion and conjecture, in the absence of witnesses, as sufficiently corroborative."[15]

I have presented Cicero, Quintilian, and the *Rhetorica ad Herennium* at some length because the categories and sometimes the very words of the ancient rhetoricians were later put to procedural and evidentiary use. There were, of course, other modes of argument, such as similarity and definition, to be found in the writings of the Roman rhetors, which though important for writers and speakers in and outside the courtroom, did not become embedded in the law of evidence. We should also point out that although it appears that some elements of Roman law found their way into medieval law, neither the Republican nor the Justinian era possessed a stable theory of evidence.

The Romano-Canon Legal Tradition

The rhetorician's treatment of inartificial and artificial proofs had a long life, and these concepts were translated, albeit somewhat incorrectly, into direct and indirect, or circumstantial, evidence in the canon, civil, and English legal traditions. Much of the content of the Roman rhetorical texts, however, was lost in the early Middle Ages. The Roman rhetorical environment and legal institutions were largely, if not completely, overlaid with or replaced by Germanic practices such as ordeals, compurgation, and oaths, which did not require what we would call argument or evidence.

The categories and arguments developed in Aristotle, Cicero, Quintilian, and the *Rhetorica ad Herennium,* however, would be adopted by medieval canonists seeking alternatives to trial by ordeal and other "irrational proofs." In the process, important elements of the rhetorical tradition became embedded in the Romano-canon inquisition process and the development of its evidentiary criteria.

The Romano-canon system featured an evidentiary scheme that developed rapidly after the 1215 abolition of "irrational proofs." Ecclesiastics first developed such concepts as "suspicion" and "common fame" to bring persons before appropriate tribunals. Confession or the testimony of two unimpeachable witnesses was required for "full" or "legal" proof in serious criminal offenses. Witnesses were examined and their testimony evaluated. Circumstantial evidence was considered inferior to direct witness testimony and was, standing alone, in most instances, insufficient for conviction. Nevertheless circumstantial evidence was considered both in the preliminary decision on whether to proceed to torture and at the actual trial. The artificial proofs of the ancient orators played an important role in determining what constituted "suspicion" and reliability of circumstantial evidence.

Rhetorical arguments were used to evaluate the credibility of witnesses and to determine whether there were sufficient and appropriate signs, circumstances, or indicia to allow judicial torture, itself designed to elicit the necessary "confession." Such rhetorical categories as family, education, habits, companions, social status, time, place, and the power and ability to do the act were deployed to provide the necessary guidance and uniformity for the judicial decision to employ torture. Rhetorically derived criteria became deeply embedded in the Romano-canon tradition of witness evaluation and judicial torture and were a familiar part of the discourse of the ecclesiastical courts and then of the various secular continental legal systems that were in the process of adopting traditional Romano-canon procedure.

The rigidity of the two-witness or confession rule proved too stringent. Here the rhetorical tradition of artificial proofs proved useful. By the thirteenth century the "undoubted indicia" or "violent presumption" might sometimes be sufficient for conviction. A category of exceptional and unlikely-to-be-witnessed crimes such as poisoning, witchcraft, and infanticide also permitted conviction on the basis of admittedly inferior circumstantial evidence consisting of signs that pointed to guilt. Still another development was the *poena extraordinaire*—sometimes called suspicion proof—that also permitted an enhanced role for circumstantial evidence. This less-than-full proof allowed for less-than-full punishment—for example, exile, monetary penalties, and sentencing to the galleys.[16] In all these developments the vocabulary and techniques of rhetoric were constantly employed.

The Romano-canon evidentiary tradition, which was so much indebted to classical rhetorical sources, was spelled out in an erudite procedural literature applicable to both ecclesiastical and secular courts, perhaps most notably in the *Carolina,* the imperial code of 1539. Its "legally sufficient signs, suspicion, and presumption" for legal torture echoed the formulations of Cicero and Quintilian.

> First: When the accused is an insolent and wanton person of bad repute and regard, so that the crime could be credibly ascribed to him, when the same person shall have dared to perform a similar crime previously or shall have been accused of having done so. However this bad repute shall not be adduced from enemies or wanton people, . . .
> Second: When the suspected person has been caught or found at a place suspicious in the context of the deed.
> Third: When a culprit has been seen in the deed or while on the way to and from it; . . . attention should be paid to whether the suspect has such a figure, such clothes, weapon, horses. . . .
> Fourth: When the suspected person lives with or associates with such people as commit similar crimes.
> Fifth: Envy, enmity, formal threat, or the expectation of some advantage.[17]

In the *Carolina* the rhetorical teachings of Cicero and Quintilian have been transformed into guidelines for jurists engaged in apprehending and processing criminals under suspicion. "Suspicion" had become a legal category.

Rhetoric and English Law

The same rhetorical sources that formed the basis for suspicion, witness evaluation, the decision to torture, and circumstantial evidence in the Romano-canon tradition also came to play an important role in English pretrial and trial procedure. It is, however, not always possible to determine whether English legal borrowing came directly from the rhetorical sources or via the Romano-canon legal tradition.

English borrowing from the rhetorical and Romano-canon traditions has both been slighted and disguised. Familiarity with the rhetorical tradition has grown so attenuated over the past century that even the most obvious borrowing was likely to be ignored by scholars. The revival of interest in the historical role of rhetoric is only now beginning to modify that situation. The association of rhetoric with deception and improper appeals to emotion also has long made an association of law and rhetoric distasteful. English pride in the common law, adulation of the jury trial, and also association of the Romano-canon legal system with the Inquisition, torture, and tyranny meant that the common lawyers drew sharp contrasts between common and civil law. Shared characteristics, such as derivation from the rhetorical tradition, were often ignored for ideological reasons. Most legal scholars and jurists writing about the common law have paid scant attention to pretrial arrest and examination. And it is in these areas that we find the first significant traces of the classical rhetorical tradition in England's legal system. Only later did the rhetorical features we have described figure prominently in evaluating circumstantial evidence and trial testimony by witnesses.

Arrest and Pretrial Examination

Evidentiary elements associated with the rhetorical tradition appeared earliest in connection with arrest — the stopping and holding of one individual suspected by another of having committed a felony. (Only later, in 1360, was arrest conceived of as an act of an official for justices of the peace). The concept of suspicion, as we have seen, was developed by medieval canonists, who were indebted to the formulations of Roman rhetoricians. Although Bracton's authoritative statements on suspicion appeared in connection with indictment, his pronouncements came to be cited as offering the appropriate criteria for arrest. Only rumor arising "among worthy and responsible men ... and wise and trustworthy persons" for repeated acts transformed mere rumor into suspicion.[18] The phrase "light suspicion" appeared in a statute of 1275, suggesting that this was already a familiar notion.[19]

The justicing handbooks that began to appear in the sixteenth century list the "causes of suspicion" in some detail. Typically, a handbook list included the age, sex, education, parentage, character, associates, and habitual behavior of the suspect as well as his capacity to commit the crime, his whereabouts at the time of the crime, the presence of witnesses, and other signs — for instance, blood, which engendered suspicion. The "causes of suspicion" justifying arrest are virtually the same as the indicia that on the Continent served to determine whether the suspect should be examined under torture. The concept of suspicion proved useful to the English for quite different institutional purposes. What was needed for arrest were guidelines that would ensure that accusations had some rational basis, while not requiring accusers to fully prove their suspicions. Over time, in granting or refusing arrest warrants, the justices of the peace came to evaluate the causes of suspicion. The more general notions of "probable cause to suspect" or "reasonable cause to suspect" came to have greater salience than the classically derived list of suspicions and the rhetorical origins of the process obscured.

Renaissance Rhetoric

It is necessary to comment briefly on the state of rhetorical knowledge in England prior to discussing the late sixteenth- and early seventeenth-century justicing handbooks. By the late sixteenth century the works of Cicero and Quintilian and the *Rhetorica ad Herennium* were available, and educational reforms had resuscitated rhetorical texts in the new grammar schools. Erasmus' widely disseminated textbook *De Copia,* designed to develop schoolboys' writing and speaking skill, treated artificial and inartificial proofs almost identically to the exposition of classical rhetoricians. Erasmus explains that "circumstances" relating to "things" involved cause, place, time, occasion, antecedents to the affair, collateral circumstances, consequences, opportunity, instruments, and methods. Circumstances relating to "persons" included considerations of family, race, country, sex, age, physical appearance, inclinations, previous acts and sayings, passion, and so on.[20] In the course of learning to produce Latin prose, schoolboys became familiar with the rhetorical categories or "places" that had found their way into the English legal system.

Although would-be lawyers were not required to spend time at university before attending the Inns of Court, many of them did so and became familiar with rhetoric in that setting. Most of those exposed to grammar school or university would have had at least a passing familiarity with Cicero and Quintilian. We know, for example, that Lord Keeper Nicholas Bacon studied Quintilian and that Sir Edward Coke's library contained rhetorical works by Aristotle and Cicero. Sir Thomas Elyot treated moots as "a shadowe or figure of the auncient rhetoric."[21] Given the importance of rhetoric in the Renaissance, it is hardly surprising to find educated Englishmen familiar with Cicero, Quintilian, and such contemporary transmitters of the rhetorical tradition as Erasmus, Thomas Wright, and Sir Thomas Wilson.

In Richard Sherry's *Treatise of Schemes and Tropes* (1550), we find not only the familiar distinction between artificial and inartificial proofs but references to signs such as the paleness of murderers and the bleeding of slain bodies when murderers approached. Inferences from such signs were frequently labeled conjecture by rhetorical writers, and these might be treated as weak or strong. Another rhetorical work, Thomas Wright's *The Passions of the Mind* (1601), suggested that the "passions" and "inclinations" are often revealed by outward behavior. The reasoning from manifest properties, effects, or signs to "cause," which is frequently invoked in Renaissance rhetoric texts, will be echoed in legal texts.[22]

Sir Thomas Wilson's *Arte of Rhetorique* (1553), a frequently reprinted English rhetoric text, most clearly indicates the transmission that took place from rhetorical texts to more obviously legal works. A civilian, Wilson borrowed heavily from Quintilian and the *Rhetorica ad Herennium,* encouraged the study of law, and made frequent use of legal illustrations. His work would serve both those seeking to rise in the world by honing conversational and writing skills and gentlemen who would become justices of the peace. The by now familiar categories of parentage, sex, education, inclination, and nature were to be employed by the orator in praising individuals. In praising or condemning an action, the orator would consider whether the action was difficult or easy to accomplish or whether it was possible or impossible to perform. Consideration of "circumstances" relating to where, when, and how the deed had been done were also part of the rhetor's task.

Rhetorical "places" were also central to Wilson's treatment of the judicial oration. Like previous authors of rhetorical manuals, Wilson focused on the "state of the cause" or the principal point at issue. We again encounter the orator's need to discuss whether the person in question had the will or power to do the act, what his inclination and occupation were, and whether he was a gamester or haunter of alehouses. Wealth, apparel, and "nature" — that is, personal characteristics such as quarrelsomeness — were also to be treated.

With respect to the "power" to do the act, alibi questions were to be addressed, as well as the issue whether the accused had been bloodstained or trembling. Wilson also invoked the "places" in connection with "confirmation," so that "greate liklihoodes maie be gathered" by both sides.[23] We shall see that Wilson's categories, and even his language, appear little changed in the new genre of manual for justices of the peace.

Pretrial Examination and the Justicing Manuals

The transition from general rhetoric manual to the specifically legal environment is readily apparent. Shortly after the justices of the peace were required by a statute of 1554–55 to examine accused felony suspects, compilers of a new genre, the justicing manual, were directing justices of the peace to utilize the "causes of suspicion" to organize their examination.[24] Suspicion proved to be a concept that could be employed in a number of different legal contexts to serve a variety of institutional and procedural functions.

William Lambarde's popular manual of 1581 provides the "Causes of suspicion" in an elaborate but compact Ramist-style diagram. Like most English writers, Lambarde would not refer to the Romano-canon filiation and suggests that the examples in this category were "collected out of Cicero and others." In a statement reminiscent of the rhetorical handbooks, Lambarde notes that the examination of an offense is a "conjectural state of a cause" and must be "weighed by matter," which he categorizes as "precedent," "present," or "subsequent" to the crime. This categorization, we should recall, is found in Cicero, the *Rhetorica ad Herennium,* and Wilson's *Arte of Rhetorique.*[25]

The "precedent" heading, roughly analogous to "before the fact," included the "will to do the fact" and the "power to commit the act." "The will to do the fact" is again subdivided to allow consideration of the disposition of the person, a category that included the character and behavior of parents, the sex of the person, and education from childhood through adulthood. The "education" heading also allowed consideration of whether the accused had an idle or honest occupation, whether he was riotous in diet or apparel, and whether he was "brawlingly quarrelsome," or "lightfingered."[26] We have met most of these in Wilson and his rhetorical predecessors, along with the assumption that it is appropriate to draw inferences from such external signs and attributes.

Lambarde's second division, "the causes inducing him to undertake" the act, might be "forcible or impulsive" — for example, motivated by revenge or "upon sudden offense" — or could be "persuasive" — that is, in hope of gain or out of fear. "Power to commit the act" called for an evaluation of the suspect's intelligence, physical capacity, and "country" and included consideration of whether the kindred, wealth, friends, or office of the accused might "cover" him.[27]

Considerations of "present state" required questioning an individual's presence at the deed and taking account of the time of day, space, and location. The "occasion," too, had to be analyzed; if it was absent, "the fact could not follow." The justice was to engage in the mental operation of "comparison," an act requiring analysis of whether "none but he, or not so commodiously as he, could commit the fact."[28]

"Subsequent" considerations, those which followed the commission of the felony, included: "common voice and fame that he did the offense. Witnesses that prove it, either probably or necessarily. Signs which discover him; as by having blood, or the goods about him; . . . flying away: . . . blushing, or change of countenance . . . . being in the company of other offenders: . . . offer[s] of composition; the measure of his foot; the bleeding of the dead body, ... Confessions, as his doubtfully or inconstantly speaking."[29] Here again we hear echoes and paraphrases of classical and Renaissance rhetorics.

Similar schemes are found in other justicing handbooks. Richard Crompton's enlargement of Fitzherbert's *L'office et auctoritie de justices of peace*, like Lambarde's, avoids mention of foreign legal sources. He does note, however, that most of the causes of suspicion are to be found in Thomas Wilson's *Arte of English Rhetorique*.[30] Given English hostility to Continental legal practice, it is not surprising that Lambarde and Crompton refer to Cicero and Wilson rather than the Romano-canon indicia, with their association with torture.

Crompton, who duplicates Lambarde's treatment of suspicion, albeit without his diagrammatic scheme, includes a similar set of screening tests. Sudden anger, hope of gain, temperament, upbringing, occupation, and trade are again to be considered, along with whether the suspect was a haunter of alehouses or a gamester.

When Crompton was replaced by Dalton's long-lived *The Country Justice,* references to Cicero and Wilson disappeared and the rules to assist magistrates in evaluating the testimony of those who come before them stood on their own authority. Dalton's treatment of suspicion included concern for parentage, background, lifestyle, and character of the accused as well as his reputation and demeanor and his motives, opportunity, and capacity to commit the crime. Justices were to consider any direct or circumstantial evidence, alibis, and supernatural indications of guilt, including the traditional bleeding of the body in the murderer's presence.[31] Post-1618 editions of Dalton added "two old verses":

Conditio, sexus, aetas, discretio, fama
Et fortuna, fides: in testibus esta requires

—verses that echo the Romano-canon legal and the rhetorical traditions.[32] Dalton's "circumstances . . . to be considered" in examining accused felons are to be found in Lambarde, Crompton, the civil law texts and, of course, in Cicero, Quintilian, the *Rhetorica ad Herennium,* and Wilson.

Although *The Country Justice* quickly acquired the status of legal authority, Dalton's more modest goal was collecting material to assist those who "have not been much conversant in the studies of the law of this realm."[33] Within a few decades, his rhetorically derived materials had become a legitimate and necessary part of the legal system. Dalton's handbook went through many editions and provided the basis for its eighteenth- and nineteenth-century successors.

The Jury and the Credibility of Witnesses

Rhetorical materials also proved useful to trial jurors in evaluating the testimony of plaintiffs, defendants, and witnesses. These developments are somewhat difficult to trace because jurors initially were expected to have personal knowledge of the facts of the case before them and only gradually became evaluators of evidence presented by others. Witnesses began to appear in the fifteenth century and became common in the sixteenth, long after their appearance in canon and civil law courts.[34] It is for this reason that rhetorical analysis is first utilized by justices of the peace rather than the jurors. The justices had acquired a duty to evaluate testimony at their preliminary inquiries before the jury's duty to evaluate testimony became clearly understood. The justices' need for a system of evaluation thus became evident earlier than that of the jury.

If jurors, who were now "judges of fact," came to hear the evidence of witnesses, their testimony had to be believable and trustworthy. Some method or at least guidance in assessing witness credibility became essential, although there was no formal printed guidance provided comparable to that in the justicing handbooks. Judges' instruction to juries in individual cases probably began to provide some guidance. Although the records of few criminal cases have been preserved, we do know that from the sixteenth century onward jurors had the responsibility of evaluating the credibility of those they heard and that by the seventeenth century such distinguished judges as Sir Francis Bacon and Sir Matthew Hale were writing about that responsibility.[35]

Although jurors were assumed to be sufficiently intelligent and morally honest to assess witness credibility, such assessment was difficult, especially because some witnesses in criminal trials testified on oath and others did not. The oath itself was thought to offer some guidance, though it was recognized that some witnesses would commit perjury even under oath. Defendants and defense witnesses in felony trials were not permitted to testify on oath, and their testimony had to be evaluated and compared for truthfulness and credibility.

The rhetorically derived criteria of the canonists and civilians contained in the justicing manuals found their way into the common-law trial. The education, social status, lifestyle, and so on, of witnesses were to be considered in giving credit to their testimony and in assessing the possibility and probability that the witness knew the fact in question. Only a generation or so after Lambarde and Dalton outlined the criteria for the pretrial examination of suspects and witnesses, common-law judges such as Francis North and Sir Matthew Hale echoed them. North thus mentioned the "inclinations" and the education of the witnesses. Those who have "habits of falsehood and are Comon and Known lyars" and those who lived "open, vitious scandalous lives" might be heard in court, but their testimony could bind jurors "no farther: than they believed it in their conscience to be true." For Hale, "light and inconsiderable witnesses" were clearly less credible, and jurors were to judge the "Quality, Carriage, Age, Condition, Education, and Place of Commorance of Witnesses" in giving "more or less Credit to their Testimony."[36]

Criminal defendants thus attempted to show that government witnesses were persons of low moral character or lacking in integrity. On trial for treason, Thomas More claimed that one of the witnesses against him was notorious as a "common lyer" and a man of "no recommendable fame."[37] Defendants in the Popish Plot trials of the late seventeenth century often emphasized the low moral status and lack of integrity of crown witnesses.

Rhetorical resonance is clear in Sir Geoffrey Gilbert's early eighteenth-century *The Law of Evidence,* the first of many evidence treatises. The testimony of a witness was suspect if he should be "a Party to the Crime, or one who swore for his own Safety or Indemnity, or be a Relation or Friend to the Party, or the like; or be of a profligate or wicked Temper or Disposition; and the Weight of the Probability lies thus; if you think the Bias is so strong upon him, as would incline a Man of his Disposition, Figure and Rank in the World, to falsify, you are to disbelieve him; but if you think him a Man of that Credit and Veracity, that, notwithstanding the Bias upon him, would yet maintain a Value for Truth and is under the force and Obligation of his Oath, he is to be believed."[38] Gilbert's authoritative treatment would be echoed and restated in subsequent treatises on the law of evidence. English legal commentators often praised the English trial process because of the opportunity it offered jurors to

assess witness demeanor and responses to questioning. The "quality and qualifications of witnesses" also included the "manner of their Testimony." How
witnesses spoke and behaved in court would be assessed along with their
social attributes, education, and reputation. "Many times the Manner of a
Witness's delivering his Testimony" provided a probable indication of whether
he spoke the truth or not.[39] "An over-forward and hasty zeal on the part of the
witness . . . his exaggeration of circumstances, his reluctance in giving adverse
evidence, his slowness in answering, his evasive replies, his affectation of not
hearing or not understanding the question. . . . precipitancy in answering
wherein, if his testimony were untrue, he would be open to contradiction, . . .
are all to a greater or less extent obvious marks of insincerity."[40]

English legal practice, which allowed public examination of speakers, put
one in a better position to "discover the Truth of Fact, than any other Trial
whatsoever." Inconsistency in a witness's testimony removed that witness
"from all credit, for things totally opposed cannot be believed from the attesta-
tion of many men." St. German was making such claims in the early sixteenth
century. Upon discovering that a witness's statements contained contradictions, juries were entitled to assume "lyghtnesse of mynde, hatred or corruption of money." Justicing handbooks also indicated that if the tales of two
persons were at odds, neither was to be credited. Among elements for evaluating witness testimony Locke, too, would list the "consistency of the parts, and
circumstances of the relation; as well as contrary testimonies."[41]

Circumstantial Evidence

English courts came to rely on indirect or circumstantial evidence, although common lawyers, like canonists and civilians, were cognizant of its
dangers. The categories "circumstances" and "circumstantial evidence," like
the criteria for witness evaluation, had their origin in classical rhetoric. We
should recall that for Quintilian and his successors signs, indications, and
vestiges "consist of some certain thing to mean and point out another." As a
sign of murder, bloodstains, when supported by other circumstances, served
as powerful testimony against an accused individual. Other circumstances
noted in the rhetorical texts were threats by the accused or the presence of that
person at the scene of a crime. Such signs could be used by both accuser and
defendant and might be decisive "as far as otherwise well supported." Some
signs were doubtful and others more certain, especially in conjunction with
additional signs and proofs.

The rhetorical distinction between inartificial and artificial proofs provided
the underpinnings for the distinction between direct and indirect proof in law.
Direct proof referred to witness testimony. Indirect proof, or circumstantial

evidence, as it was later called, consisted of fame, suspicion, and signs. Circumstances were thus the incidents of an event or particularities that accompanied an action and resulted in presumptions of varying levels of certainty.

Like the canonists and civilians, the English treated circumstantial evidence as inferior to witness testimony. It was, however, not uncommon for juries to convict on circumstantial evidence. Horse thieves, it was often pointed out, were typically convicted because they had been caught with stolen horses not because the theft had been observed by a witness. Treason trials clearly indicated that the concept of circumstantial evidence was well understood by judges and well-educated defendants and that convictions were often based on it. Judges and lawyers often referred both to the testimony of witnesses and to circumstances.

Although the English appear to have adopted the legal concept of presumption with Bracton, the doctrine gained legal currency in the writings of Sir Edward Coke. Most subsequent English legal texts cited Coke rather than its sources in the Roman legal tradition. For Bracton, rumor and suspicion might lead to "a strong presumption." Such a presumption might also arise when someone was apprehended over the body of a dead man with his knife dripping blood or when he fled from the scene of the crime. In the case of "overwhelming presumption" no further proof was necessary if there was no proof to the contrary.[42] Some presumptions were strong enough to constitute proof. Others were not.

Sir Edward Coke's treatment, cited as authority for several centuries, notes the three varieties of presumption: violent, probable, and light. "Violent presumption" was often treated as full proof. Coke, like Bracton, used the example of someone leaving the scene of a murder with a bloody sword in hand. Probable presumption, however, "moveth little," and light presumption "not at all." Presumptions or inferences drawn from circumstances in some instances could be used to convict, though Coke noted that incorrect inferences might be drawn from circumstances and the wrong persons punished. In "cases of life" it was important to "judge not too hastily upon bare presumptions."[43]

The English adopted the category of *crimen exceptum*, crimes "done in the dark," and so unlikely to be witnessed. Poisoning and witchcraft and later infanticide, rape, forgery, and assassination were crimes where conviction might rest on circumstantial evidence.

The justicing handbooks of Lambarde, Crompton, and Dalton, with their indebtedness to the rhetoricians, were undoubtedly important in familiarizing trial judges, jurors, and the literate more generally with the concept of circumstantial evidence. Its accompanying machinery of presumption may also be traced to the Romano-canon legal tradition and the writings of classical rhetoricians.

During the eighteenth century there appears to have been a curious reversal of the view that circumstantial evidence was inferior to direct testimony.[44] In the nineteenth century, evidence treatises concluded that circumstantial evidence and direct-witness testimony were equally capable of meeting the "beyond reasonable doubt" standard. By that time, however, the ancient references to habits, education, and other class attributes were disappearing from discussions of circumstantial evidence.

What conclusions can we draw from my brief sketch? First and most important is that the ancient rhetorical tradition played an important and under-recognized role in the Western legal evidentiary tradition. Although its role in the Romano-canon tradition has received some recognition, the contribution of rhetoric to the common-law system has been largely ignored. Failure to recognize that debt has resulted from adulation of the common law and the jury trial, and from the tendency of the Anglo-American legal profession and of evidence literature to ignore pretrial procedures such as arrest and pretrial examination. It is also related to lack of attention to the role of the rhetorical tradition in shaping a practical logic that deals with drawing inferences from "signs." Familiarity with the rhetorical tradition has been absent among the general public and the scholarly community for many generations. For this reason neither scholars nor lawyers have recognized or noticed a tradition once familiar to schoolboys. Although literary historians have long been aware of the important role that rhetoric played in the education of early modern Englishmen and have investigated its role in Renaissance literary culture and political argument, this tradition, or at least parts of it, also bear on the development of English law.

We have shown that portions of the classical rhetorical tradition were detached from their original oratorical context and, in combination with other cultural practices and institutions, came to serve Europe's two chief legal traditions. Although we may disagree on whether the English took the rhetorical elements directly from classical sources or indirectly from Romano-canon sources or from Renaissance rhetoricians such as Thomas Wilson, we cannot dispute that important evidentiary elements of the Anglo-American legal system are deeply indebted to classical rhetoric.

Notes

1. Richard Schoeck, "Lawyers and Rhetoric in Sixteenth-Century England," in *Renaissance Eloquence: Studies in the Theory and Practice of Renaissance Rhetoric*, ed. J. J. Murphy (Berkeley, Calif., 1983), pp. 274–91; Alessandro Giuliani, "The Influence of Rhetoric on the Law of Evidence and Pleading," *Juridical Review* 62 (1969): 216–51;

D. S. Bland, "Rhetoric and the Law Student in Sixteenth-Century England," *Studies in Philology* 53 (1967): 498–508. See also Wilfred Prest, "The Dialectical Origins of Finch's Law," *Cambridge Law Journal* 36 (1977): 316–52; Louis A. Knafla, "The Law Studies of an Elizabethan Student," *Huntington Library Quarterly* 32 (1969): 221–40.

2. The rhetorical tradition also treated the interpretation of legal documents, the distinction between letter and intent, law and equity, conflict of laws, and reasoning by analogy. See Cicero, *De inventione,* 2.10–11.

3. Aristotle, *The Art of Rhetoric,* trans. J. H. Freese (Cambridge, Mass., 1959), bk. 1, chap. 2.

4. For the influence of rhetoric on Roman law, see Hanns Hohmann, "Classical Rhetoric and the Law" (unpublished paper, Sept. 1991). See also Hanns Hohmann, "The Dynamics of Stasis: Classical Rhetorical Theory and Modern Legal Argumentation," *American Journal of Jurisprudence* 34 (1989): 171–97.

5. Cicero, *De inventione,* 2.5–8.

6. Book 1 lists name, nature, manner of life, fortune, habit, feeling, interests, purposes, achievements, accidents, and speeches (1.24).

7. Ibid., 2.9–10, 13. See also 1.24–25, 27.

8. Ibid., 2.11–12, 14. See also 1.28.

9. Quintilian, *Institutes or the Orator,* trans. J. Patsaill (London, 1777), 1.1–5.

10. Quintilian, *Institutes,* 4.9.

11. *Rhetorica ad Herennium,* trans. Harry Caplan (Cambridge, Mass., 1964), 2.3; 3.4–5; 4. 6–8.

12. Ibid., 2.5.8–9.

13. Ibid., 2.5–6, 8. The text, also discussed "confirmatory proof," employed after suspicion is established. Ibid., 2.6.9.

14. Ibid., 2.6.9–10.

15. Ibid., 2.6.11.

16. See John Langbein, *Torture and the Law of Proof* (Chicago, 1977); Alessi Palazzola, *Prova legale e pena: La crisi del sistema tra evo medio e moderno* (Naples, 1979); Richard Fraher, "Theoretical Justification for the New Criminal Law of the High Middle Ages," *University of Illinois Law Review,* (1984): 577–97.

17. John Langbein, *Prosecuting Crime in the Renaissance: England, Germany, France* (Cambridge, Mass., 1974), p. 274.

18. Henry Bracton, *On the Laws and Customs of England,* trans. and ed. Samuel Thorne, 4 vols. (Cambridge, Mass., 1968), 404, 408.

19. 34 Edw. 3. c. 1.

20. Desiderius Erasmus, *On Copia of Words and Ideas,* (Milwaukee, Wis., 1963), pp. 66–67.

21. Schoeck, "Lawyers and Rhetoric," pp. 181, 278, 279.

22. Thomas Wright, *The Passions of the Mind* (London, 1601) pp. 27, 172; Richard Sherry, *Treatise of Schemes and Tropes* (London, 1550), pp. 78–79, 83.

23. Thomas Wilson, *Arte of Rhetorique,* ed. Thomas J. Derrick (New York, 1982), pp. 184–88, 190–91, 193–94, 195, 199, 234, 236. The "places" of logic played an essential role in orations.

24. See John Langbein, *Prosecuting Crime in the Renaissance* (Cambridge, Mass., 1974). Only in the eighteenth century were suspicions transferred to the arrest section of

justicing manuals. See Barbara J. Shapiro, *"Beyond Reasonable Doubt" and "Probable Cause": Historical Perspectives on the Anglo-American Law of Evidence* (Berkeley, Calif., 1991).

25. Lambarde, *Eirenarcha* (London, 1614), p. 217. Cicero, *De inventione*, 1.34–43, 48; *Rhetorica ad Herennium*, 2.8.

26. Lambarde, *Eirenarcha*, p. 218.

27. Ibid.

28. Ibid., p. 219.

29. Ibid.

30. London, 1606, pp. 98–101. Fitzherbert was published in 1538.

31. *The Country Justice* (London, 1635), pp. 296, 297, 300. See also Shapiro, *"Beyond Reasonable Doubt."*

32. Ibid., p. 297.

33. Ibid., title page.

34. See Thomas Green, *Verdict According to Conscience: Perspectives on the English Criminal Trial Jury, 1200–1800* (Chicago, 1985); *Twelve Good Men and True: The Criminal Trial Jury in England, 1200–1800* (Princeton, N.J., 1988).

35. Francis Bacon, *The Works of Francis Bacon*, ed. J. Spedding, R. L. Ellis, D. D. Heath, 7 vols. (London, 1857–61), 1:513; Hale, *Pleas of the Crown* (London, 1736), 1:635. See also Shapiro, "Beyond Reasonable Doubt."

36. M. Macnair, " 'A Fragment on Proof' by Francis North, Lord Guildford," *Seventeenth Century* 8 (1993), p. 143; Hale, *Primitive Origination* (London, 1677), p. 128; Sir Matthew Hale, *History of the Common Law of England*, ed. Charles M. Gray (Chicago, 1971), pp. 164, 165. Juries, however, were free to make their decisions without any witnesses at all.

37. Quoted in Hubertus Schulte Herbruggen, "The Process Against Sir Thomas More," *Law Quarterly Review* 99 (1983): 113–36.

38. Geoffrey Gilbert, *Law of Evidence* (London, 1788), p. 149.

39. Hale, *Historia Placetorum Coronae*, 2:276, 277; Hale, *History of the Common Law*, p. 163.

40. William Best, *Principles of the Law of Evidence*, 6th ed. (London, 1875), pp. 18, 22. See also p. 24.

41. Gilbert, *Law of Evidence*, p. 147; Thomas More, *Complete Works*, ed. John Guy, Ralph Keen, Clarence H. Miller and Ruth McGugan, 15 vols. (New Haven, 1963–93), 10:157; Crompton, *L'office*, p. 110v; Locke, *An Essay Concerning Human Understanding*, ed. A. Fraser, 2 vols. (New York, 1959), bk. 4, chap. 4, sec. 4. The rule is also found in canon and civil law. See also Barbara J. Shapiro, *A Culture of Fact: England, 1550–1720* (Ithaca, N.Y., 2000).

42. Bracton, *On the Laws and Customs of England*, 2:330.

43. Sir Edward Coke, *The First Part of the Institutes of the Laws of England* (1628), sec. 1, 6B; Coke, *Third Part of the Institutes of the Lawes of England* (Philadelphia, 1853), chaps. 104, 232. The bloody sword example can also be found in Staunford, *Les plees del coron* (London, 1557), 1 lb. 3. c. 14., and in Bartolus.

44. See Alexander Welsh, *Strong Representations: Narrative and Circumstantial Evidence in England* (Baltimore, Md., 1992).

3

Archives in the Fiction:
Marguerite de Navarre's Heptaméron

CARLA FRECCERO

In the book from which I take the (reversed) title of this essay, *Fiction in the Archives: Pardon Tales and Their Tellers in Sixteenth-Century France*, Natalie Zemon Davis examines the fictive dimensions of pardon tales, documents presented to the king in sixteenth-century France as appeals for remission in the case of certain often capital criminal offenses.[1]

She writes, "When I was a student, we were ordinarily taught as scientific historians to peel away the fictive elements in our documents so we could get at the real facts" (3). By examining instead the "forming, shaping, and molding elements: the crafting of a narrative" in these legal documents (3), Davis undertakes an analysis of the narrative dimensions of the legal rhetorical practice, in particular the wording of appeals to a sovereign power to act in the interest of those subjects make the appeal. She compares these remission letters to other sixteenth-century French narratives, specifically the *Heptaméron* by Marguerite de Navarre, who, she remarks, "might want the king's readership, but . . . did not need his pardon" (5). Davis is thus interested in the resemblances between the *nouvelle,* which "employed many concrete details as marks of [its] reality and often claimed to be retelling actual events" (5) and "fictions in the archives." She demonstrates the extent to which these archives of crime in the early modern period are linked to the novella tradition.

Davis's admittedly parodic representation of scientific historical practice —

what might be called the "onion" theory of history — demonstrates the impossibility of separating "real facts" from the narrative forms in which they present themselves. Certainly, since Hayden White's *Metahistory,* we have become familiar with the notion that historiography itself is a genre of narrative fiction: it tells a tale about what happened and does so using literary rhetorical conventions. In this essay, then, I would like to treat both history and literature, "archives" and "fiction," as texts, to see what kinds of accounts of the past might emerge if such disciplinary boundaries were blurred. One of my texts refers to an event: the forced marriage of Marguerite de Navarre's daughter, Jeanne d'Albret, to the duke of Clèves in 1541. The other is Marguerite's collection of short stories, the *Heptaméron.* In focusing on a specific set of events in "fact" and in "fiction," I am less interested in understanding exactly "what happened" than I am in asking questions about the narratives that might be constructed from a collection of texts that includes "archives" (letters, court documents, notarial records) and "fiction."

Following Davis's line of inquiry, if letters of remission might be said to deploy the techniques of fiction to persuade a sovereign, what purpose might the claim to be "retelling actual events" serve for the novella? This question is can be posed compellingly with regard to the *Heptaméron,* whose prologue, though it places the collection within the tradition of the most illustrious Italian storytelling (Boccaccio's *Decameron*), nevertheless asserts a difference from it in aligning the work with "history" and with "truth." Parlamente declares:

> "I don't think there's one of us who hasn't read the hundred tales by Boccaccio, . . . As a matter of fact, the two ladies I have mentioned [Madame the Dauphine and Madame Marguerite], along with other people at the court, made up their minds to do the same as Boccaccio. There was to be one difference — that they should not write any story that was not truthful [*veritable histoire*]. . . . The ladies promised to produce ten stories each, and to get together a party of ten people who were qualified to contribute something, excluding those who studied and were men of letters. Monsieur the Dauphin didn't want their art brought in, and he was afraid that rhetorical ornament would in part falsify the truth of the account [*que la beaulté de la rethoricque feit tort en quelque partye à la verité de l'histoire*]."[2]

As John Lyons has noted, one of the effects of Parlamente's appeal to "véritable histoire" and her explicit elimination of authors is to locate the stories in the contemporary context of the storytellers and the writer (*Exemplum,* 79). Indeed, ever since Brantôme's *La Vie des dames galantes,* the *Heptaméron* has been read as a *roman à clef* referring to actual persons and events in the court of France.[3]

Thus, just as the addition of "fictive" narrative detail in the pardon tale adds subjective dimensions to the objective "fact" of a crime and thereby wins sympathy for its teller as both witness and perpetrator, so too the claim of verisimilitude, objective plausibility, lends to the willfully subjective domain of the fictional novella the objectivity of factual occurrence and thus contributes to the authority of its storyteller.[4] This is a fiction, then, that aspires to be an archive.

Recently, Margaret Ferguson has argued that it is precisely in relation to the question of authority that one can understand the peculiar assertions of truth-telling, peculiar because propounded within the explicitly fictional context and intertext of the address of the work (a game devised by characters to collaborate in the production of a collection of Boccaccian short stories for the French court) and elaborated through extreme indirection by Parlamente, a mediatory character (as her name attests) who is also an author-figure, a lover, a wife, and a daughter.[5]

Ferguson argues that like Castiglione, who also "rewrites" Boccaccio and stages a battle of the sexes conducted by discussants in a *locus amoenus,* Marguerite de Navarre "gives us the portrait of the author as courtier — someone who needs exquisite skills of persuasion as she attempts to play one of the most difficult of the roles Castiglione's male interlocutors discuss: the role of the courtier not only as 'ornament,' but as educator of the prince" (178).

Indeed, in story 42, Parlamente recounts just such a pedagogical tale involving a young prince (" 'the happiest and most fortunate prince in Christendom'," 385; 290), whose advances are repeatedly refused by an poor young woman of exemplary virtue, felicitously named Françoise.[6] Unlike so many of the plots of the *Heptaméron*'s novellas, where the woman in question would have been taken by force, this story results in the prince's being educated in virtuous and chaste conduct by his namesake (François/Françoise) and, it is suggested, his nation ("françoise") through the figure of a young woman.[7] As if to underline the national allegory at work in the tale, Oisille suggests that Françoise would more aptly have served as founding exemplar of virtue than Lucretia: " 'There is only one thing I would regret,' said Oisille, 'and that is that the virtuous actions of this young girl didn't take place in the time of the great [Roman] historians. The writers who praised Lucretia so much would have left her story aside, so that they could describe at length the virtue of the heroine of your story' " (389; 294).

In a passage immediately following, either Oisille (in the Penguin edition) or Hircan (in the François edition), makes the following remark: " 'I find your heroine's virtue so great, that were it not for the fact that we have solemnly sworn to tell the truth in our stories, I would find it incredible.' "[8] Whereupon

Hircan remarks: " 'I don't find her virtue quite so great as you do' " (389; "Pour ce que je les trouve si grandes [Françoise's virtues] que je ne les pourrois croyre, sans le grand serment que nous avons faict de dire verité, je ne trouve pas sa vertu telle que vous la peignez, dist Hircan," 294). In either manuscript, the narrative signals its own status as exemplary allegory: in one case, it is rendered both plausible and exemplary; in the other, its status as fact is called into question precisely because of its exemplarity. In this particular tale, then, fiction and "vérité" collude in the production of an indirect intervention in matters of state rule — the fashioning of its sovereign as a chaste and virtuous prince — that is, both marked *and* disguised as feminine. The allegorical dimensions and pointed commentary of story 42 thus support the first part of Davis's contention that "authors might want the king's readership," while the overall indirection of the authorial claim in the *Heptaméron,* its production as a collective and fictional event, casts some doubt on her statement that such an author would not need the king's pardon.

Marguerite found herself at least once urgently needing the king's pardon and protection, precisely around the crime of authorship, when she wrote and published the narrative poem *Le Miroir de l'âme pécheresse,* which was charged with heresy and placed on the Index of Forbidden Books by the Sorbonne in 1533.[9] Marguerite's involvement in doctrinal matters more than once brought her under the punitive scrutiny of both her brother and king and her husband. Jeanne, in a letter written after Marguerite's death, seems, at the very least, to have been persuaded of the threat her mother's religious activities posed and to attribute to that threat her retreat into "romans jovials": "The said Queen [was] warned by her late brother the king, François I of good and glorious memory, my much honored uncle, not to get new doctrines in her head [*mettre en cervelle dogmes nouveaux*] so that from then on she confined herself to amusing stories [*romans jovials*]. Besides, I well remember how long ago, the late King, my most honored father . . . surprised the said Queen when she was praying in her rooms with the ministers Roussel and Farel, and how with great annoyance he slapped her right cheek and forbade her sharply to meddle in matters of doctrine."[10]

But if, as Ferguson argues, the *Heptaméron* itself is a "social text" (159), through which its author aspires to influence the conduct of the ruler and the affairs of state much as Castiglione may have hoped to do, as a queen, a wife, and a woman, Marguerite ran the risk of usurping the prerogatives of a king, a husband, and a man in ways that Jeanne seems not to have perceived.[11]

Thus the obliquity of the authorial assertions in the *Heptaméron,* produced in the ambiguity of the relation between fact and fiction, suggests the political and social liabilities of female authorship — many of which, as regards the early modern period, are well known — as well as the ambition to intervene at the level of state policy and practice under the cover of fiction.

The inability of a woman to claim authority in sixteenth-century France is figured early on in the *Heptaméron* as the inability of a woman to tell the truth without herself being suspect. Brantôme claims that story 4, which recounts the attempted rape of a noble widow by a gentleman attached to her brother's household, refers to the attempted rape of Marguerite herself by the admiral Bonnivet.[12] After the attempt, during which the noblewoman has attacked the gentleman and lacerated his face with her nails, the princess informs her lady-in-waiting and triumphantly announces her intention to denounce the culprit to her brother (93; 31). In a very long speech, the lady-in-waiting articulates the all-too-familiar consequences that may befall a woman choosing to file a formal complaint against her would-be rapist:

> "Madame — if you try to make your honour even more impressive, you may only end up doing the opposite. If you make an official complaint against him, you will have to bring the whole thing into the open, whereas at the moment nobody knows anything, and he certainly won't go and tell anybody. What is more, just suppose you did go ahead, and Monseigneur, your brother, did bring the case to justice, and the poor man was put to death — people will say that he *must* have had his way with you. Most people will argue that it's not very easy to accept that a man can carry out such an act, unless he has been given a certain amount of encouragement by the lady concerned. You're young and attractive, you're lively and sociable in all kinds of company. There isn't a single person at this court who hasn't seen the encouraging way you treat the man you are now suspecting. That could only make people conclude that if he indeed did what you say, then it couldn't have been without some blame being due to you as well. Your honour . . . would be put in doubt wherever this story was heard." (94; 32)

Predictably, on the advice of the counsel, which, to counter the accusation of rape, displays every prosecutorial strategy known, the princess keeps silent. The exhaustive detailing of the reasons for silence illustrates the constraints imposed by gender on making truthful claims.

The prologue thematizes the indirection of the authorial assertion through a series of layered references to authors, narrators, and characters in the conception of the project of the work itself, which de-emphasizes Marguerite's role in the *Heptaméron's* creation. There, the narrative suggests that for Parlamente storytelling represents a compromise between her husband's one-track mind and her spiritual mother Oisille's desire to pray. In story 4, the authorial art of indirection manifests itself in slightly different techniques: the alternation within the story between narration — wherein the rapist is condemned by his own actions — and direct discourse, where the liabilities of truth-telling are relentlessly detailed, and the juxtaposition of story and frame discussion, which unmasks as hypocritical the masculine motives of the story. Within the story, as a counterpart to the noblewoman's silencing, the lacerations on the face of the nobleman shame him into silence, and he absents himself from view for the duration of the novella. It would seem then that writing — the material sign or "symptom" of which appears on the face of the nobleman as a telltale mark or wound — confers upon the woman's discourse the efficaciousness and authority that her word otherwise lacks.[13] In the discussion, when Hircan argues that the nobleman should have killed the lady-in-waiting to achieve his goal, Nomerfide gives the lie to the myth of the courtly lover by remarking: " 'Kill her!' . . . 'You wouldn't mind him being a murderer as well, then?' " (97; 34).[14] Thus the "véritable histoire," taken as a whole, intervenes in the history of an event to set the record straight.

In the matter of her daughter's marriage, Marguerite de Navarre's extratextual intervention in the practices of early modern French state-making is a matter of historical record. As Sarah Hanley notes, "early modern monarchies were characterized politically by intertwined private-public (family-state) relations," where marriage functioned as both the metaphorical and the material basis for these relations, exacerbated in the case of the royal line.[15] Marguerite's negotiations with her daughter, the king, and Marguerite's husband highlight an arena of legal contention in sixteenth-century France: the question of consent and its manipulation by institutions, families, and individuals in the matter of marriage. From the twelfth-century, with Gratien's *Concordia discordantium canonum,* which summarized case law and opinion, to the mid-sixteenth century in France, consent of the parties involved was the sine qua non of a legal marriage, which came under the jurisdiction of canon law and the ecclesiastical courts.[16]

Gratien's *Decretum* asks the telling question, "May a daughter be given in marriage against her will?" and answers it with reference to paternal authority: "A father's oath cannot compel a girl to marry one to whom she has not assented" (Hanley, "Family and State," 54). Natalie Zemon Davis argues that until 1564, when the last session of the Council of Trent established specific guidelines to ascertain the validity of a marriage, consent of the partners alone constituted a valid union, even in the absence of a priest and witnesses. "People," she argues, "used [clandestine marriage] for reasons of their own: they were minors and their parents were opposed to the marriage; they were marrying within a prohibited degree of kinship and could not get a dispensation; they wanted to have intercourse and this was the only way to do it; one of the partners was already married to a person in another place."[17] In practice, of course, families exercised the maximum control possible in contracting alliances, and Hanley argues that over the course of the Middle Ages, "a contest developed between two institutions [family and Church] for control over the connubial fate of children" (55).

In sixteenth-century France, there emerged, owing to venality, a class of professional lawyers — the *noblesse de robe* — who staffed administrative and judicial offices in the kingdom. The system of transmission of hereditary offices as family property to the next generation was subsequently legalized. This particular interweaving of private (family) and public (state) interests created an incentive — realized over the course of the sixteenth century in France — to increase the power of constitutional and civil law over that of ecclesiastical or canon law and to bring marriage, the key to state-making as well as to hereditary transmission of property and goods, under the control of secular law and thus of family and state.[18] Further, Hanley argues, with the exposure of Salic law as a forgery, and with the omnipresence of female rulers in Europe and queens as potential regents in France, the exclusion of women from political rule in France took on the character of an "obsession aimed at defining all authority to govern as fundamentally masculine in nature during a time of interrelated family formation and state building."[19] Over the course of the sixteenth century, then, legists and members of the *parlements* developed an indigenous French body of laws that Hanley characterizes as a marital regime government, that secured the legal foundations for male right to govern and definitively excluded women from the political sphere: a French legal canon encompassing public law (dealing with the constitutional foundations of the state encapsulated in the marital maxim "The king is the husband and political spouse of the kingdom"), Civil Law (governing the family and marriage), and natural law (establishing the natural superiority of males over females and the priority of male seminal transmission in matters of succession).[20]

Within the context of increasing masculine jurisdiction in political and familial matters, the issue of consent — the right of a girl not to be forced into a marriage she had not chosen poses a particular problem, one that the parlement of Paris attempted to solve definitively in 1556 by promulgating an edict against clandestine marriages, or marriages contracted by a consenting couple without parental consent.[21] In 1557, the king, Henri II, also issued an edict against them, which was to be the subject of a treatise by Jean de Coras, who would later be chancellor in Toulouse for the future Protestant queen of Navarre, Marguerite's daughter Jeanne (Davis, *Martin Guerre*, 47, 114).

In Marguerite's time, however, "consent" still offered a window of opportunity, however small, for a woman's exercise of agency. As Davis argues in relation to the question of consent, "a strategy for at least a thread of female autonomy may have been built precisely around th[e] sense of being given away." She suggests that some aristocratic women realized the economic and political importance of their bodies in contracting alliances and consolidating state power, and exploited that importance by "giving themselves away." She makes the point that "if women can think of giving themselves away, then they can also begin to think of having stronger ownership rights in their bodies."[22] In Marguerite's case, "being given away" and its relation to consent become a site of contestation at the intersection between family and state, both in the arena of law and in that of literature, where the question of clandestine marriage makes its appearance in her tales. That site — at once a legal archive and an "archive in the fiction" — constitutes one moment in an archaeology of female political subjectivity and sovereignty in France.

Christiane Klapisch-Zuber, among others, has shown how patrician women in early modern societies functioned as the sociopolitical cement of the aristocracy by maintaining strong horizontal ties of kinship even as they participated in the vertical construction of lineages through marriage.[23] Marguerite's dual position through kinship (as sister to François I) and lineage (as wife of Henri d'Albret) produced a conflict that was carried out over the body of her daughter, Jeanne d'Albret. Documents in the form of letters (by and to Marguerite) and declarations (by Jeanne), as well as a report by the secret agent of the Hapsburg Empire, Juan Martinez Descurra, outline a series of events leading to the marriage of Jeanne to the duke of Clèves and its annulment four years later. Henri d'Albret, seeking to recapture the part of Navarre that was under Hapsburg rule, entered into secret negotiations with the emperor Charles V for a marriage between the emperor's son and Jeanne d'Albret. Meanwhile, François I, Charles's enemy, sought to use Jeanne to cement his own alliances with the Germanies in order to further undermine Hapsburg control of Europe. Apprised of Henri's plan, he had Jeanne put under house arrest of sorts from the age of ten onward. In this context, Marot's famous reference to Jeanne as "the darling of two kings" seems particularly ironic.[24] Marguerite, in turn, finds herself at the center of a three-way negotiation: between her husband's and her brother's genealogical lines and property interests (a conflict between kinship and marriage), indirectly between the political interests of two monarchs (François and Charles), and finally between her daughter and these conflicting claims.

Testimony of Jeanne's opposition to the arranged marriage between herself and the duke of Clèves is provided by written declarations dating from the annulment of the marriage in 1545 (by which time Charles had taken over the duke's territory and forced him to renounce his alliance with France, thus necessitating the dissolution of his marriage). Although verb tenses suggest that the declarations antedate the annulment and the marriage itself, there is no direct evidence from Jeanne that in 1541 she actively opposed the marriage. Her opposition is alluded to, however, most notably in a letter from Marguerite to François written in 1540: "But now, Monseigneur, having heard that my daughter, knowing neither the great honor that you conferred upon her by deigning to visit her nor the obedience that she owes you nor for that matter that a girl should never have a will of her own, has had the utterly foolish notion of telling you that she begs not to be married to M. de Clèves. . . . I/we cannot imagine whence proceeds her great audacity in this matter, about which she has never spoken to us" (author's translation).[25]

In 1545, Jeanne d'Albret signed a declaration of nonconsummation of the marriage and testified to having written two earlier protests against the arranged marriage, stating that she did not consent to it. These other declarations are included in the 1545 document, prefaced by the royal notary's statement that "the said lady has presented two and a half sheets of paper, which she said were written and signed by her hand, and which contain the aforementioned declarations and protestations":

> I, Jeanne de Navarre, . . . declare and protest again that the arranged marriage between myself and the duke of Clèves is against my will; that I have never and will never consent, and that anything I might do or say from here on in, of which one might say that I consented, will have been by force, against my pleasure and my will, and from fear of the king, of the king my father and the queen my mother, who menaced me and had me whipped by my governess, who several times urged me by commandment of the queen my mother, warning me that, if I did not agree to this marriage that the king wants, and if I did not consent, I would be beaten to death, and that I would be the cause of the loss and destruction of my father and mother and of their house; of which I am so greatly fearful, also for the destruction of my parents, that I do not know to whom to have recourse except to God, when I see that my father and mother have abandoned me, they who know well what I have told them, and that I will never love the duke of Clèves and want nothing to do with him whatsoever. [Author's translation][26]

Descurra (who was relaying messages between Marguerite's husband and the emperor Charles) reports that Marguerite, having capitulated to the king's will, devised a means to prevent the marriage in 1541 and so to promote her husband's plan. According to Descurra, Marguerite writes the document that Jeanne then signs in order to fabricate nonconsent and thus provide a basis for the annulment of the marriage. Of course, neither Marguerite's letter nor Descurra's account, not to mention Jeanne d'Albret's declaration, can be read straightforwardly, given each interlocutor's position as the subject of a monarch and as articulating his or her actions to or for that monarch. Either literary historians and biographers (except Nancy Roelker) assume that Jeanne's protests expressed her opposition to the contract at the time it was proposed (rather than having been retroactively constructed), and that Marguerite desired nothing but her brother's will, or they unproblematically accept Descurra's account and assume that Marguerite set Jeanne up to it (Roelker, *Queen of Navarre*, 41–75). Those who accept Descurra's story first do not take into account the way he obtained access to information (via Henri, who had an interest in representing the situation his way to the emperor) and, second, rely the assumption that no twelve-year-old girl would be capable of mounting independent opposition to the king's will.

The question of competing wills in the matter of consent is indeed at stake in this mysterious archive, for whereas Marguerite, in her letter to the king her brother, admonishes her daughter for having the audacity to have a "will of her own" ("voulunté"), it is precisely that will ("volunté," "grey," "vouloir") and its refusal to consent that enable the timely and convenient monarchic dissolution of a politically unacceptable alliance. But because the sovereign will is being addressed in these instances, the question of whose agency and whose sovereignty is being represented remains unanswered, in the case of both Marguerite and her daughter. This is where the archival aspect in the fiction acts as commentary, inserting into the historical record a polemic regarding consent that lends "voice" to the disempowered subjects and objects of a masculine sovereign state and a marital regime.

Story 21 of the *Heptaméron*, the story of Rolandine, brings the question of consent into relief through a fictional exploration of the motives and consequences of clandestine marriage that pits "a Queen of France" (236; 158: "une Royne") against a daughter of an important noble family, a "close relative" of the queen (236; 158: "Rolandine . . . estoit bien proche sa parente"). Rolandine's story is one of the best known in the *Heptaméron*.[27] It bears a striking resemblance to the story of Marguerite and Jeanne, including the presence of a *gouvernante* through whom the royal mother mediates her commands. This story symmetrically reverses the historical situation: instead of withholding consent from an arranged union, Rolandine arranges a union for herself without parental and royal consent. Rolandine is an unmarried thirty-year-old woman whose father's economic interests prevail over his daughter's desire to marry, and whose queen dislikes her because of a grudge she holds against the father. Rolandine eventually finds consolation in the company of a "bastard," whose illegitimate birth and physical unattractiveness have kept him unmarried as well. Finally, the two hold a clandestine wedding ceremony, "in the church and in the sight of God, taking Him as witness of their vows" (240; 162). They agree not to consummate their union (another parallel with

Jeanne's situation) until Rolandine's father dies or lends his approval. When discovered together, the couple separate but continue to exchange letters through the intermediary of servants. The narrative details the queen's obsessive regulation of their speech and the eventual interception of a letter that reveals their marriage. At this point the narrator is highly critical of the queen's behavior ("The Queen was quite incapable of making a reasonable reply" [247; 169]). In the lengthy confrontation that ensues between mistress and subject, Rolandine's calm reasonableness is repeatedly contrasted with the queen's rage: "She [Rolandine] was as calm and composed as the Queen was violent and vehement" (246; 167).[28]

Rolandine's transgression of the social order constitutes a threat in that she has not obtained "parental" or royal consent: "[The Queen] . . . far from addressing her as 'cousin,' she told her repeatedly, her face contorted with rage, that she was a 'miserable wretch,' and accused her of bringing dishonor upon her father's house, upon her relatives, and upon her mistress, the Queen" (245; 167). The resemblance between this passage and what Jeanne says of her mother's reaction to her disobedience is striking. In one of the longest speeches in the *Heptaméron,* Rolandine accuses the queen of injustice and claims the right to act according to her own desires. She appeals to a higher authority to justify her actions, in legal language that echoes Jeanne's declaration in a more assertive, and therefore subversive, fashion: " 'I have no advocate to speak in my defence. My only advocate is the truth, the truth which is known to me alone, and I am bound to declare it to you fearlessly. . . . I am not afraid that any mortal creature should hear how I have conducted myself in the affair with which I am charged, since I know that there has been no offence either to God or to my honour' " (248; 169–70).

Rolandine's claim is indeed outrageous ("audatieuse" is repeated twice in the text). In story 40, Rolandine's aunt is condemned, both within the story and by the discussants, for the far more modest transgression of marrying someone she thought would meet with approval. At the end of story 40, both Parlamente and Oisille side with the social authorities: " 'Ladies, I pray God that you will take note of this example, and that none of you will wish to marry merely for your own pleasure, without the consent of those to whom you owe obedience' " (370; 277). Yet in story 21 the narrative works to justify Rolandine's claim. The state attempts to annul the union on grounds of non-consummation, while Rolandine appeals to Scripture to uphold its validity:

> However, before they sent her [to the tower], they arranged for several men of the Church and some members of the King's Council to speak with her. These men made it plain to her that since her marriage was established by nothing more than exchange of words, it could quite easily be dissolved, provided that

they gave one another up entirely. It was, they informed her, the king's wish
that she should do so, in order that the honor of her house should be upheld.
Her reply was that she was ready to obey the King in all things, provided there
was no conflict with her conscience. But that which God had joined together
no man could put asunder (250; 171)

Upon refusing to allow the dissolution of her marriage, Rolandine is returned to her father, who locks her in a castle in the forest. The bastard proves
unfaithful and dies, whereupon Rolandine's father seeks to make amends.
Rolandine marries a gentleman who bears "the same name and arms as her
father" (252; 173: "du nom et armes de leur maison"). When her brother tries
to disinherit her because of her disobedience, God intervenes and the brother
dies, leaving all the inheritance to her. God is indeed, as Rolandine asserts, on
her side.[29]

Throughout the confrontation between Rolandine and the queen and the
ensuing interrogation by the Church and the members of the king's council,
Rolandine volunteers her silence and is ordered instead to speak, to her own
detriment. And yet it is evident from the elaborate dispute the council members and the officials of the Church conduct with her that the law is unclear on
the matter of her marriage, for although the absence of witnesses and the lack
of consummation render the marriage vulnerable to dissolution, it is nevertheless recognized as a valid union, one in need of unmaking ("il se povoit facille-
ment deffaire," 171). The righteousness of her argument is further bolstered
by the mention of her age, thirty, which places her well above the age of
majority and thus beyond the requirement to seek parental consent.[30] At stake
in the matter of clandestine marriage is the ability to inherit; here it is threatened, although Rolandine is no longer involved with the "bastard," but legitimately married to a person of her father's choosing. The mention of her
brother's death only underscores the truth of her outrageously Protestant
claim that God's unmediated witness is all that is required.

The queen disappears when Rolandine returns to her father, and the discussants never mention her, although the dialogue between queen and subject
occupies a significant portion of the tale. Although the discursive confrontation with Rolandine works to discredit the queen, other events in the narrative, by contrast, seem to justify her opposition to the union. The "bastard"
proves an unworthy mate for Rolandine: "It was quite plain from his lack of
constancy that it was not true and perfect love that led him to attach himself to
Rolandine, but rather greed and ambition" (251; 172); the queen's judgment is
thus retrospectively justified on moral grounds. The unworthiness of the "bastard" reframes the queen's actions in such a way that she appears to have

been intervening in Rolandine's best interests. Earlier in the tale, the prince's mother, another queen, finds the "bastard" reading courtly romances, which serves further to undermine his moral standing. At the same time, these moral justifications for opposition to Rolandine's choice ideologically mask the threat to the sociopolitical order represented by her claims, a threat mentioned by Dagoucin in the discussion of story 40: " 'In order to maintain peace in the state ["la chose publicque," 280], consideration is given only to the rank of families, the seniority of individuals, and the provisions of the law, . . . in order that the monarchy should not be undermined' " (374; 280).

This complex — and indirect — fictional intervention into highly disputed legal territory in sixteenth-century France, and its striking resemblance to the making and unmaking of Jeanne d'Albret's marriage, suggest several ways to begin to understand one archive of female political authority and subjectivity in a context where such voices and their ability to participate in the political arena of the nation-state have been reduced to near inaudibility. In one respect, the story of Rolandine acts as a justificatory narrative exculpating the queen's intransigence in the face of the resistance of a feminine subject: if only she will obey, the sovereign will act in her interest, but submission to the will of the state is an absolute precondition for social belonging. In another way, however, the tale suggests a strategy of discursive resistance that manipulates the rule of consent in the service of the exercise of a woman's will and adds to that strategy a daring proposition: that the Protestant doctrine of "universal priesthood" might be enlisted to bolster the claims to sovereignty of the subject.[31] Davis suggests as much when she speculates that the mid-century marriage between Arnaud du Tilh (the "new" Martin Guerre) and Martin Guerre's wife, Bertrande de Rols, was inspired in part by the new Protestant doctrine: "What hope might the Protestant message have offered to the new Martin and Bertrande during the years they were living together as 'true married people'? That they could tell their story to God alone and need not communicate it to any human intermediary. That the life they had willfully fabricated was part of God's providence" (Davis, *Martin Guerre,* 50). The radical tenets of the quoted speech of Rolandine are framed, however, within a narrative that, although sympathetic to the female subject's claims, justifies the actions of the authorities by scapegoating the "bastard" and restores proper order to "la chose publicque." Story 21 thus demonstrates — as does perhaps the story of Marguerite's role in Jeanne's marriage — the extent to which this author might both want the king's readership *and* need his pardon.

It is well known that Marguerite de Navarre was a Protestant sympathizer, as patron and protectress of Protestant leaders, as a correspondent and interlocutor with Lefèvre d'Etaples, Guillaume Briçonnet, and Calvin, and as a poetic proponent of Reformist doctrine in her own right.[32] In one passage in particular in the *Heptaméron,* an exchange between Parlamente and Oisille concerning bad preachers and the "correct" interpretation of the Gospel suggests the capacity for an unmediated relation with God and divine truth: "[Parlamente]: 'I have refused to believe these preachers, unless what they say seems to me to conform to the word of God, which is the only true touchstone by which one can know whether one is hearing truth or falsehood.' 'Be assured,' said Oisille, 'that whosoever reads the Scriptures often and with humility will never be deceived by human fabrications and inventions, for whosoever has his mind filled with truth can never be the victim of lies'" (400; 304).

As Ferguson notes of this passage, "the female interpreter here becomes the judge of what 'conforms' to the Gospel's truth," although here, too, the assertion made by Oisille is immediately brought into question by some of the other *devisants* ("Recreating the Rules," 187).

The Protestant insistence, in story 21, on Rolandine's claim to be justified in her actions by the sight and witness of God alone, hints at another way in which Protestant doctrine, and specifically Calvin's speeches, inform the strategic foregrounding of feminine authority and "individual" sovereignty in the novella. Not only do the discussants never mention the agency of the queen, who acts as prosecutor and judge throughout the tale, but the king, in spite of the appeal made separately to him by the "bastard," also acts in concert with her, exercising no independent action. It is as though his presence in the tale were invoked merely to support her judgment, which, as I mentioned, is ultimately ratified by the inconstancy of the "bastard" himself. Calvin's policies regarding the relations between husband and wife, enacted into law in Geneva after 1545, undermined the strict monarchic and familial gender hierarchy of the French marital regime: Calvin permitted both sexes to instigate divorce proceedings and argued, in his sermon on *Deuteronomy,* that "authority is attributed as much to one parent as to the other . . . . God does not wish the father alone to rule the child but that the mother also have a share in the honor and the preeminence."[33]

If, then, the author-narrator of story 21 is conducting a polemic in the name of a certain (righteous) female authority — principally, it might be argued, that of the maternal sovereign — what might be the implications for the female subject of this authority? How is she being counseled to exercise her authority to act as a sovereign subject? In the story, Rolandine is allowed to "speak," and she is "heard." She claims to be justified by God in her actions, an assertion that proves simultaneously false (because the "bastard" betrays her) and true (because divine Goodness [*"la Bonté divine,"* 173] kills the "bastard," Rolandine's father absolves her, blaming himself, and Rolandine lives happily —

married—ever after). If, as Ferguson asserts, Marguerite's text can be understood to practice *The Courtier*'s indirect art of persuasion in the service of a ruler's education, might we think of that ruler as a (future) queen? And if she is one, then in the masculine state-building political arenas of France, how will she assert the sovereignty of her will, except through an appeal—the absolute appeal, one might say—to an unverifiable but supreme paternal authority, the one to whom the kings of France themselves must have recourse in justifying their claims to divine right?

Slightly over a decade after her mother's death in 1549, Jeanne d'Albret, queen of Navarre, married finally to Antoine de Bourbon, a "first prince of the blood," and mother of the future King Henri IV of Navarre, converted to Calvinism (Roelker, *Queen of Navarre*, 120–54). This was shortly after she commissioned the first authorized edition of her mother's stories in 1559 under the imprint of Claude Gruget. Jeanne also commissioned a biography of her reign, which was recorded in her day by Nicolas de Bordenave.[34]

She herself composed a political pamphlet, the *Ample déclaration* (1568), justifying her actions against the Crown.[35] Her activities as ruler, administrator, and champion of the Protestant cause in the semiautonomous territories of Navarre both before and after her husband's death have been extensively chronicled in the annals of French religious and political history. In short, Jeanne de Navarre acceded to historical subjectivity and to the political history of the wars of religion and the French monarchy. Ironically, it was also during this period after her mother's death that the Protestant sympathizer and future Protestant judge Jean de Coras, from within the Protestant territories presided over by Jeanne, composed his negative commentary on clandestine marriage in support of the king's edict of 1557. Insofar as it was associated with canon law, clandestine marriage would come to be condemned by the French state and Protestant reformers alike. On the other hand, Coras, who was lynched for his beliefs in Toulouse in 1572 in front of the parlement building, also wrote what was to become perhaps the most famous—and sympathetically recounted— French story of an illegitimate marriage. *L'Arrest memorable,* or the story of Martin Guerre, survives even today, through the intermediary of another female institution-builder, as a testament to the exercise—only partially successful—of female sovereignty.[36]

In the 1600s, the parlement of Paris began to publicize its legal decisions; these, as well as briefs, addenda, and pleadings were compiled, published and circulated by legal officials and printers; in this arena, writes Hanley, "women commanded attention," as they "wrote, dictated, or were involved in writing legal briefs, *factums* (later called *mémoires*), and addenda narrating contests with the law, hence with the monarchic state, source of the law" (Hanley,

"Social Sites," 32–33). Literate women were thus engaged in the deployment of textual and narrative strategies for intervening in the legal contexts of the state. In England in the 1640s, Sharon Arnoult argues, some radical reformist women used the concept of the "sovereignty of the soul" to justify their right to preach equally with men, to petition Parliament, and to "defy the social and political order when it conflicted with their conscience, by denying that structure any legitimate authority to keep them from fulfilling their obligation to obey God's call to them."[37] Thus, some of the particular rhetorical strategies that Marguerite, in her fictions, borrowed from Protestantism were similarly deployed to achieve female political sovereignty within the nation-state.

The *Heptaméron* was not published in Marguerite de Navarre's lifetime; it is a work of fiction, its claims to represent "histoire" asserted and denied through the distancing and relativizing mechanisms of narrative, discourse, and framing tale. Equally mysterious are the archival works of history associated with Marguerite's name and cited or addressed in the fiction (or that may themselves be citing that fiction). Together they suggest, however, a political ambition to address, if not the state itself, then at least its female subjects — herself and Jeanne de Navarre among them — through a rhetorical mode that indirectly articulates a set of strategies for achieving political voice and agency in the interests of a sovereign subjectivity. Subsequent historical moments of women's engagement in the political arena of the state support the idea that these textual and rhetorical strategies may have had some currency in early modern Europe. They certainly indicate that some women understood themselves to be leaving their mark — both "archival" and "fictional" — on the face of history.

Notes

1. Natalie Zemon Davis, *Fiction in the Archives: Pardon Tales and Their Tellers in Sixteenth-Century France* (Stanford, Calif.: Stanford University Press, 1987).

2. Marguerite de Navarre, *L'Heptaméron,* ed. M. François (Paris: Garnier, 1967), 9. For the English translation, see Marguerite de Navarre, *The Heptameron,* ed. and trans. P. A. Chilton (Middlesex, England: Penguin, 1984), 68–69. All citations from the *Heptaméron* refer to these editions, with the French page numbers following the English, unless otherwise noted. On "truth" and "story" in Marguerite de Navarre, see, among others, Marcel Tetel, *Marguerite de Navarre's Heptameron: Themes, Language, and Structure* (Durham, N.C.: Duke University Press, 1973); John Lyons, *Exemplum: The Rhetoric of Example in Early Modern France and Italy* (Princeton, N.J.: Princeton University Press, 1989); also Freccero, "Rewriting the Rhetoric of Desire: Marguerite de Navarre's *Heptaméron,*" in *Contending Kingdoms: Historical, Psychological, and Feminist Approaches to the Literature of Sixteenth-Century England and France,* ed. Marie-

Rose Logan and Peter Rudnytsky (Detroit: Wayne State University Press, 1991), 298–312.

3. Pierre de Bourdeille, seigneur de Brantôme, *Les Dames galantes,* ed. Maurice Rat (Paris: Garnier, 1960). Patricia Cholakian discusses the tradition of reading Marguerite's text as referring to actual events, in *Rape and Writing in the* Heptaméron *of Marguerite de Navarre* (Carbondale: Southern Illinois University Press, 1991). See also Margaret Ferguson, who details the critical history of reading each character as referring to historical persons of Marguerite's time, "Recreating the Rules of the Games: Marguerite de Navarre's *Heptaméron,*" in David Quint, Margaret Ferguson, G. W. Pigman III, and Wayne Rebhord, eds., *Creative Imitation: New Essays on Renaissance Literature in Honor of Thomas M. Greene* (Binghamton, N.Y.: Medieval and Renaissance Texts and Studies, 1992), 153–187, at 158–159.

4. Lyons notes that "the *Heptameron,* like many novella collections, is divided into a domain enunciated objectively as actual event (the novellas) and a domain enunciated subjectively, dialogically, as judgment and statement of alternative or potential event (the discussions within the frame-narrative). The *Heptameron* claims that *all* of the internal narratives that are enunciated 'objectively' are history in the cognitive as well as discursive sense" (*Exemplum,* 81).

5. Margaret Ferguson, "Recreating the Rules of the Games," 182–183; 187. Parlamente, as has been noted by many, is thought to be the persona of the author Marguerite; her name also refers to the name of the French semiautonomous courts of justice, the *parlements,* to which Marguerite, as Davis points out, had occasional recourse (*Fiction in the Archives,* 107; also 203, n. 72). Marguerite de Navarre also appears as a judge and one-woman "court of appeal" in the *Heptaméron,* most notably in story 22. Parlamente's name may also suggest the narrator-storyteller-author's role as producer of fictions or liar, for Parlamente is one who speaks and lies; see Freccero, "Rewriting the Rhetoric of Desire," 302. On the dilemmas of female authorship, see Ferguson, "A Room Not Their Own: Renaissance Women as Readers and Writers," in Clayton Koelb and Susan Noakes, eds., *The Comparative Perspective on Literature: Approaches to Theory and Practice* (Ithaca, N.Y.: Cornell University Press, 1988), 93–116.

6. Michel François asserts in a note that the prince is Marguerite's brother, because of the line "I shall say nothing of the perfections, of the grace and beauty of this young prince, except that in his day there was no one to equal him" (*Heptaméron,* 381, 286): "Il n'est pas de doute que Marguerite veuille ainsi désigner son propre frère, le futur François Ier; on se souvient qu'elle a déjà usé de la même périphrase dans la vingt-cinquième nouvelle" (*L'Heptaméron,* 481, n. 603). For a discussion of this story as a family romance, see Cholakian, *Rape and Writing,* 167–181.

7. For a more extensive discussion of this story as a narrative of nationalism, see Freccero, "Unwriting Lucretia: 'Heroic Virtue' in the *Heptaméron,*" in Dora Polachek, ed., *Heroic Virtue, Comic Infidelity: Reassessing Marguerite de Navarre's Heptaméron* (Amherst, Mass.: Hestia Press, 1993), 77–89; also "Practicing Queer Philology with Marguerite de Navarre: Nationalism and the Castigation of Desire," in *Queering the Renaissance,* ed. Jonathan Goldberg (Durham, N.C.: Duke University Press, 1994), 107–123.

8. The Penguin edition attributes the remark to Oisille, and cites the 1553 de Thou manuscript (ms. français 1524) as its source, but the François edition, attributing the

remark to Hircan, cites as its source *ms. français* 1512, manuscript A, from which the critical edition is derived. For a discussion of the significance of these variants, see Freccero, "Practicing Queer Philology," 113.

9. Marguerite de Navarre, *Le Miroir de l'âme pécheresse,* ed. Renja Salminen (Helsinki: Suomalainen Tiedeakatemia, 1979), 21–27.

10. The text of the letter is translated and quoted in Nancy Roelker, *Queen of Navarre: Jeanne d'Albret, 1528–1572* (Cambridge.: Harvard University Press, 1968), 127. I thank Valerie Forman for drawing this letter to my attention.

11. On the question of *The Courtier*'s failure as a text of political philosophy, see Freccero, "Politics and Aesthetics in Castiglione's *Il Cortegiano*: Book III and the Discourse on Women," in Quint et al., eds., *Creative Imitation,* 259–279. Sarah Hanley has done extensive research on the policies of the French state in the sixteenth century and on juridical developments that explicitly produced what she calls a marital regime government, encompassing both family and state units, which was designed to secure male right and definitively exclude women from participation in matters of family and state. See Hanley, "The Monarchic State in Early Modern France: Marital Regime Government and Male Right," in Adrianna Bakos, ed., *Politics, Ideology, and the Law in Early Modern Europe: Essays in Honor of J. H. M. Salmon* (Rochester, N.Y.: University of Rochester Press, 1994), 107–126.

12. See Michel François's note concerning Brantôme's account of the story, *L'Heptaméron,* 453, n. 125. Cholakian (*Rape and Writing*) builds her argument concerning the writing of the *Heptaméron* around this presumably actual event.

13. See Nancy Miller, "Arachnologies: The Woman, the Text, and the Critic," in Nancy K. Miller, ed., *The Poetics of Gender* (New York: Columbia University Press, 1986), 270–295, on the question of the telltale mark or sign within a text that allegorizes the female author's signature. Miller proposes that within female-authored texts can be found "the embodiment in writing of a gendered subjectivity," that is, that "within representation [are] the emblems of its construction" (272). The scratches on the nobleman's face are thus, I argue, the emblem of feminine writing in the text. See also my argument concerning facial disfiguration as feminine writing in Marguerite de Navarre's *Heptaméron,* "Rape's Disfiguring Figures: Marguerite de Navarre's *Heptaméron,* Day 1: 10," in Lynn A. Higgins and Brenda R. Silver, eds., *Rape and Representation* (New York: Columbia University Press, 1991), 227–247.

14. See Cholakian, *Rape and Writing,* 30: "The rapist stands accused not by his victim the princess but by the *devisant* who represents him in the book's frame. Constructing the seducer/rapist from the female point of view, Marguerite de Navarre deconstructs his fictions. Speaking through a man, she makes him define what rape/seduction signifies to a woman. The 'wise' woman's discourse sums up the way society at large deals with rape. Hircan's afterword tells the truth about rape: It is not rapture; it is violation."

15. Sarah Hanley, "Family and State in Early Modern France: The Marriage Pact," in Marilyn Boxer and Jean Quataert, eds., *Connecting Spheres: Women in the Western World, 1500 to the Present* (New York: Oxford University Press, 1987), 53–63, at 54. See also Hanley, "Engendering the State: Family Formation and State Building in Early Modern France," *French Historical Studies* 16 (1989): 4–27.

16. Hanley, "Family and State," 54; John T. Noonan, Jr., "Marriage in the Middle

Ages: 1, Power to Choose," *Viator: Medieval and Renaissance Studies* 4 (1973): 419–434; Charles Donahue, Jr., "The Canon Law on the Formation of Marriage and Social Practice in the Later Middle Ages," *Journal of Family History* 8: 2 (1983): 144–156; and Beatrice Gottlieb, "The Meaning of Clandestine Marriage," in Robert Wheaton and Tamara K. Hareven, eds., *Family and Sexuality in French History* (Philadelphia: University of Pennsylvania Press, 1980), 49–83.

17. Natalie Zemon Davis, *The Return of Martin Guerre* (Cambridge.: Harvard University Press, 1983), 46–47. At its extreme, clandestine marriage was a situation in which a couple exchanged vows in absolute secrecy; Gratian's *Decretum* determined that such marriages were valid, although undesirable. See Beatrice Gottlieb, "The Meaning of Clandestine Marriage," 50–51.

18. Hanley, "Family and State," 55; see also Hanley, "Social Sites of Political Practice in France: Lawsuits, Civil Rights, and the Separation of Powers in Domestic and State Government, 1500–1800," *American Historical Review* 102: 1 (February 1997): 27–52; and Hanley, "The Monarchic State in Early Modern France."

19. Hanley, "The Monarchic State in Early Modern France," 108–109; see also "La Loi salique," in Christine Fauré, ed., *Encyclopédie politique et historique des femmes: Europe, Amérique du Nord* (Paris: Presses Universitaires de France, 1996): 11–30.

20. Hanley, "The Monarchic State," 109–116.

21. Hanley, "Engendering the State," 9–11. Charles Donahue, in "The Canon Law on the Formation of Marriage," points out that one significant difference between England and France in the matter of clandestine marriages was that even in the ecclesiastical courts in France, such marriages were tried as criminal offenses.

22. Davis, "Boundaries and the Sense of Self in Sixteenth-Century France," in Thomas Heller et al., eds., *Reconstructing Individualism: Autonomy, Individuality, and the Self in Western Thought* (Stanford, Calif.: Stanford University Press, 1986), 53–63, at 61, 62.

23. Christiane Klapisch-Zuber, *Women, Family, and Ritual in Renaissance Italy,* trans. Lydia Cochranie (Chicago: University of Chicago Press, 1985).

24. For accounts of the events surrounding the forced marriage between Jeanne and the duke of Clèves, see, among others, Nancy Roelker, *Queen of Navarre: Jeanne d'Albret, 1528–1572* (Cambridge: Harvard University Press, 1986); Martha Freer, *The Life of Jeanne d'Albret, Queen of Navarre,* 2 vols. (London: Hurst and Blackett, 1855); P. F. William Ryan, *Queen Jeanne of Navarre* (London: Hitchin, 1911); Pierre Jourda, *Marguerite d'Angoulême, duchesse d'Alençon, reine de Navarre, 1492–1549: Etude biographique et littéraire,* vol. 1 (Paris: Honoré Champion, 1930); and Lucien Febvre, *Amour sacré, amour profane: Autour de l'Heptaméron* (Paris: Gallimard, 1944). Alphonse De Ruble, *Le Mariage de Jeanne d'Albret* (Paris: Adolphe Labitte, 1877), notes that one of the primary sources for the intrigues and conflicts that ensued between 1538 and 1541 (the year of Jeanne's marriage) is a series of reports made by Charles's secret agent Descurra, who was responsible for negotiating the alliance between Charles and Henri. For a partial translation of Descurra's report, which was written in Spanish, see pp. 80–110.

25. F. Genin, ed., *Nouvelles lettres de la reine de Navarre adressées au roi François Ier, son frère* (Paris: Jules Renouard, 1842), 176–177, letter 105: "Mais maintenant, Monseigneur, ayant entendu que ma fille, ne connoissant ne le grant honneur que vous luy faisiez de la daigner visiter, ne l'obéissance qu'elle vous doit, ny aussi que une fille ne doit point

avoir de voulunté, vous a tenu ung si fou propous que de vous dire qu'elle vous supplioit qu'elle ne feust point marié à M. de Clèves . . . je ne pouvons penser dont luy procede cete grande hardiesse dont jamais elle ne nous avoit parlé." In novella 10, a story about Floride's unhappy marriage and her attempted rape by a knight, Amadour, which her mother the countess unwittingly facilitates, these lines appear: "Pressed by the king to agree to the marriage, the countess, as a loyal subject, could not refuse his request. She was sure that her daughter, still so young in years, could have no other will than that of her mother"(137, 69). Here, the argument appears in the text that the mother is as bound by monarchical authority as is the daughter whom she constrains to marry. See Freccero, "Rape's Disfiguring Figures"; also "Marguerite de Navarre and the Politics of Maternal Sovereignty," *Cosmos* 7 (1992): 132–149. Special issue: *Women and Sovereignty,* ed. Louise Fradenburg.

26. Genin, *Nouvelles lettres,* 291: "Ladite dame a presenté deux feuilles et une demie-feuille de papier, qu'elle a dict estre escriptes et signées de sa main et contenir lesdites déclarations et protestacions dont cy-dessus a esté faicte mention, desquelles les teneurs ensuyvent." See also 291–292: "Moi, Jehanne de Navarre, continuant mes protestacions que j'ay cy-devant faictes, èsquelles je parsiste, dis et déclaire et proteste encoires par ceste presente que le mariage que l'on veult faire de moy au duc de Clesves est contre ma volunté; que je n'y ay jamais consenti et n'y consentiray, et que tout ce que je y pourray faire ou dire par cy-après, dont l'on pourroit dire que je y auroie consenti, ce sera par force, oultre mon grey et vouloir, et pour craincte du Roy, du roy mon père et de la royne ma mère, que m'en a menassé et faict foueter par la baillyve de Caen, ma gouvernante, laquelle par plusieurs fois m'en a pressée par commandement de la royne ma mère, me menassant que, si je ne faisois, au faict dudit mariage, tout ce que ledit Roy vouldroit et que si je ne m'y consentoie, je serois tant fessée et maltraictée que l'on me feroit mourir, et que je seroie cause de la perte et destruction de mes père et mère et de leur maison; dont je suis entrée en telle craincte et peur, mesmement de la destruction de mesdicts père et mère, que je ne sçay à quy avoir recours que à Dieu, quant je vois que mes père et mère m'ont délaissée, lesquelx sçavent bien ce que je leur ay dict, et que jamais je n'aymeroie le duc de Clesves et n'en veulx poinct."

27. In an important essay that serves as the foundation for my own work on the relation between history and fiction in story 21, John Lyons discusses the alternation between "recorded fact" and personal opinion in the *Heptaméron* as a deliberate intervention into the "truth" of historical discourse and a practice of critical narrative; see "The *Heptaméron* and the Foundation of Critical Narrative," *Yale French Studies* 70 (1986): 150–163. For a discussion of the differences in our arguments, see also Freccero, "Rewriting the Rhetoric of Desire in the *Heptaméron*." Lyons also discusses story 21 in *Exemplum.*

28. *Heptaméron,* 245–246 (167): "Rolandine, who had long been aware that her mistress had little affection for her, gave as good as she received. As there was little love between them, there was also little room for fear. It seemed to her that this reprimand in the presence of several people sprang not from loving concern, but from the desire to humiliate, and that the woman who was administering it was moved not by displeasure at the offence, but by pleasure in the punishment."

29. See Lyons, *Exemplum* (93–97), for a discussion of this story in terms of the transition from discourse to history; Lyons argues that in being silenced, Rolandine becomes the subject of history and as such, all the more dangerous to her enemies.

30. Hanley makes the point that the edict of 1556 raised the age of majority for both sexes: for men it was raised from twenty to thirty years, for women from seventeen to twenty-five ("Engendering the State," 9). Thus even in post-1556 France, Rolandine would have been well beyond the required age of majority.

31. For Luther's doctrine of universal priesthood, see among others, Emile Léonard, *A History of Protestantism,* trans. Joyce M. H. Reid (London: Nelson, 1965), 113. See also Marguerite de Navarre, *Le Miroir de l'âme pecheresse.*

32. See, for example, Abel Lefranc, *Les Idées réligieuses de Marguerite de Navarre d'après son oeuvre poétique* (Paris: Fischbacher, 1898); H. Heller, "Marguerite of Navarre and the Reformers of Meaux," *Bibliothèque d'Humanisme et Renaissance* 33 (1971): 271–310; Nancy Roelker, "The Appeal of Calvinism to French Noblewomen in the Sixteenth Century," *Journal of Interdisciplinary History* 2: 4 (1972): 391–418; Charmarie Jenkins Blaisdell, "Calvin's Letters to Women: The Courting of Ladies in High Places," *Sixteenth Century Journal* 13: 3 (fall 1982): 67–84; Merry Wiesner, "Beyond Women and the Family: Towards a Gender Analysis of the Reformation," *Sixteenth Century Journal* 18: 3 (1987): 311–321; also Marguerite de Navarre, *Le Miroir de l'âme pecheresse.* Marguerite is known to have corresponded with Calvin in the year of her daughter's marriage to the duke of Clèves; see Pierre Jourda, *Répertoire analytique et chronologique de la correspondance de Marguerite d'Angoulême* (Paris: Honoré Champion, 1930), 190.

33. A. Biéler, *L'Homme et la femme dans la morale Calviniste* (Geneva: Droz, 1963): 69–72. For the sermon on *Deuteronomy,* see Jean Calvin, *Joannis Calvini Opera quae supersunt omnia,* ed. Johann Wilhelm Baum et al., 59 vols. (Braunschweig, Germany: C. A. Schwetschke, 1863–1900), vol. 27: 677; cited in Biéler, *L'Homme et la femme,* 99. See also Roelker, "The Appeal of Calvinism," 406–407. Davis also argues that Bertrande may have justified her actions in relation to the new marriage law in Geneva after the Protestant Reformation: "There, marriage was no longer a sacrament; and a wife abandoned by her husband, 'without the wife having given him any occasion or being in any way guilty,' could after a year of inquiry obtain from the Consistory a divorce and permission to remarry" (*Martin Guerre,* 50). Davis cites Calvin's "Projet d'ordonnance sur les mariages, 10 novembre 1545," from the *Opera omnia,* vol. 38: 41–44. I am not suggesting that Calvin himself proposed an egalitarian alternative to the gender hierarchies of the nation-state in France; indeed, in the 1540s, he and Marguerite de Navarre had a dispute concerning his condemnation of and her support for the so-called Spiritual Libertines, precisely because they were said to reject the authoritarianism of Calvin's Geneva; see Charmarie Blaisdell, "Calvin's Letters to Women," 75–76. Rather, I am suggesting that Marguerite and other women may have made strategic use of Calvinist doctrine to claim authority for themselves.

34. Nicolas de Bordenave, *Histoire de Béarn et Navarre,* ed. P. Raymond (Paris: Société de l'histoire de France, 1873).

35. The *Ample déclaration* is published in Alphonse De Ruble, ed., *Mémoires et poésies de Jeanne d'Albret* (Paris: E. Paul, Huart, Guillemin, 1893).

36. See Davis, *Martin Guerre,* 48–49, 114–115. Davis also recounts how the story survives to the present day in Artigat (125). Jean de Coras tells the tale such that Bertrande emerges as an innocent and blameless victim of circumstance, but Davis's reading casts doubt both on his belief in this portrait of Martin's wife and on the likelihood that she was actually ignorant of the imposture. Davis's reading of the Martin Guerre story has itself been challenged on precisely the grounds that it attributes too much agency to Bertrande de Rols. See Robert Finlay, "The Refashioning of Martin Guerre," *American Historical Review* 93: 3 (1988): 553–571, and Davis's reply: " 'On the Lame,' " *American Historical Review* 93: 3 (1988): 572–603.

37. Sharon Arnoult, "The Sovereignties of Body and Soul: Women's Political and Religious Actions in the English Civil War," *Cosmos: The Yearbook of the Traditional Cosmology Society* 7 (1992): 228–249, at 231. Special issue: *Women and Sovereignty,* ed. Louise Fradenburg.

4

Gay Science and Law

PETER GOODRICH

In a mid-fifteenth century case reported in Martial d'Auvergne's *Les Arrêts d'amour* ([1460] 1951) a young woman petitioned the High Court of Love in Paris for an order against her lover. Her argument was that when they had met, he had been "the happiest, most joyful and playful person imaginable" (174). She had fallen in love with a man who was kind, gregarious, gracious, and fashion-conscious. After only a few months of intimacy, however, her lover had changed beyond recognition. Now he was pensive, distracted, and melancholic: "It seemed as if life bored him and made him world-weary" (175). He now lived in a reverie. When given flowers, he would tear them apart and throw them away; when music was played, he would weep incontinently; and when love was discussed, he would talk only of death. The petitioner requested that, insofar as it was within the power of the court, he be ordered to revert to his former self.

In his defense the young man borrowed the theme of the service of love from

Thanks to Elena Loizidou, Les Moran, and Mariana Valverde for their alternately perspicuous and kind commentaries. Especial thanks to Marinos Diamantides for amorous insights and a patrician understanding. My main gratitude, as always, to Linda Mills, and finally to Lorna Hutson for acute and constructive editorial criticisms that greatly improved these miscreant words.

the classical era of *fin amor:* the object of love was labor in the service of a pure desire. Joy was thus secondary to sorrow in the pursuit of an otherworldly or pure affection, the spiritual end of love. Similarly, material goods, physical enjoyments, and social approval were all to be abandoned as the price of giving oneself wholly to the cause of love. He asked, therefore, that the court release him from his relationship — *alliance d'amour* — and added that he was in any event indifferent to any decision the court might reach, and as happy to die as to live.

The court's poetic deliberation concluded that the lover should be "mis aux herbes" (put out to grass): he was to spend a month as a prisoner in a garden (177). It was hoped that there, as he looked only upon greenery and flowers, his amorous spirits would be revived. While enduring his floral captivity, the man was forbidden any melancholic company and instructed to remain alone, to enable the recuperation of his dreams and other amorous fantasies. The only exception to that solitude was to be the company of the petitioner who was to visit him there, engage him in joyful conversation and whenever possible read him erotic verse.

The case is a late and highly stylized example of the tradition of judgments of love. It belongs to an amorous jurisprudence, or gay science of law, that was first recorded in comprehensive detail in the twelfth-century treatise *Tractatus Amoris et de amore remedio* of Andreas Capellanus ([1176] 1993) and extends in diverse forms at least to the literary courts of the seventeenth-century *précieuses*. The long-term history of such judgments, however, is one of alternate suppression and revival, and it is against that precarious narrative that the case has to be read. In other words, the later tradition to which the judgment belongs is one that expresses the legacy of gay science in disparate and often negative or satirical forms. It is a tradition that is in a many senses foreign. It has to be read creatively as a unique and intimate casuistry that derives from the troubadour erotics and that stages the love affair according the distinctive rules or counterlaw of love.

If we turn to the details of the judgment, the key figure in the decision is that of topothesia, the description of a garden being the primary index of the jurisdiction of the laws of love from the earliest *tensons* (poetic debates) and courts of love to texts as disparate as Boccaccio's *Philocopo* ([1412] 1974) or Tilney's *Flower of Friendship*. ([1568] 1992) That the garden, and by extension the floral and rhetorical ones, should also mark a space of law already intimates something of the polemical character of this affectual site of rule. In juristic terms, the decision is remarkable for relating not to fact but to mood. Addressed to the affective space between the parties rather than to judgment of an individual, or legislation of guilt or innocence, the case clearly contradicts the procedures of positive law. This was a decision that did not adjudicate an outcome but rather suspended judgment for a period of time. This was a law that enjoined relationship, demanded that the lovers engage with each other, and proposed no less than an eroticization of their affair. Ironically, the decision attended to the particularities of subjects or a coming face to face with justice at precisely the same time as positive law was beginning to represent *Justitia* as blind (Jay, 1999, 19). More broadly still, the law of love here attended in detail to the signs of a libidinal economy that the legists had long excluded as being the inverse of the public and exterior norms of positive law.

The intimate public sphere of the laws of love, whether sung or declaimed in the tensons of the troubadours and the trobairitz or staged in the courts and trials of the judgments of love, constitutes a surprisingly comprehensive and at times radical system of amorous jurisprudence. More than that, the jurisdiction of love, marked as it is both by the figures of the garden, of arbors and flowers, and by the pursuit of an enjoyment of passion and of love, constitutes not simply a critique of legality but a positive counterlaw. The epistemic space of gay science is one that explicitly challenges the tragic-heroic rhetoric and veridical language of Western legal judgment. Gay science, too, is a rhetoric and practice of law. The questions of love (*quaestiones amoris*) are formally the mirror image of the casuistic disputations (*quaestiones disputatae*) of the glossators. The alternately chimerical and feministic jurisdiction of gay science forms an important if forgotten counterpoint to the humanistic legalism of the period. It should be remembered too that the laws of love — both the rules and the rhetoric of amorous disputation — were still well known to such late fifteenth- and early sixteenth-century legal reformers as Budé, Alciato, Forcadel, and Bodin. In short, it is modern jurisprudence that has found this counterlaw too threatening to include in its histories and too subversive to address in its practices of judgment.

The reason for that resistance to the elaboration of the laws or ethics of an intimate public sphere relates closely to the second striking feature of the case of the melancholic lover. The judgment stages a conflict between gaiety and sorrow, enjoyment and asceticism, that is crucial to an understanding of the history of gay science and of its suppression by both spiritual and secular law. The topos in question is that of the tension between physical and spiritual love, the conflict between *amor mixtus* and *amor purus*. In this case, and even more explicitly in others,[1] Martial d'Auvergne subversively formulates a defense of gay science — or of liberated love — in the face of a historical trajectory that was increasingly witness to the imposition of religious and legal codes enjoining purity, marriage, and an Augustinian solemnity of reproduction (*veritas nuptiarum*). In acceding to the woman's complaint, the court explicitly maintained the hedonistic possibility that love could be enjoyed and the amorous relation maintained. In historical terms, the decision resurrected an erotic erudition, the "delectable joy," the corporeal knowledge and pleasure of the earlier troubadours (Marol, 1998). Both the hedonism and its practice are frequently lost in later, and not least in contemporary, reconstructions of gay science.

The long-term history of judgments of love belies any attempt to define a singular erotics or law to which they refer. The diversity of the tradition, however, can usefully be formulated as a historical trajectory taking into account the fate or status of certain key themes. Understood as a knowledge and practice of relationship, as an art and aesthetic of love, gay science was a twelfth-century invention. In this early form, it was an erotic tradition of staging — and on occasion judging — love affairs. It was a theory of liberated or joyful love, a theory of physical as well as spiritual desire, and over the course of the century a casuistry of the ethical and libidinal forms of the love affair developed.

The juristic practice of twelfth-century gay science was committed to the joy or enjoyment of love, and its laws were correspondingly affective and engaged with the individuality and corporeality of lovers. The end of love or *fin amor* was thus the specific relationship between lovers, and it was that space of shared desire which the judgments or laws of love initially addressed. The physicality of the troubadour idea of the erotic is the aspect that most obviously pitches it against the prevalent Christian law and the ecclesiastical and secular legal traditions that developed from it. The gay science of law rapidly faced both physical and epistemic suppression. It was a threat to the authority of the Church and also to the reception and dominance of the Roman legal tradition. In that it was rapidly suppressed or marginalized in status and significance, the tradition of gay law is accessible mainly through texts that satirize the content, dismiss the form, or denounce the reality of the laws of love. By the fourteenth century the troubadour view of the erotic had given way to a Christian governance of relationship, and the tradition lived on only in elliptical or dissident forms. When later courts and judgments of love such as those reported by Christine de Pisan, Mahieu Poirier, or Martial d'Auvergne are examined, they have to be read against the polemic, the satire, or other forms of dismissal that surround their subject.

This essay will trace the suppression of the laws of love in the negative form of its incorporation into the rhetoric or other marginalia of law. The history is one of the displacement of the laws of love by the *legitima scientia,* or veridical purity, of early modern legalism. To look back to the sources of *Les Arrêts d'amour* in twelfth-century gay science, and to address directly what René

Nelli termed the anticonformist legal form of courts of love, requires a subtle recuperation of these laws from texts and traditions that deny their reality or their relevance to the public domain (Nelli, 1977). The key text and institution in that transition from lyric to law, and from the juristic practice of gay science to satire or farce,[2] is the mid-fourteenth-century Occitan manuscript *Las Flors del gay saber estier dichas Las Leys d'Amors* (1331–56; Gatien-Arnoult, 1841–43; Anglade, 1919–20) and the Gay Consistory and floral games that this code of the laws of love re-established.

By the end of the thirteenth century the laws of love had been judged heretical (Denomy, 1965). Any subsequent revival of such laws and judgments had to take the manifest form of literary diversion or ascetic pursuit. The laws of love fell into the hands of lawyers, a fate that can be traced explicitly to the institution of the Gay Consistory in 1323 and its interpretation of *Las Flors del gay saber,* or the rhetorical laws of desire. Composed by lawyers under the direction of Guilhem Molinier in the first half of the fourteenth century, this lengthy exposition of what was even then an ancient and faded practice takes the form of both dialogue and curricular handbook and is in substance a curious and conservative combination of ethical precepts, rhetorical figures, and poetic laws. Although historians are agreed that the codification of the laws of love "marked the definitive end of the troubadour tradition" (Huchet, 1997, 3), the juristic form and rhetorical significance of that demise has yet to be addressed. *Las Flors del gay saber* stands somewhere between the ludic and libidinal poetics of the earlier erotic genre and the stringent normativity — the legalism — of the College of the Art and Science of French Rhetoric which superseded and incorporated the Gay Consistory in the second decade of the sixteenth century. The Gay Consistory and its laws of love, in other words, stand astride two epochs, two juristic systems and two epistemic forms. Janus-faced, the gay science of *Las Flors del gay saber* was part unwitting custodian of a law of desire and part legislator of a new and broadly scholastic code of law without either poetry or love.

In what might be termed the *longue durée* of the laws of love, contemporary jurisprudence still inhabits a prosaic and veridical epistemology of law. Rhetoric, let alone some distant and to modern eyes satirical tradition of courts and laws of love, has, in this perspective, neither any place in the curriculum nor any contribution to make to knowledge of law. The logic of law — at best dialectic — has long held pride of place over any rhetoric of legal judgment or poetics of practice. Any re-examination of the gay science must thus be both partial and defensive. In the face of comprehensively negative or, more usually, laconically dismissive accounts of this erotic knowledge and law, it is necessary to sketch the trajectory, the specific forms and occasions of its suppression or dismissal. The history of the antinomies of law and love, and more specifically that of the modern legal tradition's antirhetorical — antirrhetical — form (Goodrich, 1995, 68ff), is to be addressed symptomatically. At the level of method, gay science threatened to dissolve "all distinction between legal and literary modes" (Bloch, 1977, 213) and so to put rhetoric in the same place as law. Even worse, in their casuistic and at times specifically legal practice, the courts of love subverted the imperium or jurisdiction of the science of law. In a sense, gay science represented everything that the legal tradition feared most: gaiety, aesthetics, indetermination, an ethics of the body and its emotions, and finally a tradition of feminine judges. It is that other side, or 'back face,' of legal science that this essay will address.

Adversus Amorem

It is necessary to start cautiously, theoretically. The modern historiography of gay science, and specifically of the laws and courts of love, has subjected that tradition to an overwhelmingly negative reading. With the exception of Nietzsche's ambitious but ambivalent theory of the 'gaya scienza' spelled out principally in the eponymous volume (1910), to which I will return in some detail, the preponderance of criticism, both literary and generically legal, has been concerned primarily with the question of the existence of courts of love. The principal trope of literary historiography has been that of antithesis or opposition between the laws of love and the realpolitik of literary canon and legal institutions. For Howard Bloch, to take one erudite and extreme opinion, "the *Judicia amoris* flounders on a tedious no-man's land between pseudo-document and literary text" (1977, 214). Neither properly a literature nor quite an institution, the judgment of love fails to meet the heroic standards of documented historical reality. The comedy of Eros, the law of love, is here deemed not simply lacking but tedious, and it is that tedium, that passionless detachment or even boredom, which deserves a momentary initial examination.

Leaving to one side the irony of the attribution of tedium to an explicitly gay erotic tradition of judgment, the boredom of the courts of love is explicitly referred to their ambivalent ontological status. They are neither self-evidently fictive — literary — nor tangibly real. Existing in limbo, in the in-between of the intimate public sphere, they are both defiant of spiritual law and subversive of secular laws. The tedium of the judgments of love thus appears on examination to be that of nonconformism, of a law outside established legality, of a territory or legal sphere that neither belonged to men nor observed their jurisdiction. It is this latter sense of tedium, that of a law that escapes both propriety and fraternity, that is perhaps most indicative. It is, after all, a striking feature of the amorous case law reported in Martial d'Auvergne's *Les Arrêts* that it takes an extravagantly legal form and interestingly was also subject to a lengthy juristic gloss in *The Joyful and Juridical Commentaries of the Jurisconsult Benoit de Court* (edition of 1731). In the same manner as Forcadel's *Cupido iurisperitus* (1553), the gloss collated and interpreted the decisions of the High Court of Love by reference to Roman law. If we explicitly compare one collation of case law with another, the casuistry of love to the science of law, the indissoluble relation—parodic or prosaic, satirical or serious—between the two forms is already evident and worthy of note. The judgments of love exist here in a space in between secular law and spiritual jurisdiction, between code and practice, between one writing system and another.

The intermediary or, more technically, interlinear character of the judgments of love expresses a practice that was historically a form of *vita femina,* counterposed to masculine courts and their determination according to prosaic laws. The juristic form of the judgments is in other words deceptive in the sense that they suggest a law that suspends law not only in the affect or immediacy of amorous dispute, but also in the indeterminacy, the hesitance or poetics of judgment. The decision arrived at in the case of the melancholic lover discussed earlier was a species of indecision, almost an unwitting decision, in the sense that it suspended judgment and suggested rather an exemplary indetermination, a period of waiting. The point can be illustrated further by returning to Capellanus' *Tractatus amoris* and one of the earliest of the *Iudicia amoris.*

In Judgment 16, a case heard before the court of the countess of Champagne, the question to be considered concerned communication and love (Capellanus, 1982, 264–65). A man had fallen in love with a woman, but had never had the opportunity of conversing with her at any length. Despairing of the possibility of addressing her directly, he hired a confidant to carry his declaration of love and persuade the woman to assent. The confidant agreed to act as mediator and messenger but soon afterward broke that promise and declared himself to be a suitor. Despite his evident bad faith, the woman listened to the confidant's advances and shortly thereafter consummated their relationship "fulfilling everything he asked of her."

The original suitor complained to the court of the countess of Champagne of the betrayal of friendship and of the lack of urbanity (*domina inurbane*) or amorous ethics. In view of the extremity of the case, the countess summoned sixty women to consider the issue and then pronounced judgment in the following terms: "The deceitful lover has found a woman who accords with his deserts, for she did not blush to comply with his great crime. So let him enjoy the love he has so evilly gained, and let her enjoy the kind of friend she deserves. But both must forever remain sequestrated from the love of any other individual" (264–65).

The decision was again a species of indetermination or even suspension of jurisdiction. The lovers were consigned to the purgatory or limbo of their mutual affections and to the tedium of the friendless. The determination was that judgment from then on be suspended in the abyss of nonrelation, or what might be termed the ethical space of affective incommensurability. Just as the confidant had stolen the message of the suitor, so the lovers by their actions had traversed the epistemic boundary between communication and noncommunication. The miscreant lovers were now to act out their fate on the outside of the intimate public sphere of the passions. The law of love, in other words, here recognized the limits of its law and scrupulously marked that border. What is perhaps most significant about this recognition of limits is precisely that it marks the contingency and modesty of the laws of love as a system of juristic thought. Their reality, one could say, here resides in their acknowledgment not only of the limits of judgment but also of the constraint or reality of other laws.

Returning to Howard Bloch's emblematic characterization of the tedium and pseudo-reality of the judgments of love, it would appear that their consignment to "no-man's land" not only refuses any reciprocity or recognition of difference to the jurisdiction of the laws but also marks a kind of epistemicide with regard to how the judgments of love know the object of their laws. Implicit in the dismissal of their tedium and irreality, in other words, is a very modern antinomy between the order of law and the anarchy of love, as also between the public and rational nature of legality and the privacy and madness of erotic desire. What is at stake, perhaps surprisingly, is nothing less than the mutual definition of law and love: the definition of positive law as a unified system, as legal proprium or pure norm, is simultaneously the definition of love as the obverse or antonym of law. Love becomes suddenly and perhaps rather formalistically or vacuously nothing more than the other of law (Fraise, 1998, 141–45). The reason and reality of law here depend upon the dismissal of the chimera of rhetoric and love, and this despite the paradox of the interdependence or reciprocal definition of the two orders.

For literary historicism, the laws of love thus neither exist in the real of law nor offer insight into the practice of love. Modern criticism has tended to treat the practices and judgments of the courtly tradition as merely literary diversions or aspects of theater or farce rather than the politics of the public sphere. Marginalized as feminine, derided as comic, and dismissed as tedious, the tradition from which the laws of love were drawn has suffered the unequivocal judgment of nonbeing (Rémy, 1954–55). Paradoxical though it may seem for

historians of whatever persuasion to denigrate the textual for its lack of reference, the literary-critical academy has in the main assumed that these historic
practices of love belong to the curiously or tellingly modernist category of
entertainment, diversion, or private whim.[3]

To the extent that medieval literary historicism has remained bent on strictly
philological questions of textual reception and transmission, it is perhaps
understandable that it has assumed an empiricist epistemology and a positiv-
istic conception of law, one that suppresses love in the same measure as it
inversely magnifies the value of municipal law. It is less understandable that
more contemporary work in cultural studies equally stigmatizes the dissident
and fragile world of courtly love as uniformly misogynistic (Bloch, 1991, 148–
50), narcissistic, and homosexual (Huchet, 1987), titillating and psychotic
(Lacan, 1993, 146–49), or graphically unsavory, a social game of "as if" that,
if taken seriously, is no more than a lure to servitude (Zizek, 1994, 89–91).
Without reviewing such analyses in detail—I must confess that I am not much
moved by purely academic conceptions of love—it is possible to hazard a
diagnosis of such antipathy as stemming from a resistance to any analysis of
the origins of law, and correlatively from a banalization of the erotic. The
legalistic antipathy to Eros, in other words, dismisses any expanded appreciation of the role of rhetoric and simultaneously of the laws of love in the history
and pluralistic development of early modern forms of law. At the same time
and by the same token, the reading of love through the negative lens of law
offers little insight into the history, diverse forms, and practices of love.

Lacan's theory of love, which returns time and again to the courtly tradition, is built around the lawyer's notion of the impossibility of love. The
structure of amorous desire is defined by secrecy, otherness, and inaccessibility: in the Lacanian theory of *amor interruptus,* love as passion exists only in
relation to the impossibility of its consummation. The game of courtly love, in
this perspective, expresses a narcissistic fury, a desire no more real than "the
fantasm" that emerges "from the syringe" (Lacan, 1992, 153). In Freudian
terms, falling in love or, more technically, object choice is an unconscious
repetition that will necessarily evaporate with possession of the object of desire.[4] In that the real of amorous relationship entails proximity, it will also
eventually entail recognition or more precisely misrecognition, the realization
that the beloved does not live up to the distantly installed ideal that the unconscious desired to recover. It is from this perspective that Lacan and his followers, perhaps confusing the Catharist heresy of pure love with the erotics of
gay science, depict courtly love and the doctrine of *amour lointain* as the
exemplar of love.

If love exists only in the not-yet, in the exquisitely painful desire for what the institution, law, or the other denies — in lack and impossibility — then there is self-evidently a madness (a psychosis) about love that would suggest both its futility and its irrelevance to the social. A definition of love that restricts both the concept and the practice to the unconscious offers a banal and unethical projection: love is no more than a repetition that fails even to recognize the other as a subject (Sylvestre, 1993, 135). There is, of course, good reason to adopt such a definition of love for therapeutic purposes, in that the maladies of love are frequently caused by unconscious repetitions that analysis may expose and overcome. The clinical method of drawing a solipsistic love into relationship through speech, through "pretty words" (Theweleit, 1992), is a much more complex temporal and epistemic procedure than is supposed by a definition of love that stops simply at the unconscious level of object choice. Indeed, if the impossibility of love is a symptom, the theory of psychoanalysis is one that is gauged precisely to moving beyond the image of the unattainable to an erotic conversation or practice of relationship.

If the practice of love presupposes relationship, the space and temporality of the 'entre-deux' (Irigaray, 1992), then a very different aspect of the Freudian theory of love becomes of interest. What needs to be emphasized is a different sense of the interdependence of language and love, discourse and desire. Not only is psychoanalysis committed to a theory of the reality of speech, to a practice of discourse that is predicated on both the psychic and the physical — conscious and unconscious — effects of speech, but it is also and correlatively committed to positioning desire within discourse and so blurs the boundaries that demarcate and separate psyche and socius, subject and institution. Love, like law, becomes a question of discourse and its limits, of texts and their interpretation. By the same token, law, like love, becomes engaged with the question of desire that marks its limit, the point at which law must inevitably dissolve into its opposite. To address law in the way one does love as a practice entails addressing the intimacies of the polis, the private in the public, or what Nietszche termed "the colours of existence" (1910, 42). Such colors, of course, connote the figures or schemes of rhetoric and imply attention to the affections, the imaginings, the emotions that accompany the will to knowledge and the desire to judge as well as the various other forms of Eros — the ecstasies of learning — in the study and interpretation of legal texts.

To understand love in terms of intensity and duration, and so as a form of relationship rather than its absence or lack, is to apprehend it also as a species of discourse, subject to the labor of interpretation and development. The interpretive work of relationship that constitutes the intensity and duration of love could in this regard be thought of as a diurnal form of dream work through which affect or passion is inscribed and prolonged. Love is a practice; it is discourse inscribed over time, enlaced in events, and bound up in the subjectivity of institutions and laws. The passion of the philologist, the love of the lawyer, the Eros of the scientist are thus the exact conjunctions that the 'gaya scienza' initially suggests and that Nietzsche explicitly thrusts together when he counterposes love to law as the beginning and the ending of his list of the passions that as yet lack a history: "Where would one find a history of love, of avarice, of envy, of conscience, of pity, of cruelty . . . of law?" (Nietzsche, 1910, 43)

Nietzsche Among the Troubadours

Gay science is both a theory of history and an object of history, a poetics and a practice. To understand the theoretical implications as well as the historical nuances of gay science thus requires a much more complex and optimistic definition of love than that of lack or impossibility. Specifically, in Nietzsche's words, "one must learn to love," and by that it is meant that it is only through extended attention, through patience, indulgence, goodwill, and an eye for detail, that the unfamiliar can become expected, that "it dawns on us that we should miss it if it were lacking; and then it goes on to exercise its spell and charm more and more, and does not cease until we are its humble and enraptured lovers, who want it and want it again, and ask for nothing better from the world: . . . it is precisely thus that we have *learned to love* everything that we love" (258). Love is a form of coming to know, a transitive, active, and expansive pursuit of knowledge of that which is loved. One could even say that for all its intensity, drama, and folly, the becoming of love — the process of learning, or the education *in eroticis* — signals the dissipation of the unconsciousness or psychosis of object choice that were later and inelegantly to be invested in the dismissal of gay science.

Nietzsche himself, of course, offers other definitions of love and other more or less paradoxical formulations. It is evident, however, in relation to gay science understood as the art and practice of the passion for knowledge, that it travels most easily in the habit of a wild and engaged scholarship that seeks to know more and not less of that which is desired. If love means coming over time and by virtue of infinite efforts to know the beloved — music, art, a law, a lover — it must also be recognized that such a gay or explicitly erotic knowledge implies a rending of the persona, a radical change in the gay scientist or subject that knows. The epistemic paradox of gay science lies in that when conceived as art, as an affective practice, as the Eros that grows between lovers, it necessarily implies that the subjects change and continue to change throughout the their interrelations. More prosaically, the variable intensities of love over time equate with interpretive strategies and the varying means of their expression. It is not always possible, in other words, to offer stable definitions, certain structures, or explicit parameters to the concept of gay science, for the simple reason that it is a paradoxical and at least implicitly polemical practice. It exists in the moments of its expression, in the competence or intensity of its duration; it is poetic, and it is perhaps for that reason that when Nietzsche returns briefly to the gay science in *Ecce Homo,* he links this moment of science to paradox, and specifically to the enigma of fate and the freedom that fate as lived necessity allows. The gay science is reinvoked in that later work as song and dance, as indefinable as the Mistral wind, as joy and judgment, profundity and play (1911, 95–96).

The gay science abounds with references to gaiety: the discussion of knowledge comes arrayed in "the advent of parody" (3) and is depicted as "serious frivolity" (3), "the comedy of existence" (34), "waves of innumerable laughters" (34), "the nobility of folly" (57), passion, seduction, joy, and the "good will to illusion" (146). Where later interpretations have most usually concentrated on the dimension of folly, illusion, or immeasurable laughter, the paradoxical structure of the gay science requires that such comedy or parody be understood dialectically and epistemically: What can be learned through this irreverence or by means of such belated and in essence retrospective undoing of the ideals of the serious sciences? The conjunction of passion and knowledge in scholastic terms, that of desire and wisdom — is precisely the harbinger of a "new law of ebb and flow" (35), of the plurality of practices, of the arts and their affirmation of life. The issue to attend to, however, is that of the affectivity of the practices of knowledge, and specifically those of law. Implicit in the gay science is the revival of a dissident art of law beyond the tragic and heroic form of modern legalism.

The new law, one could even say the gay law, alluded to by Nietzsche is given various formulations, but its structure is relatively consistent. The new law is introduced first, and perhaps obviously enough, in a poem against law, against the droning 'tic toc' of law's artificial reason, a critique not only of its seriousness but also of "its prejudice," namely its belief in a singular cause or measure of being.[5] (24) The structure of gay science, in other words, is at one level antirrhetic.[6] It is that of the radical critique of established science: "Free spirits take liberties with regard to science" (192); and gay scientists step out from the shadow left by the death of God in order to play "with everything that has hitherto been called holy, good, inviolable, divine" (352). At the same time that freedom of thought dictates that the gay scientist plays with the unifying rules and other earnest truths established by scientific tradition, it also expresses an active aesthetic. Imagination completes knowledge as well as expressing the pleasure of its pursuit. To such passion for knowledge and for life, Nietzsche opposes "their scientific impulse . . . their ennui" (166), the earnestness of truth, the humorless seriousness of scholarly tradition, the betrayal implicit in everything we consider important.

The opposition between moods, between pleasure and a "science perhaps best known by its capacity for depriving humanity of enjoyment, and making it colder, more statuesque, and more Stoical" (49), suggests a further feature of gay science. In essence the conflict of moods or affects dramatizes knowledge. The import of the gay science is perhaps ultimately that it reinstitutes a theater of reason and truth, and specifically a theater that develops out of the persistent antinomy of tragedy and comedy as the twin poles of dramatic tradition. If gay science is ultimately opposed to tragic wisdom (Sloterdijk, 1989, 52), Nietzsche's argument is best comprehended as intimating a theater of truth that breaks out of the stoical confines of the tragic and seeks as much to create realities — that is to say, practices of knowledge — as to describe, comply and homogenize in the manner of the laws of the tragic genre. The antiheroic and nontragic form of gay science suggests a new level of engagement and of relational expression; perhaps it even, to borrow from Freud, implies Eros in the place of Thanatos, or simply hedonism in the face of indifference or ennui.

The drama of gay science presupposes the moods or tones of historical and mundane forms of knowing. The masks and metaphors through which the drama of love unfolds are, of course, central to the earlier rhetoric of gay science. Before we turn to that tradition, however, another aspect of the dramaturgic epistemology requires brief attention. The repeated paradox of Nietzsche's conception of gay science is that it is a knowledge bound up with practice. It is a form of reason that is also tied to the irrationality of action, a logic that not only expresses but embodies affects, an analysis of the real by means of imaginative completion. In the midst of a lengthy discourse on the feminine in the social, Nietzsche also implies a more interesting and radical idea: the antinomy of the tragic and the comic, of scholastic wisdom and contemporary desire, can also be understood as masking a dramatic inversion of the public sphere. In this analysis, the public and political realm of national pride, of legal ritual and social display gives way to an internalized and private reproduction of public themes. The symbolic collapses, one could say, into the imaginary, as "the splendour in war and in the tourney, has now transferred itself into innumerable private passions, and has merely become less visible" (63–64). To this he adds that as the drama of sociality comes to be lived out on the stage of everyday practices and relationships, as the most lavish expenditures of energy turn toward the aesthetic of living and care of the self, "ardent love and ardent hatred are born, and the flame of knowledge flashes heavenward" (64).

The birth of ardent love, of extreme passions and perverse, or in conventional terms "corrupt," desires, is marked by Nietzsche and by earlier tradition as a dedication of the interior space of the social to the feminine and to the laws of love. The tenson and the judgments of love, like the "luttes poétiques," the rhetorical "tournoi," the "jeux littéraires," and "fêtes des fleurs" of the gay science are not simply new forms of knowledge; they are also a new manner of mapping the social. Whether intuitive or intentional, Nietzsche's allusion here to the Provençal gay science is an allusion to the beginnings of a longer-term emotional geography of the spaces of relationship in the public domain. The mapping of the spaces of intimacy, of the passions and intensities of a libidinal economy, suggests, at least in formal terms, the nascence of the 'patrie d'amour' or affective cartography that de Rougemont was later to invoke in his history of love in Europe (Petersen, 1998, 152). The constitution of the emotions and the corresponding history of amatory practices and their codes — in short, of the laws of love — is a history of another form of sociality and of knowledge, a history of interiority and of its expression in the space of relationship, or what might be termed the phantasmatic domain of the social.

Gay Science: Retrospect and Prospect

The nineteenth-century invocation of the gaya scienza, at least in Nietzsche's theorization, placed the poetic, rhetorical, and juristic tradition of the laws of love in the context of an ecstatic hedonism, or epistemology of corporeal enjoyment. Nietzschean gay science was a form of knowledge; it spelled out certain "laws of the soul," of desire and the spaces of its expression. It acted out a nontragic, or indeed pagan, ethos of the anarchy, the lack of *archos* or origin, of being and knowing. To place the laws of love — the flowers of gay science — within the ambivalent domain of the veridical — and specifically, to address the social significance of erotic erudition — is the primary achievement of the Nietzschean reading of the earlier poetics. It allows not only for the dramatic juxtaposition of rhetoric and the real, but also for a reading of the laws of love as an amorous jurisprudence or autonomous system of legal thought.

What is most evident from the earliest and courts of love is that the objective of the law of love was a law of enjoyment. Gay science was not simply an erotic erudition, it was also a minutely mapped practice within the affective geography, or *carte de tendre,* of relationship. To use the trobairitz, or women troubadours, as exemplary of the diversity of the gay science, the comtessa de Dia devotes one song explicitly to the joys of the love affair in an era when property rather than desire dominated marriage: "I long to hold my lover naked in my arms . . . for to him I owe my heart, my love, my reason, my eyes, and my life," and a little further on she is explicit in wishing "to sleep with you" and to experience the joy of "physical embrace," a *baiser d'amour* (Bec, 1995, 105–6).

The space of affect and Eros is in some senses an initiate space, an active space of joy that has to be seized or opened up. It may be located in the alcove, the bedroom, the arbor or public trysting place, in whispers, the anonymous proceedings of the court of love, or the physical dramas of the garden of pleasures. The hedonism of gay science connotes both a social space of intimacy and a filigreed appreciation of the intensities, the joys and sorrows, of relationship. Turning to the tensons of the trobairitz, the constant theme is not so much that of the methods of loving as that of the affects of relationship: Is the pain of love worth bearing? Is it better to have children or to remain a virgin? When should amour lointain, or distant love, give way to physical embraces? When should an errant lover be forgiven?

In one anonymous dialogue between two women, the question was whether two estranged lovers could be reconciled. The tenson in question is a debate between a young woman and an older woman who has become estranged from her lover. The younger woman, Donzela, accuses the older woman, Domna, "of committing the heinous crime of leaving her lover to die" (Bec, 1995, 128) from her indifference and neglect. His death, Donzela argues, would be on her head. Domna replies that the man in question had been disloyal, inconstant, and fickle of heart and seemingly considered their relationship to be of little significance, except when it suited him. He had been an inconstant friend and if he now appeared to be descending into madness, she could not be accused of being the cause. In response, Donzela claims that the seeming indifference of the lover is in fact lovesickness: "You could burn him, hang him, or do whatever you wish with him because he is incapable of defending himself against you, such is the power you hold over him. . . . One kiss from you opened up his heart: just like the flame that stirs cold embers" (Bec, 1995, 129). After further debate, agreement is reached. Domna's lover had been prone to acts of verbal indiscretion, pride, and deceit. She was willing to take him back if he would be "courtly and gay, sincere and humble, . . . and if he would be agreeable to the world at large" (1995, 129).

Explicitly linking friendship to love, the tenson between Donzela and Domna is particularly significant as a debate between two women and for its presentation of conversation as the form of judgment. It can serve to remind the modern reader that gay science was both an object language and a practice, a science or knowledge of emotional states and a process or mood. If love's law was that of desire, of a gay poetics, it is of particular importance to recognize the tension between questioning in the mode of conversation or of friendship and the determination of judgment. The courts of love did not seek resolutions, decisions, or the closure of secular law but rather played on the openness, variable geometry, and indefinite temporality of affective engagement. To map the intensities of relationship, the joys and sorrows of love, was a question of developing a language of intimate spaces and so keeping open the affective sites of erotic exchange.

An example drawn from a later female participant in the courts of love, Christine de Pisan's *Le Livre de trois jugemens* (1891) can embellish the theme. Consider first that Christine's book of judgments contains no judgments, only questions and the elaborate exposition of the emotional states of those caught in the web of amorous disputation. The first of the cases raises the question of a woman who is estranged from her lover. She eventually takes another lover, and the question is whether this second love affair is an infidelity in the sense of being untrue to her promises of friendship and intimacy to her former lover. Although the matter is debated in the forensic manner of the casuistic questions of love, replete with accusation and defense, duplication and replication, no conclusion is reached.

The poem lingers in the emotional history of the love affair. The couple had been lovers in both body and soul. They had pledged to love each other truthfully for the rest of their days (1891: 204). After only a few months, however, they had become estranged when the man said his heart had dulled and wearied of her. The woman had suffered inordinate grief and sorrow, endless tears and sighs, as a consequence of this rebuff. She felt tormented and deceived and for long months agonized over whether to await the return of his heart and his sanity or to leave him. She grew ill from the loss of both his friendship and his love, and only finding a new lover cured her malaise.

The original lover now claimed that she had broken her promises to him and that he felt deceived, betrayed, and cheated. He asked that she return to him. Her response was disbelieving: it was he who had emotionally abandoned her and broken his word. It was too late now, after wounding and rejecting her to ask her to return. In his duplication he argues that he has over the years protected her name from gossip and criticism, even though he never sees her, and that he has not taken any other lover or friend. The woman, however, has the last word: "You wish me to love you whether you deserve it or not" (620); and as for the argument that he has been platonically faithful over the years, she argues that his love has been invisible and reason dictated that what was not expressed and could not be seen could not be known or enjoyed.

The poetic and public staging of the emotions in Christine's tenson belongs within an erotic tradition that consistently weighed, interpreted, and adjudicated the comparative degrees of suffering and the occasions and intensities of erotic pleasure. In this vein, common themes of tenson and of judgment were questions such as: Who suffers more, someone whose lover dies, or someone whose lover is unfaithful? Similarly, is it better to sleep once with a beloved and never see him again, or never to sleep with him and to see him daily for the rest of one's life? These and further questions relating to the affective signs and emotional states of falling in love, being in the presence of a lover, pursuing love, and maintaining love or curing lovesickness pervade the tradition and were codified most visibly in works such as Capellanus' *Tractatus,* Mahieu le Poirier's *Court d'amours* (edition of 1976), and Martial d'Auvergne. It is that tradition which the troubadour college, or Gay Consistory, both preserved and suppressed in *Las Flors del gay saber.*

Standing somewhere between the classical tradition of troubadour erotic regimen and a law that would come to define itself as the antithesis of love, wisdom without desire, the Gay Consistory is probably the ultimate emblem of what de Rougemont described as "a pagan middle ages tormented by Christian law" (1983, 185). The attempt to impose a style on the life of the passions was both the virtue and the failure of the college. The Gay Consistory was established in 1323 in Toulouse, ostensibly as a revival of the poetic tradition of courtly love, of the pursuit of joy, and of other amatory strategies and practices, including the oratorical contests that accompanied the more casuistic tradition of questions and judgments of love. The consistory was also a more systematic and seemingly doctrinal attempt to codify and promulgate the rules and ethics of poetry defined as the search for or finding (*trouver*) of love. Appropriately enough for a self-styled gay academy, the precise character and composition of the consistory remains somewhat mysterious. Aside from the chancellor of the consistory, Guilhem Molinier, "one learned in law," and Berthemieu Marc, doctor in law (Anglade, 1920, t IV 25), the names of those who participated in the compilation are as encrypted or absent as the extravagant and ludic use of nomination in the earlier tradition would suggest was appropriate (Dragonetti, 1982, 17–25). It is best, in other words, to treat the gay science of this latter day troubadour college not as a referent composed of historical personages but rather as an experiment in thought, as a system of texts and rules, inscriptions and practices, whose initial reality necessarily resides in the epistemic system that they set down. The work of the college was in this sense to be understood as a kind of *corpus iuris amoris* or monument to the geography and laws of love.

The project explicitly espoused by the Gay Consistory was both juridical and ethical. The founding charter appears to have aimed at re-establishing a jurisdiction of love, a "gay and feminine knowledge" of desire "by means of which gay science of the rules for composing poems in the vernacular tongue . . . the ignorant can be educated, the madnesses and idiocies of lovers can be judged, and equally the means of living in joy and amorous rapture, free of melancholy and indifference" could also be inscribed (Anglade, 1919, 1: 8–9). The general form of the consistory was to be that of a judicial college which would both expound and apply the laws of love. The authors of the laws specifically stipulated that "we have set down the precise rules by reference to which [the authors] are to arrive at their judgments" (4: 25). Although the moralizing tone of some of the subsequent statement of project and design cannot be denied, and indeed codes and their consistories always come after the event and are in one dimension necessarily conservative, the ethical and casuistic trajectory of the code and its progeny is depicted as that of seeking and of learning the joy and lightness of love: "It is through poetry that joy" and the practical knowledge of love is inscribed in the soul (4: 48).

The *scientia,* "saber," or knowing of fourteenth-century gay science has varied and complex meanings, and it is only at the risk of severe reductionism that I draw attention to three connotations in particular. One starting point is the tripartite definition of "this ancient knowledge" offered at the start of the Gatien-Arnoult manuscript of *Las Flors del gay saber:* finding, learning, and judging the practices of love. It should be noted also that the figure under which these definitions travel severally is that of the recollection and recon-stitution of laws of love that time and social circumstance—not least the hostility of the Church—had let fall into disuse. The art of love, defined as poetry, is thus buried in the ancient practices of the troubadours, and hidden even there in a lyric that is described as often "obscure" and at times in-felicitous or wanting (Gatien-Arnoult, 1841–43, 1: 4). The first and perhaps the most radical characteristic of the fourteenth-century laws of love is thus that in defining their object as the recollection of the antique science of "trou-ver," of searching, finding, or meeting love, they also locate their own practice in relation to a comparable epistemic search.

While some have attempted to bolster the definition of love as lack by referring to the derivation of *trouver* from *trou,* meaning hole, gap, or lack (Huchet, 1987), it is significant that the substantive definition of this genre of love poem depends in fact on two manners of finding love, by chance and by endeavor. The first is defined as a form of anamnesis. To find love by chance is to refind something that has been forgotten or that one only imagined to be lost. In a modern terminology, this kind of love is characterized by the repeti-tion of a pattern, and fortuitous or unconscious trouver being does not mea-sure up to the rules of the art of love. The love that is valuable and just is the love that is built through rhetorical labor. The stronger definition of finding is thus formulated in light of the art of love: to find is to invent a work of love, to create something new and express the new emotion in a new and "perfectly measured" composition (Gatien-Arnoult, 1841–43, 1: 9). The measure in question, I shall argue, is not only explicitly defined according to the laws of love and the rhetorical rules of composition, appropriateness, beauty, and "syllable and rhyme," but also in terms of the justice of the poem understood as the expression of love (Gatien-Arnoult, 1841–43, 1: 10).

In *Las Leys d'amors* the finding of love is the result of a lengthy process, of a labor or education in the art of relationship and the spirit of love. The ethics of love was built around the mapping of the process of building an erotic relationship, of learning to love. Lack, therefore, had little to do with the definition of love as the reality and justice of its expression and duration. More than that, however, the notion of finding love has not only an ethical connotation, that of seeking to deserve love, but also an epistemic valence. The laws of love institute a jurisdiction or space of relationship within the social. The various codes of love spell out certain principles of affect and intimacy in the public sphere. Paradoxically, however, the code of amorous interaction was also cryptic in the senses both of disguising the authors and judges of such laws and of demanding secrecy with respect to the identities of the subjects engaged in amorous relationships.

The paradox of finding love was that of composing a discourse, a poem or letter, that would both serve the specific desires of the lovers and guard their identity from the Church or marital state. The practice of love was enlaced in an erotics of disclosure and encryption, of declaration and seclusion. The poem "is made out of nothing," refers to no one and signifies only through metaphor: "The place of courtly poetry is no place, in the sense that there is absolutely no way of naming or of knowing the identity of the poet or of the characters in the poem. The work itself, in its precariousness and fragility, resting in the space of fiction" is our only guide to the allegory of names and places (Dragonetti, 1982, 25). If the space of love is a nonplace, an idealization or internalization, then one might well argue that it truly concerns a space of laws, of norms that attach to the relationship between lovers or to practices of love rather than to any specific individual. In defining the "propriety" or ethic of the name, *Las Leys d'amors* thus offers a lengthy discourse on names as the signifiers of substances and qualities, rather than identities or individuals. Thus the name will represent either a corporeal or an incorporeal quality, pursuant to a predetermined theme or idea. (Gatien-Arnoult, 1841–43, 3: 17). Following this law of reference, "names of first imposition" are those which derive from the senses (18). They exist in the body as feelings or sensations and can be mapped and expressed directly. Names of "second imposition exist only in the understanding; they are incorporeal and are forged by the imagination" (19).

Gay science refers to knowledge and participation in the nonplace of thought. In that counterintuitive sense of the governance and growth of the social space of amorous relationship, the laws of love offer principles for the expression of the corporeal and spiritual intensities of desire, as well as for judging the duration of love and the disputes attendant on loving. As a system of thought, the laws of love institute a rhetoric and practice of love in the most concrete of physical and emotional forms, and yet they are also an art that escapes the *principium individuationis,* or tragic juristic principle of nominate singularity, of identity as title and name. The radical character of the gay science is thus attached at a fundamental level to the trajectory of a system of thought that exists not so much in the domain of fiction as in that of the drama or theater of plural desires. Borrowing their names from body parts and sensations as well as from emotions and virtues, lovers were free to play with names and the other masks of identity as occasion and desire suggested. The theater of love was staged precisely to escape the legislation of reference according to the laws of property. It juxtaposed passion and property, the rhetoric of the real and the dogma of law.

The play of substitution of names was no doubt in part a dimension of the subversive and dissident character of the pursuit of a corporeal love. It was also, however, a displacement of the object of love. In the place of God or the unified object of marital exchange, the laws of love "imposed," not once but twice,[7] the artistic or constructed space of amorous relationship. Within the play made possible by artifice, and particularly by the rhetorical art of staging the love affair, it was impossible to know the identity of the subjects in love. The incidents of relationship, and at times even the most intimate aspects of what parts of the body could be touched, were lauded or lambasted, sung or sobbed, never the irrelevance or property in a name.

If amorous relationship was the internality or emotional life of the social, it is worth observing that the play of identities was also, at the level of theory but equally and necessarily in practice, a play of sexualities. To the prevalent notion of the homosexuality of courtly love argued most ably by Jean-Claude Huchet, one should therefore add the other possibilities of bisexuality and of lesbian desire. It is not only that the trobairitz includes both tensons debating the greater merit of women's love for women over women's love for men, and instances of love poems addressed to feminine others, but also and more important that the focus of the laws of love upon the relationship, on subjects rather than objects, precluded any prior definition of the gender of the persons between whom love was shared. The laws of love may have looked to the most intimate of corporeal signs and tests of love yet they did so not in terms of the prior construction of sexual identity but rather as a means of mapping the requisite forms of expression and the duration of relationship. The justice of love was the most intimate or proximate of forms of judgment and it entailed addressing the face-to-face, mouth-to-mouth, body-to-body of desire. Its judgments, however, are marked not only by the intimacy made possible by the seclusion of identity, but also by an epistemology addressed to the emotional space created between subjects.

Intensity is not the same thing as duration. Perhaps in part in relation to this distinction, the chronology or historicity of the laws of love is obscure. They need to be read through the indefinite or plastic temporality of the passions, and their history narrated as that of the historical geography of desire. In this regard, it should be noted that the southern French reception of classical rhetoric and poetics, including the translation and adaptation of Ovid's *Ars amatoria,* should be set in the context of the revival of all the rhetorical genres. Within this tradition, rhetoric was not simply the appropriate form of knowledge of all that related to human affairs, to probability, but was in its Ciceronian guise the means of acting upon and staging the real. That orators were *actores veritatis* meant that they were those who enacted the real, rather than simply imitating or being faithful to an external truth. The orator was an actor on the stage of law, politics, or in our case the enactment of love. Reality was a matter of what words were made to mean, a matter of staging the drama of relationship and the questions of love. Yet in 1355 when the lawyer Arnaut Donat won the laureate of gay science, truth had become abstract and external. In place of a rhetoric that staged the real, the poet now spoke of a spiritualized love and of a world that was "faithful to the truth" (Gatien-Arnoult, 1849a, 21).

The author of the first poem to win the poetic tournament and so the first person to receive the accolade of "doctor in gay science" was Arnaut Vidal, also a lawyer by training. His poem was a song of love to the Virgin Mary and distinctly Christian in tone. In its practice the Gay Consistory presided over a rapid formalization and purification of the earlier tradition and art. The Christianization and legalization of the laws of love coincided with the demise of the Catharist heresy and with the return of Toulouse to France. When Mathieu d'Artigeloube received the doctorate in gay science in 1468, his poem was addressed explicitly "to all those experts in the art of Rhetoric (*Rectorica*) — vulgarly (*vulguarement*) known as the Gay Science — whose work is customarily read out on the first of May — in the city of Toulouse" (Gatien-Arnoult, 1849a, 235). In the hands of jurists and presided over exclusively by men, the antique joy of gay science had become vulgar and the knowledge of the body, relationship, and desire that it had cultivated had been displaced by a normative rhetoric — appropriately enough, *rectorica* — and its abstract rules of formulaic exposition.[8] By the time, in the second decade of the sixteenth century, that the Gay Consistory was replaced by the College of the Art and Science of French Rhetoric, the practice of relationship had given way to the abstraction of truth, and the dogmas of law had triumphed over the language and art of love.

The trajectory that leads from the Gay Consistory to the college of rhetoric is one of suppression, of conformism and obedience to the reception of secular law. It is not insignificant that it was jurists, and most particularly Coras and Forcadel, the framers of the French constitutional state, who held custody of the tradition of the laws of love in the sixteenth century and who ensured in effect that gay science lived on, if at all, in a negative and displaced form (Fell, 1983–86, 1: 25–47). In the hands of lawyers, the laws of love were treated as the archaisms of a ludic and uncultivated private realm. The memory of this vulgar art stood in rank opposition to the heroic and public norms of Salic law, under which no woman could own property, hold office, or play any public role in the kingdom of France. The gay science, an art and knowledge of both the sexes, a dramatic libidinal expression of an erotic *vita femina*, and of the rules and judgments of women's courts and laws of love now belonged truly to the "tedious no-man's land" that Bloch earnestly and retrospectively predicted. The feminine had become private, and formal rules of presentation had replaced rhetoric as a practice of truth.

Divagations on the Return of Gay Science

What is carried within a tradition, however obscurely and however often denied, is far from lost. The advent of the college of rhetoric may finally and unequivocally have sealed the fate of gay science as a political practice or as the ambiguous code of the laws of an intimate public sphere, but it is equally arguable that the courts of love continued to press against the fence that contained them. Even if the later tradition is at times satirical, at times ludic, and on other occasions oneiric, it carries the possibility of recuperating the laws of love from the negative effect of longstanding legal hostility to their resurrection. Thus, to take a final example, this time from Mahieu le Poirier's mid-fourteenth-century *Court d'amours,* the antinomy of love and law, of Eros and legal proprium, is explicit. The form the conflict takes is that of a series of judgments on questions relating to marriage.

In Judgment 12, the Bailiff of Love is asked whether a married man or a married woman can love someone other than his or her spouse (Poirier, 1976, 29–30). His judgment is that although it appears disorderly in nature — "because one has no right to such love" — it is also possible to excuse such affairs outside marriage where, "perhaps through bad advice" a couple has entered into marriage inappropriately, as may happen between partners of radically different ages (30). Having admitted the exception, the bailiff proceeds to a normative peroration in which the love of a married man is described as "neither cultivated nor valuable and it is indeed dangerous to the soul because it is a breach of faith. Such covert love leads to confusion and is contrary to common usage; it is a mad theft of pleasure — it is nature run wild without meaning, without care and without reason" (321). In short, the norm is here honored only in the exception, and the law of love is subject to what might prosaically be called the law of law.

In Judgment 31, the bailiff hears the case of a man who complains that his lover is too demanding, that she wants him to love her wisely, to promise to have no other lover save his wife, and to carry a token of her on all public occasions. His plea is that he loves his wife, that he married her for love, and that she pleases him. He also loves his lover but her demands now force him to choose between them. The bailiff offers the opinion that loyalty requires one to be bound to a lover and not to leave the lover without good cause. The complainant should thus remain loyal to his wife, because he is "longer and more greatly bound to her. Such should be your honor and your joy . . . just as it is the coat armor you wear and the arms that you bear" (Poirier, 108). Again, fidelity, in the legal sense of obligation, of service to an institution and proprium, is privileged over the pursuit of passion.

In brief, a dramatic and evidently transitional ambivalence places these fourteenth-century laws of love midway between the earlier judgments of love, which mentioned time and again that marriage and love were incompatible and that spouses could not be lovers, and the Christian law of true marriage that prohibited love outside of conjugal reproduction. To take the point further, consider the penultimate judgment of *La Suite anonyme de la Court d'amours* in which the Bailiff of Love upholds the view that love is not the same thing as marrying one's lover — *amers n'est mie mariers* (Poirier, 1976, 227). As much by indirection as by purpose, these latter-day judgments of love nonetheless hold open a precarious intimate public space between the institution and desire, marriage and love. As the law of marriage took hold of the social space of love, the passions came to be marked increasingly by secrecy, obscurity, and nonknowledge. When the bailiff admits that to be married is not necessarily to enjoy one's true love, he offers an aperçu which presents love as an illicit passion or secret infidelity, a view that finds dramatic instantiation in an anecdote relayed by the humanist lawyer Vives.

In a discussion of marriage in *De Institutione foeminae Christianae,* Vives remarks that when he was in Paris he called on the house of a fellow jurist, Guillaume Budé. While they were talking in his library, Budé's wife came past, and he remarked, "This is my wife, who so diligently follows my pleasure that she treats my books as well as she treats her children" (Vives, 1523: fol. Z1a). Through or across his wife, one might say, the bibliophile humanist pursues an even greater love, that of books, of literature and the history of law. Budé the lawyer loves his wife because she attends to his love of texts, a point that is substantiated in his work on philology, where he explicitly admits, "I have also a second spouse [*altera coniux*], whom I often call Philologia" (Budé, 1536: sig. 26v). Elsewhere in the same work Budé talks of this lover as "literarum studium" and even "literarum optimarum studium" and admits that it is to her that he devotes "the ardor of my soul and all the energy of my nature" (sig. Vv).

For Budé, love as passion is in itself an infidelity, a secret and illicit desire, a Pandora's box. It would seem that Budé was fearful of losing himself in texts and in an erotic and ungoverned passion for literature. His greatest love thus had to be subjected to the order of law and to become the altera, or other. Marital fidelity and obedience to law meant that the ardor of his soul, his love for his mistress literature, can be glimpsed only by accident, in lapses and occasional allusions. In the same vein, the constitutional tradition that Budé was so central to inaugurating retains only elliptical signs of the earlier jurisdiction and rhetorical laws of love. A few maxims related to justice rather than law,[9] occasional introductory comments on rhetoric in treatises on Book 50 of the *Digest, De verborum significatione,* and a few long forgotten glossatorial works on the jurisprudence of love are all that remain of any explicit tradition of the laws of the first Venus, or judgments of love.

The revival of Scholasticism and the subsequent concentration on method (*scientia scientiarum*) in law as in the other disciplines definitively displaced rhetoric from the field of law to that of literature, and correlatively from jurisprudence to aesthetics. It also and even more clearly expunged the practices or stagings of gay science from the solemn discussions of community, constitution, and obligation that accompanied the rites of the legal form. The lawyer was a priest (*sacerdotes legum*) and a politician — "jurisconsultus hoc est homo politicus"; and there was little place in such a mystic and regal practice for levity — or erotic ideals of friendship and love (Baudouin, 1559, 20). At best the lawyer would secretly love texts (Budé's mistress philology, "princess and source of all thought"), but he did so in the epistemic mode of law, thereby consigning his passion to a truth that lay beyond both body and text in the spirit of the laws. It is that bleak history which we modern jurists have inherited and indeed until recently have unquestioningly accepted as our fate. Rhetoric, and specifically that art and practice of gay science that underpinned the *Las Leys d'amors,* did not and has not found a place within *legitima scientia* or professional knowledge of law. Gay science was not legal science, just as humor was alien to sanctity and imagination was foreign to the dignity of law.

The Gay Consistory, however, had explicitly revived a tradition and practice and even if there was pervasive aura of legalism to its practices and judgments, the codification of laws of love could not wholly obscure the counterlaw that lay at its root. The "flowers" of the gay saber were many and historically various, their claim to knowledge and to law self-evidently subversive and also explicitly pluralistic. The gay science plucked the flowers of a specific knowledge and practice; its laws were those of one jurisdiction amongst many. The epistemic modesty or legal pluralism within which the gay science exercised what the modern lawyer would term a consensual and so voluntary jurisdiction should not be treated as an occasion, yet another occasion, for dismissing the significance or status of a rhetoric that played the law. Few if any who currently study or teach law would maintain that law could be defined by some external or behavioral characteristic. For some time now, it has been recognized that law is a system of communication among other such systems. It has no foundation external to its own elaboration or, more obliquely, its self-founding. In short, the contemporary conception of law, whether it be termed autopoietic, deconstructive, or simply pragmatic, is one which necessarily recognizes that law is no more than a system of thought, a pattern of discursive practices, that exist heterarchically within a plurality of social systems of communication.

To adopt the definition of law just loosely sketched — as a system of thought — even a mentality — circumscribed by the internal rules of its elaboration rather than by any exterior force or foundation is to begin to recognize the potential comedy or at least paradox of legality (Luhmann, 1988, 161). The lawyer, as Legendre has somewhat seriously remarked, is in one interesting sense an imbecile, a bureaucrat who puts texts into social circulation, an idiot savant or wise fool (1983, 161). Such ambivalent scholarship, such arcane chattering or hotchpot textuality not only marks law as profoundly rhetorical but also opens up the question of the status of rhetoric as law. Returning to the gay science and to a tradition in which rhetoric had neither severed its links with dialectic — with argument or the reason of law — nor broken its ties to practice, it is perhaps easier to begin to understand the senses in which the laws of love deserve belated recognition as a legal system or body of norms and judgments that make up a significant casuistry or amorous jurisprudence.

To take the point further, law is increasingly defined as one of the many discourses competing to express and at least retrospectively to govern the various and increasingly fragmentary forms of social becoming according to its own peculiar temporality of precedent and rule (Murphy, 1997, 186–88). To the extent that the forms of social becoming are diverse and increasingly varied, law too fragments and itself becomes a plurality of systems of communication. The changing character and plural roles of the legal system require the development of a new terminology, a new rhetoric within which to think through the paradoxes and comedies of a legality that occupies ever more social space, that pervades the symbolic dramas of the public sphere, while simultaneously suffering the loss of its epistemic status or claim to universality and truth.

The rhetorical critique of law has consistently maintained that the tragedy or corruption of legality was constituted in large measure by the disjunction between legal communication and social practices. The space, the language and experience, of law was corrupt to the extent that it was dissonant with, or simply could not know, the relations and institutions that it claimed to govern. Gay science suggests a local, specific, and limited digression on the same theme of the critique of law: in essence, that a pluralistic conception of legality would frame specific systems of laws within their expression of, and interaction with, the practices that they sought to govern. In this sense, gay science and the laws of love form one of the most ethically appropriate, politically coherent, and jurisprudentially elegant of legal frames. They form a rhetorical system, a continuity of practices, and a corpus of principles and judgments expressive of them. Rhetoric, in short, here came to play the law, to stage the real and act out the truth.

I cannot hope, in the present, very preliminary discussion of gay science, to capture adequately the resonances or possibilities that the laws of love can convey. In the spirit of offering at least an intimation of the contemporary potential of this medieval art, it may be useful to focus finally on the Eros of its subject matter. Gay science was concerned with the rules that should govern or hold open the space of intimacy and affectivity in the public sphere. Recognizing with what might be viewed as proleptic acuity the importance of affect and desire, of Nietzsche's ardent loves and ardent hatreds, to all aspects of social relationship, gay science sought to treat that most significant and often most unwitting of all the domains of practice in its own terms. The laws of love were in this sense the rhetorical rules that expressed the ethics or justice of the varied forms and intensities of expression of affect, of intimacy in the public domain of relationship. In a sense the significance (and failure) of this science can be measured against the later history of the figures of speech and the recognition that trope and figure are always to be understood as signs of the affect or force, the Eros or drive, of language use.

A more extreme interpretation of gay science is also possible. Its focus was on amatory and sexual practices, on physical experience, the incorporation and expression of desire. How were the various signs or marks of love, the diverse jealousies, sicknesses, tokens, embraces, and consummations of passion, ranging from flirtation to estrangement, from epistolary love to nights spent naked together in bed without touching, or without kissing or without consummation, to be mapped and measured? How were lovers to act in the institution, in front of their parents, their guardians, their spouses, their employers, their friends? How could one move from falling in love to learning to love? These and countless other questions relating to justice or to the ethics of relationship were the questions around which gay science developed its rules of expression and its judgments of love. It was not simply or only, it should be noted, a rhetoric attached to the verbal expressions of love, but also and perhaps most fundamentally a knowledge of corporeal, gestural, and in particular chiromantic signs. Precisely for this reason, gay science was suppressed: it threatened the spiritual ideals and abstract principles of law with a knowledge of the erotic body.

I would like to suggest in conclusion that these corporeal signs of affect, these incorporations of passion and relationship, are intrinsic to the more radical possibilities of the laws of love. At issue is a rhetoric of the senses, a practice and ethic of passion, a knowledge or system of thought addressed to the affective bonds, the intensities and durations, of erotic relationship. For the gay science, and here I risk a certain polemical invention, the justice that the laws of love sought to introduce was one not geared simply to the face-to-face but concerned with the minute mapping of the erotic spaces of the body next to the body of the other. Addressed to the zones of pleasure, the and libidinal surfaces of love, the gay science did not and could not distinguish or name the gender or sexual identity of lovers. The elaborate play of metaphor and mask is simply a reflection of an Eros attached not to the unity of a gender or sex but to the unstable space of body parts, to the performative domain of movements and gestures, touch, excitation, and caress.

Gay science was also historically a rhetoric of the body and its passions, and it included a lexicon of physical and verbal expressions of emotion which coded such corporeal signs as blushing, palpitations, sweating, sleeplessness, arousal, trembling, nausea, lack of appetite, and the like. It also symbolically marked the zones of the body and the forms, places, and times of touch and embrace. Appearing not as a gender, sex, rank, or name but simply as a lover in relation to the beloved, the subject of desire was in these most intimate terms of the *carte de tendre* an erotic and rhetorical possibility, a site of the libidinal inscription of relation, and precisely not a name or status. If in contemporary terms, gay science displaces sexual identities and transgresses the heterosexual norms of amorous expression, if it is in form a modern species of outlaw culture, then the history of gay science may well contribute to the epistemic as well as the rhetoric of such collective practices.

Notes

1. In judgment 37, for example, the plaintiff was a woman who had entered a formal *alliance d'amours* with a young man who, shortly after entering into their pact — sworn before friends and sealed with tears and kisses — joined *Les Cordeliers de l'observance d'Amours*. Her plea was that the order be enjoined to release the man so that he be could be made to appear before the justices of love and account for whether he intended to keep his promise or not. The decision was in the petitioner's favor and, although the rules of the order forbade members to talk to women, the defendant was enjoined to appear, but the order was allowed to blindfold him during his testimony (169).

2. The later tradition of parody is also of course open to reconsideration, and it is worth noting Michelle le Doeuff's remark in a footnote to *Le Sexe du savoir*, although she is discussing Rabelais's reference to gay science in *Gargantua*: "Could feminism not also in its turn produce a 'gay science,' an epistemology of a lost learned culture like that of Gargantua?" (1998, 371).

3. Benton, 1981. A much longer account of the historiographical issues has yet to be written. For present purposes, in addition to works specifically discussed, the most useful philological recuperations of the tradition are those of W. A. Neilson, "The Origins and Sources of the Court of Love" (1899); Vilho Puttonen, *Etudes sur Martial d'Auvergne* (1945); and Roger Dragonetti, *La Vie de la lettre au moyen âge* (1980).

4. It bears passing observation and is scarcely simply coincidental that this definition of love is also that spelled out in Giacomo Casanova, *History of My Life* (edition of 1968), vol. 5, p. 71: "If they love us they must fear to lose us and hence must do all that they can to keep alive our desire to attain possession of them. If we attain it nothing is surer than that we will no longer desire them, for one does not desire what one possesses."

5. In that it is good to acknowledge the influence of friends and the virtual community of scholarship, I would like to note that this point arrived by way of an e-mail from Mariana Valverde and her kind animadversion to Klossowki's wonderful French translation of *The Gay Science*.

6. The rhetorical figure of antirrhesis is defined by Henry Peacham as "a form of speech by which the orator rejects the opinion of some person, for error or wickedness" (*The Garden of Eloquence*, 1593, [London: Jackson] fol. N4r). As Peacham goes on to note, the figure of antirrhesis was most commmon in discourses against heretics and in the various later apologies or defenses of the Christian faith. For a discussion of this tradition, see Goodrich, *Oedipus Lex*, chap. 3.

7. It is difficult to resist referring here to the concept of double meaning that derives initially from Capellanus and the definition of the *iudicis amoris* in terms of *duplicem sententiam*.

8. Assuming that it has a Latin root, *rectorica* suggests both *oratio recta,* direct speech, which is associated historically with equity, and also a root close to *rego,* meaning "to rule or govern," and by association, straight, right, or lawful.

9. From the many tags and maxims that early modern jurists were fond of, one might single out a few, from those which derive from Boethius and the principle "Maior lex amor est," to rules of method such as "In lectione non verba sed veritas est amanda," or more broadly still, "Corde creditur ad iustitiam." In aesthetic terms, one might add the principle of *elegantia iuris,* and the even fonder observation "Nihil pulchrius ordine" — nothing is more beautiful than order.

Works Cited

Anglade, Joseph (ed.). 1919–20. *Las Leys d'amors: Manuscrit de l'académie des jeux floraux.* Toulouse: Privat.

D'Auvergne, Martial. 1951 [1460]. *Les Arrêts d'amour* (Paris: Picard).

Baudouin, François. 1559. *Commentarius de iurisprudentia Muciana.* Paris: n.p.

Bec, Pierre (ed.). 1995. *Chants d'amour des femmes-troubadours.* Paris: Stock.

Benton, John F. 1981. "Collaborative Approaches to Fantasy and Reality in the Literature of Champagne," in G. Burgess, ed., *Court and Poet.* Liverpool: Cairns.

Bloch, Howard. 1977. *Medieval French Literature and Law.* Berkeley: University of California Press.

———. 1991. *Medieval Misogyny and the Invention of Western Romantic Love.* Chicago: Chicago University Press.

Bozzolo, C., and Loyau, H. 1982. *La Cour amoureuse dite de Charles VI.* Paris: Léopard d'or.

Budé, Guillaume. 1536. *De philologia.* Paris: Vascosan.

Capellanus, Andreas. 1982 [1176]. *On Love.* P. G. Walsh, trans. and ed. London: Duckworth.

Clanchy, M. T. 1983. "Law and Love in the Middle Ages," in J. Bossy, ed., *Disputes and Settlements: Law and Human Relations in the West.* Cambridge: Cambridge University Press.

Court, Benoit de. 1731 ed. *Commentaires juridiques et joyeux.* Paris: Gaudoin.

Denomy, A. J. 1965. *The Heresy of Courtly Love.* Gloucester: P. Smith.

Dragonetti, Roger. 1980. *La Vie de la lettre au moyen âge.* Geneva: Droz.

———. 1982. *Le Gai Savoir dans la rhétorique courtoise.* Paris: Seuil.

Fraise, Arlette. 1998. *Les Femmes et leur histoire.* Paris: Gallimard.

Gatien-Arnoult, ed. 1841–43. *Las flors del gay saber estier dichas las leys d'amors,* 3 vols. Toulouse: Privat.

———. 1849a. *Las Joyas del gay saber.* Toulouse: Privat.

———. 1849b. *Recueil de poésies.* Toulouse: Privat.

Goodrich, Peter. 1995. *Oedipus Lex: Psychoanalysis, History, Law.* Berkeley: University of California Press.

———. 1996. *Law in the Courts of Love.* London: Routledge.

Gordon Fell, A. 1983–86. *Origins of Legislative Sovereignty and the Legislative State,* 3 vols. Cambridge: Greenwood.

Huchet, Jean-Claude. 1987. *L'Amour discourtois: La "Fin Amors" chez les premiers troubadours.* Toulouse: Privat.

———. 1997. "Introduction," in Arnaut Vidal, *Le Livre des aventures de Monseigneur Guilhem de la Barra.* Paris: Champion.

Irigaray, Luce. 1996. *I Love to You: Sketch for a Possible Felicity Within History.* London: Routledge.

Jay, Martin. 1999. "Must Justice Be Blind?" in C. Douzinas and L. Nead, eds., 1999, *Law and the Image.* Chicago: Chicago University Press.

Lacan, Jacques. 1992. *The Ethics of Psychoanalysis.* New York: Norton.

———. *The Psychoses.* London: Routledge.

Legendre, Pierre. 1983. *L'Empire de la vérité.* Paris: Fayard.

Luhmann, Niklas. 1988. "The Third Question: The Creative Uses of Paradox in Law and Legal History," *Journal of Law and Society* 15: 153.

Marol, Jean-Claude. 1998. *L'Amour libérée.* Paris: Dervy.

Murphy, Tim. 1997. *The Oldest Social Science? Configurations of Law and Modernity.* Oxford: Oxford University Press.

Neilson, W. A. 1899. "The Origins and Sources of the Court of Love" *Studies and Notes in Philology* 6: 1–269.

Nelli, René, 1974, *L'Erotique des troubadours,* 2 vols. Toulouse: Union Générale des éditions

———. 1977. *Ecrivains anticonformistes du moyen âge occitan: Les femmes et l'amour,* vol. 2. Paris: Phébus.

Nietzsche, Friedrich. 1910. *The Joyful Wisdom (La Gaya Scienza),* trans. Thomas Common. Edinburgh: Foulis.

———. 1911. *Ecce Homo.* Edinburgh: Foulis.

Petersen, Hanne (ed.). 1998. *Law and Love in Europe.* Aldershot: Dartmouth.

Pisan, Christine de. 1891 ed. *Le Livre des trois jugemens,* in *Oeuvres poétiques de Christine de Pisan,* vol. 2. Paris: Firmin Didot.

Poirier, Mahieu le. 1976 ed. *Le Court d'amours de Mahieu le Poirier.* Waterloo, Ontario: Wilfred Laurier University Press.

Puttonen, Vilho. 1945. *Etudes sur Martial d'Auvergne.* Helsinki: Suo Malainen.

Rémy, Paul. 1954–55. "Les 'cours d'amour': Légende et réalité," *Revue de l'Université de Bruxelles* 7, 179.

Reynouard, François (ed.). 1821. *Choix des poésies originales des troubadours.* Paris: Firmin Didot.

Rougemont, Denis de. 1983 ed. *Love in the Western World.* Princeton, N.J.: Princeton University Press.

Sloterdijk, Peter. 1989. *The Thinker on Stage.* Minneapolis: Minnesota University Press.

Stone, Gregory. 1994. *The Death of the Troubadour.* Philadelphia: University of Pennsylvania Press.

Sylvestre, Michel. 1993. *Demain la psychanalyse.* Paris: Seuil.

Theweleit, Klaus. 1994. *Object-Choice: All You Need Is Love.* London: Verso.

Vives, Jan Luis. 1523. *De institutione foeminae Christianae.* London: H. Wykes.

Zizek, Slavoj. 1994. *Metastases of Enjoyment.* London: Verso.

5

Bribery, Buggery, and the Fall of Lord Chancellor Bacon

ALAN STEWART

Over the past twenty years, the legal history of homosexuality in early modern England has come under intense scrutiny. Yet scholars remain largely mystified by their researches, which seem to yield a set of contradictions. First, on the one hand, sodomy appears to have been taken very seriously as a crime: "the detestable & abominable vice of buggeri committed with mankind or beast" was among the first offenses to be taken from the ecclesiastical courts in Henry VIII's legal reformation and designated a capital offense without benefit of clergy.[1] On the other hand, the number of known prosecutions over the next 150 years is negligible.[2]

Second, sodomy was dubbed, in indictments and legal commentaries, the crime *inter Christianos non nominandum,* not to be named among Christians.[3] As Leslie Moran has argued, this produced an anomaly: "In order to

Some ideas on Bacon, buggery, and bribery were developed in collaboration with Lisa Jardine in chapter 16 of Alan Stewart, ed., *Hostage to Fortune: The Troubled Life of Francis Bacon, 1561–1626* (London: Gollancz, 1998); the present chapter, however, takes a different path. I am grateful to Lorna Hutson and Victoria Kahn for their comments, which have helped to shape the final version. The research for this chapter was generously funded by a British Academy Postdoctoral Research Fellowship, and by the Birkbeck College Research Fund.

speak of buggery within [the common law] tradition, the speaker had to proceed according to a command to remain silent."[4] The "speaking" of sodomy is often therefore bewildering in its allusions. Critics have followed Michel Foucault, who asserted famously that sodomy was "that utterly confused category"[5] which seemed to attach itself opportunistically to other crimes: atheism, witchcraft, treason, conjuring, rape, adultery, and so on. Ed Cohen has claimed that sodomy "indicated a spectrum of nonprocreative sexual practices ranging from use of a dildo for birth control to anal intercourse (between men or between men and women) and bestiality."[6]

Yet in practice, in order to define the crime more particularly, lawyers were forced not only to name the unnameable but to specify the act(s) in detail.[7] This did not necessarily lead to clarity of the nature of sodomy. In *The Third Part of the Institutes,* for example, Sir Edward Coke writes, "*Emissio semenis* [the emission of seed] maketh it not Buggery, but it is an evidence in cases of buggery of penetration," while in *The Twelfth Part of the Reports* he contradicts himself, stating that both penetration and emission of semen are required: "To make that Offence *Oportet rem penetrare, & semen naturae emittere, & effundere* [it is right and proper to penetrate the thing, and to emit the seed of nature, and to pour it forth]"; he notes that the indictment contains the phrases "*rem habuit & carnaliter cognovit,*" implying "penetration and emission of seed."[8] A contemporary manual by Michael Dalton privileges seminal emission as proof: "And this can be without penetration because the use of the body to spend seed in such cases makes this Buggery in the Statute without penetration.'[9] In court, defendants were interrogated and required to supply intimate physical details. In the most widely reported English legal case of the early modern period to involve sodomy, that of the second earl of Castlehaven, the witnesses were required to specify who was lying with whom, and where; on what side of the bed; whether on top or at the side; whether the body was being held down (and how); whether the body was penetrated; and whether the body emitted semen.[10]

In this chapter, I attempt to explain how these apparent contradictions, far from obscuring the nature of sodomy, might in fact enable us to understand its place in early modern England. I focus on a notorious accusation of sodomy which appears to be inexplicably "utterly confused" with (or tacked on to) a more concrete accusation, of bribery. I suggest that, by investigating the relation between these two accusations — one prosecuted, the other not — we can begin to understand how sodomy functioned in relation to the law, and in relation to society more generally, in early modern England.

My inquiry was prompted by a chance reading of two variations on a single libel aimed in 1621 at Francis Bacon, viscount St. Albans and baron Verulam, lord chancellor of England. In April of that year, Bacon was found guilty of having accepted gifts in money and goods from various petitioners, against whom he nonetheless then ruled in cases brought to the court of Chancery. He was deprived of all public office and his place in the House of Lords for life, fined £40,000, and sentenced to indefinite imprisonment in the Tower of London. As it turned out, the imprisonment lasted less than a week, and by some creative accountancy he avoided the financial penalties, but Bacon never re-entered public life.[11]

Contemporary reports refer to a spate of libels against the lord chancellor. On 27 March 1621, Samuel Albyn wrote to John Rawson, mentioning "Certayn Lybles" against, among others, "Sir francis bacon who is in his sty, at york House."[12] Two months later, on 23 June 1621, the newsletter writer John Chamberlain reported, "Many indignities are said and don against him [Bacon], and divers libells cast abroad to his disgrace not worth the repeating or savoring of too much malice and scurrilitie."[13] It is possible that the two libels I explore here can be traced originally to this wave. The first is in a commonplace book entitled "Vpon Sr F Ba," now in the Folger Shakespeare Library:

> Within this sty heer now doth ly
> A hog well bred wth bribery
> A pig, a hog, a boare, a bacon
> Whom God hath left, and ye Divel taken.[14]

The second version is contained in a manuscript account of Bacon's life by Sir Simonds D'Ewes, now in the British Library's Harley collection. It reads:

> Within this sty a hogg* doth ly:
> that must bee hanged for Sodomy
> *Alluding both to his surname of Bacon & of that swinish abominable sin.[15]

These are clearly in essence the same rhyme, but where the Folger manuscript has "bribery," the crime for which Bacon was impeached, D'Ewes has "sodomy." How can these two discrete accusations be linked?

It is generally accepted that the acknowledged fact of Bacon's sodomy took hold of the public imagination at a particular historical moment, after his fall. As Mario DiGangi argues, "Bacon's continuous homosexual activity . . . became the subject of discourse—was identified as disorderly sodomy—only after *he* had been identified as a disorderly subject. . . . Before Bacon was stigmatized as a disorderly subject, his 'sodomy' was simply the *status quo* of mastery."[16] This follows the argument of Jonathan Goldberg that sexual acts between men "went on all the time, unrecognized as sodomy, called, among other things, friendship or patronage, and facilitated by the beds shared, for instance, by servants or students." Sodomy was what these acts were called on particularly loaded occasions, "only in particularly stigmatizing contexts."[17]

But we might temper that claim. The association of bribery and sodomy hinted at by these libels is reinforced in other, lengthier writings. In the manuscript on which his "Brief Life" of Bacon is based, John Aubrey has three sentences, written in the left-hand margin of a sheet, as a single block of text: "He was a paiderastos [pederast]. His Ganimeds and Favourites tooke Bribes; but his Lordship always gave Judgement secundum aequum et bonum [according as was just and good]. His Decrees in Chancery stood firme, i.e. there are fewer of his Decrees reverst then of any other Chancellor."[18]

In three short sentences, the paragraph moves from Bacon as *paiderastos* to the fact that his degrees in the court of Chancery tended not to be reversed. This is not, I shall argue, sloppy thinking on the part of John Aubrey. Instead, it suggests that we need to conceive of a society where pederasty might reasonably be thought of in terms of the reversal or otherwise of the alleged pederast's decrees in Chancery. The key lies in the second sentence: "His Ganimeds and Favourites tooke Bribes; but his Lordship always gave Judgement secundum aequum et bonum." The issue that links pederasty and durable Chancery judgments for Aubrey is servants and bribery: while Bacon's servants, who were linked to him by ties of pederasty ("Ganimeds" strengthens this), may have taken bribes, he himself was not vulnerable to bribery. There are two possible interpretations of this. The simple point is that Bacon's conduct as a judge was unaffected by the actions of his servants. But the phrasing suggests something more specific: that strangely enough for a pederast, Bacon remained fair in his legal judgments. The tacit implication here is that pederasts are precisely those people who normally take bribes, whose professional opinion can be swayed in this way.

The lengthiest exploration of Bacon's "notorious & base briberie" and buggery comes in the journal of Simonds D'Ewes:

> Neuer had anie man in those great places of gaine hee had gone thorough hauing been attornie generall before hee was Lorde chancellour, soe ill husbanded the time, or prouided for himself; but his vast prodigalitie had eaten vpp all his gaines; soe as it was agreed on by all men that hee owed at this present at least 20000l more then hee was worth . . . Though he weere an eminent scholler, & a reasonable good lawer; both which hee much adorned with his elegant expression of himselfe & his graceful deliuerie Yet his vices were so stupendious & great, as they vtterlie obscured & outpoized his vertues. For hee was immoderatelie ambitious, & excessivelie proud, to maintaine which hee was necessitated to iniustice & bribery, taking sometimes most baselie of both sides. To this later wickedness the favour hee had with

the beloued Marquesse of Buckingham [George Villiers, James's favorite] emboldened him, as I learned in discourse from a gentleman of his bedchamber, whoe told me hee was sure his lorde [Bacon] should neuer fall as long as the saied Marquesse continued in fauour. His most abominable and darling sinne I should rather burie in silence then mention it, weere it not a most admirable instance how men are enslaued by wickednes & held captiue by the deuil. For wheereas presentlie vpon his censure at this time his ambition was moderated his pride humbled, & the meanes of his former iniustice & corruption remoued, yet would hee not relinquish the practice of his most horrible and secret sinne of Sodomie keeping still one Godrick a very effeminate faced youth to bee his catamite and bedfellow. Men begann to discourse of that his unnaturall crime, which hee had practiced manie yeares; deserting the bedd of his Ladie; which hee accounted as the Italians & Turks doe, a poore & meane pleasure in respect of the other; & it was thought by some that hee should haue been tried at the barre of iustice for it, & haue satisfied the law most seuere against that horrible villanie *with* the price of his bloud which caused some bolde & forward mann to write these verses following in a whole sheete of paper, & to cast it downe in some part of Yorkhowse in the strand wheere Viscount St. Alban yet lay.

Within this sty a hogg* doth ly:
that must bee hanged for Sodomy
*Alluding both to his surname of Bacon & of that swinish abominable sin.

But, D'Ewes notes, "hee neuer came to any publike triall for this crime; nor did euer that I could heare forbeare his old custome of making his seruants his bedfellowes."[19]

Here Bacon's "most admirable and darling sinne . . . his most horrible and secret sinne of Sodomie" is presented as "a most admirable instance how men are enslaued by wickednes, held captiue by the deuil" — as precisely the kind of thing one might expect from a generally wicked man. However, the vagueness of this formulation is belied by the position which sodomy takes in the construction of the passage. The precise progression of ideas and association of vices produces a clear path: "vast prodigalitie," extravagant debts, immoderate ambition, and excessive pride, moves him "to iniustice bribery, taking sometimes most baselie of both sides." This is precisely the banal argument from which Aubrey is at pains to extricate Bacon. According to D'Ewes, Bacon's sodomy is the culmination of this decline and underpins and explains his bribery. According to Aubrey, Bacon was a pederast, but it was his favorites who took bribes; his own judgments always remained fair. In other words, the two biographical accounts, by Aubrey and D'Ewes, often used to bolster each other to invoke a "gay Bacon," in fact contain entirely contradictory verdicts on the lord chancellor. Taken together, however, they provide evidence of a set of assumptions linking pederasty and bribery which are evidently so entrenched and beyond question that they are open to manipulation in opposite arguments.

But to represent the two accusations of bribery and buggery as analogous underscores their essential difference. Bacon was tried for bribery, but never tried for buggery (a capital offense), although D'Ewes claims the latter was public knowledge: "It was thought by some that hee should haue been tried at the barre of iustice for it, & haue satisfied the law most seuere against that horrible villanie *with* the price of his bloud." In the remainder of this chapter, I shall argue that the defense mounted by Bacon in response to the bribery charges was what left him (at least in theory) open to charges of buggery. The very nature of that bribery defense, however, also precluded any prosecution of the buggery charge.

In understanding the bribery charges against Bacon, we have to reconstruct a mindset that is now utterly alien. What seems to us remarkable about the accusations is not that Bacon may or may not have *taken* bribes, but that the accusers should come forward and declare that they had *given* bribes to ensure their suits' easy progress through Chancery. These men were annoyed, not that there was a lord chancellor who accepted bribes, but that there was a lord chancellor who failed to deliver the goods on receipt of those bribes — Bacon had apparently taken the money and then ruled *against* the suits. These petitioners were not overcoming guilt in making their complaint against Bacon: they were overcoming their embarrassment at having paid out for a decision which did not go their way.[20]

This explains why Bacon argued, quite fairly, that his crimes were *"vitia temporis,* and not *vitia hominis"* — vices of the times, shared by many, and not vices specific to the man.[21] In his "particular confession" on twenty-eight counts (based on twenty-one cases), which the Lords demanded, Bacon adopted three identifiable defense strategies. All involved the fact, as Joel Hurstfield writes, that "Bacon appears to have kept the gift and the judgment in two separate compartments of his mind."[22] First, Bacon claimed that the final decree was already passed by the time he received gifts from the litigant, so that the gift did not affect his judgment: for example, four hundred pounds was "delivered unto me in a Purse . . . but, as far as I can remember, it was expressed by them that brought it, to be for Favours past, and not in respect to Favours to come." Second, that the gift had been received at an occasion when gifts were perfectly natural, for example at New Year: "I received at New-year's Tide, an Hundred Pounds from Sir John Treavor; and, because it came as a New Year's Gift, I neglected to enquire whether the Cause was ended or depending." Both these strategies fit a tried and tested defense, namely that, as Bacon claimed, "a defence might in diverse things extenuate the offense in respect of the time or the manner of the gift."[23] However, significantly in this case it did not work, perhaps because, as Linda Levy Peck has argued, these traditional, customary models were in decline: "Time and manner, which served to contextualise transactions and distinguish between gifts and bribes, had increasingly been renounced in contemporary prescriptive literature and now were disregarded in political action."[24]

We therefore have to turn to Bacon's third strategy: his assertion that the transactions had involved his servants, as he acknowledged in answer that charge that he had "given way to great Exactions by his Servants, both in respect of Private Seals, and otherwise for sealing of Injunctions," that it was "a great Fault of Neglect in me that I looked no better to my Servants." For example, money is given by Holman "to my Servant Hatcher; with that certainly I was never made privy"; his servant Hunt received £200 from Smithwick, and only "after I had understood the Nature of it, I ordered him to repay it, and to defaulk it of his Accompt."[25]

At one level, the inability of the lord chancellor to control what his servants accepted might be seen, as J. H. Baker has pointed out, as a fundamental practical flaw in the composition of the court of Chancery. All the responsibility for the thousands of cases that passed through Chancery rested ultimately on the shoulders of the lord chancellor. Indeed, in a letter to the House of Lords, Bacon asked, "If there come any more Petitions of like Nature [i.e., against him], that your Lordships would be pleased not to take any Prejudice or Apprehension of any Number or Muster of them, especially against a Judge that makes Two Thousand Decrees and Orders in a Year (not to speak of the Courses that have been taken for hunting out Complaints against me); but that I may answer them, according to the Rules of Justice, severally and respectively."[26] Lower down the scale, also, Chancery seemed to be an example in extremis of a system that was quickly disintegrating: the fees providing the income of most offices had remained fixed since the times of Henry VIII.[27] Chancery officials were worse off, however: unsalaried, they relied on payment in cash or in kind from the litigants whose cases they facilitated. Thus, writes Baker, "for [the] subordinates [of a lord chancellor] gifts were almost respectable. Gold or silver could open paths through the Chancery morass, and by long usage many 'presents' became fees which could be demanded as of right with an untroubled conscience."[28]

There is, however, an important difference between this accepted state of affairs and the particular circumstances of Bacon's case. As John Chamberlain writes, in the course of their investigation the Lords "proceed very orderly and warilie and *will not admit any accusation of what was geven to his servants or frends,* but what came directly to his owne handes, and that proved by oath."[29] According to this, the Lords perceived the problem of the dispersed nature of the gift economy and wanted to hold Bacon responsible only for what was given to him directly. But it is at this moment that Bacon's defense breaks down, because such a clear distinction was for Bacon, as his confession demonstrates, an impossibility. The accusations of personal bribery attached themselves so readily to Bacon because the relationships he enjoyed with his servants and subordinates were perceived to be too confused — it is not clear, as it were, where the master ends, and the servants begin. Instead of forming the glue of the social structure, gift-giving to Bacon is going astray: rather than cementing the relationships and understanding between the lord chancellor and his suitors, the gifts are lining the pockets of his "Ganimeds and favourites," not his Chancery subordinates, but his household servants.

It is precisely the domestic dangers of the judge's life which are highlighted in the 1631 pamphlet entitled *The iust Lawyer His Conscionable Complaint against Auricular or private Informing and soliciting of Iudges.* The anonymous author (whom I shall call the Just Lawyer) was "pathetically moved," according to his publisher George Purstowe, "with the corrupt courses used, and the excessive *bribery* affected in those dayes by this brethren learned in the *Lawes,* especially the more eminent sort; and the continuall condescending or proclivity of the *Iudges,* not onely to their uniust *motions,* but to the private and undue *solicitations* of their owne *Menials,* besides their *Friends* & *Favourites* at large; and their partiall preferring or hearing of some *Pleaders* before others at the *Barre of Iustice.*"[30]

Although a judge's "favorites at large" (defined as being "neither of counsell nor houshold" [B2r]) and his counselors are dangerous, the "most pernicious" is the "meniall" (B2v) — the low-ranking servant whose characteristic is that he is a domestic, household servant:[31]

> This *Meniall* or *Familiar,* if he may finde the *grace* to be in the eye and stand at the elbow of his *Master* (especially in the *closet*) then shall hee not want his *Suitors,* and then also will he take the courage to board his *Master,* not onely in lawfull *Petitions,* but also in *Causes* meerely *judiciall;* and by reason that hee is neere at hand to take hold of every advantage, and may best watch both the time, the place, and good cheere of his *Lord,* and the absence of the *adversary* and of his friends, hee will make his gaine thereby both in jeast and earnest, though now and then he doe but *fumum vendere,* sell smoke, and pay *Alchyme* for good and currant money. (B2v–B3r)

The menial's power lies in his constant and intimate access to his master, "especially in the closet," the supposedly solitary "private" space that in fact constituted the locus of secret political transactions between men. The judge's "good quiet and repose" is "interrupted by often obtunding [rendering obtuse] that in his privie *Closet,* which he might dispatch with once hearing in open *Court*" (B4r–v). The Just Lawyer goes on to suggest that the closet effectively confuses the discrete identities of the master and menial, so that the menial starts to speak *for* his master:[32]

> For of these, some will sooner use (or abuse) the name of their *Master* (as if were by way of a message to others, where it may prevaile) than take the paines to speake unto himselfe, lest they discover a suspition that they be hired for money: By these and such other meanes the innocent *Iudge,* like to *Actæon,* becommeth *præda canibus,* devoured of his owne dogges, who care not what dishonorable *staine* they cast upon him (whom they are most bounden to honour) so as they may reape the *harvest* of their most greedy and ravenous *lucre.* (B3r)

Interestingly, in *The Wisedome of the Ancients* Bacon explains the story of Actaeon as symbolizing the dangers faced by a master from his servants, although he sees the master's vulnerability as lying in his intimacy with the prince:

> For those that are neare about Princes, and come to the knowledge of more secretes then they would haue them, doe certainly incurre great hatred. And therefore (suspecting that they are shot at, & opportunities watcht for their ouerthrow) doe lead their liues like Stagges, fearefull and full of suspition. And it happens oftentimes that their Seruants, and those of their houshould (to insinuate into the Princes fauor) doe accuse them to their destruction: for against whomsoeuer the *Princes* displeasure is knowne, looke how many seruants that man hath, and you shall find them for the most part so many traytours vnto him, that his end may proue to bee like *Actaeons.*[33]

The specific danger with bribery comes, according to the Just Lawyer, because the menials do not possess the judge's ability to discern right from wrong; as a result, they accept bribes from both parties in a particular case: "For as those men commonly cannot judge of the state of a cause in controversie; so neither doe they greatly care whether that part which they favour, be right or wrong; But doe onely fasten their *eye* upon that *money,* which may be coyned out of it. . . . And in this part, some of them be so miraculous *Machiavellians* that they be able to expresse *two* sundry liquors out of one same vessell, making their owne profit by both the parties to one same suit and controversie" (B3r).

Another image emerges in contemporary literature on the bribable judge: that of sexual uncleanness. In his 1613 *Fovre Treatises, tending to disswade all Christians from foure no lesse hainous then common sinnes; namely, the abuses of Swearing, Drunkennesse, Whoredome, and Bribery,* John Downame discusses the sin, particularly heinous in a judge, of taking bribes:

> It cannot be but great preiudice to the vprightnesse of a Iudge, and a shrewd presumption of his corruption, when as he receiueth gifts of those who haue suites depending before him; for as a wife or maide would incurre the danger of iust suspition, of hauing an vncleane heart, who being solicited by a fornicator to commit whoredome, should receiue his gifts, although she should deny his suite: for howsoeuer in word she refuse his wicked motion, yet indeed she receiued pledges of his loue: so likewise are such Iudges not without cause to bee suspected, who receiue gifts of those who labour to peruert iudgement; for howsoeuer in outward shew, they make profession of integritie, yet in action they receiue the pawnes of vnrighteousnesse, which will cawse them to preiudice the cause, and to halt in the administration of iustice, and to respect the cause of one, more then of another, and the cause for the persons sake.[34]

The judge who accepts gifts is like the wife or unmarried woman who accepts gifts from a suitor, gifts which (whatever they may say) are the "pawnes of vnrighteousnesse." Downame's analogy is echoed by the Just Lawyer: "For as it is hardly credible, that any *Castle* which is continually battered should not be taken at the *length,* or that any *Woman* which admitteth all *Wooers,* should not apply to some *one:* So can this man never excuse himselfe to the worldward" (Cr–v).

The Just Lawyer concludes: " let every good and true *Friend, Favourite* and *Follower* of the *Iudge . . .* hold it for meere *Sacriledge* and prophanation of *Iustice,* once to attempt him in the part of his *jurisdiction,* which ought to be unto him a most chaste and undefiled *Virgin*" (C2r).[35]

These uses of the analogy of the judge and/or his jurisdiction as a virgin woman whose chastity is called into question simply by the acceptance of gifts both precede and follow Bacon's fall in 1621. It is intriguing, then, that Bacon himself plays on this image in his attempts to win royal favor at the time he is under attack. In a clean, but incomplete draft entitled "Memoranda of what the Lord Chancellor intended to deliver to the King, April 16, 1621, upon his first access to his majesty after his troubles," Bacon declares in the preamble that he will "deal ingenuously with your Majesty, without seeking fig-leaves or subterfuges,"[36] a striking image to which he returned compulsively over the following days.[37] A related image appears in his "final" letter to the king, dated 21 April 1621: "This is the last suit I shall make to your Majesty in this business, prostrating myself at your mercy-seat, after fifteen years' service, wherein I have served your Majesty in my poor endeavours with an entire heart, and as I presumed to say unto your Majesty, am still a virgin for matters that concern your person or crown; and now only craving that after eight steps of honour [his career promotions] I be not precipitated altogether."[38]

But he was wrong when, writing to his patron Buckingham, he declared, "I know I have clean hands and a clean heart; and I hope a clean house for friends or servants."[39] It was precisely the unclean state of his house, his domestic housekeeping, which was about to come under scrutiny.

Bacon clearly recognized his Achilles' heel. He publicly pinned the blame for his downfall on his servants, as Moses Pitt relates: "Much at the time he was put out of the Chancellorship, he happen'd to come into his Hall where his Gentlemen were at Dinner. As soon as they see my Lord, they all rose up, but his Lordship calls to them to sit still, For, saith he, your Rise has been my Fall."[40] The financial malpractice of Bacon's servants remained widely rumored. John Aubrey recalled how "the East Indian merchants presented his lordship with a cabinet of jewels, which his page, Mr. Cockaine, received, and deceived his lord." The profits were such that "three of his lordship's servants kept their coaches, and some kept racehorses."[41] One of his loyal servants, Thomas Bushell, alleged later that some of Bacon's servants, "insinuating caterpillars," as he called them, "ministered those hellish pills of bribery, gilded them over, not only at first with a show of gratuity, or in the love of courtesy, but waited the opportunity of his necessity."[42]

But no matter how widely acknowledged the guilt of the servants, that guilt remains, ultimately, the responsibility of the master. As the Just Lawyer declares, it is up to the judge himself to change the situation:

> The *Remedy* of all which evils is . . . in the very hand and power of the *Iudge* himself: For if he be willing to maintaine the authority and countenance of his *call*, he may *alto vultu,* with a lofty looke take it unkindly at the hands of his better, Equall or inferiour Friends; blaming them with the touch of his credit for their so advised tampering with him in matter of his *judiciall* and sworne *Dutie.* Hee may also with one word of his mouth command his owne *Curres* to couch and to cease their *barking:* He may likewise send the *Suitor* to the Court, and his *Counsellor* to the *Barre,* and consequently rid himselfe and his house of all this unquiet *kennell,* and thereby redeeme many a good houre. (B4v–Cr)

Bearing in mind these images — the household menials improperly admitted to places of intimacy, the bribable judge as the unchaste woman — it is striking to see how anxieties about Bacon's alleged sodomy are figured as anxieties about admittance into his bedchamber, a place of intimate influence and of course of potential unchastity. D'Ewes gossips about Bacon's "keeping still one Godrick, a very effeminate faced youth, to be his catamite and bedfellow" and his being unable to "forbear his old custom of making his servants his bedfellows, so to avoid the scandal that was raised of him."[43] A contemporary satirical verse alludes to the manner in which Bacon's servant Thomas Bushell had obtained his much marveled-at many-buttoned cloak: "His lord's posteriors makes the buttons that he wears": Bacon shits gold for Bushell, or possibly it is Bacon's arse which is Bushell's route to success.[44] In 1655 a bookseller's assistant overheard a conversation between two customers, one of whom had been in his youth to see Lord Chancellor Bacon at this Hertfordshire estate, Gorhambury. While Bacon was temporarily absent from the room, he related,

> There came into the Study, one of his Lordship's Gentlemen, and opens my Lord's Chest of Drawers wherein his Money was, and takes it out in Handfuls and fills both his Pockets, and goes away without saying one word to me; he was no sooner gone, but comes a Second Gentleman, opens the same Drawers, fills both his Pockets with Money, and goes away as the former did, without speaking a word to me; at which I was surpris'd, and much concern'd, and was resolv'd to Acquaint my Lord with it. As soon as my Lord return'd into his Study, I told him, my Lord, here was a very odd passage happen'd, since your Lordship went to Ease your self; upon which he Ask'd me what it was, I told the passage as here related. He shook his Head; and all that he said was, Sir, I cannot help myself.

The customer opined that "my Lord had a Fault, whatever it was he could not tell" — the standard early modern formulation for referring obliquely to sodomy, the crime inter Christianos non nominandum.

So why then, if the bribery charges against Bacon, and indeed his defense, played so much on his relations with his male servants, was Bacon not prosecuted for buggery? Or if indeed he was innocent of the imputation, why did he not pursue a suit for slander? There are of course many eminently practical reasons why neither course was pursued — who would bring the case against Bacon? how would it be proven, given that the other men involved would also risk the death penalty if they gave evidence? However, I shall suggest in closing that there are, as it were, "figurative" reasons why such charges of buggery slipped through early modern English legal practice.

The sixteenth century witnessed a significant upturn in what we might call "sexual defamation" or "sexual slander" cases, and the rich records have been well investigated by, among others, Christopher Haigh, J. A. Sharpe, Martin

Ingram, and Laura Gowing.[45] Most of these were concerned with allegations of cuckoldry, whoredom, pimping, bastardy, and adultery — all crimes under the jurisdiction of the ecclesiastical courts. Sodomy or buggery, however, was among the first offenses to be reassigned as a secular offense in the 1534 parliament. As J. H. Baker and R. H. Helmholz have shown, there was, in post-Reformation slander law, very little controversy on which court had jurisdiction over which defamation. Helmholz writes: "The courts of the Church heard causes involving the imputation of 'spiritual' crimes like simony, sorcery or adultery, but not causes involving imputations of temporal crimes, which they had heard in medieval practice. The common law courts dealt with these, under the rubric of the action on the case for words. The sensible principle underlying this sharing was that only where the ecclesiastical courts had jurisdiction over the principal matter should they also hear cases involving the accessory matter, that is the slanderous imputation."[46] This might in itself explain why there appear to have been no slander cases concerning sodomy: quite simply, the courts to which people were accustomed to turn for slanders of their personal morality or sexuality had no jurisdiction over that offense.

As a result, early modern English legal commentaries do not have a place for sodomy slander. There is no mention of sodomy or buggery in connection with defamation in John Godolphin's *Repertorium Canonicum* (1678),[47] and John March's *Actions for Slaunder* (1647) discusses only the "Buggering of a Mare," which had excited legal interest in determining the status of local dialect in a slander (apparently, "in Yorkshire strayning of a Mare, is all one with Buggering of a Mare.")[48] The only legal manual I have read that does discuss the slander of sodomy is W. Sheppard's *Action upon the Case for Slander. Or A Methodical Collection under certain Heads, of Thousand of Cases* (1662), in which the insults "sodomite" and "buggerer' " are lined up alongside other accusations of felonies: "Hee is a Traitor, a Murtherer, a Thief, a Robber, a Church-robber, a Sacrileger, a House-robber, a Buggerer, a Sodomite, or the like." However, the point Sheppard is making is simply that these crimes are felonies: the only cross-references are to the statutes which make buggery a felony, and to Coke's commentaries, and there is no suggestion that such slanders have ever been prosecuted.[49]

Laura Gowing is, to date, the only social historian who has explored in print the lack of a tradition of sodomy slander. Noting that "there was much established mythology and satire around sodomy" but that "none of this found an echo in the language of insult reported to the church court," she follows Alan Bray in asserting that "Renaissance thought pictured sodomy through distant metaphors, not the realm of daily life; and it was daily life with which . . . defamers were most concerned."[50] Against this, it should be noted that this treatment of sodomy appears to be local to England: as Peter Burke has shown, in societies as different as medieval Iceland and Renaissance Rome sodomy slander was widespread (as indeed it is in modern Spain and Turkey).[51] I suggest therefore that we need to examine how sodomy was construed specifically in early modern England.

Although Gowing is right in noting that most defamation "focused around the street, market, and the household," sodomy is not only a matter of "distant metaphors." Instead, I would argue, its place can be understood only through an appreciation of the different ways in which men and women were perceived in relation to the domestic household. J. A. Sharpe notes: "It is striking that males were more likely than females to be described [in slander cases] as perjurers, liars, or . . . usurers. . . . It is difficult not to see the wider types of defamation against which men litigated as a consequence of their more varied involvement in the affairs of the world."[52] Gowing concurs: "Sexual insult belonged to a culture that perceived women's virtue, honour, and reputation through their sexuality, men's through a much wider range of values."[53]

One way in which this difference played out was spatially: a woman's alleged infidelity by necessity included the crossing of household boundaries — either the woman's entering another man's house, or the male lover's entering the house of the woman's husband. A man's sodomy, by contrast, was often essentially a household crime, taking place within the walls of his house.[54] And this difference between the illicit sexual activities of women and men was necessarily replicated in the varying forms of sexual insult. Sexual insult against heterosexual relations is proffered in public, but insult about sodomy is by its very nature a domestic matter, and thus not amenable either to prosecution or to defense by prosecution of the slanderer. Therefore, Bacon is attacked privately — domestically — as a corrupt husband (in the widest sense) and publicly as a corrupt judge. This explains why the scurrilous note recorded by Simonds D'Ewes had to be "cast . . . downe in some part of Yorkhowse in the strand wheere Viscount St. Alban yet lay" — placed very precisely *within* Bacon's residence York House, rather than in the street in the Strand.[55]

Bacon's bribery and buggery figure in contemporary reports in the same manner: as a failure properly to manage his male servants. Through this figure, Bacon's "buggery" is generated, which in turn "explains" his susceptibility to bribery — thus his buggery is both an effect of and an explanation for his failings as lord chancellor. We might say that the buggery charge is a way of discussing his professional legal conduct by figuring it in domestic terms; conversely, it could be argued that his professional fall depends on pre-existing doubts about his domestic ménage. Ultimately, as this enduring sodomy slander bears witness, the two areas of his life were — and will always remain — inexorably linked.

Notes

1. For the statute see *Anno .XXV. Henrici VIII.actis made in the session of this present parliament holden vppon prorogation at Westmynster, the .XV. Januarye, in the XXV. yere of the reigne of our moste dradde soueraygne lorde kynge Henry the .VIII. and there contynewed and kepte tylle the XXX. daye of Marche than nexte ensuinge* (London: Thomas Berthelet, 1534), B.i.v–B.ii.r.

2. See Alan Bray, *Homosexuality in Renaissance England,* 2nd ed. (London: Gay Men's Press, 1988), 38–49.

3. For the indictment, see Edward Coke, *A Booke of Entries* (London: Societie of Stationers, 1614), Ooo.iij.v–Ooo.iiij.r; see also the indictments against the earl of Castlehaven: *Cobbett's Complete Collection of State Trials and proceedings for high treason and other crimes and misdemeanours from the earliest period to the present time,* vol. 3 (London: T. C. Hansard, 1809), col. 402.

4. Leslie J. Moran, *The Homosexual(ity) of Law* (London: Routledge, 1996), 33–35.

5. Michel Foucault, *The History of Sexuality,* vol. 1, *An Introduction,* trans. Robert Hurley (London: Allen Lane, 1976), 101.

6. Ed Cohen, "Legislating the Norm: From Sodomy to Gross Indecency," in *Displacing Homophobia: Gay Male Perspectives in Literature and Culture,* ed. Ronald R. Butters, John M. Clum, and Michael Moon (Durham, N.C.: Duke University Press, 1989), 173.

7. See Bray, *Homosexuality in Renaissance England;* Bruce R. Smith, *Homosexual Desire in Shakespeare's England: A Cultural Poetics* (Chicago, Ill.: University of Chicago Press, 1991), 41–53; Ed Cohen, *Talk on the Wilde Side: Toward a Genealogy of a Discourse on Male Homosexuality* (New York: Routledge, 1993), 103–25; Alan Stewart, 'The Bounds of Sodomy: Textual Relations in Early Modern England,' unpublished Ph.D. dissertation, University of London, 1993, chap. 4.

8. Edward Coke, *The Third Part of the Institutes of the Laws of England: concerning High Treason, and other Pleas of the Crown, and Criminall Causes* (London: W. Lee and D. Pakeman, 1644), 59; Coke, *The Twelfth Part of the Reports* (London: Henry Twyford and Thomas Dring, 1656), 37.

9. "Et ceo poet estre sans penetration; Car le use del corps despend le sede in tiel cases, fait ceo Buggery deins ceo Stat. sans penetration: Et issint fuit tenus in le case le Sign'A. come ieo oye." Michael Dalton, *The Countrey Justice,* 6th ed. (London: Richard Best, 1643), 337.

10. The most accessible account of the Castlehaven trial is in *Cobbett's State Trials,* vol. 3, cols. 402–26. All previous critical work on the trial has now been superseded by Cynthia B. Herrup, *A House in Gross Disarray: Sex, Law and the Second Earl of Castlehaven* (Oxford: Oxford University Press, 1999).

11. For accounts of the complex impeachment, see Robert Zaller, *The Parliament of 1621: A Study in Constitutional Conflict* (Berkeley: University of California Press, 1971); Joel J. Epstein, *Francis Bacon: A Political Biography* (Athens: Ohio University Press, 1977), 133–57; John T. Noonan, Jr., "Angelo," in *Bribes: The Intellectual History of a Moral Idea* (London: Macmillan, 1984), 334–65, 751–58nn; Jardine and Stewart, *Hostage to Fortune,* 444–69.

12. Samuel Albyn to [?John Rawson], 28 March 1621. British Library, London [hereafter BL], Harley MS 383 folios 13–14, quoted in David Colclough, "Freedom of Speech

and the Law in Early Modern England," paper delivered at *Renaissance Law and Literature,* Wolfson College, Oxford, July 1998. I am grateful to Dr Colclough for permission to quote from his paper.

13. John Chamberlain to Sir Dudley Carleton, 23 June 1621, London. Public Record Office, State Papers [hereafter PRO SP], 14/121, art. 121, printed in *The Letters of John Chamberlain,* 2 vols., ed. Norman Egbert McClure (Philadelphia Pa.: American Philosophical Society, 1939), 2: 383–86 at 385.

14. "Vpon Sr F Ba." Folger Shakespeare Library, Washington, D.C., MS 5.a.345, p. 25. Also in the Bodleian Library, Oxford [hereafter Bodl.], Douce MS 5, folio 16a. See Arthur Marotti, *Manuscript, Print, and the English Renaissance Lyric* (Ithaca, N.Y.: Cornell University Press, 1995), 105, n.66.

15. BL, Harley MS 646, folios 58b–59b at 59b, printed (with some errors) as *Extracts from the ms. Journal of Sir Simonds D'Ewes, with several letters to and from Sir Simonds and his friends* (London: J. Nichols, 1783), 25–26 at 26. Marotti does not record this variation.

16. Mario DiGangi, *The Homoerotics of Early Modern Drama* (Cambridge: Cambridge University Press, 1997), 73–74.

17. Jonathan Goldberg, *Sodometries: Renaissance Texts, Modern Sexualities* (Stanford, Calif.: Stanford University Press), 19. In fact, the knowledge that Bacon was a man who had intimate relations with other men and whose professional opinion could be swayed by gifts had been exploited long before March 1621. During a sermon at St. Paul's in May 1619, one Isaac Singleton, who had been the loser in a Chancery decision, "declaimed bitterly against his [Bacon's] court, and glanced (they say) somewhat scandalously at him and his catamites as he called them." Chamberlain to Carleton, 5 June 1619. Chamberlain, *Letters,* 2: 243. In *Calendar of State Papers, Domestic Series, of the Reign of James I,* ed. Mary Anne Everett Green (London: Longman, 1858), the editor reads "Latinities" for "catamites."

18. John Aubrey, *Brief Lives,* ed. Oliver Lawson Dick, 3rd ed. (London: Secker and Warburg, 1958), 11. For information on the format of the manuscript, I am grateful to Dr. Kate Bennett.

19. BL, Harley MS 646, folios 58b–59b, printed in D'Ewes, *Extracts,* 25–26.

20. This discussion is taken from Jardine and Stewart, *Hostage to Fortune,* 462.

21. Lambeth Palace Library, London [hereafter LPL], MS 936, art. 146; Bacon, *Letters and Life,* 7 vols., ed. James Spedding (London: Longmans, 1861–1974) [hereafter *LL*], 7: 235–36.

22. Joel Hurstfield, *Freedom, Corruption and Government in Elizabethan England* (London: Jonathan Cape, 1973), 145–47 at 146.

23. For Bacon's confession, see *Journal of the House of Lords* 3: 98–101; *LL,* 7: 252–62.

24. Linda Levy Peck, *Court Patronage and Corruption in Early Stuart England* (Boston: Unwin Hyman, 1990), 187.

25. *Journal of the House of Lords* 3: 98–101; *LL* 7: 252–62.

26. Bacon to the Lords, 19 March 1620/21, PRO SP 14/120, art. 28; *Journal of the House of Lords* 3: 54; *LL,* 7: 216.

27. Peck, *Court Patronage and Corruption,* 4.

28. J. H. Baker, *An Introduction to English Legal History,* 3rd ed. (London: Butterworths, 1990), 112–34 at 128–29.

29. Chamberlain to Carleton, 24 March, 1621, PRO SP, 14/120, art. 38; Chamberlain, *Letters,* 2: 355. My emphasis.

30. *The iust Lawyer His Conscionable Complaint against Auricular or private Informing and soliciting of Iudges. By their Menialls, Friends and Favourites* (London: George Purstowe, 1631), A2r–v. My attention was drawn to this work by Peck, *Court Patronage and Corruption,* 199.

31. *OED,* s.v. "menial," 9: 605.

32. For this notion of the closet, see Stewart, "The Early Modern Closet Discovered," *Representations* 50 (1995), 96–100.

33. Francis Bacon, *The Wisedome of the Ancients,* trans. Arthur Gorges (London: John Bill, 1619), C2v–C3r. The image of Actaeon being devoured by his own dogs also echoes Christopher Marlowe's play *Edward II,* where the "menial" Piers Gaveston fantasizes about how he will sway "the pliant king" to his own ends. Christopher Marlowe, *The troublesome raigne and lamentable death of Edward the second, King of England* (London, 1594).

34. John Downame, *Foure Treatises, tending to disswade all Christians from foure no lesse hainous then common sinnes; namely, the abuses of Swearing, Drunkennesse, Whoredome, and Bribery* (London: Michaell Baker, 1613), Gg 2v.

35. Early on in the parliamentary debate on the case, Coke pointed out that the testimony of those who had given bribes to Bacon had to be admitted. A participant in the crime was "often taken for two good witnesses. And therefore we have a rule that if an offense be committed in a brothel-house, the testimony of brothels shall be admitted." Wallace Notestein, Frances Helen Relf, and Hartley Simpson, eds., *Commons' Debates, 1621,* 4 vols. (New Haven, Conn: Yale University Press, 1933), 2: 241–42, 4: 168, discussed in Noonan, *Bribes,* 347.

36. LPL, MS 936, folio 26; *LL* 7: 237–38.

37. In a letter to James dated 20 April 1621, Bacon promised, "I shall without fig-leaves or disguise excuse what I can excuse, extenuate what I can extenuate, and ingenuously confess what I can neither clear nor extenuate." Bacon to James, 20 April 1621; *Letters and Remains of the Lord Chancellor Bacon,* ed. Robert Stephens (London: W. Bowyer, 1734), 138; *LL* 7: 240. His letter to the House of Lords, dated 22 April 1621, similarly tells all "without Fig-leaves," *Journal of the House of Lords* 3: 84–85; *LL* 7: 242–45 at 243.

38. Bacon to James, 21 April 1621. Bodl., MS Tanner 73 (1), folio 3; *LL* 7: 240–42 at 241–42.

39. Bacon to Buckingham, 14 March 1620/21. LPL, MS 936, art. 220; *LL* 7: 213.

40. [Moses Pitt], *The Cry of the Oppressed* (London: Moses Pitt, 1691), (a4)v.

41. Aubrey, *Brief Lives,* 10.

42. Thomas Bushell, *First Part of Youths Errors* (London, 1628), 16v–18v.

43. BL, Harley MS 646, folios 58b–59b; D'Ewes, *Extracts,* 25–26.

44. BL, Harley MS 7009, folios. 324a–325b.

45. See C. A. Haigh, "Slander and the Church Courts in the Sixteenth Century," *Transactions of the Lancashire and Cheshire Antiquarian Society* 88 (1975), 1–13;

J. A. Sharpe, *Defamation and Sexual Slander in Early Modern England: The Church Courts at York* (York: University of York [Borthwick Papers, no. 58], 1980); Martin Ingram, *Church Courts, Sex and Marriage in England, 1570–1640* (Cambridge: Cambridge University Press, 1987); Peter Christie, *Of Chirche-Reves, and of Testamentes: The Church, Sex and Slander in Elizabethan North Devon* ([Barnstable?]: Devon Family History Society, 1994); Laura Gowing, *Domestic Dangers: Women, Words, and Sex in Early Modern London* (Oxford: Clarendon Press, 1996).

46. R. C. Helmholz, *Roman Canon Law in Reformation England* (Cambridge: Cambridge University Press, 1990), 56–69 at 56; J. H. Baker, introduction to his edition of *The Reports of Sir John Spelman*, vol. 2 (London: Selden Society [vol. 94], 1978), 236–48, esp. 238–39.

47. John Godolphin, *Repertorium Canonicum; or An Abridgment of the Ecclesiastical Lawes of this Realm, Consistent with the Temporal* (London: Christopher Wilkinson, 1678), 514–27.

48. Jo[hn] March, *Actions for Slaunder, or, A Methodicall Collection under certain Grounds and Heads, of what words are actionable in the Law, and what not?* (London: M. Walbank and R. Best, 1647), Cr–v.

49. W. Sheppard, *Action upon the Case for Slander. Or A Methodical Collection under certain Heads, of Thousand of Cases* (London: Ch. Adams, J. Starkey and T. Basset, 1662), Jr, Mv. I am grateful to Lorna Hutson for this reference.

50. Gowing, *Domestic Dangers,* 65, citing Bray, *Homosexuality in Renaissance England,* chaps. 1–2.

51. Peter Burke, "The Art of Insult in Early Modern Italy," *Culture and History* 2 (1987), 68–79, esp. 70, 77.

52. Sharpe, *Defamation and Sexual Slander,* 28–29.

53. Gowing, *Domestic Dangers,* 2.

54. Compare the gender-specific attacks on nuns and monks in Reformation propaganda, discussed in Stewart, *Close Readers: Humanism and Sodomy in Early Modern England* (Princeton, N.J.: Princeton University Press, 1997), chap. 2.

55. This aspect of sodomy slander in the Jacobean period is being fascinatingly developed by James Knowles (Stirling). I am grateful to him for allowing me to read his unpublished paper, " 'To Scorge the Arse | Jove's Marrow so Had Wasted': Scurrility and the Subversion of Sodomy."

6

Ben Jonson and the Law of Contract

LUKE WILSON

My topic is the relation between Ben Jonson's work and the legal developments which transformed the English common law of contract in the sixteenth and seventeenth centuries. I refer particularly, of course, to the rise of the action of assumpsit, whose dominance was finally secured in the ruling in Slade's case (1597–1602), and out of which modern contract doctrine developed. Assumpsit (literally, *he promised*) takes its name from the wording of an action under which more and more contractual disputes came to be tried during the early modern period of English legal history.

As readers of Renaissance drama will at once recognize, the most obvious point of connection to Jonson is the celebrated contractual Induction to *Bartholomew Fair*. In an influential essay published in 1982, Don Wayne noted that the ruling in Slade's case represents a crucial step in what Henry Sumner Maine called the transition from a status to a contract society; and he argued that, similarly, Jonson's proposal in *Bartholomew Fair* of a contract stipulating what his audience was to get in exchange for its money, and laying out the limits and conditions of its right of censure, reflected "an unmistakable tension between, on the one hand, the traditional moral doctrine of social obligation according to status, and, on the other, the more modern principles of rational self-interest and voluntary contractual obligation."[1] Wayne continues:

First published in *Cardozo Studies in Law & Literature* 5, no. 2 (1993).

> The legalistic device of the "Articles of Agreement" reflects the weakening in the early seventeenth century of a reliable order of shared assumptions, embodied in popular tradition, religious ritual, and dogma, upon which to base moral and aesthetic judgment in the public playhouse. The feigned necessity of a contract mediating the relationship between independent parties to a literary or theatrical communication focuses, at the plane of the aesthetic, what is becoming a fundamental problem in all aspects of social life.[2]

Where social relations had once been understood as depending on who you were (your status), they were increasingly determined by what you did, that is, by the legal relationships you voluntarily entered into. As a general proposition this seems to me essentially correct. It is true that Maine's notion of a fundamental shift from status to contract has been challenged, and the suddenness of the shift designated by Slade's case can easily be exaggerated. It nevertheless seems beyond dispute that the meaning of contractual relations was a matter of particular concern in the last decade of the sixteenth century and the first decades of the next. Contractualism and contract-related terms like *assumpsit* and *consideration* appear with striking frequency in the nontechnical literature of the period; and this sense that new kinds of wrongs might in theory be actionable under assumpsit corresponded with legal fact, because the triumph of that action did in fact entail, as A. W. B. Simpson puts it, "the extension of promissory liability into areas previously outside the scope of the common law" — promises to marry, for example, or to build houses or return lost dogs — which fell outside debt because they did not involve fixed sums.[3] It was this extension of liability that necessitated the rise of the doctrine of consideration as a means of distinguishing actionable from inactionable agreements; and with this formalization modern contract doctrine began to take shape.[4] Clearly, then, the contractual Induction to *Bartholomew Fair* reflects awareness of this extension; and it is even conceivable, though I think unlikely, that assumpsit could have been brought to cover a situation where someone felt he had not gotten the theatrical entertainment for which he had bargained.[5]

An increased awareness of contractualism in legal and political relations may also be observed in the contemporary notoriety of what from the start was known as the Great Contract of 1610, an unsuccessful proposal, offered by the lord high treasurer, Robert Cecil, earl of Salisbury to the House of Commons, to trade certain royal prerogatives for set amounts of support and supply. English parliaments had negotiated with monarchs for a long time; but the agreements sought after had not before been conceived or spoken of as contractual.

Jonson, as it happens, knew several men involved in the debates surround-

ing the Great Contract, among them Salisbury himself, the contract's archi-
tect, to whom he had addressed two epigrams several years earlier as an
expression of thanks for his support during the legal difficulties arising out of
Eastward Ho, The Isle of Dogs, and *Sejanus.*[6] Jonson also knew Thomas
Egerton, Lord Ellesmere, who acted as a liaison between the Lords and the
Commons during the 1610 debates; Robert Cotton, who goes on record as
supporting the contract; and John Hoskins, who spoke in support of parliamentary rights against royal prerogatives.[7] Although this range of connections
does not of course point us toward Jonson's own attitude toward the Great
Contract, about which in any case he may not have know much, it does
represent support for an argument I won't make here, that the contractualism
of *Bartholomew Fair* ought to be examined in light of the Great Contract. In
the present context it serves the more general function of indicating that in his
relationships with these men, and later, around the time of *Bartholomew Fair*
(1614), with the members — most of them lawyers — of the Mermaid Club,
Jonson was almost certainly exposed to a good deal of legal discussion during
this crucial period in the history of the law of contract.[8]

My present objectives are more limited. I will argue here that the tactical
uses to which Jonson puts contractual relationships are similar to some of the
devices that arise in the complexities of contract law and appear to derive from
similar conceptual constraints and opportunities. I will ask what authorial
strategies and tactical maneuvers, what difficulties, advantages, and aesthetic
effects, the deployment of these structures enables in Jonson's poetic and dramatic enterprises. The triumph of assumpsit over its rival form of action, the
action of debt, involved the redeployment in a new social context of conceptualizations of the temporality of intentional action; the move from the essentially atemporal action of debt to the complex temporality of assumpsit is
both reflected in and paralleled by Jonson's own work. Both may be understood as gestures toward a reorientation of human interiority in terms of
intentional action. I am interested particularly, therefore, in the temporal
shape of what are called executory contracts (contracts whose completion is
deferred), though what I have to say also should have some bearing on the
temporality which seems to be essential to the practice of gift-exchange, as
Bourdieu's critique of Lévi-Strauss's critique of Marcel Mauss's account of the
gift suggests.[9] These forms of temporality are related, I think, to the represented and representational temporality of the theater and of theatrical performance, spectatorship and composition; but they are present even where, as in
the poetry, Jonson seems determined to exclude them.

What I am concerned with, then, is how Jonson uses contractual constructions of human relationships to open narrative spaces in which he can pursue a

range of tactical advantages and aesthetic effects. In referring to tactics I mean to evoke de Certeau's distinction between tactic and strategy. Tactics are the necessary recourse of those who do not own property and who, thus forced to operate in alien territory, have no place to secure their winnings. The tactician lacks the insulation from time that is the privilege of the strategist, but he is thus also in a position to put time to imaginative uses. A successful tactic depends on seizing the right moment in time (*kairos*) and effecting changes by means of a combination of memory and anticipation. As de Certeau puts it, "A certain duration is thus introduced into the relationship of forces and changes it. *Métis* [cunning] in fact counts on an accumulated time, which is in its favor, to overcome a hostile composition of place."[10] For Jonson, particularly, the public theater was such a place; and it is through his manipulation of temporal relationships in the theater that he attempts to make his way in this alien territory. Jonson's relation to the theater, one might say, was simultaneously tactical and strategic: to the extent that he was able to impose his own conditions of reception and dramaturgic practice, he maintained the position of the strategist; but this position was always in doubt, owing to the form of the theater itself, which required intervention at the tactical level.[11]

The "Epistle to Mr Arthur Squib"

The same thing is true of Jonson's poetic engagements, and that's where I begin, by considering some of the ways Jonson conceives debt, obligation, and contractual relations in social and patronage relationships in his poems. Stanley Fish has argued persuasively for the importance to Jonson's poetic practice of a "community of the same" at once established and presupposed in the epigrams Jonson wrote for those friends and patrons he considered his moral and intellectual equals.[12] These poems tend to concern themselves with the act of praise in which they are engaged, and often seem in danger of canceling themselves out because they suggest that the merit in question cannot be stated but can only be performed or pointed toward. It is the fact of their being read and understood by their recipient that affirms an affinity (in fact an identity) between writer and addressee. No praise is possible because there is no difference between the two; each knows his own worth in his friend's. Thus, says Fish, the "state [these poems] would celebrate is one of epistemological immediacy and ontological self-sufficiency."[13]

In the closed economy of this scheme, "proof" is not a matter of corroboration by reference to an objective standard, but rather the mutual examination by which poem and reader test one another and confirm one another's inclusion within the community of the same. Fish shows, for example, how the epigrams addressed to the earl of Salisbury represent the relationship between poet and patron in such a way as to foreclose the possibility of any indebtedness or owing—any temporally structured inequality. The self-sustaining operation of the community of the same through the medium of these poems of praise occurs outside and independently of the temporal dimension that characterizes real-world systems of social (especially economic) exchange—not least of which, of course, is the system of patronage in which Jonson is wholly enmeshed and to which this poetic strategy is, it has been argued, a defensive response.

Thus in Fish's account the Jonsonian poem of praise is "a transaction of perfect if closed reciprocity in which to give something—a poem, a praise, a liking, a reading—is at the same moment to be getting it back." This pseudo-exchange is "bidirectional and instantaneous, and leaves no room—no temporal space—for the usual (and invidious) distinctions between creditor and debtor, petitioner and petitioned, client and patron."[14]

Yet even in the poems there can be a tension between what Katherine Maus calls Jonson's ideal economy, in which there is always plenty of everything, and therefore never any debt, and a contractualism in which time and owing necessarily imply one another.[15] Typically, this tension is in part imposed on Jonson by the circumstances under which he is writing, and in part deliberately heightened *by* him in a gesture of aesthetic control. Consider, for example, the second of Jonson's two epistles to Arthur Squib, a short poem in which he asks Squib for a loan.[16]

> I am to dine, friend, where I must be weighed
> For a just wager, and that wager paid
> If I do lose it: and without a tale
> A merchant's wife is regent of the scale,
> Who, when she heard the match, concluded straight,
> An ill commodity! 'T must make good weight.
> So that upon the point, my corporal fear
> Is, she will play Dame Justice, too severe;
> And hold me to it close; to stand upright
> Within the balance; and not want a mite;
> But rather with advantage to be found
> Full twenty stone; of which I lack two pound:
> That's six in silver; now within the socket
> Stinketh my credit, if into the pocket
> It do not come: one piece I have in store,
> Lend me, dear Arthur, for a week five more,
> And you shall make me good, in weight and fashion,

> And then to be returned; or protestation
> To go out after — till when take this letter
> For your security. I can no better.

The poem implies two grounds of indebtedness or sources of consideration. In the first, the poem is a request, and Jonson proposes that once Squib has lent him five pounds he will be bound to pay him back. In the second, the poem itself constitutes consideration, and Squib involuntarily incurs an obligation to pay the five pounds which are now, in effect, demanded. In the second sense the poem itself is a preposterous (inverted or reversed) payment of a loan that has not yet been granted. Jonson undoubtedly knew his poems had a certain market value, and he may well have felt that Squib ought to prefer to keep the poem rather than demand repayment. Even so, as Jonson tells him at the end, the poem is also, alternatively, a promissory note guaranteeing a monetary repayment.

The implicit tension between these two aspects of the exchange emerges in the clever presumptuousness of preposterously *supplying* that which you profess only to *offer,* contingently, as your part of a mutual quid pro quo. By the indebtedness incurred in the act of its coming into Squib's hands and before his eyes, the poem virtually creates the obligation for which it appears to sue. The exchange is oddly coercive; and this coercive disorganization of offer and acceptance (you've got the poem, now give me the money) is framed within a second exchange relationship that also can be construed as contractual, namely the wager that Jonson recounts to justify his need. Such cleverness as the poem possesses has to do with the relation between these two anticipated contractual exchanges. Jonson has wagered a certain sum that he will weigh in this evening at twenty stone, or 280 lbs.[17] Unfortunately, however, he is two pounds short. Now six pounds worth of silver weighs about two pounds, and carrying this on his person would make up the difference and enable him to win the bet.[18] He already happens to have one pound, and therefore requires Squib to lend him five more. This witty play on the difference between what money is materially, and what it is symbolically, its power to pay for things (food and drink for Jonson's consumption, for example), is not immediately apparent. It appears at first that Jonson is asking for the loan to cover his loss should he lose the wager. As it turns out, however, he wants (or claims he wants) to borrow the money for its material weight rather than its symbolic or monetary value.

This willful subversion of the *very idea* of borrowing money — of what it *means* to "borrow money" — wittily negotiates the socially delicate task Jonson has (or at any rate pretends to have) in hand. But it also problematizes the meaning of the *period* proposed for the loan: Jonson promises to pay Squib back after a week, a duration that is meaningful only if he is borrowing the money to spend it, and won't be able to repay it immediately. But the poem also renders the money in question monetarily inert — in effect transforms it *directly* into corporeal substance and thus removes it from the temporal circulation implied in the stipulated period; it makes the transaction something not quite identical to the borrowing of a sum of money. This figurative transformation, which is the work the poem performs, appears to derealize the debt, so that Jonson and Squib can remain uncontaminated by the temporal inequality or unevenness of the relationship between debtor and creditor. But in stipulating the period for repayment Jonson acknowledges with deliberate wit that in truth he just needs a loan for the usual reasons, that he cannot really add to his substance, or make money work for him, except through the hazardous mechanisms of exchange. The two possible purposes for borrowing the money (the sensible, strictly pecuniary one we expect but don't get and the nonpecuniary, insane one Jonson gives us) have a reciprocal relation within Jonson's story. If he needed the money to pay off the wager should he lose, he would not need to lose, since he could use the money to win the wager. But if he does use it for this purpose, he will also — as the proposed repayment schedule implies — spend it afterward on something else. The nonpecuniary purpose pre-empts the sensible purpose, but then the two get turned inside out and end up pretty much the same.

The epistle to Squib gestures toward the atemporal condition of instantaneous reciprocity that Fish identifies as characteristic of Jonson's epigrams. But it also deliberately repudiates this condition, first in allowing a narrative contingency to enter into relation with the proposed loan, and second in stipulating a period of repayment that dispels the pretense of an intention to put the loan to a nonmonetary, and therefore socially uncompromising, use. The epistle thus establishes two interrelated forms of duration which together make up the situation upon which the poem is predicated: on the one hand, the imaginary duration of the week for which, playfully, Jonson proposes that the debt shall endure, and on the other, the contingent inner contractual narrative of dinner, weighing, judgment and paying, which raises imaginary questions of sequence, motive, and causality. Squib, reading the poem, would presumably wonder about the relation between Jonson's dinner engagement and his wager. Will the weighing occur before or after dinner? That, presumably, would make a difference. Or, for that matter, does getting dinner depend on winning the wager? We hear about the negative stake involved; but what about the positive? If Jonson doesn't get dinner for winning, does he get something else? And so on. These persistent but unanswerable questions constitute a kind of duration that is purely or open-endedly narratological in the sense that it consists of temporal relations among potentially coordinated events while lacking any particular sequential coherence. The period of one week stipulated for the loan both participates in this narrativity and stands in contrast to it as a wholly liquidated, stipulated quantity. Similarly, in offering this piece of writing both as collateral or surety for a future payment, and as itself payment for a condition of owing it itself produces in Squib, Jonson establishes two opposed accounts of the temporality of contract which we will encounter again: one that is executory in structure, and the other that attempts atemporality but which, insofar as human experience is inescapably temporal, tends in fact toward the preposterous.[19]

Slade's Case and the Action of Assumpsit

In 1597 John Slade brought against Humphrey Morley a bill claiming Morley had reneged on a promise — an assumpsit — to pay Slade sixteen pounds in return for the harvest of a field of wheat and rye. In a special verdict, the jury found that there had been a bargain and sale, as Slade alleged, and that there had been no other promise made between them. The primary issue therefore was whether a simple bargain and sale involved an assumpsit, that is, when you made a bargain whether you also implicitly *promised* to uphold your part of it.[20]

Several related difficulties were involved in this question. The case was brought as an action on the case for assumpsit, and because an action of debt also lay, the question arose whether assumpsit should be allowed, given that the so-called double remedy doctrine forbade an action on the case — a form designed to accommodate exceptional legal situations — where one of the actions provided in the ancient Register of Writs could be had instead. Also, since debt allowed the defendant the right of compurgation (wager of law), and assumpsit, owing to its origin in the tortious writ of trespass, did not, the question arose whether, if assumpsit were allowed, the defendant was being improperly denied this ancient right accorded all Englishmen.

These concerns, in turn, were situated in the context of a dispute between the court of King's Bench and the court of Common Pleas. The former, which was the more progressive and less expensive of the two, had for many years allowed assumpsit in lieu of debt, while the latter had not. Assumpsit could be brought in either King's Bench or Common Pleas, while in theory debt could be brought only in the latter, raising the possibility that the practices of both courts in this respect were motivated by competition for business.[21] As J. H. Baker points out, however, King's Bench had for a long time entertained actions of debt by means of a simple fiction, so they had nothing to gain by seeking to supplant debt by assumpsit.[22] In any case, the jurisdictional conflict came to a head when the statutory court of Exchequer Chamber was substituted for Parliament as the court to which writs of error were directed from King's Bench. The new statutory court was composed only of Common Pleas judges and barons of the Exchequer, and not surprisingly it began routinely to reverse King's Bench assumpsit convictions in cases where debt lay.

Slade's case, which was argued several times between 1597 and 1602, brought the matter before an ancient assembly (also called the Exchequer Chamber and not to be confused with the statutory court of the same name) of all the judges of all three courts. These arguments, which engaged the best legal minds of the time—most notably Edward Coke for the plaintiff and Francis Bacon for the defendant—finally resulted in the apparently unilateral announcement by King's Bench that the issue had been decided in favor of both the plaintiff and assumpsit: the use of assumpsit in lieu of debt was definitively allowed. Specifically, as Coke put it in his report of the case, published a few years later,

> every contract executory imports in itself an *assumpsit,* for when one agrees to pay money, or to deliver any thing, thereby he assumes or promises to pay, or deliver it, and therefore when one sells any goods to another, and agrees to deliver them at a day to come, and the other in consideration thereof agrees to pay so much money a[t] such a day, in that case both parties may have an action of debt, or an action on the case on *assumpsit,* for the mutual executory agreement of both parties imports in itself reciprocal actions upon the case, as well as actions of debt.[23]

In other words, as Simpson puts it "wherever a situation has arisen where the writ of debt *sur contract* would lie against a person, and that person has not paid the debt ('executory') an assumpsit to pay the money will be implied."[24]

For Don Wayne, the ruling in Slade's case is important because it "brought to a culmination a gradual process whereby the mercantile notion of contract had been encroaching on the common law through the evolution of the action of assumpsit" (118–19); and this encroachment contributed to the demise of status-oriented modes of social relation. The shift could equally well be regarded, however, in an almost opposite way, as the invasion of business relationships by criteria—above all the presupposition that actions are intentional—deriving from the tortious law of trespass. As Charles Spinosa has recently argued, the ruling in Slade's case means that when you make parole contracts you are legally responsible for the states of mind—intentions and motives, and so on—which the law may decide to find in those contracts.[25]

Slade's case marks the shift from a customary culture in which social actors operate in habitual ways without formulating accounts of their intentions and reasons for acting to an assumpsit or contract culture in which social actors are required, at their peril, to be able provide an account of the motives and intentions according to which they are supposed to have acted. As a result, social actors are forced to assume a habit of constant self-examination, attending to their own consciousness and continually constructing intentional accounts of their accounts. Interiority, consisting largely of the maintenance of a sort of inventory of intentional states, develops because the law demands that people think this way about themselves. It is thus important that assumpsit arose from the tortious action of trespass on the case, since such actions tend to assume *intentional* wrongdoing; in Coke's report, Slade claims Morley has not paid, "his assumption and promise little regarding, but endeavouring and intending the said John of the aforesaid 16l. in that part subtilly and craftily to deceive and defraud."[26]

In this view, Slade's case is important because it heralded a new self-consciousness in social actors, who were forced to leave their customary, unreflective ways of operating, and to engage in vigilant self-inspection in order to monitor the intentions with which the law now presumed them always to act. Such an argument may not do justice to the forms of self-consciousness medieval people perhaps in fact possessed; David Aers complains about the presupposition among Renaissance scholars that the history of the subject gets interesting only *after* the medieval period, a presupposition which derives from Burckhardt and is entirely traditional.[27] What is genuinely new in early modern thought, however, is that intentional conceptions of interiority have found their way into the discursive logic of the law, and that this logic has assumed a new degree of importance in conceptualizations of person and action in the theater and in the shapes of popular consciousness generally.[28] What follows addresses particularly the temporal aspects of intentional action in contract law and theatrical performance.

Assumpsit, Debt, Time

In the history of contract law, the displacement of debt by assumpsit in Slade's case represented a shift from the *things* with which the action of debt was concerned to the actors and intentional actions construed in assumpsit and understood as generating contractual relations.[29] In his argument for the defendant at Serjeants' Inn on 13 May 1602, Bacon claims that no deceit (and therefore no action on the case) can properly be involved in a debt situation, since the transaction from which debt arises is by definition complete, in the sense that even if the plaintiff does not have possession, the undelivered item belongs to him.[30] Bacon cites Bracton's formula: "contractus est permutatio rerum [contract is the exchange of things]." In debt, contract is conceived as a relation between things and where they are located relative to where they ought to be located. The contrary way of conceiving contract is to think of it as the work of social actors, and to emphasize the fact that it is often — and in a minimal sense, *necessarily* — executory: not completed at the time of the bargain but only upon mutual performance.

In debt, therefore, contract is conceived in atemporal terms. Rather than an interval between promise and performance, there is only a condition which signifies by its structure that money or goods bargained for are not in the possession of the person who has a right to them. Everything happens at the moment of the bargain; a failure of the items to pass from one person to the other must be corrected by the law because it is, in some sense, *unreal*.[31] Circumstances must be brought into line with the relations that obtain legally: the plaintiff *really* has the thing sued for, therefore he *should* have it.

By "every contract executory imports in itself an *assumpsit*," Coke means that where the contract transaction is incomplete on one side, the agreement that is the contract *is* a promise, or *signifies* a promise made, to execute the remaining terms of the agreement. The manuscript of Coke's case report, according to J. H. Baker, shows that Coke first wrote "implies," and then changed it to "imports," as though he were at some pains to express the relationship precisely.[32] Whereas "implies" suggests a fiction or presumption and seems to locate the promise off to one side of the agreement, "imports" perhaps better conveys the notion that the promise *informs* the agreement, or that there is an identity between them.

At the same time that Coke's argument closes the gap between the objective act of entering into a debt relation and the subjective act of making a promise, it delineates the temporal structure of the assumpsit, in which the promise and the interval that divides it from performance, logically implied in the qualification "executory," are mutually affirming. If you have a promise, you have an interval; if you have an interval, it becomes relevant to ask whether there has been a promise. The action of assumpsit distracts or distends the structure of the contract into a futurity that retroactively precipitates the promises, intentions, deceits, motives, and considerations according to which the action organizes itself.

Slade's case thus represents one version of a tendency to invest contract with an intentional temporality. Other uses of assumpsit not directly at issue there had handled the problem rather differently. Because before Slade's case it was vital for actions of assumpsit, in order to avoid the double-remedy doctrine, to provide a ground of action distinct from the obligation to repay arising from the contract itself, assumpsit was plead in a variety of forms designed to establish logical and temporal distance between the original contract and a subsequent promise to pay. (This strategy, it should be noted, is the opposite of that pursued on behalf of the plaintiff in Slade's case. In one of these forms the plaintiff alleges that the defendant, being in debt to the plaintiff, promises repayment in return for the plaintiff's promise not to sue.[33] Toward the end of the sixteenth century this subsequent promise became more and more openly fictional, and the interval of forbearance claimed was reduced to a purely symbolic dimension. Alternatively it was alleged that a small sum had been paid at the time of the contract and that there had been a subsequent promise to repay the rest.

A more common way of pleading an assumpsit was what was known as indebitatus assumpsit, which typically alleged that the defendant, being in-debted, *postea assumpsit solvere* (thereafter promised to pay). The insertion of *postea* served two purposes, according to Simpson: first, it ensured that the indebtedness served as consideration for the assumpsit, as it could only do if it was alleged to have preceded it; and second, it helped evade the double-remedy doctrine by establishing the promise as a basis of liability distinct from the obligation to repay the contract.[34]

These complex examples show some of the ways in which manipulations of legal situations depended on subtle temporal constructions. But what, specifi-cally, is the conceptual topography of the region created by the temporal distance between the contract and the subsequent, fictional promise? This distance, used here to establish a separate basis of liability, is not the same kind of distance as the one we have already looked at, between the promise and the performance in Slade's case, but the effect is similar. Here, the fiction of a subsequent promise produces a *fiction of subsequence* integral to that promise. In practice, any debt will entail temporal tensions associated with perfor-mance, regardless of the legal view of the matter. Here, the entry into practice consists in the adaptation of assumpsit to particular cases by means of this fic-tion of subsequence. Just as the adjustment of the letter of the law by equity in particular cases may be understood as the principle of legal performance (and, as I argue elsewhere, theatrical performance as well), legal *procedure* here precipitates the temporal dimension of practice as such.[35] The *fictionality* of the subsequent promise seems intimately tied to the peculiar tense logic gov-erning it: it is *subsequent* to the indebtedness both in the sense that it is alleged to have come after it and in the sense that it has, in fact, been invented after the fact in order to furnish a ground of liability that will support assumpsit.

Jonson and the Temporality of Contract

This fictionality, I think, is related to a move in Jonson from a world of ideal relationships (of the kind which for Fish constitute Jonson's "community of the same") into a less-than-ideal world of practice — particularly but not exclusively theatrical practice, or performance. In Jonson's theater, the ideal "community of the same" Fish describes cannot be sustained, both because Jonson was never satisfied with his audiences and because, even if he had been, theatrical experience cannot occur atemporally. The temporal dimension excluded from the epigrams tends to intrude disruptively, and, forced to cope with this inevitability, Jonson takes the initiative, deliberately opening or reopening the temporal space of exchange, rehearsing the inception of performance, initiating action by means of contractual constructions. While the concession that relationships of human exchange have a temporal structure brings with it all sorts of problems which render the monetary reality of patronage difficult to conceal, it also makes this limitation a potential source of control where — as in the theater — such relationships were for Jonson characterized by open hostility and contempt on either side.

Jonson's obsession with futurity and with the play between epistemic and deontic modalities of the verb "to will" — that is, between saying what one *believes* will happen and saying what one intends *should* happen — represents an attempt pre-emptively to occupy the tactical space of temporality in the theater.[36] Jonson makes this pre-emptive gesture, for example, at the opening of *The Alchemist* (1610). Like many of Jonson's plays, this one is structured as a series of bargains and agreements, of mutual promises to do or refrain from doing; and, in fact, the very first utterance of the play itself consists of a promise, and an assurance that the promise is good: "Believe 't, I will" (1.1.1), Face tells Subtle as they appear on stage in the midst of a bitter dispute.[37] The promise (which, despite its promissory form, is a threat) has no content, since it equally refers backward into the silence preceding the play's opening; it exists as the pure *form* of a promise, an oddity not otherwise possible in the sense that a speech act that promises must in theory have intentionality, must promise *something*. We are free, of course, to construe the content of the promise as we see fit. But what is important to know is not what Face is promising, but simply the fact that the play emerges into language *as* a promise, and establishes itself in a promissory temporality. I see this empty, initiating promise, moreover, as an openly *translocutionary* speech act, in which Jonson reabsorbs into his own tactical design the temporal structure of the speech act he has transmitted to Face.

Subtle and Face eventually suspend their differences and together with their Doll Common agree to cooperate in the enterprise of sharking London's gulls. Subtle is to play a doctor of alchemy, and Face is to bring him victims, the first of whom is Dapper, a lawyer's clerk who seeks a familiar to help him to win at cards and at the track. The strategy here is for Subtle to compound Dapper's interest by feigning reluctance to obligate himself by accepting Dapper's money. Face, pretending offense at this reluctance, threatens to leave, and the roles are reversed when Dapper must himself intercede to patch up the quarrel between the two. Thus Face pretends to deal with Subtle through Dapper: "Will he take then?" (1.2.67), he demands. Subtle insists Face hear him out, but Face is adamant: "Upon no terms but an *assumpsit*," he says, to which Subtle, feigning reluctance, replies "Your humour must be law," and, Jonson's stage direction informs us, "He takes the money."

The stage direction is, I think, pedantically and parodically legalistic, in the sense that it is intended to underscore the receipt of money as constituting the consideration that makes the assumpsit, in theory, legally binding. Legal terminology serves here as a linguistic irritant, provoking impatience at the way the law manhandles human relations supposedly antecedent to and independent of it. It is as though the law were branded with its subsequence to practice. Contracts themselves — not to mention the openly fictional promises on which liability in actions of assumpsit was based — were often legal constructions imposed on social exchanges only retroactively. Similarly, Jonson's representations of action as contractual thematize, directly and indirectly, a retroactivity specific to the legalization of the world. Jonson's plays develop the political, social, and ontological implications of this logic of subsequence and antecedence. Thus where Face insists that Subtle furnish an assumpsit, that he formally "take" (1.2.67), Jonson rehearses, parodically, the retroactive assimilation of social action to legal construction. In doing so, he not only points out the spread of mercantile thought beyond its immediate sphere of influence, as Wayne argues, but also anatomizes a habit of language and a mode of conforming human experience to conceptual (specifically legal) categories.[38] At the same time, while Face's insistence on an assumpsit implicitly satirizes the subjection of the individual will to perverse and dehumanizing linguistic rituals, this rehearsal of the law's infiltration of categories over which it should not maintain jurisdiction itself seems to precipitate a vigorous, almost excessive, linguistic energy; legal rhetoric is powerfully instrumental in the construction of human action, and, as Wayne argues, Jonson knows he is implicated in the social reorganizations this rhetoric supports and articulates. We are reminded that the law is itself a form of practice.

Bartholomew Fair: *The Contractual Induction*

Like the assumpsit which in *The Alchemist* produces the performed action designated in the stage direction "He takes the money," the contractual Induction to *Bartholomew Fair* juxtaposes the legal performance of a promise with the theatrical performance of the play. The contract, recited during the Induction by a Scrivener at the Book-holder's direction, sets forth the terms under which Jonson is to provide the play and under which the audience is to attend to it:

> Articles of Agreement indented between the spectators or hearers at the Hope on the Bankside, in the county of Surrey, on the one party, and the author of *Bartholomew Fair* in the said place and country, on the other party, the one and thirtieth day of October, 1614, and in the twelfth year of the reign of our Sovereign Lord, James, by the Grace of God King of England, France, Ireland, Defender of the Faith; and of Scotland the seven and fortieth.
>
> INPRIMIS, It is covenanted and agreed by and between the parties above-said and the said spectators and hearers, as well the curious and envious as the favoring and judicious, as also the grounded judgments and under-standings do for themselves severally covenant and agree, to remain in the places their money or friends have put them, with patience, for the space of two hours and a half and somewhat more. In which time the author promises to present them, by us, with a new sufficient play called *Barthol'mew Fair,* merry, and as full of noise as sport, made to delight all, and to offend none; provided they have either the wit or the honesty to think well of themselves. (Ind. 57–75)[39]

The contract goes on to provide that members of the audience are entitled to "their free-will of censure, to like or dislike at their own charge, the author having now departed with his right" — but only proportionate to the amount each has paid for his seat, according to what Wayne calls a "strictly quantitative equity":[40] "if he drop but sixpence at the door, and will censure a crown's worth, it is thought there is no conscience or justice in that" (Ind. 76–86). Throughout, the contract reflects Jonson's recurrent anxiety about the reception of his work; he concerns himself specifically here with the temporal organization of acts of aesthetic judgment. Repeatedly in his plays Jonson seems concerned with the maintenance of a sort of temporal equilibrium apparently essential to proper judgment and to a centered sense of self.[41] An auditor, Jonson feels, should keep his place in the temporal order of performance through strict control of the mental play of past, present, and future that constitutes *attendance* to the action (and I mean to invoke the root sense of attend: to stretch). The spatial and temporal form this general anxiety takes helps explain the temporal complications created by the concluding sentences of the contract: "In witness whereof, as you have preposterously put your seals already (which is your money), you will now add the other part of suffrage, your hands. The play shall presently begin" (Ind. 135–38). This makes the contract "preposterous" (inverted or reversed, like the payment Jonson offers in his epistle to Squib) because sealing, which should come last, has come first; the audience, having paid its money, now finds itself *further* obligated to undertake additional terms — and by precisely the gesture that should have discharged its part of the bargain. But the contract becomes yet more preposterous when Jonson adds the condition that his audience "will now add the other part of suffrage, your hands." Richard Burt points out that by this unusual requirement — that applause be supplied before the play can even be begun — Jonson seems to imply that his audience cannot be trusted to appreciate his work, and must be forced by legal mechanisms to furnish, beforehand, the applause that is his proper due.[42]

Jonson does undoubtedly mean to suggest this; but the ambiguity of the play on "hands" — which suggest both those used to applaud and those used to affix a signature — complicates the joke, since at this moment it is legitimate to ask for a signature in a way that it is not legitimate to ask for applause (let alone that it seems entirely crazy to ask a theater audience to sign a contract in the first place). This play on the legal and the theatrical "hand" at once links legal and theatrical practice and distinguishes between them by suggesting that the temporalities of performance they imply contradict each other.

Moreover, the principle of partitive suffrage displayed here — the distribution of suffrage between money payment and "hand" — would normally act to rationalize the interval between the entry into a bargain and the mutual execution of that bargain. But here it works in the opposite way, to collapse this interval in on itself. In a maneuver that in effect reverses the limit case of the strategy involved in pleading assumpsit — allegation of an initial payment followed by a promise to pay the balance at a future date — Jonson elides any structurally significant duration between the payment of money and the addition of applause. Where assumpsit pleas are trying to open up an intentional space in which to operate, Jonson here appears to be attempting to close one down.

The trace of the expected rationalization remains, however, as a tension built into the "now" (of "now add the other part of suffrage, your hands"), which thus both designates a present instant and points toward the moment of the conclusion of the play; the pressure that the "now" thus comes under represents and produces the temporal rift or fissure that opens out into the space of performance itself — the "space of two hours and a half and somewhat more" initially stipulated. Thus, although the version of *Bartholomew Fair* performed at the Hope Theater lacked an epilogue, precisely in its "now" the Induction serves this function as well as its introductory one.[43]

So in the Induction contract Jonson seems to be playing with a problem that could be described in terms of the difference between the atemporality of debt and the temporal structure of assumpsit. There is on the one hand the contract in its preposterous aspect: in this aspect everything happens at once, or, at least, everything is crowded into a small, complicated space, as though Jonson were insisting on immediate performance in order to dispense with the uncertainties attaching to promises and the intentional states they bring into play, though at the cost of a sort of structural compression amounting to inversion.

On the other hand, the Induction can also be read as seeking out or constructing the interval between promise and performance in such a way that the interval is *itself* that in which the play is enacted. To make a contractual agreement and its attendant mutual promises the founding act of a theatrical performance is to construct the space of that performance — the "space of two hours and a half and somewhat more" — as a specifically contractual interval. Jonson seems torn between giving in to the temporality of performance as construed in assumpsit (with all the uncertainty that must come with it) and insisting on a debt-based notion of contractual performance in which everything is already accomplished in an instant and the material world needs simply to catch up with what is already, by law, the case. A world where this would be possible would be much like the ideal world of the "community of the same" described by Fish.

Cokes and Trouble-All

The plot that constructs the world of *Bartholomew Fair* itself consists of intervals opened within relationships of exchange, and it is through these intervals between promise and performance that the theatrical performance occurs. One form of contract nests within another. The exchanges that organize the plot, like the Induction contract, manifest a tension between an understanding of the exchange as at least in part executory, on the one hand, and as executed, on the other. Typically the two parts to the bargain are not carried out at once; one performance or both are delayed. Jonson is interested in what happens during these "executory" intervals, how they organize plot and structure time, how bargain and sale, promise and performance enclose and delimit small and large stretches of dramatic time, how futurity is contained in present moments as the structure of anticipatory practical judgment and calculation.

A single, exemplary contractual interval may be noted here. Its subject is

Bartholomew Cokes, and it occurs during his visit to the fair that bears his first name. Moneyed and affable, guileless and simple-minded, Cokes has proved no match for the wit of the Bartholomew birds, who by the fourth act have picked his pockets clean. Lost, penniless and in despair, he asks the enigmatic Trouble-all to take him home, in exchange for a payment when they get there. Trouble-all, who throughout the play demands of those he meets a warrant from Justice Overdo sanctioning whatever it is they happen to be doing, agrees to do so on condition that Cokes provide him such a warrant for *this* undertaking. Now Overdo, as it happens, is Cokes's brother-in-law, and one house is home for both. The problem is that Cokes must find his way there in order to get the warrant, but he can't find his way alone, which is why he needs Trouble-all to guide him. Trouble-all, willing to be helpful, offers a solution: "Go you thither yourself, first, alone; tell your worshipful brother your mind; and but bring me three lines of his hand, or his clerk's, with 'Adam Overdo' underneath. Here I'll stay you; I'll obey you, and I'll guide you presently" (4.2.94–97). The deal proposed is of course preposterous: the only way for Cokes to secure the benefit he seeks is to do so in such a way as no longer to need it. Trouble-all's demand for a warrant is usually read, no doubt correctly, as expressing an ironic nostalgia for a time when warrants really did provide authority. But, more to the point here, the demand necessitates a specifically preposterous contract precisely because of the way in which contracts depend on a system of enforcement that has itself come to be understood as contractual. Although the Great Contract of 1610 had recently failed, and the doctrine of consideration had just begun to assume a coherent shape, social-contract theory had yet to acquire political significance. Later in the same century, John Selden was to write in *Table Talk*:

> Lady *Kent* Articled with Sir *Edward Herbert,* that he should come to her when she sent for him, and stay with her as long as she would have him, to which he set his hand; then he Articled with her, That he should go away when he pleased, and stay away as long as he pleased, to which she set her hand. This is the Epitome of all the Contracts in the World, betwixt Man and Man, betwixt Prince and Subject, they keep them as long as they like them, and no longer.[44]

As with the agreement proposed by Trouble-all, the contracts between Lady Kent and Sir Edward founder on a collapse of temporal distinctions. Each party can come and go when he or she pleases, and since this coming and going constitutes the performance of the agreements, precisely what is leveled here is the efficacy of the contract in fixing human behavior in time. In each case the cause of this temporal collapse is the disappearance or demystification of the authority of enforcement. When it turns out that personal contracts depend for their enforcement on a social contract, that authority itself is merely contractual, then the distinction between the (divine) authority requiring one to *keep* one's contracts, and the freedom one preserves in *making* one's contracts, disintegrates.[45] Trouble-all's proposed agreement stages this displacement of the mechanism of enforcement as a specifically temporal paradox. Like Bartholomew Cokes confronted with Trouble-all's proposal, Jonson finds himself in an impossible position in *Bartholomew Fair,* since it is only by temporal means, through a similarly preposterous performance, that he can approach the atemporal certainty whose temporary suspension he played with in his poems.

Notes

This chapter has benefited from a stimulating discussion following my presentation of an earlier version at a meeting of the Law & Humanities Institute, New York City, 19 May 1992. Thanks are due to Richard Weisberg for inviting me to present the paper and to Leslie Katz and John G. Norman for reading the essay and offering suggestions.

1. Don E. Wayne, "Drama and Society in the Age of Jonson: An Alternative View," *Renaissance Drama* 13 (1982): 104. For Maine's seminal idea of the displacement of status by contract, see *Ancient Law: Its Connection With the Early History of Society and Its Relation to Modern Ideas* (1861; Dorset, 1986), esp. pp. 139–41, 252–305.

2. Ibid., 115.

3. A. W. B. Simpson, *A History of the Common Law of Contract: The Rise of the Action of Assumpsit* (Oxford: Oxford University Press, 1975), p. 316.

4. On the early history of the doctrine of consideration, see ibid., 316–405; J. H. Baker, "Origins of the 'Doctrine' of Consideration, 1535–1585," *On The Laws and Customs of England: Essays in Honor of Samuel E. Thorne,* Morris S. Arnold, Thomas A. Green, and Stephen D. White, eds. (Chapel Hill: University of North Carolina Press, 1981), pp. 336–58; J. L. Barton, "The Early History of Consideration," *Law Quarterly Review* 85 (July 1969): 372.

5. I know of no such cases. There were, of course, cases where playwrights hired to produce plays were sued for failing to do so; see Laurie E. Maguire, "A King's Men's Contract and Dramatic Output," *Notes and Queries,* n.s. 32 (1): 73–74; R. Mark Benbow, "Dutton and Goffe versus Broughton: A Disputed Contract for Plays in the 1570s," *Records of Early English Drama* 2 (1981): 3.

6. See David Riggs, *Ben Jonson: A Life* (Cambridge: Harvard University Press, 1989), pp. 124–26. By 1609 Jonson had already become disaffected with Salisbury. Salisbury died in 1612.

7. On Jonson's connections with these figures, see I. A. Shapiro, "The 'Mermaid Club,'" *Modern Language Review* 45 (1950): 1, 6–17. On the debates surrounding the Great Contract, see Samuel Rawson Gardiner, ed., *Parliamentary Debates in 1610,*

edited, *From the Notes of a Member of the House of Commons* (Westminster: Camden Society, 1862); Alan G. R. Smith, "Crown, Parliament and Finance: The Great Contract of 1610," *The English Commonwealth 1547–1640: Essays Presented to Joel Hurstfield,* Peter Clark, Alan G. R. Smith, and Nicholas Tyacke, eds. (Leicester: Leicester University Press, 1979), pp. 111–27; Roger Lockyear, *The Early Stuarts: A Political History of England, 1603–1642* (London: Longman, 1989), pp. 173–82.

8. Shapiro determines that the group was primarily one of lawyers, and that Jonson's presence there was one of a few exceptions. The poets were joining a lawyer's fraternity, not the other way around.

9. Pierre Bourdieu, *Outline of a Theory of Practice,* Richard Nice, trans. (Cambridge: Cambridge University Press, 1977), pp. 1–15.

10. Michel de Certeau, *The Practice of Everyday Life,* Steven Rendell, trans. (Berkeley: University of California Press, 1984), p. 82.

11. Thus Iago, the tactician par excellence, instructing Roderigo to be patient, can remark that "wit depends on dilatory time," when moments later, alone, he can urge himself to headlong action: "Dull not devices by coldness and delay" (*Othello, The Riverside Shakespeare,* G. Blakemore Evans, ed. (Boston: Houghton Mifflin, 1974), pp. 373–88. Iago's wit is precisely the ability to negotiate between the precipitate and the dilatory; and it thus recapitulates the compositional negotiation Shakespeare himself attempted in the notorious "double time" of the play.

12. Stanley Fish, "Authors-Readers: Jonson's Community of the Same," *Representing the English Renaissance,* Stephen Greenblatt, ed. (Berkeley: University of California Press, 1988), pp. 231–63. First published in *Representations* 7 (1984): 26–58.

13. Ibid., 240.

14. Ibid., 253, 255.

15. Katherine Eisaman Maus, "Facts of the Matter: Satiric and Ideal Economies in the Jonsonian Imagination," *Ben Jonson's First Folio,* Jennifer Brady and W. H. Herendeen, eds. (Newark: University of Delaware Press, 1991), pp. 64–89. First published in *English Literary Renaissance* 19 (1989): 42–64.

16. The text used is that of *The Complete Poems,* George Parfitt, ed. (New Haven: Yale University Press, 1982), pp. 200–201.

17. On the relation between Jonson's poetic practice and his corporeal substance, see Joseph Lowenstein, "The Jonsonian Corpulence, or the Poet as Mouthpiece," ELH 53 (1986): 491; Bruce Thomas Boehrer, "Renaissance Overeating: The Sad Case of Ben Jonson," *PMLA* 105 (1990): 1071.

18. Jonson's 1:3 ratio of weight to value appears to be consistent with the coinage practices of the period. In *The Tudor Coinage* (Manchester: Manchester University Press, 1978), C. E. Challis records that in 1603, 63,890 pounds of sterling silver coins were minted with a face value of 198,059 pounds (Appendix 2, 306), for a ratio of 3.1 pounds value per pound of coin. Before the great debasement of the 1540's, the ratio had been closer 1:2; see J. D. Gould, *The Great Debasement: Currency and the Economy in Mid-Tudor England* (Oxford: Oxford University Press, 1970). The traditional sterling degree of fineness (11 oz. 2 dwt.) was restored in 1551 and maintained, with slight fluctuations, until the death of Elizabeth. See also J. Geoffrey Dent, "The Pound Weight and the Pound Sterling: The Relationship Between Weight and Coinage and its Consequences," *Folk Life: Journal of Ethnological Studies* 27 (1989): 80.

19. I owe my interest in the preposterous to Joel Altman, " 'Preposterous Conclusions': Eros, *Enargeia,* and the Composition of *Othello,*" *Representations* 18 (1987): 129; Patricia Parker, *Literary Fat Ladies: Rhetoric, Gender and Property* (London: Methuen, 1987). See also Parker, "Preposterous Events," *Shakespeare Quarterly* 43 (1992): 186.

20. The primary sources of information about *Slade v. Morley* are Coke's report of the case, 4 *Reports* 91a–95b in *English Reports* (Edinburgh: William Green & Sons, 1907), vol. 76; and the additional reports excerpted and discussed in J. H. Baker, "New Light on *Slade's Case,*" *Cambridge Law Journal* 29 (1) pt. 1 (Apr. 1971): 51–67; 29 (2) pt. 2 (Nov. 1971): 213–36. See also Simpson, *History of the Common Law of Contract,* 292–302; Simpson, "The Place of Slade's Case in the History of Contract," *Law Quarterly Review* 74 (July 1958): 381–96; H. K. Lucke, "Slade's Case and the Origin of the Common Courts," *Law Quarterly Review* 81 pt. 1 (July 1965): 442–45; 81 pt. 2 (October 1965): 539–61; 82 pt. 3 (January 1966): 81–93.

21. T. F. T. Plucknett, *A Concise History of the Common Law.* 5th ed. (Boston: Little, 1956), pp. 644–45.

22. Baker, "New Light," pt. 2, p. 215.

23. Coke 4 *Reports* 94a–94b.

24. Simpson, *History,* 292–302.

25. Charles Spinosa, "The Transformation of Intentionality: Debt and Contract in *The Merchant of Venice,*" *Cardozo Studies in Law and Literature* 5 (Spring 1993): 65. I thank Spinosa for making a copy of his essay available prior to its publication.

26. Coke, 4 *Reports* 91a–b.

27. David Aers, "Reflections on Current Histories of the Subject," *Literature and History* 2 (2) series 2 (Autumn 1991): 20–34.

28. I argue this thesis in relation to early modern homicide law in "*Hamlet, Hales v. Petit,* and the Hysteresis of Action," *ELH* 60 (1993): 17–55.

29. See Spinosa, "Transformation." A related move can be detected in the developments of homicide law. See Thomas Glyn Watkin, "*Hamlet* and the Law of Homicide," *Law Quarterly Review* 100 (April 1984): 282–310.

30. Baker, "New Light," pt. 1, p. 60.

31. Bacon's sensitivity to the temporal dimension of contract is reflected in his admission that where a contract is "distracted and divided" an action on the case may lie (ibid., p. 62). He appends this exception to his list of "collateral circumstances" that would support an action on the case independently of debt. These exceptions include a specified place of delivery, but not as a rule a specified time, so it seems a little odd that he does except the "distracted and divided" contract. I suggest that it is because such cases problematize the atemporality attributed to contracts plead as debt *sur contract.* True, Bacon is attempting to rationalize cases where assumpsit has been allowed instead of debt, and he needs to account for cases like these. At the same time, one could also say that "distracted and divided" contracts managed to get accepted as actions on the case because they presented this feature.

32. Baker, "New Light," pt 1, p. 12, p. 226n.

33. Simpson, *History,* 301–2.

34. Ibid., at 304–5, where Simpson corrects his earlier assumption (in "The Place of *Slade's Case* in the History of Contract") that Slade's Case involved an indebitatus assumpsit plea. The advantage of indebitatus assumpsit for the plaintiff was that, because

the basis of liability was the subsequent promise and not the indebtedness itself, he did not need to allege any specifics about the indebtedness itself; for the same reason it was somewhat unfair to the defendant (ibid., at 305). But indebitatus assumpsit could only be pled in lieu of debt; other actions of assumpsit (breach of promise to deliver a thing sold, or to marry, etc.), as well as some assumpsits in lieu of debt, were plead *specially;* i.e., the full circumstances of the indebtedness were set forth. These were therefore called actions of special assumpsit (ibid., at 306–307). See also Lucke, "Slade's Case," pt. 2, pp. 548–61 and pt. 3, passim.

35. On equity in legal and theatrical performance see Luke Wilson, "*Hamlet:* Equity, Intention, Performance," *Studies in the Literary Imagination* 24 (Fall 1991): 91.

36. For a discussion of the shift from deontic or intentional futurity to epistemic futurity in the use of "will" and "shall" during the medieval period, see Leslie K. Arnovick, *The Development of Future Constructions in English: The Pragmatics of Modal and Temporal* Will *and* Shall *in Middle English* (New York: Peter Lang, 1990), esp. pp. 91–103.

37. Quotations from *The Alchemist* are from the Penguin edition, Michael Jamieson, ed., *Ben Jonson: Three Comedies* (Harmondsworth: Penguin, 1966).

38. The same claim might be made for the much more prominent use of alchemical language in the play as a rhetorical instrument of social interaction and self-construction and -transformation.

39. Quotations from *Bartholomew Fair* are from the Yale edition, Eugene M. Waith, ed. (New Haven: Yale University Press, 1963).

40. Wayne, "Drama and Society," 115.

41. On the figure of the "centered self" in Jonson, see Thomas M. Greene, "Ben Jonson and the Centered Self," *Studies in English Literature* 10 (1970): 325–48.

42. Richard A. Burt, "'Licensed by Authority': Ben Jonson and the Politics of Early Stuart Theater," *ELH* 54 (1987): 539–40.

43. For the performance at court, on the other hand, Jonson omitted the Induction and substituted for it a prologue and epilogue addressed to the king. To presume to bargain with the king, to offer him a coercive contract, would seem to be intolerable, even in jest. Contracting with the king had been attempted, unsuccessfully, as we have seen, in 1610, and it would not do to appear to parody the Great Contract, the failure of which had not made either side look especially good, in the royal presence.

44. John Selden, *Table Talk* (London: Gibbings, 1897), p. 41.

45. In some sense, in the common law this had always been understood. Thus, in *Bromage v. Genning* (1616), Coke objected to the legal enforcement of specific performance, on the grounds that in entering into an agreement, one of the options was to pay damages rather than perform. To the plaintiff's remark that Chancery routinely provided specific relief it was retorted that

> Without a doubt it ought not to do so, for then to what purpose is the action on the case and covenant; and COKE said that this would subvert the intent of the covenantor, since he [the defendant] intended to have his election to pay damages or to pay the lease, and they would compel him to make the lease against his will; and so it is if a man binds himself in an obligation to enfeoff another, he cannot be compelled to make the enfeoffment. (1 Rolle 368 in *English Reports*)

In this scheme, the intention to have a choice supplants the intention to enter into a legally binding obligation. The reversibility this way of thinking forecloses is compensated for by the way in which performance itself becomes liquid, measurable quite precisely in terms of the money it is worth. All this is predicated, it is important to notice, on the notion that there are no *moral* imperatives to make good one's promises, only strategic ones; and if you find that not doing so is a more profitable course of action, it is your right to perform or pay damages, at your preference. The intervention of the law is an opportunity rather than an inconvenience; the intention behind a promise implies — one might even say "imports" — an intention *not* to perform at one's election.

7

Not the King's Two Bodies: Reading the "Body Politic" in Shakespeare's Henry IV, *Parts 1 and 2*

LORNA HUTSON

The extent to which people in late sixteenth-century England could be said to have any kind of "civic consciousness" remains a matter of debate among historians and literary critics.[1] J. G. A. Pocock's brilliant analytical overview of the classical republican tradition in the early modern period argues that sixteenth-century English thinkers, though clearly affected by Italian civic humanism, were prevented from fully grasping the idea of the state as a "polis" maintained by the active and deliberative virtue of its citizens because they were still dominated by the idea of the state as *corpus mysticum,* a mystical body.[2] Though Pocock does not refer to the famous book by Ernst Kantorowicz, *The King's Two Bodies* (1957), it is fair to suppose that his views on the impossibility of a sixteenth-century English civic consciousness have gained credibility from the widespread currency of Kantorowicz's version of the corpus mysticum.[3] Kantorowicz, of course, is only tangentially concerned with Renaissance England. Nevertheless, the conceptual debt to Kantorowicz in Foucault's *Surveiller et punir* (1975), coupled with the fact that Kantorowicz's thesis takes its departure from two sixteenth-century English texts, has ensured that recent critical work on the literary and political culture of the late sixteenth century acknowledges the dominance of the symbolism of the monarch's natural and political bodies.[4] In a recent article, David Norbrook, taking a skeptical look at claims made for the ubiquity of the two-bodies metaphor in seventeenth-century political thought, argues that it acquired, at most, a temporary prominence during debates over the nature of the allegiance owed by James' English and Scottish subjects after the union of the crowns.[5] Yet the problem of the obscuring effects of the two-bodies metaphor goes further back, past the radical developments of seventeenth-century political thought, to their mid-sixteenth-century legal roots. Kantorowicz's study of medieval political theology opens with a chapter entitled "The Problem: Plowden's Reports." I shall argue that as a result of encountering the great sixteenth-century jurist, Edmund Plowden (1518–85), exclusively in the pages and footnotes of Kantorowicz's scholarly and persuasive book, literary critics and historians have, with a few exceptions, almost entirely missed the political significance of Plowden's *Commentaries* of 1571. In the pages that follow I deny that Edmund Plowden was primarily famous in his own time for establishing the theory of the king's two bodies and argue in addition that the intellectual innovation for which he did become famous — the introduction into English common law of an Aristotelian theory of equitable interpretation — not only lies behind what Alan Cromartie has called "the constitutionalist revolution" of the seventeenth century but also relates to contemporary innovations in the dramatic representation of monarchy in ways which must challenge Pocock's assumptions about the nonexistence of Elizabethan civic consciousness.[6]

Back to Plowden's Commentaries

If the name Edmund Plowden means anything at all to literary critics working on the Renaissance, it evokes the man who gave a new currency to the medieval doctrine of the state as corpus mysticum. Historicists new and old make reference to Plowden when they mean to invoke this doctrine, and, more often than not, their footnotes show that they have been reading only those pages of Plowden which Kantorowicz makes available. Thus, in an influential essay on Spenser's construction of his readers as subjects of an absolutist queen, Louis Montrose has written: "The political fiction of 'the queen's two bodies' — one natural, fallible, mortal; the other, 'not subject to Passions . . . nor to death' — occupied a transitional position between the medieval theological doctrine that all Christendom was a collective *corpus mysticum*, and what Quentin Skinner has called 'the distinctly modern idea of the State as a form of public power separate from both the ruler and the ruled, and constituting the supreme authority within a certain defined territory.' . . . At this historical juncture, the body politic inhered in the body of the prince."[7]

In his footnotes, Montrose glosses the first quotation as "the words of

Edmund Plowden, Elizabethan common lawyer, as quoted in Ernst Kantorowicz, *The King's Two Bodies*," and he goes on to refer the reader to Kantorowicz more generally and to Marie Axton's development of his theories in *The Queen's Two Bodies* (1977). Though Kantorowicz offered the doctrine as one that could legitimize both absolutism and regicide, the argument that sixteenth-century political thought was dominated by such a personification of the state in "corporeal, sacramental terms" tends, as Norbrook points out, "to work against a more radically abstract concept of the state."[8] Indeed, the metaphor of the state as corporate personality encourages a scholarly focus on the charisma and image manipulation of the ruler; David Starkey's invocation of Plowden and Kantorowicz in a discussion of how Henry VIII's subjects tended to "fuse" the monarch's bodies natural and politic is a case in point.[9] The attractions of reading Plowden thus are almost irresistible. If Kantorowicz's erudition were not enough to make the point seem conclusive, Marie Axton's discovery that Plowden used the two bodies argument in his 1566 manuscript treatise on the Elizabethan succession would seem to clinch the matter.[10] And yet there is a real problem in taking such a selective reading of so influential a book as *Les Commentaries ou Reports de Edmund Plowden* (1571) as evidence of its impact on contemporary thought and practice.[11] We need to beware, as Quentin Skinner has argued, of that form of intellectual history which assumes that "an ideal type of a great doctrine" was and is "always in some sense immanent in history."[12] In question is not whether Edmund Plowden and the lawyers whose speeches he recorded deployed a conception derived from medieval political theology, but rather what kind of meaning in institutional terms we can attach to that deployment. Skinner's own adaptation of Austinian speech-act theory, and the work on the history of reading practices associated with historians such as Roger Chartier, textual critics such as the late D. F. McKenzie, and others, might prompt us to reconsider the meaning of Plowden's *Commentaries* not as the final emanation of a nearly vanished political theology, but as a decisive event in the history of the common law's institutional transformation through the rhetorical, philological, hermeneutic, and print-oriented practices we call humanism.[13]

Kantorowicz's interest in Plowden was stimulated by reading F. W. Maitland.[14] It is now clear that that great historian of English common law underestimated its humanistic transformation in the sixteenth century.[15] J. H. Baker's critique of Maitland's famous 1901 Rede lecture "English Law and the Renaissance" challenged the argument that the cessation of the yearbooks in the year of Thomas More's execution marked the beginning of the isolation of English common law from developments in humanistic jurisprudence on the Continent.[16] On the contrary, Baker argued, humanism transformed the English common law by encouraging "procedures which enabled the law to become more detailed."[17] Baker's work makes it clear that changes were taking place in the way in which the judicial role was coming to be perceived, a change reflected in the greater decisiveness of the law reports of Edmund Plowden by comparison with the reports in the yearbooks:

> In point of detail the English story could not be more different from Continental legal history. But in the shift of emphasis from *doctrine* (or common learning) to *jurisprudence* (or judge-made law) the similarity is striking. On the Continent the change is marked by the increasing publication of *decisiones*, and in England — where law reporting had passed through an earlier stage — by the greater decisiveness of reports such as Plowden's or Coke's. . . . The reason why Plowden is so different from the typical year books is not merely that he was the first reporter to revise his own proofs. . . . It is that he *deliberately refrained from reporting inconclusive or extempore discussions, and published only set-piece debates about formal demurrers, special verdicts, writs of error and motions in banc after trial*[18] [my italics].

In spite of its rhetoric of continuity and insularity, then, English common law underwent a transformation of its own status and agency, perceptible in the dissemination of reports of cases which were seen to generate forms of legal action by deciding a dubious point of law (a demurrer) or the application of the law to the facts found by the jury (a special verdict). Plowden himself draws readers' attention to the basis of his enterprise in humanistic pedagogic practice. His preface describes how he attended the debates of the most eminent lawyers, resolving to

> commit to wrytting those thinges which I hearde, and the Iudgement theruppon. . . . And finding great profit therby, I disposed my selfe at last to reporte the arguments and Iudgements made and geuen in the kynges courtes uppon demurrers in lawe, as those of which I might reape more fruit and perfection in Iudgement . . . in this book there is no Recorde entered, but such vpon which there is a Demurrer in lawe, or a special veredict conteigning a matter in lawe, which bothe were debated by those of the barre and benche to the uttermost, and in thende allowed, or for the causes shewed in this booke disalowed by the iudgement of the court, and so most firme to trust unto.[19]

Plowden's focus on demurrers, or doubtful points of law, as yielding more "fruit and perfection in Iudgement" to the student, links the project of reporting, which enabled the law to become more detailed, with the humanistic practice of exemplary reading, for which gathering and collecting arguments became, in itself, a form of dialectical analysis and a method of improving the invention and judgment.[20] This, in turn, suggests that Plowden and the lawyers whose arguments he reported did not subscribe to these discursive proofs as theories or beliefs but applied them as they were likely to turn, or alter, the direction and outcome of a certain case. Marie Axton, establishing Plowden's precedence among the anti-Suffolk writers of treatises on the Elizabethan succession, assumes that the currency of the proverb "The case is altered, quoth Plowden," refers to the prevalence of what she calls "Plowden's theory and figural technique, his miracles of the Crown" (that is, the wonders wrought by the metaphor of the state as the monarch's "political body").[21] In fact, as most of the cases in Plowden's *Commentaries* make no mention of "miracles of the Crown" but inevitably feature ingenious reversals and resolutions of dubious points of law, it seems far more likely that the proverb refers to the textual and legal innovations of the *Commentaries*. In any case, the succession treatise — arguably an attempt to restrict the monarch's right to will away the Crown through an appeal to common-law doctrine — could hardly have gained Plowden a reputation for supporting royal miracles. Early in Elizabeth's reign he had argued a case protesting against the right of the Crown to impose customs by virtue of prerogative alone. Plowden proposed, quoting a statute passed in the reign of Edward I, that "it doth appear amongst other things how the custom of wool and skins and leather was first granted by parliament. And how that rules and precedents shall not be any title to the king other than is expressed by parliament."[22] William Hakewill remembered Plowden's arguments against royal prerogative in his speech against impositions in the 1610 Parliament.[23]

Plowden's argument in the case on customs on wool and leather proceeded by reconciling two sources of law — statutes and common law — relating to the freedoms of merchants in exports and imports. Many of the demurrers raised in the cases of the *Commentaries* were resolved by the same sort of reconciliation. The fiction of corporate personality, or the symbolic embodiment of the polis in the figure of the monarch is, in other words, merely one of the argumentative resources enabling the more general project of squaring an unwritten common law with a rapidly increasing corpus of statute law to enable individual legal actions which would, in aggregate, be distinctly "beneficial a le common weal."[24] At its most comprehensive, this project is identifiable with the application of an Aristotelian theory of equity (*epieikeia*) to the interpretation of statute law. Before I go on to discuss equity in relation to the interpretation of statutes, however, a few words of clarification on the nature of sixteenth-century thinking on equity are required.

Sixteenth-century discussions of epieikeia take their departure, via the writings of Jean Gerson, from that passage in the *Nicomachean Ethics* in which Aristotle declares it right, when a case arises the particular circumstances of which have not been anticipated by the general words of the positive law, to "rectify the defect by deciding as the lawgiver would himself decide if he were present on that occasion."[25] Guided by Maitland, however, twentieth-century literary critics have until quite recently assimilated Tudor thinking on equity to a notion of the arbitrary exercise of an individual judge's conscience in merciful judgment and have associated the exercise of such conscionable jurisdiction with absolutism. These critics thus equate the Aristotelian injunction to "decide as the lawgiver himself would decide" with the Lord Chancellor's overturning of common-law decisions in the prerogative court of Chancery.[26] The constitutional crisis that manifested itself in the dispute between the common-law courts and Chancery in 1616 makes this equation understandable, but it is, in fact, a teleological distortion of history.[27] While it is true that one branch of the application of Aristotelian epieikeia to English law was concerned with the possibility of remedial action in the court of Chancery, another and equally important branch developed the idea of equity as a *principle of interpretation* within the common law itself. As such, equity was, in the words of Christopher St. German, "an excepcion secretly vnderstande in euery generall rule of posytyue lawe," permitting a judicial decision that "rather followeth the intent of the lawe than the wordes of the lawe."[28]

The principles that would enable lawyers to engage in a responsible reconstruction of legislative intention were merely hinted at in St. German's treatise. The imperative to develop these hints into a full and complex body of theoretical and exemplary knowledge came about subsequently, as a direct result of the unprecedented increase of the written component of English law, in the form of post-Reformation statutory legislation. And it was as the unrivalled textbook of this body of knowledge that Plowden's *Commentaries* became famous in his lifetime. "Nothing," as Samuel Thorne remarked, "is more apparent in Plowden's *Commentaries* than his interest, and that of his contemporaries, in equity and equitable interpretation."[29] Thorne has described, in his introduction to the manuscript attributed to Sir Thomas Egerton and entitled *A Discourse upon the Exposicion & Vnderstanding of Statutes,* the transformation of the theory and practice of statute interpretation in the sixteenth century. In the fourteenth and fifteenth centuries, statutes were not perceived as a cognate body of legislation, and judges had happily exercised what they called "lequity del estatute," extending individual statutes beyond their express words to cover analogous cases without theoretical justification, or any sense of potential conflict between legislative and judicial authority. In the sixteenth century, however, "extensions of acts to analogous cases were now made by judges in the light of a controlling *Equitas*" which was explicitly concerned with the concepts of *interpretation* and of the *reconstruction of legislative intention.*[30] In 1530 St. German had given examples of "dyuers statutes" in which exceptions were usually understood by common-law judges, "for *that* the mynde of the makers of the sayd estatute shalbe taken to be that case shuld be exceptyd,"[31] but by the time Sir Thomas Egerton wrote his discourse, the "Construction de Statute per Equytye" had become a strategy for identifying the intentions of the law with the interests of the commonweal. Egerton observes that "the opynion of some be that it forceth not what the commen lawe was, sence it is certen what the lawe is nowe by estatute," yet knowledge of the common law enables the exposition of statutory legislation in doubtful cases, "where there are no wordes in the statute, and yet a case happenethe upon an estatute, the common lawe shall make a construccion."[32]

A version of Egerton's manuscript, which was evidently revised after the publication of Plowden's *Commentaries* in 1571, has an annotation at this point referring the reader to the *Nicomachean Ethics,* and to classic discussions of Aristotle in Plowden, notably *Stowell v. Lord Zouch.*[33] Samuel Thorne, as Egerton's editor, was in a position to appreciate the centrality of Plowden's *Commentaries* to sixteenth-century legal thinking on the issue of statute interpretation, and Egerton's manuscript was far from being the only text on the subject that gave evidence of extensive reliance on Plowden for its examples. Others include Edward Hake's *Epieikeia* (presented in manuscript to James I in 1604); the *Treatise Concerning Statutes, or Acts of Parliament: And the Exposition thereof* (attributed to Sir Christopher Hatton); and Thomas Ashe's *Epieikeia* a comprehensive index to cases "queux concerne le exposition des Statutes per Equitie," dedicated to Sir Edward Coke in 1609.[34] Abridgements of Plowden composed by Thomas Ashe (1607) and by Sir John Walter (1659) are further testimonies.[35] Literary critics may have been deterred from attending to this material by the dismissive attitude of such influential legal historians as C. K. Allen, for whom "Plowden's attempt to build round statutes . . . an Aristotelian *epieikeia* analogous to the *synderesis* of Chancery was artificial and unfruitful."[36] The institutional "failure" of an intellectual enterprise, however, is not a reason to ignore its impact on thought and practice; Plowden's record of the concerted and persistent attempts of the Tudor lawyers to apply an Aristotelian epieikeia to a burgeoning body of legislation was central to the emergence of the kind of political consciousness that later brought the issue of parliamentary sovereignty into sharp focus, as Stuart Prall explains: "It was really around this point that the controversy over equity was to rage, because the struggle for primacy in the English legal system would not only be that between the common law courts and the Chancery, but also between Parliament and the courts—common law or prerogative. The right to *extend* and *restrict* the meaning of statutes was hardly compatible with the principle of parliamentary sovereignty which would begin to raise its head obliquely by the end of the century, and which would become a *casus belli* by the mid-seventeenth century."[37]

Plowden seems to have been virtually identified with the range of learning associated with the equity of statutes. Before Thomas Ashe wrote his treatise on equity, *Epieikeia,* he had been busy with an abridgement of Plowden, which offered summaries of what was to be learned from each case; for example, from *Reniger v. Fogassa,* the student could expect, "Mult bon matter & bon learnings touchant lexpositions de statutes & le*qui*tie de eux."[38] When Edmund Hake moves on to the capacity of equity to supply actions denied by the rigidity of the common law, he refers the question of "actions that have bin taken by the *Equity* of Statutes . . . to our olde stoarhowse, *Mr. Plowdens Commentaries,* where yow shall fynde plentifully thereof."[39] Finally, describing how epieikeia governs the exposition of statutes, Hake remarks, "If I should take it upon me to speake of all Statutes that have bin expounded by *Equity,* assuredly I should take upon me an endlesse piece of worke. . . . And in the dooing thereof I should but *actum agere,* for that if yow will but looke unto the tables that are extant . . . of *Mr Plowden's Commentaries* . . . there yow shalbe dyrected unto whatsoever yow would desier in that behalf."[40] The "tables" of which Hake speaks probably refer to the index composed by William Fleetwood, and appended to the 1578 edition of the *Commentaries.*[41]

There is evidence, too, that the "stoarhowse" aspect of the text, and the dialectical activity it was thereby designed to promote, was part of the author's design. In an aside to the reader of *Eyston v. Studd* which has not been retained in the eighteenth century-translation from the text's original law-French, Plowden writes,

> Et ieo exhort toy (O Student) quaecunque soyes, que voyes ensuer mo*n* aduise, dauer ceux Equities prist en tien ment quant conceues ascun doubt sur ascun statute, & ensues le dist document, & toy trouueres ex ceo grand lumyer, come ieo ay deuaunt.
> [And I exhort you, O student, whoever you are, to follow my advice, to bear these equities in mind when you conceive any doubt on any statute, and follow the said document, and you will find it greatly illuminating, as I have done before.][42]

The link between the practical orientation of the book and the specificity of its concern with enabling individual lawyers to engage in equitable reconstructions of legislative intention appears to have been picked up by a contemporary reader, whose marginal notes, written in a late sixteenth-century hand, remain in a Bodleian copy of the first (1571) edition of the *Commentaries,* pressmark KK.10.Jur. This reader has annotated every one of the well-known discussions of equitable interpretation that occur in the first part of the *Commentaries,* as well as others less often cited. On folio 10r of the case of *Fogassa v. Reniger,* he has bracketed the text and written in the right-hand margin, "Intents of *the* Makers of Statutes." At the bottom of folio 17r, before one of the classic discussions of equity, the reader has underlined an argument that penal statutes should not be extended by equity against the party to be penalized, and has written, "Penall Statutes taken favourably"; he then brackets the whole Aristotelian discussion of equity that follows on folio 17v. His interest in the concept of intention continues in the case of *Colthirst v. Benjushin,* where he makes a note of "Lentent del condicion" on folio 23v. In the case of *Wymbishe v. Talboys* he makes note at the bottom of folio 46v of a "Statute penall not taken by Equity," whereas on folio 53r he finds a "Statute taken by Equity"; in the left hand margin of folio 57v he notes the "Intent of *the* statute" and, at the bottom right of folio 59r, he finds the conclusion "Within Equity of the Statute." In *Partridge v. Strange and Croker,* another locus of equity doctrine, the whole of Saunder's important discussion on folio 82v is bracketed, and the marginal note "Within *the* Equity of *the* Statute" adjoined. In *Stowell v. Zouch,* another classic discussion on folio 363r, which defined Acts of Parliament as positive laws consisting of the letter and the internal sense, is underlined and bracketed against the marginal note, "acts del Parl*ement*." Against Serjeant Catlin's citation of Aristotle's definition of equity on folio 375r, he writes in the margin, "Aequitas".

The reader of Bodleian KK.10.Jur has relatively little interest in the case of the duchy of Lancaster, the citing of which by Maitland drew Kantorowicz's attention to the Tudor subscription to the fiction of corporate personality. He does, however, underline a reference to the "corps politique" in the case of *Hill v. Grange* (which I shall discuss). My argument is not, however, simply that this reader's references to equity outweigh those to the king's body politic (though they clearly do). It is, rather, that this reader's response supports my argument that the two features I have been trying to identify as characteristic of Plowden's *Commentaries* — the concern with the practical application of equitable principles of interpretation to parliamentary legislation, and with enabling the reader's judgment of individual, concrete instances — encourage, in themselves, a distinct form of political consciousness which is not quite that supposed by those readers of Kantorowicz for whom the King's body is the "master symbol" of his absolute power.[43] The kind of thing I am thinking of is best illustrated by an example. A declamatory exercise familiar to the Romans and designed to debate the letter (*scriptio*) versus the intention (*voluntas*) of the law concerns the question of whether a penal law forbidding men to climb the walls or open the gates of the city should be equitably disregarded in the case of one who committed the offense in order to drive back the city's enemies in time of war.[44] The example occurs twice in Plowden, once, in *Eyston v. Studd* among a cluster of references to Aristotle, St. German, and others, and again, in *Fogassa v. Reniger* when Sergeant Pollard, setting out to prove that Fogassa's agreement with the Southampton collector of customs lies within the intent of the statute requiring the payment of subsidies on imports, declares,

> And I have read in Books that amongst the *Romans* there was a Law, that every one that scaled the Walls in the Night Time should be condemned to Death, and a certain Person in the Time of Night scaled the Walls in Time of War to discover the approach of the Enemy, and he was not only discharged by the Senate from penalty of Death, but besides was well rewarded for the Action, and yet he had thereby broken the Words of the Law, but the wise senators expounded it to be no Breach of the Intent of the Law, *because that Law was made to prevent the Hurt and Danger that would come to the Romans by scaling of the Walls, and not to inhibit Benefit and Safety to the City.* [my italics][45]

Pollard, unlike his sources, presumes to expound the *intention* of the legendary penal law: "That Law was made to prevent the Hurt and Danger that would come to the Romans by scaling of the Walls". No other user of the example, as far as I know, offers precisely this hypothesis, and indeed, in Quintilian, the law is supposed to have been a law against the scaling of the city walls by *foreigners,* not by Romans, while in St. German the law requires that "no man vnder payne of deth shuld open the gates of the cytie before the sonne rysinge."[46] Clearly, while all commentators agree to understand that the disregarding of the law in this exemplary case respects the legislator's intention, they would hardly be in agreement about the nature of that intention. Thus it becomes clear that the imperative to hypothesize, to reconstruct the intentions of the absent legislators, necessarily inherent in the rationale of equitable jurisdiction, compels an implicit but distinctive form of political action. The judiciary finds itself, in construing the letter according to the intention of the law, obliged to suppose a governing principle of legislative intention, which unsurprisingly turns out to be the principle of prevention of mischief, or enlargement of benefit, for the citizens or the polity as a whole.[47] This, in turn, of course, encourages the conceptualization of the judicial function as the abstraction and exposition, from the phrases and clauses of particular statutes, of details of the public benefit or commonweal to which each statute tends. The judiciary thus glosses the legislature, and the gloss delineates the features of the "body politic."

The judicial function, thus conceived, is occasionally made explicit in Plowden and in Plowden-derived discourses on equity and statutes. Thus, for example, in *Partridge v. Strange and Croker* (in a discussion noted by the reader of Bodleian KK.10.Jur) Chief Justice Saunders argues that a statute which made it unlawful for a man to sell or bequeath land of which he had not been in possession for a full year should be construed equitably, in spite of its being penal, since it was intended for the good of the public:

> And then I say, although the statute gives a Penalty, yet seeing it is very beneficial to the public Weal [beneficial al publique weale] things which are out of the Letter shall be within the Equity of it: And if the Words of it are obscure, they shall, for the same Reason, be expounded most strongly for the publick Good[pur le weal publique]. For Words, which are no other than the Verberation of the Air, do not constitute the Statute, but are only Images of it, and the Life of the Statute rests in the Minds of the Expositors of the Words, that is, the Makers of the Statutes. And if they are dispersed, so that their Minds cannot be known, then those who may approach nearest to their minds shall construe the Words, and these are the Sages of the Law Whose Talents are exercised in the study of such matters.[48]

Drawing on Saunders's argument here, a treatise attributed to Sir Christopher Hatton observed that the equitable interpretation of statutes constituted a new form of political agency which no one as yet had seen fit to check. Legislators, as the author pointed out, were necessarily absent if elected, and this absence was supplemented by the interpretative activity of the judiciary: "The Assembly of Parliament being ended, *Functi sunt officio,* and their Authority is returned to the Electors so clearly that if they were altogether assembled again for interpretation by a voluntary meeting, *eorum non essent interpretari.* For the Sages of the Law, whose wits are exercised in such matters, have the interpretation in their hands, and their Authority no man taketh in hand to control, wherefore their power is very great, and high, and we seek these interpretations as Oracles from their mouths."[49] The author acknowledges that "all Statutes may be expounded by Equity so far forth as *Epicaia* goeth, that is, an exception of the Law of God, and the Law of Reason, from the general words of the Law of Man," but in practice the considerations governing such exceptions must be political: "In all Expositions by Equity, there must be . . . good judgement of evident Utility publick."[50]

If we return, at this point, to *The King's Two Bodies,* we must be struck by the fact that Kantorowicz's decision to ignore the hermeneutic activity promoted by the *Commentaries* has also led him to ignore the extent to which the vision of the "weale publique" that emerges from the text actually marginalizes, rather than makes central, the symbolic power of the monarch.

In support of his thesis of the survival of a form of political mysticism among the Tudor lawyers, Kantorowicz quotes a reference to the eternal nature of the king's political body from the case of *Hill v. Grange* (1556).

The case itself turns, at this point, on the question of whether the statute 32. Hen.8 c.34, designed to give remedy for rent in arrears to grantees or patentees of monastic lands from Henry VIII, should extend, on the grounds that the king "never dies," to the patentees of Edward VI.[51] Kantorowicz, however, does not explain the case; neither does he point out that the argument of the king's eternity, which he chooses to cite as an impressive ending to his chapter on Plowden,[52] was actually rejected by the lawyers, who concluded, on the grounds that the preamble to a statute is the key to legislative intention, that the statute was in this case decisive in specifying the king as a mortal, historical agent: "But in our Case here the Act first names the King in the Preamble with a special mark of Distinction adapted to himself, for, it says, *as also all Grantees and Patentees of the King our Sovereign Lord, of sundry Manors, &c. late belonging to Monasteries, &c., come to the Hands of the King's Majesty* . . . where this Addition of the Monasteries coming into his Hands is as strong and lively a demonstration of King *Henry* 8. as if a Man was to point him out with a Finger."[53]

Sometimes it is in the interest of the commonweal to say that the king never dies, but here the case is altered, quoth Plowden. And though the judges finally resolved to extend the words of the statute to the patentees of Edward VI, they were swayed not by the two bodies argument but by the contention of Chief Justice Brooke that the statute should be interpreted equitably in respect of the *intention of the legislators*: "*Brook,* Chief Justice, argued that the Words (*the Patentees of the said Sovereign Lord*) could not extend to the Patentees of other Kings than *Henry* 8. and that other Clause could not contain the Patentees of *Edward* 6. and that the Patentees of *Edward* 6. were out of the Words of the said Statute. But he argued that the Patentees of *Edward* 6. should be taken within the equity of the said Statute. For, he said, the *Statute was made to remedy the Mischief generally*" (my italics).[54]

Clearly, the "body politic" envisaged in this case depends for its health upon the common landlord's ability in law to take remedial action against tenants who refuse to pay their rent. Brooke's subsequent speech, a set piece on the giving or equaling of common-law actions by equity, was the one alluded to by Hake in his reference to Plowden as "our old stoarhowse."

Monarch, Justice, and "Body Politic" in Shakespeare

The Plowden who has been invoked by Anglo-American literary critics to prove the indispensability of the monarch's body to sixteenth-century conceptions of the commonweal is, then, a fiction. The principles of the equitable interpretation of statutes established in Plowden's *Commentaries* were developed in politically radical directions in the first eleven volumes of the

Reports of Sir Edward Coke (1552–1634). Coke's emphasis on the freedom of the judiciary to construe the words of statutes "according to the true intent of the makers of the Act, *pro bono publico*" had the effect, as Alan Cromartie has written, of conceptually reducing the king to the position of instrument of the public good, and of binding him to the priorities of the common law.[55] In 1607 Nicholas Fuller could invoke Plowden's idea of equitable interpretation as proof of the common law's guardianship of the subject's liberties: "Is it not apparent, that, to uphold the right of the lawes of England, the Iudges in the past have advisedly construed some wordes of divers statutes contrary to the common sence of the wordes of the statute, to uphold the meaning of the common lawes of the Realme?"[56] The fact that, in practice, this view over-stated the power of the judiciary in relation to Parliament does not detract from its importance in helping to bring about a transformation in the political imagination. Indeed, in Cromartie's view the immediate political future be-longed not to those who insisted on the distinction between Parliament and the bench, but to those who, like Coke, "made no clear distinction between a legislature's role and that of a court or council," thereby making it possible to imagine a process of collaboration and debate between Parliament and judiciary concerning the public good, a process from which the king was excluded.[57]

If the effect of Plowden's writings on the political imagination of Englishmen at the turn of the seventeenth century has been so misunderstood, it is surely worth asking how differently we might, in the light of this new evidence of Plowden's political influence, interpret the dramatic products of that imagination in the same period. Decades after Kantorowicz's influential reading of the deposition in Shakespeare's *Richard II* as a tragedy of the king's two bodies, the same play became pivotal, through the records associating it with the failed Essex rising of 1601, to the attack on formalist literary criticism launched by American new historicism and British cultural materialism.[58] For these critical movements, the commissioning of a play "of the killing of Richard the Second"[59] by the Essex conspirators on the eve of their rising became an exemplary instance of the political impact of theater, a refutation of the notion that literary texts are insulated from the materiality of power and its effects. Although attempts were made to qualify, or even deny, the evidence of any connection between Shakespeare's *Richard II* and the events that led to the rising, it is now generally conceded that Shakespeare's play permits a skeptical view of Richard's absolutist claims, and a critical view of his actions as a king.[60] Indeed, according to Donna Hamilton's persuasive reading, *Richard II* works to promote a discernible civic consciousness, a consciousness of the public weal as distinct from its embodiment in the king.[61] Hamilton's conclusion, however, suggests that this civic consciousness disappears with

Henry IV, Parts 1 and 2, when Shakespeare's interest in the commonweal is overtaken by an interest in "the threat to the realm where the king is not legally titled."[62] This view of the Henry IV plays as centrally concerned with legitimizing illegitimate power fits within the broad lines of new historicist and cultural materialist arguments, according to which the skepticism employed to expose or subvert Richard's absolutist pretensions in *Richard II* becomes, in the course of Parts 1 and 2 of *Henry IV,* the skepticism with which we watch a monarchy deprived of the signs of legitimacy go about, like the ill-equipped governor of a newly founded colony, improvising supplementary forms of power by manipulating belief. In Stephen Greenblatt's words, an audience of *Henry IV,* Part 2, watches a play in which "the illegitimacy of legitimate authority is repeatedly demonstrated" and the "commonwealth" revealed as an empty name: "The whole state seems — to adapt More's phrase — a conspiracy of the great to enrich and protect their interests under the name of commonwealth."[63] What chiefly distinguishes cultural materialist criticism on the *Henry IV* plays from its new historicist counterpart is the extent to which the former is prepared to concede agency to the figures, such as Falstaff, who in both are given the part of the colonial "Other" in this critical narrative: "Royal meanings do not go uncontested," writes Catherine Belsey, among the cultural materialists, "In the *Henry IV* plays it is Falstaff who consistently represents the refusal of monarchic order."[64] Greenblatt, by contrast, speaks of Shakespeare's "absolutist theatricality" and concludes of 2 *Henry IV* that although "Falstaff's cynical wisdom can make this opaque hypocrisy transparent," paralysis ensues: "subversive perceptions are at once produced and contained."[65]

Where, then, has the "anachronistic inflection of civic humanism" which David Norbrook, like Donna Hamilton, detects in Shakespeare's depiction of the feudal society of *Richard II,* gone by the time we come to *Henry IV,* Parts 1 and 2? Norbrook identifies this quality in Richard II with the play's concern with the suppression, under tyranny, of "full and open speech."[66] He points to the continuing anticlimax of the opening scenes, in which Richard aborts the trial by battle that should prove the justice of the cause between Bolingbroke and Mowbray. Thus, Richard's tyranny as it emerges through repeated references to the suppression of frank speech is closely related to the definition of his tyranny as an extension of royal prerogative in the direction of "wrest[ing] the sence of the law"[67] to please the prince. These connections are more explicit in *The Mirror for Magistrates,* and in the anonymous play of *Woodstock* (where Richard's lord chief justice Robert Tresilian makes the law an agent of the king's unjust taxes) than they are in Shakespeare's play, but they are nevertheless present in the latter.[68] Of course, I am not saying anything new in pointing out that the baronry's charges against Richard were dominated by the accusation that he thought himself the embodiment of the law. Kantorowicz pointed out that Richard was said to have asserted that "laws are in the King's mouth, or sometimes in his brest" (although he seems to have mistaken the spirit in which this was said; in a copy of Halle's *Chronicles* which belonged to Philip Sidney's father and mother, Henry and Mary, a fuller version of this accusation against Richard has been underlined: "*He said that the lawes of the realme were in his head, and sometime in his brest, by reason of which fantasticall opinion, he destroieth noble men and empouerisheth the poore commons*").[69] What is less frequently acknowledged, however, is that a concern with the problem of distinguishing what the law intends from what is in the monarch's head, or breast, does not simply disappear in *Henry IV*, Parts 1 and 2.[70] Indeed, the motif of Hal's youthful prodigality, around which Shakespeare constructs the dramatic narrative of Henry IV's reign, is no less than the development of a legal anecdote which offers the disturbing specter of a repetition of Richard's tyranny in the disregard shown for the common law by the young Prince Hal. If we look more closely at the way in which Shakespeare handles the common-law material of his sources and relate that in turn to the contemporary developments in the equity of the common law under discussion, we may find that the elements of a civic humanist concern with the "commonwealth" which are discernible in Shakespeare's treatment of Richard II's deposition return in *Henry IV*, Parts 1 and 2, to effect a distinction between the institutions of the monarchy and the judiciary which, far from consolidating Hal's power by containing all subversion, enables the audience to recognize the constitutional limits of royal power. It should be obvious that I am not trying to argue that Shakespeare's second tetralogy is in any way *republican* in sympathy. What I am suggesting, however, is that as well as more information about the connections between Shakespeare's company and the Essex circle in the 1590s, we need an approach to Shakespeare's plays which pays more attention to their humanistic qualities, both formal (that is, rhetorically concerned with the achievement of dramatic verisimilitude) and thematic (that is, *civic* humanist — concerned with the problem of corruption in political states, or bodies).[71] We have seen how, in the debates over equitable interpretation of statutes, a civic conception of the "body politic" emerges through judicial hypotheses of what might constitute the public good intended by the act. I'd like to suggest that it is something like this "body politic" that an audience of Shakespeare's *Henry IV*, Parts 1 and 2, are gradually enabled to imagine, as the dramatist uses Falstaff to displace and rework the play's founding legal anecdote — Sir Thomas Elyot's account of how the youthful Prince Hal violated the common law and defied the lord chief justice.[72]

Elyot's anecdote also forms the basis of an acknowledged source for *Henry IV*, the anonymous *Famous Victories of Henry the Fifth*, which, like Shakespeare's play, shapes the story of Henry V's accession as the gradual resolution of the disregard for justice shown by the future king. Elyot's moral exemplum tells how the prince, furious at the arrest of one of his servants for felony, enters the courts of the King's Bench and demands that the lord chief justice set his man free. The lord chief justice orders him to go to prison for defying "the auncient lawes of this realme."[73] In the *Famous Victories* this story functions as an ineffective attempt at paternal chastisement within the narrative of the prince's prodigality. Thus, the prince boxes the ear of the lord chief justice, who imprisons him, and appeals for authority to Henry IV, who lamentingly concedes the righteousness of the law. The prince's punishment at law thereby becomes a tautology of his filial status within the prodigal son narrative; his father is the law, and the lord chief justice is his father's representative.[74] This, in turn, means that a simple forward dramatic movement toward the illness and death of the old king is meant to suffice to transform the thuggish and frankly terrifying son into the personification of the law in the monarch. The transitional motif is that of sudden conversion; the prince, having just promised his cronies, Sir John Old-Castle and Ned, that as soon as he is king, he will appoint the latter lord chief justice, is immediately informed of his father's sickness. He hastens straight from his companions to the court, dressed in a cloak full of needles, and with a dagger in his hand. "There is never a needle in thy cloke," says his stricken father, "but it is a prick to my heart."[75] After the encounter with his father, the prince is conscience-stricken, repenting of his vengeful fantasies against the lord chief justice. In a speech which moves from accusing himself of "neglect . . . from visiting" his "sicke father" to the realization that the body of the king which lies before him is beyond visiting, he offers to weep: "Oh my dying father . . . if weeping teares which come too late, may suffice the negligence neglected too soone, I will weepe day and night until the fountaine be drie with weeping."[76]

Of course it is a condition of prodigality that "weeping tears" come too late; prodigality is, as it were, the antithesis of timely reciprocity, in which obligations are duly met and promises fulfilled. And yet the problem here is precisely not that the tears come too late, but rather that they arrive on cue, in too timely a fashion to be plausible. A more ambitious dramatist (such as Shakespeare) would face, in the reworking of this play, the problem of rendering the conversion believable in terms of the prince's *character*. This is precisely what the dramatist of *The Famous Victories* fails to do, and it is quite important, I think, to recognize how this failure limits, rather than enables, an audience's political imagination. The timing of the prince's abjuration of his cronies (the equivalents, of course, of Falstaff, Bardolph, Poins, and the rest in Shakespeare's play) to coincide precisely with his father's illness and death makes the prince's behavior look like the merest pragmatism. His simultaneous reconciliation with the lord chief justice leaves the political status quo unchanged:

the lord chief justice saw himself as representing the majesty of the king/father in chastising the prince/son, and now by the simple logic of time the son has become the king, subsuming the person of the lord chief justice into his own majesty. There appears to be nothing to prevent this new king from saying that "the lawes of the realme were in his head, and sometime in his brest".

Thus, when Stephen Greenblatt observes in passing the extent to which an audience of Shakespeare's play all along *knows* that "when Prince Henry comes to be king he will assume a character suitable to his dignity,"[77] he encourages our failure to appreciate that this knowledge, this conviction, marks both the technical advance and the shift in political consciousness represented by Shakespeare's *Henry IV* plays over a play like *The Famous Victories*. One reason that Falstaff can be idealized by critics like Greenblatt and Belsey as dispossessed Other, one of the "alien voices" recorded by the improvisations of an illegitimate power in the making, is that the credit we are prepared to give to Hal's conversion means that Falstaff's fantasies of dominating the law are no longer threatening, no longer a sinister repetition of the realized fantasies of Robert Tresilian. Yet compare Robert Tresilian's words with those of Falstaff. "It shall be law, what I shall say is law, / And what's most suitable to all your pleasures," promises Tresilian to Richard's counselors on the eve of Richard's attaining his majority, and Falstaff similarly exclaims on learning of Hal's accession: "The laws of England are at my commandment. Blessed are they that have been my friends, and woe to the Lord Chief Justice."[78]

The techniques of probability or verisimilitude that Shakespeare employs to make the timing of Hal's reformation seem credible are, I propose, self-consciously related to the techniques of proof characteristic of the equitable development of the common law in this period. As J. H. Baker has argued, equitable notions of proof as the detailed deliberation of evidence relating to the individual circumstances of the case were offering a challenge to the persistence of "archaic methods of proof, designed to settle general issues but not to answer specific questions." These "archaic methods of proof" were, he observes, "symptoms of the old concept of the judicial function as the more or less withdrawn supervision of a contest" which could only ultimately be decided by God.[79]

One aspect of the law in which the survival of such a concept of proof was increasingly being perceived as problematic related to the making and breaking of informal contracts, those extensions of trust on which the sixteenth- and seventeenth-century "culture of credit" depended, not only economically, but ethically and socially as well.[80] Sixteenth-century common law actually offered no legal remedy for the enforcement of simple contracts, beyond an action of debt according to which the accused might defend himself by "waging his law"; that is, by swearing, along with eleven other compurgators, that he owed nothing. That wager of law was being felt to be inadequate to the increasing need to ensure the eventual repayment of long-standing debts is suggested by the admission, from the mid-sixteenth century onward, of breaches of informal contract to be sued as a type of action on the case which originated as an action for the breach of a prior undertaking, known as an assumpsit.[81] For our purposes here, however, there are two crucial points to be made about the consequences for a reading of Shakespeare's second tetralogy of the transition from wager of law to assumpsit. The first is that in wager of law, as Baker suggests, the judicial function is seen as "withdrawn," merely facilitating the arbitration of God. An oath was said to be the invocation of God as witness.[82] The correspondence between a man's words and the secret knowledge in his heart was thus understood to be offered, in the act of swearing, as an anterior and interior truth to be externalized or revealed by God. Originally, of course, this divine revelation was imagined as an inscription on the body in the form of miraculous immunity to the effects of an ordeal, or in the outcome of combat. Nor had this idea, as the rationale for wager of law, been forgotten by the 1590s: "In secret things the trial of them is *per Deum et victoriam,* as in battle, or *Deum et partem,* as in wager of law," argued Francis Bacon in his defense of wager of law in 1597.[83] In assumpsit, however, the truth of a debt's existence was thought to depend on whether or not an undertaking, or a promise, might be inferred from the "consideration" or motivating reason a person might have had for offering to pay. In A. W. Simpson's words, "The actionability of informal promises is made to turn upon an analysis of the motivating reasons which induced the promissor to make the promise — the consideration or considerations for the promise."[84] Such an analysis, as Luke Wilson's chapter shows, "tends to invest contract with an intentional temporality,"[85] but it also insists that "intention" is inaccessible except as inferred, or except as *hypothesis.* In other words, in the action of assumpsit, what Bacon calls secret things — promises for which no witnesses exist, implied promises, mere *intentions* — are not imagined as anterior and interior truths to be disclosed, but as retrospectively argued inferences, the relative probability of which may be enhanced by oratorical techniques of "artificial proof."[86]

The second crucial point to be made is that this conceptual distinction between the judicial function as the facilitation of divine arbitration and the judicial function as the forensic invention of probable hypotheses was coming under intense and well-publicized scrutiny in the very years in which Shakespeare's *Richard II* and *Henry IV,* Parts 1 and 2, were first written and staged.[87] For in those years, as David Harris Sacks and Luke Wilson discuss elsewhere in this volume, the famous case brought by John Slade against Henry Morley for the breach of promise on failing to pay for goods sold was being argued in the

Exchequer Chamber.[88] At issue, as Sacks ably demonstrates, was the very viability of wager of law. Ostensibly grounded in God's intolerance of perjury, wager in fact made sense as the guarantee of good faith in a community of credit in which the parties involved knew one another.[89] Increasingly in the years before Slade's case, however, the sanctity of the oath in wager of law was becoming subject to opprobrium and ridicule. Although the courts appear to have taken steps to ensure that the defendant was aware of the gravity of the oath sworn, they were also complicit in providing professional oath-helpers, known as knights of the post, to help make up the required eleven.[90] References to the encouragement of corruption by "knights of the post" accumulate in literature published between the 1570s and 1600. In George Whetstone's *Promos and Cassandra* (which was dedicated to the lawyer William Fleetwood in the year that he compiled the index to Plowden's *Commentaries*) a wicked magistrate, confronted by an equitable judge, who accuses him of abusing the sentence of the "stryckt law" for his own ends, turns immediately to look for oath-helpers: "O Lord God is there no knyghtes of the poste heare?" he asks, "Well then, of force I must sing *Peccaui.*"[91] Thomas Nashe has the devil appear to Pierce Penniless in the form of "a knight of the Post . . . a fellowe that will sweare you anything for twelue pence," who takes on this particular human shape "onely to set men by the eares and send soules by the millions to hell."[92] Nashe's personification perhaps alludes to a proverb against judicial oaths; at any rate, Sir Edward Coke was remembered, in Slade's case, to have "sayd well, that in criminal causes, an oath in a man's own cause is the device of the devil to throw the poor souls of men into hell").[93] Shakespeare's *Henry IV,* Parts 1 and 2, engages — literally — with this contemporary discourse on the abuses of knights of the post. Thomas Harman's *Caveat for Common Cursitors* has been invoked, along with Thomas Harriot's Algonquin glossary, as analogies for the governmental strategy behind Hal's attempts to "gain the language" of his thieving companions.[94] Yet the Eastcheap scenes in fact derive from the milieu described in the anonymous pamphlet of *The Discouerie of the Knights of the Poste,* published in 1597, both the year in which *Henry IV,* Parts 1 and 2, was first performed and the year in which Slade's case moved to the Exchequer Chamber. Like Harmon's *Caveat,* the *Discouerie* sits uneasily between jest-book and instrument of reform. The first-person narrator is a justice of the peace whose Falstaffian interlocutors proceed to enlighten him on the practices of "our ancient acquaintance, the good oath-takers, or common baylers: *Alias* the knights of the post . . . heires apparent to the pillory."[95] The first interlocutor straight away sets up the justice as a fall guy for his one-liners. "[I]t is pitty you should be made a Justice of the peace that can examine a cause no better," he says.[96] (The justice ends up buying his meals.) The "acquaintance" who participate in and form the subject of the subsequent convivial discourse recall the Boar's Head crowd. There is a hostess who attacks one of the speakers for wanting credit, one knight of the post who boasts "a tun" belly, another who "will neuer be pleased when he hath bailed one, except he giue him more then his promise, and stop his mouth with a pint of old sack," another who, like Pistol, "looks very high . . . as if he would quarrell with the Moone," and another whose "firie face," like Bardolph's, makes other knights of the post "utterly deny to go before a Judge with him, for feare the fire in his face should set the J[udge's] chamber in a flame."[97] Shakespeare's Falstaff even quotes the pamphlet: "I would to God thou and I knew where a commodity of good names were to be bought" (I.ii.80–81), says the knight to Hal, in one of the heart-warming moments of "communitas" between the prince and his companions. The phrase is straight from *The . . . Knights of the Poste,* alluding to the practice of penurious knights of the post impersonating bail: "If they knew where a commoditie of good names were to be sould, yet I think all the money in their purses could not buy it."[98] Shakespeare's immersion of his Eastcheap characters in the milieu of the late sixteenth-century knight of the post inflects the frustrations and abuses of the judicial system as represented in *Richard II* with more topical meaning. As we have seen, the emphasis in other literary treatments of Richard II's abuse of the law (such as *Woodstock* and *The Mirror for Magistrates*) tends to be on Tresilian's manipulation of the words of the law to fit the prince's pleasure. Shakespeare's emphasis, apparent in the accumulated frustrations of the aborted trial by battle, is rather on the censoring effects of a judicial function conceived as the facilitator of a divine revelation of a hidden (anterior and interior) truth. Shakespeare is not sparing of references to such a concept of judicial proof. "I wish — so please my sovereign — ere I move / What my tongue speaks my right drawn sword may *prove*," declares Bolingbroke, and again: "Look what I speak, my life shall *prove* it true," and another time: "Besides I say, and will in battle *prove*" (my italics, I.i.44–45, 87, 92). Poststructuralist critics read lines like these, and the frustrated trial by battle in general, as representative of a passing world of certainty in meaning, and legitimate absolutism. Phyllis Rackin argues that trial by combat is "a crucial ritual in the scheme of divine right" and that its failure to take place in *Richard II* is consequently significant of a vanishing world of providential belief: "Richard is the only king in the two tetralogies with an unambiguous hereditary claim to the throne, rooted in an uncontested genealogy and ratified by divine right. The medieval world — and with it the possibility of ritualized judicial combat — disappears with his deposition."[99]

For Catherine Belsey, similarly, though the "vanishing world" where "the essential link between signifier and referent had not been broken" is an "imaginary one," yet its loss through Richard's failure to hold the signifier and signified together in his title means that "Bolingbroke's reign becomes in consequence one of bitter uncertainties, conflicts for meaning which are simultaneously conflicts for power."[100] A nostalgia for the world of immanent justice and sacramental kingship is implied, if only to give meaning to the postmodern "crisis" of meaning and legitimacy of Bolingbroke's reign. And yet the associations of trial by battle were not exclusively royal and did not necessarily imply absolutism. In earlier sixteenth-century literature, combat can be seen as much the same thing as wager of law. Thus, in the mid-century interlude *Impacient Poverty,* the hero, furious at being arrested for a debt of elevenpence, vows to wage his law, or "let it be tryet by manhode."[101] Moreover, the lawyers and antiquaries of the turn of the century were far from suggesting that the significance of the Mowbray-Bolingbroke trial was its being, as Rackin claims, the end of an era, "the last formal trial by battle in English history."[102] These writers were concerned to distinguish trial by battle as being comparatively "rational" ("not without reason") when contrasted with trial by ordeal: "for indeede," as one wrote, "in the triall by red-hot iron and boiling water a miraculous preservation is to be expected," whereas in trial by battle, "the strength, the spirit and the powers of nature decide the controversy."[103] Indeed, one of Richard II's violations of the common law consisted precisely in abusing this *rational* aspect of trial by battle. It was said that "he contrary to the Great Charter of England caused dyvers lustie men to appele diuers olde men, upon matters determinable at the common law, in the Court Marcial, because in that court is no triall, but only by battaile: whereupon the said aged personnes fearynge sequel of the matter submitted themselfes to his mercy."[104]

It is possible, then, that Shakespeare employs the idea of trial by battle, with its emphasis on the unity of word and body ("Look what I speak, my life shall prove it true") not to represent the always already lost unity of the body politic and the body of the king, but to suggest an impasse in the judicial system. Nor is this system wholly identified with Richard as "the only king in the two tetralogies with an unambiguous hereditary claim to the throne . . . ratified by divine right." For Bolingbroke's first act in the Parliament in which one might have expected a denunciation of Richard's crimes is actually to reopen the investigation into the undisclosed truth of Gloucester's death. The terms in which Bolingbroke invites disclosure — "Now, Bagot, freely speak thy mind" (IV.i.2) — seem to offer relief from the censorship associated with Richard's reign, yet as the barons proceed to give evidence by throwing down their gages in readiness to wage battle, it becomes clear that the terms in which "proof" is conceived remain, as they were in the first trial, entirely those of compurgation, the danger of invoking God as witness to be borne upon the swearer's body. The conclusion to this strange little scene is a sense of frustration: the only reliable witness (Thomas Mowbray) turns out to be dead, yet Bolingbroke nevertheless defers the trial—"Your differences shall all rest under gage," he declares (IV.i.105).

For Shakespeare to place such an emphasis on the frustration of the oath as the instrument of justice is to engage with a growing body of opinion which opposed the pretensions of canon law to have access, through compurgation and the abuses of the ex officio oath, to the secrets of men's consciences. As Sacks observes in Chapter 1, Christopher St. German's *Doctor and Student* had, as early as 1530, offered a common-law objection to the canon-law argument that an intention to perform makes the promise liable. The Student argues to the Doctor that "no accyon can lye ... vpon suche promyses, for yt is secrete in hys owne conscyence whether he entendyd for to be bound or naye. And of the entent inward in the herte: mannes lawe cannot Juge ... and yf an accyon sholde lye in that case in the law Canon: than sholde the law Canon Juge vppon the inwarde intente of the herte / whyche can not be as me semeth."[105]

Wager of law might be defended by common lawyers concerned to attack the canonists' abuse of the ex officio oath (James Morice, for example, argued that the situation of "the defendant ... voluntarilie offring an oath for his clear discharge" was acceptable in an action of debt, whereas Nicholas Fuller distinguished between the use of the oath in wager for debt and its use in criminal causes, which he saw as devilish[106]). Nevertheless, the increasing use of pleas of assumpsit in local courts dealing with broken credit agreements, as well as the outcome of Slade's case itself, demonstrates a widespread dissatisfaction with the practice of compurgation.[107] In literary texts, the openness of wager of law to abuse became symbolic of wider corruption in judicial and political systems; in Whetstone's *Promos and Cassandra,* the king assumes that the corrupt magistrate he examines will wage his law: "You may be bold these faults for to deny / Some lyttel care upon their othes to lye."[108] Shakespeare's hint at the problems of a justice based on purgation under Bolingbroke is followed up by an allusion to the anecdote in Elyot's *Governour* according to which Bolingbroke's son threatened the lord chief justice for imprisoning his man. The prince not only hangs around with men who, we are told, "stand in narrow lanes, and beat our watch and rob our passengers," but "takes it on point of honour to support / So dissolute a crew" (V.iii.8–12). In the course of *Henry IV, Part 1,* the "dissolute crew" is clearly identified as enjoying, in Hal's friendship, immunity before the law. Indeed, the one occurrence of the word "commonwealth" in the play alludes to this immunity: Gadshill says that the members of the nobility with whom he steals "pray continually to their saint the commonwealth, or rather not pray to her, but prey on her, for they ride up and down on her, and make her their boots." "What, the commonwealth their boots?" asks the chamberlain, "Will she hold out water in foul way?" "She will, she will," Gadshill replies; "justice hath liquored her" (II.i.78–84).

How does Shakespeare suggest the possibility that this political status quo will ever change? In *Henry IV,* Part 2, the force that slowly erodes the well-being of Falstaff and his companions is rightly linked by critics to the inevitable exhaustion of carnival: "Age and diseases encroach upon him, supplanting the carnivalesque image with warnings of decrepitude," says Neil Rhodes. To this recognition Greenblatt gives a Foucauldian inflection: "In 2 *Henry IV* the characteristic operations of power are less equivocal than they had been in the preceeding play. . . . Falstaff, whose earlier larcenies were gilded by fantasies of innate grace, now talks of turning disease to commodity."[109]

Yet Falstaff's "decline" is not simply carnivalesque, or rather Lenten, in form; it is linked to our gradual hypothesizing both of Hal's intentions with regard to justice and of a general good intended by justice which will curb Hal's magisterial power. The whole of *Henry IV,* Part 2, is shaped around the material signs of a diminishing of Falstaff's *credit* in the security of a promise —an assumpsit—which everyone imagines to have been made to him by his prince. The second scene of the play opens with Falstaff's frustration at being unable to purchase a new short coat and slops on the strength of Bardolph's bond; his tailor "liked not the security" (I.ii.33). In a parallel scene a group of disaffected noblemen dispute whether they should rely on the supposition that Northumberland will supply them with twenty-five thousand men at arms. Like Falstaff's tailor, Lord Bardolph is one who "likes not the security"; "we fortify in papers and in figures," he says, "using the names of men instead of men" (I.iii.56–57). "Using the names of men instead of men" recalls the "commodity of good names" hoped for by knights of the post impersonating bail; the parallel diffuses the sense of overextended credit, of encroaching bankruptcy. Immediately afterward, act II opens with Mistress Quickly asking the officers, Fang and Snare, if they have entered her action against Falstaff: "He's an infinitive thing upon my score," she complains (II.i.23), proceeding, before the lord chief justice, to plead his implied promise to marry her (II.i.83–101). The peculiar sense of paralysis, of marking time, which characterizes the action of *Henry IV,* Part 2, is intimately related to the play's progression through these scenes of the erosion of credit, which in turn refer obliquely to the way in which competing hypotheses of intention sustain dramatic action. Uncertainty, for example, around the intentions of Northumberland is deliberately sustained for two whole acts. At the beginning of act III, in a speech which critics often cite in support of the proposition that the second tetralogy is ultimately providentialist, Henry IV recalls and gives credit to Richard's prophecy because he has just received letters suggesting that the rebels can count on reinforcements of fifty thousand men. Henry infers from this that Northumberland has become his enemy:

> "The time shall come" — thus did he follow it —
> "The time will come, that foul sin, gathering head,
> Shall break into corruption" — so went on,
> Foretelling this same time's condition,
> And the division of our amity. (III.i.75–79)

Warwick, however, elicits from Henry the grounds of this conviction: "They say," he replies, "the Bishop and Northumberland / Are fifty thousand strong" (III.ii.95–96). This fifty thousand is a rumor; these reinforcements, as Hastings previously admitted, merely "live . . . in the hope / Of great Northumberland, whose bosom burns / With an incensed fire of injuries" (I.iii.11–12). Pretensions to know exactly what burns in the bosom of Northumberland (the "inward intent of his heart") are doomed to failure; the rebels have, like Hotspur, eaten "the air and promise of supply" (I.iii.28), and Warwick takes a chance with this probability: "It cannot be, my lord. / Rumour doth double, like the voice and echo, / The numbers of the feared" (III.ii.96–98). Rumor, the presiding genius of the play, supplies motivation and sustains action even when credit has almost entirely run out. Throughout *Henry IV, Part 2*, the diminishing credit the play is prepared to accord to Hal's inferred promise — the belief that he *assumpsit*, or undertook, to place the laws in the hands of Falstaff and his other companions — acquires a material force, indeed, generates such action as there is. We note it in the churlishness of Falstaff's tailor, in Mistress Quickly's bawdy reference to her long-deferred litigation ("A hundred mark is a long one for a poor lone woman to bear, and I have borne, and borne, and borne, and have been fubbed off, and fubbed off, and fubbed off" II.i.30–33), and in Shallow's queasy plying of Falstaff with hospitality in Gloucestershire. The sense of tardiness, of reluctance to make a decisive move, is characteristic of the temporality of credit, of "living in the hope" of another's intentions; the play "loiter[s]" as the lord chief justice accuses Falstaff of doing (II.ii.181). At the same time, this refusal of *timeliness* is crucial, as we have seen, to the resolution of the dramatic problem of Hal's credibility. In *The Famous Victories*, the prince's weeping arrived on cue after the boxing of the justice's ear and in time for the illness of his father. In *Henry IV, Part 2*, Shakespeare has Hal allude to the importance of not showing grief when it is expected. When Poins berates him for "talking idly" when his father is so sick, he replies, "it is not meet that I should be sad now my father is sick. . . . What wouldst thou think of me if I should weep?" Naturally, Poins answers, "I would think thee a most princely hypocrite," and so, implies Hal, would the audience (II.ii.29–55). The refusal to show what burns in his bosom, in other words, is crucial to our crediting him with something burning there, with interiority. Thus the delaying of the action in *Henry IV,* Part 2, by what amounts to a series of hypotheses over the likelihood of what others are thinking and feeling has the positive effect of producing Hal's reformation into someone emotionally credible and politically transformative. As part of this, Shakespeare reworks the supposed event of the prince's striking of lord chief justice into the interstices of *Henry IV,* Part 2, into spaces of hearsay and rumor. Significantly, the incident becomes an allusion among a number of self-consciously retarding exchanges between Falstaff and the lord chief justice. Falstaff, anticipating his later triumph over the lord chief justice, savors a moment of condescension: "As for that box of the ear the Prince gave you, he gave it like a rude Prince, and you took it like a sensible lord. I have checked him for it, and the young lion repents — [*Aside*] marry, not in ashes and sack-cloth, but in new silk and old sack" (I.ii.194–98).

According to Catherine Belsey, Falstaff's "emblematic significance" as resistant to monarchic order "reaches its climax when he performs in play the role of king to Hal's prince."[110]

Yet at this moment, the effect is just the opposite. Falstaff's words, mocking those of Henry IV in Elyot's anecdote and in *The Famous Victories,* spell out the disturbing implications of those versions of the story. What would have happened if Henry IV had, in fact, indulged his son's action, bidding the magistrate take the blow "like a sensible lord"? The significance of Shakespeare's evasion of the staging of the boxing of the ear incident, and of his deferral of the final hostile confrontation between Hal and the lord chief justice, through scene after scene of implied deliberation over the nature of Hal's intentions, becomes clear. It is through uncertainty, in the form of scope for hypothesis, that both forensic and dramatic arguments constitute our knowledge of the intentions of others. In retrospect we can "see all along" that Hal's intentions were as Warwick glosses them, because the competing and cynical hypotheses enacted by court and companions invite us to engage skeptically with the Tacitean claustrophobia of Henry IV's warning to Thomas of Clarence that Hal's "temper . . . must be well observ'd" (IV.iv.36). At the same time as techniques of artificial proof work against our thinking of Hal's "sadness" as the mask of a hypocrite, they help to defer Hal's confrontation with justice until after the death of Henry IV. The effect is to dissociate the drama of filial succession and inheritance from the resolution of the problem of litigious agency in the commonwealth, and so to prevent the conceptual subsuming of justice under the idea of the monarchy. Although, in the final confrontation, the common law still expresses itself as representative of the monarch in judgment — "Your Highness was pleased to forget my place / The majesty and power of law and justice / The image of the king whom I presented" (V.ii.77-79) — the prince's striking the lord chief justice is held to have been obstructive to his office, "Whiles I was busy for the commonwealth" (V.ii.76). Whereas *Richard II* opens with the king pretending to the position of judge: "face to face, / And frowning brow to brow, ourselves will hear / The accuser and accused freely speak," *Henry IV,* Part 2, ends with a declaration of the monarch's readiness to let his "intents" be a product of the hermeneutic directions of the sages of the law:

> You did commit me:
> For which I do commit into your hand
> Th'unstained sword that you have us'd to bear,
> With this remembrance — that you use the same
> With the like bold, just, and impartial spirit,
> As you have done 'gainst me. There is my hand.
> You shall be as a father to my youth,
> My voice shall sound as you do prompt mine ear
> And I will stoop and humble my *intents*
> To your *well practis'd wise directions.* (V.ii.112–121)

The echo here of Plowden, as he would be quoted and summarized in numerous epitomes and treatises well into the seventeenth century, is surely striking. And while none of this, perhaps, denies the final effect of an increased governmentality in Shakespeare's play, it does, I think, make us able to counter Greenblatt's famous proposition that in *Henry IV,* Part 2, "subversive perceptions are at once produced and contained"[111] with the reflection that we may have been looking for perceptions "subversive" of absolute monarchy in the wrong parts of the play.

Notes

1. The classic statement of the case against the emergence of "civic consciousness" in sixteenth-century England can be found in J. G. A. Pocock, *The Machiavellian Moment: Florentine Political Thought and the Atlantic Republican Tradition* (Princeton, N.J.: Princeton University Press, 1975), 333–60. It is countered by Patrick Collinson, *Elizabethan Essays* (London: Hambledon Press, 1994), 17–27 and 30–57, and by Markku Peltonen, *Classical Humanism and Republicanism in English Political Thought, 1570–1640* (Cambridge: Cambridge University Press, 1995). See also David Norbrook, *Writing the English Republic: Poetry, Rhetoric and Politics, 1627–1660* (Cambridge:

Cambridge University Press, 1999), 5–17. I would like to thank David Norbrook, Quentin Skinner, J. H. Baker, Victoria Kahn, Erica Sheen, and Paul Hamilton for reading and commenting on earlier drafts of this paper, and the audiences at seminars at the Universities of Oxford, Bangor, Berkeley, Hull, Sheffield, and Sussex for criticism.

2. Pocock, *Machiavellian Moment,* 334–35.

3. See Ernst H. Kantorowicz, *The King's Two Bodies: A Study in Medieval Political Theology* (Princeton, N.J.: Princeton University Press, 1957).

4. Michel Foucault, *Discipline and Punish: the Birth of the Prison,* trans. Alan Sheridan (Harmondsworth: Penguin, 1977), 28–29; 208–9. Foucault's homage to Kantorowicz and his influence on recent Anglo-American critical discourse is noted by David Norbrook, "The Emperor's New Body? *Richard II,* Ernst Kantorowicz, the Politics of Shakespeare Criticism," *Textual Practice* 10 (1996): 329–57, at 329.

5. Norbrook, "Emperor's New Body?" 343.

6. See Alan Cromartie, "The Constitutionalist Revolution: The Transformation of Political Culture in Early Stuart England," *Past and Present* 163 (1999): 76–120, especially 97–100. Cromartie's article is exceptional in its appreciation of the significance of Plowden's legacy for Sir Edward Coke, and so for subsequent political culture; thanks to David Colclough for alerting me to it.

7. Louis Montrose, "The Elizabethan Subject and the Spenserian Text," in *Literary Theory/Renaissance Texts,* ed. Patricia Parker and David Quint (Baltimore: Johns Hopkins University Press, 1986), 307.

8. Norbrook, "Emperor's New Body?" 344.

9. David Starkey, "Representation Through Intimacy: A Study in the Symbolism of the Monarchy and Court Office in Early Modern England," in *Symbols and Sentiments: Cross-Cultural Studies in Symbolism,* ed. Ioan Lewis (Academic Press, 1977), 187–225.

10. Marie Axton, "The Influence of Edmund Plowden's Succession Treatise," *Huntington Library Quarterly* 37 (1973–74): 209–226; Axton, *The Queen's Two Bodies: Drama and the Elizabethan Succession* (London: Institute of Historical Research, 1977).

11. In the course of this essay, I shall be referring to three different editions of Plowden, but all of them retain the same foliation, so references to the folio numbers which the editions have in common are interchangeable. The editions are *Les Commentaries ou Reports de Edmund Plowden* (London: Richard Tottel, 1571); *Les Commentaries ou Reports de Edmund Plowden,* 2 parts (London: Richard Tottel, 1578 and 1584), and *The Commentaries or Reports of Edmund Plowden of the Middle Temple esq.,* 2 parts (London: S. Brooke, 1816).

12. Quentin Skinner, "Meaning and Understanding in the History of Ideas," *History and Theory* 8 (1969): 10. Marie Axton's study, of course, is not of this "history of ideas" type.

13. Quentin Skinner, "Motives, Intentions and the Interpretation of Texts," *New Literary History,* 3 (1972): 393–408; Roger Chartier, *Cultural History: Between Practices and Representations,* trans. Lydia G. Cochrane (Cambridge: Cambridge University Press, 1988); Chartier, *The Cultural Uses of Print in Early Modern France,* trans. Lydia G. Cochrane (Princeton, N.J.: Princeton University Press, 1989); D. F. McKenzie, *Bibliography and the Sociology of Texts* (London: British Library, 1986).

14. Kantorowicz, *King's Two Bodies,* 3; F. W. Maitland, "The Crown as Corporation,"

in *Selected Essays,* ed. H. D. Hazeltine et al. (Cambridge: Cambridge University Press, 1936), 104–27.

15. S. F. C. Milsom, *Historical Foundations of the English Common Law,* 2nd ed. (Toronto: Butterworths, 1981), vi. On the difference between Maitland's and Milsom's approaches, see Norman F. Cantor, *Inventing the Middle Ages* (New York: William Morrow, 1991), 66–69. See also L. W. Abbot, *Law Reporting in England, 1485–1585* (London: Athlone Press, 1973), 9.

16. F. W. Maitland, "English Law and the Renaissance," in *Selected Historical Essays of F. W. Maitland* (Cambridge: Cambridge University Press, 1957), 143. J. H. Baker, "English Law and the Renaissance," in *The Legal Profession and the Common Law* (London: Hambledon Press, 1988), 461–76; see also Donald Kelley, "History, English Law and the Renaissance," *Past and Present* 65 (1974): 24–51.

17. Baker, "English Law and the Renaissance," 473; see also R. M. Fisher, "Thomas Cromwell, Humanism and Educational Reform," *Bulletin of the Institute of Historical Research* 50 (1977): 151–63.

18. Baker, "English Law and the Renaissance," 474–75. For the political significance of the enhancement of the judicial role in this period, see Cromartie, "Constitutionalist Revolution," 81–86.

19. "The prologe of the Auctor, yelded in English by E.M.," *Les Commentaries, ou les Reports de Edmund Plowden* (London: Richard Tottel, 1571), sigs. ¶5r-v. Italicized letters such as the *m* at the beginning of this quotation were contracted in the original.

20. Victoria Kahn, "Humanism and the Resistance to Theory," *Literary Theory/ Renaissance Texts,* 373–96.

21. Axton, *Queen's Two Bodies,* 28, 37.

22. Quoted from B. L. Harg, MS 27, fols. 84–85v, by Geoffrey de C. Parmiter, *Edmund Plowden: A Elizabethan Recusant Lawyer* (Catholic Record Society, 1987), 72.

23. William Hakewill, *The Libertie of the Subject: Against the Pretended Power of Impositions Maintained by an Argument in Parliament An° 7° Jacobi Regis* (London: 1641), 95; noted by de C. Parmiter, *Edmund Plowden,* 72.

24. See Samuel Thorne, *A Discourse upon the Exposicion & Understanding of Statutes with Sir Thomas Egerton's Additions* (San Marino, California: Huntington Library, 1942), 60.

25. Aristotle, *Nicomachean Ethics,* trans. H. Rackham (London: William Heineman, 1932), 5.x.5, 315–17; see Christopher St. German, "What is Equytie," *Doctor and Student* [1530], ed. T. F. T. Plucknett and J. L. Barton (London: Selden Society, 1974), 95–111; Jean Gerson, *Oeuvres Completes,* ed. P. Glorieux (Paris: 1960–67), vol. 5, 177; Zofia Rueger, "Gerson's Concept of Equity and Christopher St. German," *History of Political Thought* 3 (1982): 1–30; John Guy, "Law, Equity and Conscience in Henrician Juristic Thought," John Guy and Alistair Fox, *Reassessing the Henrician Reformation, 1500–1550* (Oxford: Basil Blackwell, 1986), 179–98; John Guy, *Christopher St. German on Chancery and Statute* (London: Selden Society, 1985).

26. F. W. Maitland, *Equity: A Course of Lectures* [1909], rev. ed. John Brunyate (Cambridge: Cambridge University Press, 1936), 1–9. For an example of the literary-critical equation of equity with the conscionable jurisdiction of the prerogative courts, see Arthur Kinney, who writes, "It is just this distinction between the unalterable law and its

literal representation in the courts of common law and the explosively multiplying cases of equity, or individual exception and mercy in Chancery, that is Shakespeare's basis for the great debate in the trial scene of *The Merchant of Venice,* "Sir Philip Sidney and the Uses of History," *The Historical Renaissance,* ed. Heather Dubrow and Richard Strier (Chicago: University of Chicago Press, 1988), 304–5. A challenge to this view comes from William Chester Jordan, "Approaches to the Court Scene in the Bond Story: Equity and Mercy or Reason and Nature," *Shakespeare Quarterly* 33 (1982): 49–59. The present study is indebted to the excellent explorations of the relation between the equitable reconstruction of intention and the rhetorical category of hypothesis which may be found in Kathy Eden, *Poetic and Legal Fiction in the Aristotelian Tradition* (Princeton, N.J.: Princeton University Press, 1986), and Luke Wilson, "*Hamlet* Equity, Intention, Performance," *Studies in the Literary Imagination* 224 (1991): 91–113, and "*Hamlet, Hales v. Petit,* and the Hysteresis of Action," *ELH* 60 (1993): 17–55. See also Ian Maclean, *Interpretation and Meaning in the Renaissance: The Case of Law* (Cambridge: Cambridge University Press), 181–85.

27. Charles M. Gray, "The Boundaries of the Equitable Function," *American Journal of Legal History,* 20 (1976): 192–226; Stuart E. Prall, "The Development of Equity in Tudor England," *American Journal of Legal History* 8 (1964): pp. 1–19; Baker, *Reports of Sir John Spelman,* vol. 2, 40–43.

28. St. German, *Doctor and Student,* 97–99.

29. See Samuel Thorne's preface to Edward Hake, *Epieikeia: A Dialogue on Equity in Three Parts,* ed. D. C. Yale (New Haven, Conn.: Yale University Press, 1953), v.

30. Thorne, "Introduction," *Discourse upon the Exposicion,* 55–62.

31. St. German, *Doctor and Student,* 103.

32. *Discourse upon the Exposicion,* 140–41.

33. Ibid. There are two manuscripts of the *Discourse* in the Huntington Library, EL 2565 and EL 496. One of these appears to be a condensed version of the other, with additions from Plowden's *Commentaries.* See Thorne's introduction, 92–100.

34. Hake's *Epieikeia* exists in an elegant, vellum-bound MS, written in a italic hand, BL. Add. MS, 35, 326; Sir Christopher Hatton, *A Discourse Concerning Statutes, or Acts of Parliament: And the Exposition thereof* (London: Richard Tonson, 1677); Thomas Ashe, *EPIEIKEIA Et Table generall a les Annales del Ley, per facilement troueres touts les cases contenus in yceux; queux concerne le exposition des Statutes per Equitie* (London: Society of Stationers, 1607).

35. *Abridgement des touts les cases Reportes alarge per Mounsieur Plowden . . . composee . . . per T. A.* (London: 1607); *An Exact Abridgement of the Commentaries or Reports of the Learned and Famous lawyer, Edmund Plowden . . . digested by Sir John Walter . . . Englished by Fabian Hicks* (London: 1659).

36. C. K. Allen, *Law in the Making* (Oxford: Clarendon Press, 1964), 455.

37. Prall, "Development of Equity," 6.

38. Ashe, *Abridgement des touts les cases,* fol. 2v.

39. Hake, *Epieikeia,* 108.

40. Hake, *Epieikeia,* 85.

41. Les Commentaries ou Reports de Edmund Plowden . . . Ouesque vn table perfect des choses notables contenus en ycell nouelment compose per William Fleetwood Recorder de Londres, & iamme cy deuaunt imprimer (London: Richard Tottel, 1578).

42. *Les Commentaries,* 2 parts (1578 and 1584), fol. 468v.

43. As David Starkey suggests in "Representation Through Intimacy," 187–225.

44. See Stanley F. Bonner, *Education in Ancient Rome* (London: Methuen, 1977), 301; Quintilian, *Institutio Oratoria* trans. H. E. Butler (London: Heineman, 1936), vol. 3, 138; VII.vi.7; Guy, "Law, Equity and Conscience," 185; St. German, *Doctor and Student,* 97–98.

45. *The Commentaries,* fol. 18v.

46. St. German, *Doctor and Student,* 97.

47. Samuel Thorne says as much: "As enactments acquire formal rigidity their words must be saved by regarding departures from them as 'interpretations' made by judges. . . . In Plowden this is taken in its widest sense — as the desire to reach results 'beneficial a le common weal' or to avoid 'enconuience & mischiefe' — and under so broad a concept of legislative intention, similarly equivalent in all respects to that of justice, acts could be boldly extended," *Discourse upon the Exposicion,* 62.

48. *The Commentaries* (1816) and *Les Commentaries* (1578 and 1584), fol. 82v.

49. Hatton, *Treatise Concerning Statutes,* 29–30.

50. Ibid., 31, 36–37; "Utility publick," which has a very late seventeenth-century ring, denies the authorship of Christopher Hatton, who died in 1591. The treatise is possibly not by Hatton, but it may be a translation of a sixteenth-century law-French original, in which case the original phrase may have been something like "weal publique."

51. Kantorowicz, *King's Two Bodies,* 13; *Les Commentaries* (1571), fol. 176 v.

52. Kantorowicz, *King's Two Bodies,* 23.

53. *The Commentaries,* fol. 176v; for the preamble of an act of parliament as a key to legislative intention, see Hake, *Epieikeia,* 83 and Plowden, *The Commentaries* (1816), fols. 10v, 369r, 464r.

54. Ibid., fol. 178r.

55. Cromartie, "Constitutionalist Revolution," 99.

56. *The Argument of Master Nicholas Fuller in the Case of Thomas Lad, and Richard Maunsell, his Clients* (1607), sig. D2v.

57. Cromartie, "Constitutionalist Revolution," acknowledges the "unrealistic demands made on the judiciary" by Coke's and Fuller's theoretical positions but nevertheless sees them as agents of conceptual transformation, 97, 102, 107. For a historian skeptical of the claims made for the hermeneutic power of the judiciary, see J. P. Sommerville, *Politics and Ideology in England, 1603–1640* (London: Longman, 1986), 95–100.

58. See Stephen Greenblatt, "Introduction, in *The Power of Forms in the English Renaissance* (Oklahoma: Pilgrim Books, 1982), 4; Jonathan Dollimore and Alan Sinfield, eds., *Political Shakespeare* (Manchester: Manchester University Press, 1985), 8; Jonathan Dollimore, *Radical Tragedy* (Hassocks, Sussex: Harvester Press, 1984), 24.

59. See Evelyn May Albright, "Shakespeare's *Richard II* and the Essex Conspiracy," *PMLA,* 42 (1927): 686–720, at 689.

60. Leeds Barroll attempted to cast doubt on evidence that Shakespeare's play had "any political relevance" in "A New History for Shakespeare and His Time," *Shakespeare Quarterly* 39 (1988): 441–64, at 452. Critics who have convincingly argued for the play's antiabsolutist elements include Donna Hamilton, "The State of Law in *Richard II,*" *Shakespeare Quarterly* 34 (1983): 5–17; David Norbrook, "A Liberal Tongue: Language and Rebellion in *Richard II,*" in *Shakespeare's Universe: Renaissance Ideas and*

Conventions: Essays in Honour of W. R. Elton, ed. John M. Mucciolo, Steven J. Doloff, and Edward A. Rauchert (Scolar Press), 37–51; and Margaret Healy, *William Shakespeare: Richard II* (Northcote House, in association with the British Council, 1998).

61. Hamilton, "State of Law," 5–9.

62. Hamilton, "State of Law," 15.

63. Stephen Greenblatt, "Invisible Bullets," in *Shakespearean Negotiations* (Oxford: Clarendon Press, 1988), 55.

64. Catherine Belsey, "Making Histories Then and Now: Shakespeare from *Richard II* to *Henry V,*" in *Uses of History: Marxism, Postmodernism and the Renaissance,* ed. Francis Barker, Peter Hulme, and Margaret Iverson (Manchester: Manchester University Press, 1991), 24–45, at 42.

65. Greenblatt, "Invisible Bullets," 56, 65.

66. Norbrook, "A Liberal Tongue," 41.

67. This is what Richard's Lord Chief Justice was said to have done: see "The fall of Robert Tresilian chiefe Iustice of Englande . . . for misconstruyng the lawes, and expounding them to serue the Princes affections," in *The Mirror for Magistrates* ed. Lily B. Campbell (Cambridge: Cambridge University Press, 1938), 73.

68. See previous note, and *Woodstock: A Moral History,* ed. A. P. Rossiter (London: Chatto and Windus, 1946), especially 85–89, 111–16, 123–37, 145–50, 159–69. Hamilton, "State of Law," points out the consistency of Shakespeare's portrayal of Richard's violation of the common law with the *Mirror,* with Holinshed, and with *Woodstock,* 8.

69. See Kantorowicz, *King's Two Bodies,* 28–29. The copy of Edward Halle's *Union of the Two Noble and Illustrious Fameilies of Lancastre and York* (posthumously edited by Richard Grafton in 1550), is in the Folger Shakespeare Library, STC 12721, copy 2. Verses by Henry and Mary Sidney may be found on fol. 61v. The underlined charge against Richard II is on fol. 7v.

70. Donna Hamilton acknowledges this point, in "State of Law," 17.

71. Among the commentators who point out the need for more information on Shakespeare and the Essex circle are Richard Tuck, *Philosophy and Government, 1572–1651* (Cambridge: Cambridge University Press, 1993), 106–7, and Norbrook, "A Liberal Tongue," 40. On humanism as a political discourse concerned with causes and remedies for corruption in the commonweal, see Peltonen, *Classical Humanism and Republicanism,* 54–118. On humanist readings of Terentian comedy as enabling dramatic verisimilitude, see Joel Altman, *The Tudor Play of Mind* (Berkeley: University of California Press, 1978), and Lorna Hutson, *The Usurer's Daughter: Male Friendship and Fictions of Women in Sixteenth-Century England* (London: Routledge, 1994), 163–87.

72. Sir Thomas Elyot, *The Boke named the Governour* [1531] (London: Dent, 1907), 139–141.

73. Elyot, *Governour,* 139.

74. *The Famous Victories of Henry the Fifth* (1598), in *Narrative and Dramatic Sources of Shakespeare,* vol. 4, ed. Geoffrey Bullough (London: Routledge, 1962), 308–14. For Shakespeare's indebtedness to *The Famous Victories,* see Bullough, 167–79.

75. *Famous Victories,* 315–17.

76. Ibid., 317.

77. Greenblatt, "Invisible Bullets," 41.

78. *Woodstock,* p. 86; Shakespeare, *Henry IV,* Part 2, ed. A. R. Humphreys (London: Routledge, 1967), V.iii, 133–34, p. 176. Further references to this edition will appear in the text.

79. Baker, *Reports of Sir John Spelman,* 37–38.

80. Baker, *Reports of Sir John Spelman,* 38; Hutson, *Usurer's Daughter,* 139–50; Craig Muldrew, *The Economy of Obligation: The Culture of Credit and Social Relations in Early Modern England* (Basingstoke: Macmillan, 1998).

81. On the rise of *assumpsit,* see A. W. Simpson, *A History of the Common Law of Contract: The Rise of Assumpsit* (Oxford: Clarendon Press, 1971); Baker, "The establishment of *assumpsit* for nonfeasance," *Reports of Sir John Spelman,* vol. 2, 255–98; S. F. Milsom, "Growth of the Modern Law of Contract," *Historical Foundations of the Common Law,* 2nd ed. (Toronto: Butterworths, 1981), 322–60.

82. See Paul R. Hyams, "Trial by Ordeal, in *On the Laws and Customs of England,* ed. Morris S. Arnold, Thomas A. Greene, Sally A. Scully, and Stephen D. White (Chapel Hill: University of North Carolina Press, 1981), 91; James Morice, *A briefe treatise of Oathes exacted by Ordinaries* (Middleberg: 1590), sig. A2r.

83. See J. H. Baker, "New Light on Slade's Case," *Cambridge Law Journal* 29 (1971): 59.

84. Simpson, *History of Contract,* 326.

85. See Chap. 6.

86. On the relationship between sixteenth-century legal conceptions of proof and discussions of "artificial proof" in classical and humanist rhetorical treatises, see Barbara Shapiro's chapter in this volume.

87. *Richard II* was entered on the Stationers' Register in 1597; it is usually dated as having been written in 1595–96. A. R. Humphreys suggests that *Henry IV* was played in the winter season of 1596–97, and that both parts of *Henry IV* were revised in response to the objections of William Brooke, Lord Cobham in the summer of 1597, and played on the reopening of the theaters in the autumn. See *Richard II* ed. Peter Ure (London: Routledge, 1956), xxix, and *Henry IV,* Part 1, ed. A. R. Humphreys (London: Routledge, 1960), xiv. Further references to these editions will appear in the text.

88. See Chaps. 1 and 6. The case was argued from 1595 to 1602, moving to the Exchequer Chamber during Michaelmas 1597, when *Henry IV,* Parts 1 and 2, were playing. See also A. W. Simpson, "The Place of Slade's Case in the History of Contract," *Law Quarterly Review* 74 (1958): 381–96; Simpson, *History of Contract,* 205–97 and Baker, "New Light on *Slade's Case,*" 213–36. For an illuminating discussion of the bearing of Slade's case on *Cymbeline* see Constance Jordan, *Shakespeare's Monarchies* (Ithaca, N.Y.: Cornell University Press, 1997), 76–80.

89. See Chap. 2. Hyams finds a similar rationale in the ordeal prior to the twelfth century, "Trial by Ordeal," 95.

90. Baker, "New Light on *Slade's Case,*" 228n; Simpson, *History of Contract,* 298; Baker, *Reports of Sir John Spelman,* vol. 2, 115; Baker, *Introduction to English Legal History,* 64–65.

91. George Whetstone, *Promos and Cassandra* [1578] in Geoffrey Bullough, *Narrative and Dramatic Sources of Shakespeare,* vol. 2, *The Comedies, 1597–1603* (London: Routledge, 1958), 491 and 497.

92. *The Works of Thomas Nashe,* ed. R. M. McKerrow, rev. ed. F. P. Wilson, 5 vols.

(Oxford: Blackwell: 1966), vol. 1, 164. McKerrow gives further references to knights of the post in the works of Robert Greene and Thomas Dekker in vol. 4, 94.

93. *Argument of Master Nicholas Fuller,* sig. B2r.

94. Greenblatt, "Invisible Bullets," 49–50.

95. E. S., *The Discouerie of the Knights of the Poste: Or the Knightes of the post, or common baylers newly Descried* (London: 1597), sig. B1r.

96. *Discouerie,* sig. A4r.

97. *Discouerie,* sig. B1v–B2r, sig. C1v.

98. *Discouerie,* sig. B2v. Thanks to Professor J. H. Baker, who explained to me the practice of impersonating bail in debt cases.

99. Phyllis Rackin, *Stages of History* (Ithaca, N.Y.: Cornell University Press, 1990), 52.

100. Belsey, "Making Histories," 35–37.

101. *A Newe Interlude of Impacyente Poverte,* ed. R. B. McKerrow (1911), *Materialen zur Kunde des älteren Englischen Dramas,* 44 vols. (Louvain), vol. 23, 10.

102. Rackin, *Stages of History,* 52. John Selden, in *The Duello, or Single Combat* (London: 1610), says that the trial was "in euery mans mouth famous" because "of the great consequences of Crown-conuersion thence following," 34–35. Selden also mentions an instance of champions delivering challenges in Elizabeth's reign, 49–50. On the connection between Selden's *Duello* and the handling of the same topic by several members of the Society of Antiquaries, see Paul Christianson. "Young John Selden and the Ancient Constitution," *Proceedings of the American Philosophical Society* 128 (1984): 271–315.

103. Mr. Davies, "Of the Antiquity, Use and Ceremony of lawful combats in England," in Thomas Hearne, *A Collection of Curious Discourses written by Eminent Antiquaries upon Severall Heads in our English Antiquities,* 2 vols. (London: W. & J. Richardson, 1770), vol. 2, 180.

104. Halle, *Union of the . . . Famelies of Lancastre and York,* fol. 7v.

105. St. German, *Doctor and Student,* 230. See Chap. 2, and Donna Hamilton, *Shakespeare and the Politics of Protestant England* (New York: Harvester Wheatsheaf, 1992).

106. Morice, *Briefe treatise of Oathes,* sig. D2r; *Argument of Master Nicholas Fuller,* sig. B2v.

107. On the increasing use of assumpsit in local courts from the end of the sixteenth century on, see Muldrew, *Economy of Obligation,* 207. On discontent with the outcome of Slade's case as enabling professional perjurers to become hired witnesses, however, see Baker, *Introduction to English Legal History,* 288–89.

108. Bullough, *Narrative and Dramatic Sources,* vol. 2, 497.

109. Neil Rhodes, *Elizabethan Grotesque* (London: Routledge, 1980), 113; Greenblatt, "Invisible Bullets," 47–48.

110. Belsey, "Making Histories," 42.

111. Greenblatt, "Invisible Bullets," 56.

8

Law and Political Reference in Montaigne's *"Apologie de Raimond Sebond"*

CONSTANCE JORDAN

An ancient [philosopher] who was reproached for professing philosophy, of which nevertheless in his own mind he took no great account, replied that this was being a true philosopher. They wanted to consider everything, to weigh everything, and they found that occupation suited to the natural curiosity that is in us. Some things they wrote for the needs of the society, like their religions; and on that account it was reasonable that they did not want to bare popular opinions to the skin, so as not to breed disorder in the people's obedience to the laws and customs of the country.
— *Michel de Montaigne, "Apologie de Raimond Sebond"*

Michel de Montaigne's "Apologie" has long been recognized as a monument to sixteenth-century skepticism. Its readers have understood its disclaimers as providing the pretext for its author's fideist rejection of any connection between his or any human reason and an experience of faith. Trust in knowledge derived from rational deliberation is similarly undermined: the

Epigraph: *The Complete Works of Montaigne: Essays, Travel Journal, Letters*, trans. Donald Frame (Stanford, Calif.: Stanford University Press, 1943, 1971), 379. Also *Les Essais de Michel de Montaigne*, ed. Pierre Villey (Paris: Presses Universitaires de France, 1965), 511–12. Further citations of Frame's translation appear within parentheses in the text of my essay; each of these citations is be followed by a citation of Villey's edition in brackets. The most politically heterodox statements in the "Apologie" come from the text

"Apologie" asserts that whatever is true in an absolute and unchanging sense lies beyond human apprehension and therefore cannot be communicated in human discourse. In what follows, I address an ancillary feature of these positions: Montaigne's identification of law as essentially positive and his vision of the political order as a historical artifact.[1] No law, he argues, can be plausibly regarded as either divine or natural; no politics, of whatever type, can be reliably identified as illustrating a divine will. Law and politics are local and temporal institutions and have no demonstrable relation to a transcendent order of things. At the time of its publication, the "Apologie" was virtually unique in making these claims; they were nevertheless claims that conveyed Montaigne's own timely awareness of the distress caused by the wars of religion through which he and his readers were living and suffering.

The implications of Montaigne's argument are twofold. On the one hand, by making human experience the foundation of society, and dismissing as merely human inventions both divine law and the rules apparently implicit in nature, it forestalls practically any justification for revolution by denying its premise. As neither God nor reason speaks to man in a human language, neither can support a move to change the status quo; to deny human beings access to a transcendent, absolute, and changeless source of truth disarms the revolutionary, whose actions are typically justified by extraordinary insight or divine inspiration. Without such access, what speaks to the possibilities for change is rather the confusing and haphazard laws and customs of a citizen's own time and country. At the same time, the programmatic mutability illustrated in the "Apologie" — its affirmation of a historicist and ethnocentric view of human society — was incompatible with the main tenets of contemporary political thought. Without the conviction that God's will was always at work in the fate of a people, there was no reason not to attribute to history a purely human agency. The galvanizing fiction of a sacred monarchy had possessed the power to summon all subjects to a duty justified by a transcendent will; by 1580, when the first version of the "Apologie" came into print, after eighteen years of civil war, it was unclear how a national politics could do without such a reference. The paradox here is patent: the nature of political society is to be regarded at once as inherently instable, lacking absolute guarantees; and as functionally stable, forbidding change not provided for by positive law.

---

written for the first edition of the *Essais,* published in 1580; this, together with minor emendations from editions published through 1587, is designated as the A text in Villey's edition. Following Villey, I have cited later additions to the "Apologie" as it was published in 1588 as the B text; and posthumously in 1595 as the C text. Unless so noted, all quotations in my essay come from the A text as noted by Villey.

Despite its skepticism with respect to divine law, reason, and the status of nature, however, the "Apologie" illustrates a state that is both lawful and able to command the allegiance of subjects. Positive law, Montaigne insists, has a real and definitive presence within history. A people can and should obey its positive laws, its customs, and those forms of religious worship which they have inherited, even though these are productions of anomalous and imponderable forces operating through time. Like Plato's written law, which was to overrule the dictates of a philosopher king, Montaigne's notion of positive law establishes a second-best form of government.[2]

The epigraph to this essay suggests that Montaigne knew the risks he took in publishing the "Apologie." Citing with approval the practice of ancient Pyrrhonists, he notes that they restricted their skeptical inquiries to themselves, while publicly supporting the "laws and customs" of the country (379 [512]). He warns his noble reader (almost certainly Marguerite de Valois) against using the very tool — skepticism — with which he has attacked the assumptions sustaining notions of transcendence and unchanging truth: Practice "moderation and temperance," avoid "novelty and strangeness," he tells her (419 [557–8]).[3] A reader must therefore assume that in some way Montaigne regarded his thorough and explicit contravention of the principal assumptions supporting the laws and customs of France and its monarchy as less dangerous to the health of the body politic than the convictions he sought to dispel. Weighed in the balance, a state whose subjects believed in its divine and rational foundation was less secure than one whose institutions were historical, ad hoc (to some degree), and not to be explained absolutely. The historicity of such institutions did not provide subjects with any special leverage for vindicating changes in their order or character. In other words, no aspect of government was capable of justifying more than its continuance on the terms on which it had been established.

In taking this position, Montaigne obviously alluded to a contemporary crisis in government whose conceptual underpinnings were both the monarchomach sentiments of Protestant as well as Catholic thinkers and the absolutist tactics of the Crown and its apologists, who sought to contain such sentiments. Practically all his contemporaries agreed that divine law and the rules apparently evident in nature were the final arbiters of positive law and, as it were, the court of last appeal. To represent concepts of divinity and nature as merely projections of human desire or a record of human practice implied that there was no way other than by reference to positive law to distinguish monarchic or indeed any political will from being better than tyrannical or anarchic. Justified by collective agreements over time, such projections could become the basis of custom and positive law, but they could secure no other kind legitimacy. Because the "Apologie" was so heterodox, the fact of its publication remains intriguing.

Montaigne had answered the question of what to publish and what to suppress in the public interest well before he took the first version of the "Apologie" to Simon Millanges in Bordeaux, who would publish the first edition of the *Essais* in 1580. Entrusted with the works of his friend and colleague Etienne de La Boétie, who died in 1563, Montaigne had omitted from the 1571 edition of La Boétie's *Oeuvres complètes* two treatises he considered inflammatory: the *Discours de la Servitude volontaire* (c. 1548) and the *Mémoire de nos troubles sur l'édit de janvier 1562*, composed during that year. He later considered including the *Discours* in the *Essais* of 1580 but once again rejected the idea.[4] Explaining his position in "De l'amitié," Montaigne states that he will not publish the *Discours*, "because I have found that this work has since been brought to light, and with evil intent, by those who seek to disturb and change the state of our government without worrying whether they will improve it" (144 [154]). His anxiety on this score is consistent with his rejection of revolution in the "Apologie": of interest is how and why he saw that La Boétie's treatises might have been understood as arguments for revolutionary political action.[5]

The *Discours* represents the obedience of the subject under tyranny or when the authority and power within a state are held by only one governor. In such cases, "to obey" is actually "to serve," and "to govern" is effectively "to tyrannize."[6] Subjects of a tyrant are horribly demeaned by their dependence, their servility, and their abdication of what La Boétie calls a freedom of being that is instinctive and desired even by domestic animals (136, 141). But if, despite their servitude, the subjects also enjoy the protection of the tyrant, they risk becoming complicit in their own enslavement, and thus no better than expendable cogs in a vast mill of oppression. There are, however, important contradictions in La Boétie's argument, and they suggest why Montaigne's characterization of the *Discours* as disturbing has merit. Although La Boétie formally forbids violence even in the interest of securing freedom, his examples of freedom are predicated on the use of violence. He represents violence as an instinctive recourse of creatures who are in some way captive to a superior power or force. Liberty among human beings is a "natural right" predicated on their fundamental equality: "it must not be doubted that we are all naturally free because we are all comrades" (*compagnons;* 140–41). It is abrogated only in part by the natural law requiring obedience to parents: "If we lived with the rights that nature has given us, and with the instructions she has provided us, we would be naturally obedient to our parents, subject to reason, and slaves to no one" (139). A love of liberty exists among all animals; in beasts, it provokes a violent reaction against captivity, which they fight with their teeth, horns, and claws. And the annals of the past testify to bloody battles fought by human lovers of liberty to overthrow tyrants.

True, elsewhere La Boétie insists that the defeat of tyranny is primarily a matter of insight and will. The overthrow of a tyrant leaves the structures of command untouched; they are overthrown only when the subjects decide to tolerate them no more. "One must take nothing away from the tyrant, but only not give him anything. . . . When the people stop serving him, they will be free of him" (136). La Boétie's interpretation of servitude is brilliant and subtle. It becomes clear when he distinguishes between servitude and obedience: servitude requires subjects to forfeit their powers of judgment to the prince; by contrast, obedience demands only that subjects follow the law. Subjects who are truly in a state of servitude not only do what they are told (a condition that might be true of those coerced to perform a certain action) but think what the tyrant thinks: "Often, to satisfy him [the tyrant], they [those in servitude] anticipate even his thoughts. It is not enough for them to obey him; they must also please him" (165). In these passages, liberty is an intellectual capacity, not a physical condition. That is why it does not entail any kind of overt resistance, whether active or passive, to authority. What it does entail is a recognition that politics is lived out in a divided world. In a real sense, it is a world in which subjection to the power of an authority is inevitable and probably harsh; considered as a feature of an individual's inwardness, however, politics is rather the ground upon which to make judgments about the wisdom and justice of a particular rule. Was it La Boétie's fascination (despite his aversion to violence) with the historical existence of revolution that made his text attractive to writers apparently committed to revolution, writers that Montaigne remembers when he declares that La Boétie's text has been used to "disturb and change the state of our government?" It seems likely. The *Discours* was, in any case, a text that saw freedom in nature—a concept too susceptible to volatile interpretation for Montaigne to endorse openly. His refusal to print the *Discours* signals his approval of the Pyrrhonist rule.

Whatever its primary intention—to defend Sebond or to attack Sebond— the "Apologie" recasts the thesis of the *Discours* so that it forbids any possibility of seeking a redress of tyranny through an appeal to nature and rather defines freedom as purely the exercise of judgment. It makes the subject's obedience to political order a merely physical and material affair—one, as Montaigne would say, "of the body." It also provides for the subject's independence relative to opinion and popular belief, by recommending a rigorous observance of the law and custom informed by a skeptical vision of life, to introduce the necessary basis for the recomposition of the historical conditions of government. For Montaigne, the knowledge upon which human beings could rely had neither a divine nor an extracultural source; it was only local and historical. Nor was this all. Not only were subjects governed by their own human constructions of a moral code; heads of state, emperors and kings, also human, were similarly positioned.

La Boétie's *Mémoire de nos troubles sur l'édit de janvier 1562,* the second of his friend's works that Montaigne refused to publish in 1571, also contains hints about why it was subject to his censure. It actually recommends royal intervention in what was a settled, customary, and legal institution. Unlike the theoretical *Discours,* the *Mémoire* was timely and practical, an argument for one church, both Catholic and French. For, La Boétie stated, were France to tolerate two religions, Protestant and Catholic, she would in effect become two nations — a situation in itself intolerable and a violation of the fundamental law of the kingdom. Instead, La Boétie proposed a Catholicism *reformed* to satisfy Protestants.[7] His recommendation, rejecting the tolerance supported by the regent, Catherine, and the chancellor Michel de l'Hôpital in the Edict of January, would result in a new state, Catholic yet imbued with the spirit of Protestantism. The institution uniquely destined to effect this reform was the monarchy, always the "protector of the Gallican church" (162): "There is nothing the king cannot do with his authority" (164). In print nearly two decades later, the "Apologie" would repudiate the reform La Boétie had proposed and rather support the idea of one nation united by a single religion, traditional, venerated, and adequate in all respects. This union, Montaigne would state, exists and is satisfactory; did it not exist, Montaigne implies, it would have to evolve from licit and popular beginnings. It could not be created through human prerogative, even royal prerogative, because there was no authority or power that could supersede the broad consensus of centuries past. If the king is only human (and Montaigne said he was), he has no authority to speak divine law. In the light of the *Discours,* the *Mémoire* seems rather paradoxical. While the former provides a rationale against absolute rule, the latter defends the exercise of such rule — particularly with respect to the Church.

Montaigne may well have regarded the position taken by La Boétie in the *Mémoire* equivocally. Although, like La Boétie, he rejected tolerance for Huguenots, he saw no reason to compromise Catholic practice; he stood for a French church justified by tradition, unreformed, whether by revolution or royal fiat. And like La Boétie (who seems to have changed his mind on the matter of religious reform), Montaigne took the oath of loyalty to the Catholic Church required of all officers of the Crown by the Parlement of Paris in June 1562, an oath that flatly defied the spirit of the Edict of January.[8] Montaigne may not have been unsympathetic to a policy of tolerance in principle, but in practice he saw its dangers: civic unrest in general and the unwarranted use of royal authority in particular. Both parties to the religious conflict that began in 1562 — Catholics and Huguenots alike — had sought justification for their actions in the concepts of divine will and natural law. The consequences of this presumption had proved dire: both sides suffered terrible assaults on their lives and property.[9] The Edict of January had assumed the exercise of the prerogative over a matter that touched the lives of all subjects and ordinarily required registration by their courts, the regional parlements, and the principal parlement in Paris. The fact that the parlement balked initially, registering the edict only in March, suggests its resistance to royal authority in the matter of religion; three months later, it defied entirely the spirit of the edict by requiring its officers to take the oath of fidelity.[10]

The "Apologie" opens by ridiculing the presumption that human reason is competent to challenge "the authority of the laws or the reverence of ancient usage" (320 [439–1]). The "plague of man is the opinion of knowledge" (360 [488]).[11] When the conduct of religion is at stake, the act of passing "judgment" becomes more presumptuous, as judgment is exercised to give "personal consent" to articles of faith that are essentially expressions of a profound "mystery" (320–21 [441]). Condemning the exercise of reason in a believer motivated by a "pious zeal," Montaigne repeatedly insists that the experience of faith is mysterious and lies outside any system of discursive representation: faith is "extraordinary" (321 [441]), exhibited by the "miraculous" (322 [442]); "private considerations" in matters of faith are inherently doubtful (323 [444]); "our considerations, our reasons and passions" are irrelevant, as we are given grace only by God's "supernatural clasp" (326 [446]); God's promises are "ineffable" (385; [*indicibles,* 518]); the believer rises to God only by "exception" (457; [*extraordinairement,* 604]); his is a "divine and miraculous metamorphosis" (604C). Deprived of "divine grace and knowledge" and "armed solely with his arms," no human being can comprehend God's creation (328 [449]). These claims put religious doctrine out of the philosophical running, as it were; they also explain Montaigne's assertion that what passes for religion is a human artifact, designed for human ends. Human beings may receive grace, but its effects on their conscious thought are communicable only in local and historical terms.[12] "I do not think it is good to confine the divine power . . . under the laws of our speech" (392 [527]), Montaigne declares; yet, inevitably, religion is established in and by speech. In other words, divine power will exceed and escape the terms in which religion describes it.

The experience of faith is generally misunderstood, Montaigne argues; it too often leads to powerful and dangerous delusions. He deplores the tendency of the faithful to equate human invention with the vast creativity of God, to understand the world in images derived from human experience. "Man equals himself to God, attributes to himself divine characteristics, picks himself out and separates himself from the horde of other creatures" (331 [452]); "we prescribe limits to God, we hold his power besieged by our reasons. . . . We want to enslave [*asservir*] him to the vain and feeble approximations of our understanding" (389 [523]); "to have made gods of our condition . . . [indicates] a marvelous intoxication of the human intelligence" (383 [516]); " 'men,' says St. Paul, 'professing themselves to be wise, became fools, and changed the glory of the incorruptible God into an image made like to corruptible man' " (394 [529]); "of all forms, the most beautiful is that of man; so God is of that form" (397, C [532]). A correlative of this specious identification of man with God is the human self-interestedness of all action taken to institute, promote, or reform the practices of religion. The most dire of such actions is of course a war of religion, the ultimate instance of a delusional conviction in divine inspiration.

On the "wars which at this moment are oppressing our state," Montaigne has this to say: "The justice that is there in one of the parties is there only as an ornament and a covering; it is indeed alleged, but it is neither received, nor lodged, nor espoused; it is there as in the mouth of the advocate, not as in the heart and affection of the party"[13] (323 [443]). Self-interestedness becomes identified with revelation or truth when its reflections are taken to be expressions of divine or natural law: "Men's opinions are accepted in the train of ancient beliefs, by authority and on credit, as if they were religion and law. They accept as by rote [*jargon*] what is commonly held about it [that is, authority and law]" (403 [539]). This is typically a consequence of persuading others of one's superhumanity: "Whoever is believed in his presuppositions, he is our master and our God" (404 [540]). The social norms that are created by such a fallacious sense of competence are, inevitably, transient and topical; they are tied to contingency and circumstance. At worst, as in France, they condone war against the nonconformist. At best, and in any case, they are no better than other social norms. Their relative authority implicitly acknowledges the gross and imposing fact that, in Montaigne's words, "we have no communication with being" (455 [601]):[14] "We receive our own religion only in our own way and with our own hands, and not otherwise than as other religions are received. We happen to be born in a country where it was in practice; or we regard its antiquity or the authority of the men who have maintained it; or we fear the threats it fastens upon unbelievers, or pursue its promises. Those considerations should be employed in our belief, but as sub-sidiaries; they are human ties. Another region, other witnesses, similar prom-ises and threats, might imprint upon us in the same way a contrary belief" (324–25 [445]). Nor is our understanding of nature, its order, its liberties and its impositions free from this autoaffectionate bias: "Everything that seems strange to us, we condemn" (343 [467]). "To us, to go according to nature is only to go according to our intelligence. . . . What is beyond is monstrous and disordered" (391 [526]). These kinds of distinction are, however, routine, made "by each man and each nation according to the measure of his igno-rance" (391, C [526]). They fail to convey a truth because to investigate the workings of nature means to reason from data the senses give us:[15] "To judge the appearances that we receive of objects, we would need a judicatory instru-ment; to verify this instrument, we need a demonstration; to verify the demon-stration, an instrument: there we are in a circle" (454, C [601]). Strictly speak-ing, there are no natural laws; if there were, they would be "universal" laws and obeyed everywhere: "Not only every nation, but every individual would resent the force and violence used on him by anyone who tried to impel him to oppose that law [of nature]. Let them show me just one law of that sort — I'd like to see it [*Qu'ils m'en montrent pour voir, une de cette condition*]" (437 [580]).[16]

No one — not even a king, an emperor, or any head of state — who is not at all divine and in fact like any other man (350 [476]) — can read such a law, because it simply does not exist in any way that human beings can recognize. Animals seem to respond to "natural laws," but "human reason" has not allowed humankind to recognize and report them (438, B [580]). Like di-vinity, nature is an unwritten book; it has no systematic representation. Na-ture may at some level be intuited to be "universal" and even to have "com-mon laws" [*loix communes*], but they elude our powers of conceptualization and expression (333–34 [456], 356 [483]).[17]

The state Montaigne outlines in the "Apologie" is therefore purely secular. Divinity and universality surround it but are apprehensible only through grace or by instinct; what they mean defies articulation. To announce a divine or natural law is no better than to speak of some kind of human desire, whether monarchic or popular. At the same time, this secular state must be protected, if not by God then at least by a positive law that grounds its artificial and man-made institutions so that violation of them can find no justification in either religious inspiration or the exercise of reason. Hence Montaigne's insistence in the "Apologie" that the French must profess allegiance to the historic Catholic Church of France: "The knowledge of his [religious] duty should not be left to each man's judgment; it should be prescribed to him" (359 [488]). Although such "duty" is no more than "accidental" — for if "justice" had a "real existence," it would not be tied to "the condition of the customs of this country or that" — it must not be devalued on that account. "Reason" — which cannot explain God's promise of immortality (415, C [554]) — will nevertheless tell a man "to obey the laws of his country" (437 [579]).[18] In other words, in the "Apologie" we seem to looking not at the outlines of a theocracy in which a state realizes the divine will (Calvin's Geneva), but rather at something like its inversion, in which the divine will appears to the rational mind as a strategic fiction of the state.

Although the period from 1562 to the publication of the "Apologie" was agitated by monarchomach protest, the dominant political philosophy of the time was generally conservative, deriving the foundations of government, including the monarchy, from divine and natural law and placing the monarchy under providential care. At the very least, the succession was divinely ordained: a monarch was crowned "par la grace de Dieu."[19] Guillaume Budé, composing his *De l'institution du prince* about 1518–19, also regarded the monarch as the particular vessel of God's will: he is assumed to be so "perfectly prudent, so outstandingly and supremely noble, so imbued and endowed with justice and equity" as not to need the law, as God "guides [his] free will and through divine inspiration which is beyond human knowledge . . . directs [him] to the straight path of reason."[20] Claude Seyssel, whose *La Grande Monarchie de France* (1519) exemplifies contemporary constitutionalist thought, saw that the power and authority of the monarch were hedged by custom and divine and natural law; he also saw the "head" and "members" of the monarchy were so "regulated" that they could not fall out, "at least until by the will of God and by the common course of nature . . . the time of decline and dissolution comes." The fate of the monarchy was in any case providential: if the "ordinance of God's vengeance smite the realm," it has been preordained "by divine wisdom and providence which human reason and prudence cannot resist."[21] Michel de l'Hôpital, pleading for tolerance and, as he thought, an end to religious conflict in 1570, represented the king as one who, when God had given his kingdom peace, was obliged to keep it; to this end, God would open his heart.[22] Late in the century, François de L'Alouette, while maintaining that kings were under the law, also believed that the kingdom of France was protected by the "Esprit Divin," its princes "divinely ordained" and imbued with a "spirit from on high to rule and guide their subjects" as Moses did the Israelites.[23] It was of course one thing to see the king as inspired and protected by God; it was quite another to recognize in the king a figure of divinity itself. Jean de La Madeleine, who had followed Seyssel in his view of a mixed monarchy, insisted that because God protected all human government, monarchs represented "the authority and majesty of God on earth." Barthélemi Chasseneuz, repudiating the spirit of Seyssel's distinctions altogether, declared that the king was unequivocally "God on earth."[24] There was general agreement that the king was not only a person categorically different from his subjects but also in some way or other in God's care. These were articles of a faith that the ties between the institutions of government and God's will were knowable and could be articulated, articles that Montaigne rejected.

Thinkers justifying violent resistance to tyranny often argued from assumptions that mimicked those of absolutists: as government was grounded in divine and natural law, a head of state who violated that law could be deposed. Important in such cases was the primacy of the people, who had given the monarch power to rule over them in accordance with divine law. His power was in that sense provisional; it had to answer to the judgment of subjects who had heard divine law and were under a covenant to observe it. Théodore Bèze, in his *Du Droit des Magistrats sur leurs Subjets* (1574), citing numerous examples of his conception of rule in scripture, argued that although a private person ought not to resist his government unless "he has a special calling from God," and nations with a "rightful case against oppressors" were sometimes denied redress, albeit "in accord with the just decree of God," a remedy for tyranny lay in "human institutions," which were designed to protect subjects.[25] The monarchomach treatise entitled *Vindiciae contra tyrannos* (1579), supposed to be the work of Philippe de Mornay, makes a comparable point: "If [the king] neglects God, if he goes over to His enemies and is guilty of felony towards God, his kingdom is forfeited of right [*ipso iure*] and is often lost in fact [*ex facto*]. . . . Hence, a religious people not only will restrain [*coercebit*] a prince in the act of doing violence to God's law, but will, from the beginning, prevent gradual changes arising from his guilt or negligence. . . . As a whole people is permitted to oppose a tyrant, so also are the principal persons of the kingdom, who represent the body of the people."[26] François Hotman, whose *Francogallia* (1573) was in Montaigne's library, argues strictly from history rather than from scripture and the assumption of a divine law and states that the Franks, having overthrown the Romans, remained a "free" people and were in fact the "authors of liberty"; hence, when threatened with servitude, they had the right to depose their monarchs.[27] Despite his avoidance of any reference to providence, Hotman's conclusion implies what the works of Bèze and de Mornay also imply, that is, the people's right to act on their conscientious judgment of their monarch, whether inspired by God or informed by history. Montaigne does not so much deny this right as much as ridicule its presumption: human beings can know nothing absolutely by reason; hence they cannot know certainly what to do in a political crisis. Skepticism remains a matter of judgment and does not justify taking action of any kind.

The work to which Montaigne's "Apologie" seems most responsive is Jean Bodin's *Six Livres de la République* (1576) — certainly the most imposing work on political philosophy of the period, and one that Montaigne owned. In many respects, their texts represent the elements of secular government in similar ways. But while Bodin, like most political philosophers of the period (except Hotman), derives the authority of government from natural law and places the power of the sovereign under God, Montaigne *divorces* human society from both these metaphysical connections to a perfect truth and justice. That is, Montaigne acknowledges neither the sovereign nor the people as being linked in any way to a discursively recognized transcendence, whether natural or divine, by which a political decision or action could be justified. True, Bodin argues that no single religion can claim to be the true religion. But he does not abandon a belief in a broadly universal and entirely "natural" religion or, more important, in a natural law. Bodin acknowledges these as the foundations of government and also of individual liberty: while the power of princes is absolute, it "does not extend in any way to the laws of God and of nature"; "every prince on earth is subject to divine and natural laws."[28] Bodin further deduces from natural law the right of individuals to possess property that the monarch could not appropriate without consent: "If the prince does not have power to overstep the bounds of natural law, which has been established by God, of whom he is the image, he will also not be able to take another's property without just and reasonable cause" (1.viii, 39). And he concludes his argument with a syllogism: "If justice is the end of law, law the work of the prince, and the prince the image of God, then by this reasoning, the law of the prince must be modelled on the law of God" (1.viii, 45).

Adhering to his position on the primacy of divine and natural law as the final guarantee of political order, however, Bodin has to make exceptions to the rule against disobedience. Divine inspiration could sanction not only the thought of regicide but the act itself, as in the case of Jehu's killing King Ahab "by a special and unquestionable mandate from God" (2.v, 118). More generally, a subject could be expected to recognize divine and natural law in order to know when not to obey a prince: "It is certainly possible not to obey him [that is, the prince] in anything that is against the law of God or nature: to flee, to hide, to evade his blows, to suffer death" (2.v, 120).[29] Bodin recognizes an abuse of magisterial power when that power is used against royal authority, and he criticizes magistrates who fail to administer the law on the grounds of a personal judgment, especially when such a failure leads to civil war: "We oft times see the subjects to take up armes against their prince . . . for the false opinion that the people have of the equitie and integritie of the judges, refusing to verifie and put in execution the Edicts and commaunds of their prince."[30] Yet here too Bodin makes an exception for violations of divine and natural law, including, in this instance, the natural law that protects personal property: "How should the magistrat then be bound to obey or to put into excecution the prince's commaunds in things unjust and dishonest, the prince in this case transgressing and breaking the sacred bounds of the lawes both of God and nature" (*Six Books,* 3.iv, 312). These are exceptions that Montaigne's theory does not need to entertain, because it severs any connection between the experience of a mysterious God and nature on the one hand and political action on the other.

As illustrated in the "Apologie," Montaigne's state thus appears to be a perfectly self-referential entity. God intervenes in the life of the people only extrapolitically, and his influence is ineffable. Positive law alone provides the foundation of a stable state. Having wrenched the idea of government from its foundations in divine and natural law, the "Apologie" was quite useless as a pretext for violent change — unless, of course, positive law itself allowed for such change.

The evocation in the "Apologie" of its author as a revolutionary conservative who rejected the idea of government justified by forms of transcendence yet also maintained that government must be obeyed recalls one of the text's most arresting figures, cited in the epigraph to this essay (379 [511, 512]). Montaigne's portrait of the Pyrrhonist shows that he exhibits "a pure, complete and very perfect postponement and suspension of judgment." In the absence of belief, Montaigne declares, followers of this school "lend and accommodate themselves to natural inclinations, to the impulsion and constraint of passions, to the constitutions of laws and customs and to the tradition of the arts. . . . They let their common actions be guided by those things, without any taking sides or judgment" (374 [505]). Theirs is a "useful" philosophy, which represents man as "naked and empty. . . . Not setting up any doctrine [*aucune dogme*] . . . [they are] consequently free from the vain and irreligious opinions introduced by the false sects" (375 [506]). Here Montaigne illustrates a mentality wholly uncommitted to any kind of proposition that could challenge "the constitutions of laws and customs" of his country, but also one entirely incapable of belief in the merit of such laws and customs.[31] As Montaigne continues to explain his own obedience to positive law, however, it becomes clear that his position is not exactly like that of his model. Montaigne never denies belief; in fact, he affirms it; what he does claim is that there is no language proper to its communication. There is an obvious difference between a statement declaring that it cannot be known whether or not a thing exists (God, truth, and so forth) and one declaring that nothing can be said about it. It is the fact of belief—in the sense of what cannot be said—that eventually comes to complicate Montaigne's attitude toward positive law. His contact with society is vexed in ways that it is not for the Pyrrhonist. This vexation is evident in Montaigne's preface to the *Essais*.

Representing himself to his reader, Montaigne measures the distance between a nudity of self he desires to portray, presumably the naked emptiness and freedom of mind of the Pyrrhonist he describes in the "Apologie," and the clothes that decency requires him to wear. Were he to be living "in the sweet freedom of nature's first laws," he would show himself "wholly naked": as it is, he goes only as far in that direction as "respect for the public" will permit (2 [3]). Authorial nudity and the freedom it stands for is thus metaphorically at one with a privacy entirely theoretical and nowhere to be realized except as thought.[32] Expression of any kind is tantamount to a clothed truth, dressed up in terms that are conventional and easy to understand.[33] In this perspective, all writing is necessarily inflected to meet the requirements of prevailing law and custom. But it also responds to an imagined freedom; it is produced from a consciousness of virtual independence from the needs of society.[34]

Social behavior must of course conform to the dictates of positive law and the religion of the state. We must accept religion as we receive it "by external [*estranger*] authority and command" (369 [500]); the limits to intellectual expression must be "artificially determined" (419 [559]). But a subject's obedience does not mean that he should remain blind to the very local and temporal (that is, relativistic and thus also mutable) nature of the law he is obeying—a law that Montaigne then disparages as "the undulating sea of the opinions of a people or a prince, which will paint me justice in as many colors and refashion it in as many faces as there are changes of passion." It is the law as partial and limited that a skeptic cannot afford to leave unexamined. He must object to accepting its vagaries as instances of true justice; as Montaigne declares: "I cannot have my judgment so flexible" (437 [579]). In other words, his judgment of the law will remain above the law, even while his person follows the law. To obey positive law does not mean to refrain from thinking critically about it—thought is free because there is no agent or institution to control it—not only as this law may instantiate an injustice but, more important, because it is a purely human artifact and therefore always subject to interpretive reform.

Montaigne's ambivalence here can be understood in several ways: one, conventionally philosophical, is the legacy of Pyrrhonism; the second is specifically political; and the third is, I think, properly a reflection of the literary.

First, it is reason's job to turn on itself routinely, to use its powers to defy a desire to make any claim to objectivity: the power of man "is to have learned to acknowledge his weakness" (370 [500]). Truth, insofar as it is apprehensible, is announced only as a *de-articulation* of its various and accepted definitions. This philosophical antitruth is radical in that it undermines the belief that human language can convey certain and absolute knowledge. Second, the practical use to which Montaigne's skepticism is put when directed to politics results in a notion of the state that is, if not unprecedented, at least unique in its own time. By eliminating any recourse to an authority whose source is or pretends to be supra- or ahistorical, the "Apologie" puts all consideration of political thought and action into a social context that history allows us to see as evolving. Action that claims a privilege in inspiration is thereby ruled out; action that is not provided for during the usual evolution of positive law is forbidden. The "Apologie" leaves divine and natural law outside discourse. It posits an encounter with divinity that is exclusive of language and seeks to persuade us that what we experience of truth is incommunicable and "a sign that [we] have grasped it [the truth] by some other means than by a natural power that is in [us] and in all men" (423 [562]). Nature as natural law is simply unreadable. The human condition of an aphasic illiteracy requires the faithful — *who may actually have been graced with divine yet ineffable insight and knowledge* — to show a "bodily" reverence for the positive laws and customs of their country. In this respect, Montaigne differs from his Pyrrhonist model, who believes nothing, and for whom the obligation to obey the law is presumably easy. Montaigne never denies his belief or the power of ineffable grace. He makes them the pretext for an unwritten text that remains as a record of resistance to but also acceptance of change, which is acknowledged as inevitable and therefore in some sense open to determination.

And finally, considering himself as a political subject, Montaigne illustrates his political position in autobiography:

> From the knowledge of this mobility of mine I have accidentally engendered in myself a certain constancy of opinions [*j'ay par accident engendré en moy quelque constance d'opinions*], and have scarcely altered my original and natural ones. . . . I do not change easily, for fear of losing in the change. And since I am not capable of choosing, I accept other people's choice and I stay in the position [*me tiens en l'assiette*] where God put me . . . in the ancient beliefs of our religion, in the midst of so many sects and divisions that our century has produced. (428 [569])

His account conveys the distinct stages in the evolution of his practice: his sense of his ignorance creates ideological stability; this stability corresponds to the condition of an originary and "natural" self; this condition is manifest in a refusal to choose; this refusal justifies remaining where God placed him. What paraphrase does not reveal, however, is the extent to which an apparent condition of impotence and passivity is actually the self-reflexive creation of the agent in whom the condition is registered: Montaigne is not capable of choice, yet he chooses to *hold himself* in the position his condition has designed for him. In effect, he retains a kind of authorial creativity. The condition itself, described as both self- and divinely validated, is something other than an index of a bare conformity. Rather, it is the product of *conscious* although random (accidental) thought whose resolution is apparent although asymptotic (it produces only a "certain constancy"). Montaigne's pious obedience is therefore not typically conformist. Nor, considered as a fact of social history, is it necessarily hostile to a kind of change, one that responds to the flexibility implicit in the notion of a "certain constancy." Montaigne's freedom is not to be derived from the dicta of divine or natural law but from the evidently mutable terms of history, the only condition of life he can know, however imperfectly.

The "position" in which Montaigne found himself was in another and more prosaic sense one of a recent prosperity and distinction, given the social norms of his day, and moreover one for which he was considerably indebted to others. His château, a "noble house" which conferred a "minor nobility on its owner" (Frame, vii), had been acquired in 1477 by his great-grandfather Ramon Eyquem, whose family in Bordeaux engaged in an international trade in dried fish and wine. Montaigne's father Pierre Eyquem *de* Montaigne (his status having come to him with his property) was the first of his family to renounce trade and live as a gentleman on his considerably enlarged and improved estate. Records of his substantial expenditures and improvements survive. Montaigne himself dropped "Eyquem" from his name and became simply Michel de Montaigne. His intervention in politics was, initially, at the instigation of his uncle Pierre de Eyquem, who in 1554 purchased a position in the Cour des Aides de Périgueux (an official body created to collect taxes) and resigned that position to his nephew Michel in 1557. Montaigne remained in public service in various capacities intermittently until 1585.[35] Montaigne's mother, Antoinette de Louppes, came from a family of Portuguese Jews, the Lopès, who converted to Christianity in the fifteenth century. They were also engaged in commerce.[36] One or perhaps two of Montaigne's siblings were Huguenots.

Evidently God had placed Montaigne in a position that was fraught with aspects of contingency; despite his official duties, his was not a family deeply invested with the attributes of a noble and Catholic inheritance or ancient seigneurial status. As Pierre Villey notes, "his nobility was of a recent date."[37]

Nor was his family unified in its religion. There was of course every reason for Montaigne to insist on the privileges of his position and the permanence of his place; it was the common practice of rural gentry to do so, however new their status. But Montaigne's association of his "position" in life with divine will rather than with the aggregate of historical factors actually responsible for it is more than an expression of pride in his gentle condition. It is also testimony to the particular self-interestedness that, he has insisted throughout the "Apologie," shapes all human knowledge.

Notes

1. For studies of the *Essais* as political literature see Géralde Nakam, *Montaigne et son temps: Les événements et les Essais,* 1982 (Paris: Gallimard, 1993); and *Les Essais de Montaigne: Miroir et procès de leur temps* (Paris, Nizet, 1984). For an overview of Montaigne's political ideas, see David Lewis Schaefer, *The Political Philosophy of Montaigne* (Ithaca, N.Y.: Cornell University Press, 1990); for Montaigne's political persona, see Timothy J. Reiss, "Montaigne and the Subject of Polity," in *Literary Theory/ Renaissance Texts,* ed. Patricia Parker and David Quint (Baltimore, Md.: Johns Hopkins University Press, 1986), 115–49. For Montaigne in relation to contemporary political thought, see Zachary Sayre Schiffman, *On the Threshold of Modernity: Relativism in the French Renaissance* (Baltimore, Md.: Johns Hopkins University Press, 1991), 53–77; Nannerl O. Keohane, *Philosophy and the State in France: The Renaissance to the Enlightenment* (Princeton, N.J.: Princeton University Press, 1980); and Peter Burke, *Montaigne* (New York: Hill and Wang, 1981). For the "Apologie" and Montaigne's religion, see Henri Weber, "L'Apologie de Raymond Sebond et la religion de Montaigne," *Bulletin de la Société des amis de Montaigne* 33–34 (1993): 183–96. For background to the skeptical impulse in early modern political philosophy, see Richard H. Popkin, *The History of Skepticism from Erasmus to Descartes* (Assen, Netherlands: Van Gorcum, 1960); and Richard Tuck, *Philosophy and Government, 1572–1651* (Cambridge: Cambridge University Press, 1993); for the development of legal concepts during this period, see Donald Kelley, *The Human Measure: Social Thought in the Western Tradition* (Cambridge: Harvard University Press, 1990). For the history of religious ideas and their relation to events in the wars, see Myriam Yardeni, *La Conscience nationale en France pendant les guerres de religion, 1559–1598* (Paris: Nauwelaerts, 1971).

2. See *Politicus,* i.e., *The Statesman.* Montaigne cites the *Laws* as an instance of Plato's Pyrrhonism: "Where he writes on his own, he makes no certain prescriptions. When he plays the lawgiver, he borrows a domineering and assertive style" (379, C [512]).

3. On the status of women in the "Apologie" and particularly in this passage, see François Rigolot, "D'une théologie 'Pour les dames' à une Apologie 'per le donne,'" in *Montaigne, Apologie de Raimond Sebond: De la theologia à la théologie,* ed. Claude Blum (Paris: Champion, 1990), 261–90, esp. 283–87.

4. Montaigne mentions but does not comment on the *Mémoire* in "De l'amitié." For

accounts of Montaigne's decision, see Nakam, *Montaigne,* 238–41; *Les Essais,* 180; Donald M. Frame, *Montaigne: A Biography* (New York: Harcourt Brace, 1965), 70–73. See also Etienne de la Boétie, *Discours de la servitude volontaire,* ed. Simone Goyard-Fabre (Paris: Flammarion, 1983), 39–42. For a complete edition of La Boétie's treatises, see *Discours de la servitude volontaire suivi du Mémoire touchant l'Edit de janvier, 1562,* edited with an introduction by Paul Bonnefon (Abbeville: Frédéric Paillart, 1922). For a study of the *Mémoire,* see Malcolm C. Smith, *Montaigne and Religious Freedom* (Geneva: Librarie Droz, 1991).

5. La Boétie's antityrannical text — also known as *Le Contre Un* — was printed in two pirated editions of 1574 and 1576. Montaigne appears to have in mind the critique of royal power and authority in such works as François Hotman's *Francogallia* (1573), Théodore Bèze's *Du droit des magistrats sur leurs sujets* (1574), and Philippe de Mornay's *Vindiciae contra tyrannos* (1579). For English translations of the significant portions of Hotman, Bèze, and de Mornay, see Julian H. Franklin, *Constitutionalism and Resistance in the Sixteenth Century: Three Treatises by Hotman, Beza, and Mornay* (New York: Pegasus, 1969). For an assessment of this literature, see Quentin Skinner, *The Foundations of Modern Political Thought* (Cambridge: Cambridge University Press, 1978), vol. 2, 302–38; and Keohane, *Philosophy and the State,* 25–82.

6. *Discours,* ed. cit., 133. Further citations to this work follow in the text of my essay; translations are my own.

7. *Mémoire,* ed. cit., 139. Further citations to this work appear in the text of my essay.

8. For Montaigne's decision to take the oath, see Frame, *Montaigne,* 53; Nakam, *Montaigne,* 144–46; Smith, *Montaigne,* 99–100.

9. For a description of the violence, see Kathleen Parrow, *From Defense to Resistance: Justification of Violence During the French Wars of Religion* (Philadelphia: American Philosophical Society, 1993); for the conduct of the wars, see Mack P. Holt, *The French Wars of Religion, 1562–1629* (Cambridge: Cambridge University Press, 1995); for Montaigne's treatment of the wars, see Nakam, *Montaigne,* 167–99; and for Montaigne's view of war in general, see David Quint, *Montaigne and the Quality of Mercy: Ethical and Political Themes in the Essais* (Princeton: Princeton University Press, 1998).

10. Montaigne's position on the monarchy and its powers is complex. On the one hand, Nakam is certainly right to say that he supported "the principle of monarchy" against those who engaged in feudal rivalry (*Montaigne,* 179). On the other hand, as she notes, he thought changes (*mutations*) in established custom were dangerous, and was especially repelled by the example of the English church (215). Moreover, his defense of "custom and the law" was energized by a radical argument: "Far from being narrowly conservative, it was opposed to every authoritarian tradition on the one hand, and, on the other, to the introduction of tyrannical novelties" (*Les Essais,* 178). Smith supports this view of Montaigne's politics and finds that he generally distrusted "the use of extrajudicial means" to ensure public order (*Montaigne,* 113). Evidence suggests that Montaigne would have been suspicious of any use of prerogative, as against custom or positive law; the suspicion reflected his belief that the monarch could not claim an understanding of suprapositive law, any more than could his subjects.

11. This observation is substantially repeated elsewhere in the *Essais* as published in editions before 1588: see remarks on opinion, 1.14 (33 [55]); local norms, 1.31 (152

[205]); imposture, 1.32 (159 [215]); custom and self-reference, 1.49 (215 [296]); partial vision, 2.1 (239 [331]); and projection, •2.32 (548 [725]).

12. David Lewis Schaefer understands Montaigne's statements on ineffable grace to mean that its possibility is denied (man is informed only by human agents): "Montaigne's proposal to consider man 'armed solely with his arms' turns out to be no hypothesis at all, but rather *the essayist's true view of the human condition*" (*The Political Philosophy of Montaigne*, 56, Schaefer's emphasis). It is important, however, that Montaigne's own theory of language admits a prediscursive consciousness that precedes speech and would allow for the experience of grace, although not the articulation of its terms in language. For a discussion of Montaigne's conception of human speech and speakers, see Ian Maclean, "'Le Païs au delà': Montaigne and Philosophical Speculation," in *Montaigne: Essays in Memory of Richard Sayce* (Oxford: Clarendon Press, 1982), 101–32.

13. The historian and magistrate Jacques-Auguste De Thou reported that Montaigne said of Guise and Navarre, the Catholic and Protestant leaders respectively, that "religion, which is alleged by both, is used speciously as a pretext by those who follow them; for the rest, neither one regards it" (quoted in Frame, *Montaigne*, 140–41).

14. The source of this dictum is Plutarch's "On the Meaning of *Ei*" in *Moral Essays;* cited in Frame, *The Complete Works of Montaigne*, 455, n. 64. For the relation between these texts, see Géralde Nakam, "Le Dieu de 'L'Apologie de Raimond Sebond': De Plutarch à Montaigne," *Bulletin de la Société des Amis de Montaigne,* series 7, vols. 33–34 (1993): 131–48.

15. On the notion of working from appearances, see Ian Maclean's analysis of Montaigne's understanding of *locus a simili,* "Montaigne et le droit civil romain," in *Montaigne et la rhétorique: Actes du colloque de St. Andrews, 28–31 mars 1992* ed. John O'Brien, Malcom Quainton, and James J. Supple (Paris: Champion, 1995), 163–76, 172.

16. The larger question of Montaigne's notion of nature throughout the *Essais,* and whether it provides human beings with laws other than fixed, absolute, irrevocable ones, is beyond the scope of this paper. My own view is that of the three conceptions of nature Montaigne discusses — that is, the nature of creation in its diversity, the nature of human needs and aspirations, and the nature of instinctual behaviors (for these categories, see Keohane, *Philosophy and the State,* 103), only nature as instinct, experienced outside language or any other form of communication, can survive the critique of reason and understanding expressed in the "Apologie." For Montaigne's definition of "natural law" as "any instinct that is seen universally and permanently imprinted in both the animals and ourselves," and so on, see 2.8.279 (386). Richard Tuck thinks that Montaigne's idea of self-preservation implies self-interest though not "vulgar self-aggrandizement": *Philosophy and Government, 1572–1651* (Cambridge: Cambridge University Press, 1993), 51. Instances of self-interest in the *Essais* are not, however, invariably linked to an instinct for self-preservation; characters deliberately sacrifice themselves in order that their interests may prevail.

17. As critics have recognized, the absence of a connection between God, nature as an index of a rational creation, and human intelligence implies a theory of language and sign systems in general. See Mary B. McKinley, "Traduire/Ecrire/Croire: Sebond, les anciens et Dieu dans le Discours des *Essais,*" in *Montaigne: Apologie,* ed. Blum, 167–86. See also C. Blum, "Les *Essais* de Montaigne: Les Signes, la politique, la religion," in *Columbia*

Montaigne Conference Papers, ed. Donald M. Frame and Mary B. McKinley (Lexington, Ky.: 1981), 9–30.

18. For other statements on the need to conform in editions of the *Essais* published before 1588, see comments on conformity, 1.23 (86 [118–9]); prayer, 1.56 (229 [317–18]; 232 [320]); and "monstrous law," 2.17 (497–98 [655]).

19. See, for example, Bernard de Girard, Seigneur du Haillan, *De l'Estat et succez des affaires de France* (Paris, 1580), 289. For an excellent summary of French political opinion in this period, see William Farr Church, *Constitutional Thought in Sixteenth-Century France* (Cambridge: Harvard University Press, 1941).

20. "On the Education of the Prince," trans. Neil Kenny, in *Cambridge Translations of Renaissance Philosophical Texts: Political Philosophy,* ed. Jill Kraye (Cambridge: Cambridge University Press, 1997), 258–73; 259, 268. See also Church, 47, n. 8, quoting "De l'institution du prince," *Bibliothèque de l'arsenal,* Paris, MS 5103; dated 1519, 31v.

21. *The Grand Monarchy of France,* trans. J. H. Hexter, ed. Donald R. Kelley (New Haven: Yale University Press, 1981), 49–50. See also Church, 23, n. 5, citing *La Grande Monarchie de France* (Paris, 1588), 9b, 10a, who mentions the king's miraculous powers of healing; and Marc Bloch, *The Royal Touch: Sacred Monarchy and Scrofula in England and France,* trans. J. E. Anderson (London: Routledge and Kegan Paul, 1973). For the status and powers of the monarchy, see Roland Mousnier, *The Institutions of France Under the Absolute Monarchy, 1598–1789,* trans. Brian Pearce, 2 vols. (Chicago: University of Chicago Press, 1979), vol. 1, 653–79.

22. "Le But de la guerre et de la paix, ou discourse du chancelier l'Hospital pour exhorter Charles IX à donner la paix à ses subjects, 1570," in *Mémoires,* ed. P. J. S. Duféy, 3 vols. (Paris, 1824), vol. 2, 212, 214.

23. *Des Affaires d'Estat: des Finances du Prince et de sa noblesse* (Metz, 1597), A, A3v.

24. Jean de la Madeleine, *Discours de l'estat et office d'un bon roy, prince ou monarque* (Paris, 1575), 3b; quoted in Church, 94. Barthélemi Chasseneuz, *Consuetudines ducates Burgundiae* (Paris, 1547), 62a; quoted in Church, 47–48. For reference to other authors endorsing a notion of the king as a quasi-divine being, see Church, 48, n. 14.

25. "The Right of Magistrates," in *Constitutionalism and Resistance,* trans. and ed. Julian Franklin, 97–135, at 103, 106, 108.

26. *Vindiciae contra tyrannos,* quoted in Franklin, 138–99; 143, 149, 151. For the original text, see Stephano Iunio, *Vindiciae contra tyrannos* (Edinburgh, 1579) STC 15211, sig. B5, D6, D8v.

27. *Francogallia,* Latin text ed. Ralph E. Giesey, trans. J. H. M. Salmon (Cambridge: Cambridge University Press, 1972), 204–5, 234–35.

28. Jean Bodin, *On Sovereignty,* trans. and ed. Julian Franklin (Cambridge: Cambridge University Press, 1996), 1.viii, 13; see also 4, 8, 10, 25, 31, 32 for further comments on monarchic authority and power as they are circumscribed by divine and natural law. For the original text, see *Les Six Livres de la République,* ed. Christiane Frémont, Marie-Dominique Couzinet, and Henri Rochas, 5 vols. (Paris: Fayard, 1986). Further citations of this translation appear in the text of my essay. For an analysis of opinion on divine and natural law as checks on the monarch's power and authority, see Skinner, *Foundations,* vol. 2, 294–95; the fundamental study of Bodin is Julian Franklin, *Jean Bodin and the Sixteenth-Century Revolution in the Methodology of Law and History* (New York: Columbia University Press, 1963).

29. Here Bodin permits the subject's reading of natural law as a pretext for passive obedience. In practice, however, as Julian Franklin asserts, Bodin would have denied the validity of such a reading on the part of the subject because he could not attribute to the subject the ability to discern and interpret natural law: Bodin "cannot imagine any power remaining in the people authoritatively to take cognizance of a violation of a law of nature" (*On Sovereignty,* 129, n. 17).

30. *The Six Bookes of a Commonweale,* trans. Richard Knolles, ed. Kenneth Douglas McRae (Cambridge: Harvard University Press, 1962), 3.iv, 323.

31. This portrait appears indebted to the philosophy of Sextus Empiricus. Speaking of obedience to a tyrant who orders "something forbidden," presumably by law and custom, Sextus says that the skeptic will "choose the one course and avoid the other on the basis of the common understanding of the laws and customs of his country" (Sextus Empiricus, "Against the Mathematicians," 11, 165–66, cited in Benson Mates, *The Skeptic Way: Sextus Empiricus's Outlines of Pyrrhonism* (Oxford: Oxford University Press, 1996], 71–72). Like Montaigne, Sextus repeatedly insists that the skeptic follow a politics of the "common way"; his thoughts, having the status of mere speculation and hypothesis, do not therefore disturb the law; see Sextus Empiricus, *Outlines of Pyrrhonism,* bk. 1, chap. 11, article 24; 1: 33, 226–27; 3: 3, 2; III 24, 235; ed. and trans. Mates, in *The Skeptic Way,* pp. 92, 121, 169, 173, and 210, respectively.

32. Nannerl O. Keohane suggests that Montaigne's privacy is less theoretical than I regard it, stating that it is both in "solitary meditations and among close friends": *Philosophy and the State,* 109. As she points out, he sends his friends who want to know his "secret knowledge" to the bookseller (3.9.750, C). To me, Montaigne's instruction implies irony: thought expressed in language and published in a book cannot be secret. Montaigne's real secrets are protected by silence. Montaigne distinguishes between the privacy of thought and the fundamental publicity of every form of expression in "Of Custom" when he declares: "Society can do without our thoughts; but the rest—our actions, our work, our fortunes, and our very life—we must lend and abandon to its service and to the common opinions" (1.23.86).

33. Describing for his reader a place of study that would appear to allow for complete nudity, Montaigne makes a distinction between inwardness which is an uncommunicable condition and degrees of going public, of which the privacy of a study is the least ostensible (1.39, 177 [241]).

34. Montaigne's recourse to imaginary states and entities allows him to judge affairs as if there were some absolute standard (whatever is not "opinion") on which he could draw. For Montaigne's understanding of the counterfactual, see Ian Maclean's analysis of topoi in the practice of Roman law, "le domaine de prémisses dites probables," especially the *locus a simili* "Montaigne et le droit civil romain." 172.

35. In 1571, having been refused admission to the Grand'Chambre of the Parlement of Bordeaux, he retired to his château, only to return to Bordeaux as mayor in 1581, an office he held until 1585. See the comprehensive outline of his life in *Essais,* ed. Villey, xxxiii–xxxix.

36. See Frame, *Montaigne,* 21–24. For the Jews in Bordeaux in this period, see Mousnier, *The Institutions of France,* 1, 413–28.

37. *Essais,* ed. Villey, vii.

9

Mens sine Affectu?
Algernon Sidney's Ideal of Law

ANNABEL PATTERSON

When John Adams, a rising young colonial lawyer, agreed to defend the British soldiers who fired on a riotous Boston crowd in 1770 in the so-called Boston Massacre, he had recently been rereading Algernon Sidney's *Discourses Concerning Government*. Adams knew that he took considerable risks in defending Captain Preston, a symbol of British oppression, and he began with a florid self-justification from Beccaria's *Essay on Crime and Punishments:* "If, by supporting the rights of mankind, and of invincible truth, I shall contribute to save from the agonies of death one unfortunate victim of tyranny, or of ignorance equally fatal, the blessing and tears of transport will be a sufficient consolation to me for the contempt of all mankind."

If this seems rhetorically excessive and self-serving, the same cannot be said of Adams's peroration, where he reached for something larger than himself. He announced his intention to use "the words of a great and worthy man, a patriot and a hero, an enlightened friend to mankind, and a martyr to liberty — I mean Algernon Sidney." Adams then cited from the *Discourses* Sidney's definition of the ideal nature of Law: "The law no passion can disturb. 'Tis void of desire and fear, lust and anger. 'Tis *mens sine affectu,* written reason, retaining some measure of the divine perfection. It does not enjoin that which pleases a weak, frail man, but, without any regard to persons, commends that which is good, and punishes evil in all, whether rich or poor, high or low. 'Tis deaf, inexorable, inflexible. *On the one hand, it is inexorable to the cries and lamentations of the prisoner; on the other, it is deaf, deaf as an adder, to the clamors of the populace.*"[1]

What caught Adam's eye here was the classical claim of law's impartiality, *mens sine affectu,* ultimately derived from Aristotle's *Politics* (3:5). But the italicized last sentence was Adams's addition. He thereby translated both an ancient commonplace and an early modern argument — that monarchs, given their human failings, must always be subordinate to the laws of their land — into a modern claim for law's necessary impassivity — its ignoring of passions and special interests — especially when political feelings run high. It was also partly Sidney's way with words, especially the positive valence of words we usually hear as negatives ("deaf, inexorable, inflexible") that had captivated Adams and contributed to his courtroom victory; the paradox of a Law immune to affect, whose definition nevertheless moves us extremely. But the fact that these words were Algernon Sidney's tripled their effect and endowed Adams, by proxy, with charisma. For Sidney had died a political victim of the law whose indifference he championed theoretically. This essay expands on the idea of Sidney's rhetorical understanding of law (as distinct from legal rhetoric): the historical circumstances that generated it, its subsequent codification and transmission in the Whig canon, and some at least of its formal features.

Just after the Revolution of 1688, Sir John Hawles, who would later become William's attorney-general, published a commentary on some of the more notorious state trials of the reign of Charles II. The purpose of this publication, impossible while James II was on the throne, was in part to justify the revolution in terms of legal theory. A series of "undue Prosecutions in criminal, but more especially in capital matters," that is to say, treason trials, had so undermined the public trust in the legal system that the political system itself had become suspect and due for reform. Hawles's *Remarks upon the tryals of Edward Fitzharris, Stephen College, . . . the Lord Russel, Collonel Sidney,* published in 1689, was therefore structurally related not only to Locke's *Two Treatises,* which contained a similar argument in its closing sections, but also to the first published edition of Algernon Sidney's *Discourses,* produced in 1689 by John Darby, Sr., with a brief preface by John Toland. During the eighteenth century three other important editions of the *Discourses* helped to create for the Whig reader at home and the potentially revolutionary reader in the American colonies the idea of Algernon Sidney as victim of an unjust legal regime and theorist of a just one; the rhetorical force of the pairing of roles occurring precisely at the moment of Sidney's execution, at the juncture of short-term defeat and long-term victory.

In his commentary on the trial of Stephen College, the joiner executed in 1681 for insulting the king and the duke of York in conversation and cartoons at the time of the Oxford parliament, Hawles paused to sum up what he called the legal "practise of late times" — "late" implying recent and very topical. Hawles deserves quotation at some length, not least because his account of late Stuart juridical practice in trials for treason reads today like something out of Kafka:

> It is so very much like, or rather worse than the practise of the inquisition, as I have read it, that I sometimes think it was in order to introduce popery, and make the inquisition, which is the most terrible thing in that religion, and which all nations dread, seem easy in respect of it. I will therefore recount some undeniable circumstances of *the late practise:* a man is by a messenger, without any indictment precedent, which by the common law ought to precede, or any accuser or accusation that he knows of, clapt up in close prison, and neither friend nor relation must come to him, he must have neither pen, ink or paper, or know of what, or by whom he is accused. . . . If any persons advise or solicit for him, unless assigned by the court by which he is tried, they are punishable: he is tried as soon as he comes into the court, and therefore of a solicitor there is no occasion or use. . . . The prisoner indeed hath liberty to except to thirty-five of the jury peremptorily, and as many more as he hath cause to except to, but he must not know beforehand who the jury are; but the king's counsel must have a copy of them; . . . there is a proclamation to call in all persons to swear against him, none is permitted to swear for him; all the impertinent evidence that can be given is permitted against him, none for him; as many counsel as can be hired are allowed against him, none for him. Let any person consider these circumstances, and it is a wonder how any person escapes: it is downright tying a man's hands behind him, and baiting him to death, as in truth was practised in all these cases. The trial of Ordeal, of walking between hot iron bars blindfold, which was abolished for the unreasonableness of it, though it had its [biblical] saying for it too, that God would lead the blind so as not to be burnt if he were innocent, was a much more advantageous trial for the suspected than what was *of late practised,* where it was ten to one that the accused did not escape.[2]

I cite Hawles, himself a rhetorician of no mean qualifications, from the *State Trials,* a collection begun with Whig motives and which today constitutes our greatest resource for studying the convergence of English law and rhetoric from the sixteenth century onward. When Thomas Salmon brought out (anonymously) the first edition of *State Trials* in 1719, he initiated a kind of reporting that we associate with Whig or liberal principles, especially the public's right to know how the law is being administered.[3] The ideal of verbatim reporting, however, which governs the collection, even for the earliest trials, where some degree of collation and invention must have filled out actual note-taking by witnesses, also permits us to relive as drama the hours in those tense courtrooms and listen with our inner ears to the proceedings — especially, of course, to the defense.

Hawles included in his remarks on College's trial a specific attack on the denial of legal counsel to the accused. The practice was archaic in two senses; first, that to defend a person accused of treason was held to be speaking against the monarch; and second, that the accused was required to speak for himself, in the full expectation that he *would* incriminate himself; in other words, self-defense was expected to serve, in the traditions of the residually magical political rituals of early modern state, as a form of confession. Yet what was not fully grasped by the legal institution was the rebarbative force of this compulsion to bear witness, a force increasingly understood and manipulated by the dissenting and liberal communities. When accused men defended themselves with intelligence and passion, their trials became dramatic representations of issues that, if left to lawyers, might have been rendered safely professional and obscure. And when the accused defended themselves, others of similar views would be taking notes in the courtroom and could (by flouting the press laws) make the drama of the treason trial available in print to a larger audience.

The result was the creation of an alternative legal canon, as it were: the records, most often produced surreptitiously and printed illegally, of what were seen as unusually unjust trials, providing ethical and emotional support to any temporarily disadvantaged party or actively persecuted minority. But in addition, this alternative legal literature (of which the *State Trials* served as a canonizing and legitimating mechanism) could actually serve a practical legal purpose: that of providing instruction in the ways of courts and the strategies of self-defense which could literally be passed on from one defendant to another. In the rare case (one in ten) suggested by Hawles, this educative process allowed the defendant to escape conviction. In the case of Algernon Sidney, this strategic use of the precedent trials became, precisely because the "law" was itself unstable and liable to judicial manipulation, a snare and a delusion.

This "trial" literature, which had by the Restoration become a significant genre with well-defined conventions, made its first appearance in the middle of the sixteenth century, in a case that laid down both some effective strategies of self-defense and the importance of making such trials available to a broad reading public. This was the trial of Sir Nicholas Throckmorton in 1553 for complicity in the uprising led by Sir Thomas Wyatt the Younger against Mary Tudor. As we know from the account subsequently published in Raphael Holinshed's *Chronicles* in 1577, Throckmorton managed to conduct his defense with such a mixture of legal sophistication and moral superiority that the jury acquitted him.[4] Its members were thereupon themselves thrown into prison and fined so exorbitantly that the case became something of a skeleton in the closet of British legal history. We know, however, that it was seen at the time as potential "trial literature." John Bradford, the Protestant martyr, was given a manuscript transcript of Throckmorton's trial while in prison in London in the spring of 1555, awaiting execution for heresy, and wrote in it "Remarks" evidently intended as a preface with a view to its publication.[5]

Bradford began his "Remarks," delivered *e carcere*, by testifying that this "book" was "worthy to be had in print, and diligently read of all men, but especially of the nobility and gentlemen of England." His repeated injunction, "Read this book," is a striking early illustration of what such trial literature was meant to accomplish. The "houses and names" of the nobility and gentry, Bradford asserts,

> could not but continue, if that yet now they would begin to take this gentle-man a sampler to ensue, and a pattern to press after: For here thou, good reader, shalt perceive a gentleman in deed, and not in name only: his trust was in the Lord, and not in man, and therefore he was not confounded: he honoured God, and therefore God hath honoured him accordingly. His study was in God's word, and therefore found he comfort: by it he found more wisdom and had more knowledge than all his enemies, which were not few nor foolish to the judgement of the world. They came to him as Goliah the mighty giant, harnessed and armed cap-a-pie: he came as a little David with his sling, and had the victory. . . . What wisdom, what grace, what audacity, did God give to him in his need! What could all the learned lawyers, which better might be termed lewd losels of the realm, do against him? What could all the power of the queen's highness prevail?

Clearly, the first benefit would be solidarity among the Protestant leaders of England during the Catholic reaction. But a specific defensive technology is also involved: "Read the book," Bradford continued:

> and thou shalt see what knowledge this gentleman had in the statutes, laws, and chronicles of the realm, to teach the nobility and gentlemen, which are and would be magistrates and rulers of the realm, to spend more time to attain wisdom and knowledge to execute their offices than they now do. Read this book, and thou shalt see what false packing there is against the simple and plain truth. Read this book, and thou shalt see how unrighteousness sitteth in the place of justice.

And finally Bradford turned to the example set by "the good men em-
panelled of the quest," that is, the jury:

> A greater honour never came to the city of London than by those twelve men.
> What said I, to the city of London? Nay, to the whole realm of England: for,
> alas! if they had not more conscience and truth than king, queen, lords,
> counsellors, judges, sergeants, attornies, solicitors, lawyers, &c., England had
> been guilty of innocent blood;
>
>   But what reward had this good jury? Well, I pass over that: a papistical
> reward. What is that? Forsooth, such as Julianus Apostata gave to the faithful
> Christians.
>
>   God our Father look better on this gear in his good time, which in respect of
> his enemies is at hand; "for they have scattered abroad his law."

Thus a proper reading of the Throckmorton trial will provide the following
benefits: religious consolation; pragmatic and stateworthy instruction in the
laws and statutes; skeptical awareness of the brute fact that "false packing"
exists and that often "unrighteousness sitteth in the place of justice"; and a
reminder of the fundamental importance in English law of the jury system. In
Bradford's Protestant rhetoric, however, the sanctions are exclusively religious, and the metaphors, with Throckmorton as "little David with his
sling," appropriately biblical.

When Algernon Sidney was himself tried for treason in 1683, it appears that
he had taken Bradford's advice and informed himself of Throckmorton's defense, along with those of John Lilburne and Sir Henry Vane,[6] transcripts of
whose trials had also been published by their supporters.[7] Sidney was tried for
complicity in a plot against Charles II, to whom, on being allowed to return to
England in 1677, he had promised obedience. Only one witness could be
produced against Sidney, Lord William Howard, a co-conspirator who was
evidently embroidering his tale to enhance his own chances of survival; and
the Crown therefore had to improvise, producing as the second "witness" to
the charge of imagining the death of the king the manuscript of Sidney's
republican answer to Filmer's *Patriarcha* which had been found among his
private papers. Jonathan Scott, the historian who has done most to put Sidney
back in focus, cites the various commentators, including the conservative John
Evelyn and the French ambassador Barillon, who felt that the injustice of the
trial had seriously damaged the government's reputation.[8] As Scott put it,
"Sidney's trial and execution established, and slightly exceeded, the limits of
public tolerance."

Scott makes the important moral point that there was nothing unique about

Sidney's trial in terms of early modern jurisprudence, in which the "unjust tribunal" was never confined to one side of the political spectrum. In the denial of counsel and of a copy of the indictment, at least to commoners, Sidney's trial ran true to form, including the precedents of the trials of those accused during the Popish Plot, when Slingsby Bethel, the London sheriff, and Attorney General Jones had managed manifestly unjust trials with Sidney's oversight and approval. Sidney had informed himself of the precedents in the attainder of Strafford, whom Vane had helped to destroy, and Stafford, for whom Sidney had done the same. Yet Sidney's trial proved more powerful as an agent of later political and legal thought than any of its predecessors, precisely because of its imbrication with his *Discourses*. As the *Discourses* were used as evidence against him, so Sidney's obsession with the law and its abuses pervades the *Discourses* and was revealed by his trial as a self-fulfilling prophecy.

Sidney was arrested on June 26, 1683, a week before the government had anything other than hearsay evidence against him: technically an illegal arrest. On the same day his papers, including the manuscript of the *Discourses,* were confiscated. Direct evidence of a plot of which Sidney was one of the six designers would follow on July 9, when Lord Howard was taken, who, according to Gilbert Burnet, "at his first examination . . . told, as he said, all he knew."[9] Later he would tell a good deal more than he knew. Sidney was then held in the Tower until early November, while the government attempted to build its case on firmer ground. In late October Sidney and Hampden filed a writ of habeas corpus; and the government responded by moving ahead with his trial, having come up with the expedient of using the *Discourses* in place of a second human witness. The charge of "imagining the king's death" was to be supported by Sidney's own words in an unpublished manuscript. In the meantime Lord Russell, with two material witnesses against him, had been successfully prosecuted under Justice Pemberton and executed on July 21. Sidney included those proceedings in his material for study.

In this instance, in contrast to the case of Lord Russell, where the government tried in vain to suppress publication of the proceedings, the transcript of Sidney's trial was published by authority early in 1684, to pre-empt surreptitious editions, with their editorial coloring, as also, presumably, to show to the world the weakness of Sidney's defense.[10] Judge Jeffreys himself ordered its assignment to Benjamin Tooke "and that no other Person presume to Print the same." It was, however, reprinted in Dublin by Joseph Ray, who also reprinted, as had Mary Crooke before him, *The very copy of a paper delivered to the sheriff,* that is to say, Sidney's scaffold speech, which Sidney had made no attempt to deliver *as* a speech, but of which he had rather handed one copy to the sheriff, advising him that another resided in safe hands. Its publication was promptly prohibited, but a Dutch edition appeared almost immediately, spawning so many manuscript copies that the government threw in the towel and permitted a London edition.[11]

Six years later, as mentioned earlier, John Darby published the first edition of the *Discourses,* with Toland's preface. Darby and Toland thereby began the gradual process of accretion and consolidation of the Sidney legend, which thereafter became monumental. In 1705, John Darby, Jr., published a second edition of the *Discourses,* with a portrait of Sidney, Toland's preface, and the *Last Paper.* This volume also added an excellent if highly tendentious index, in which, for example, the subheadings under "Absolute power and Monarchy" include "Burdensome and dangerous," "The sad effects of it," "Encourages venality and corruption," and "Few or none long subsist under it."

Half a century later, in 1751, Andrew Millar published a third and new edition by Richard Baron. This volume included Toland's preface, Baron's "Memoirs" of Sidney's life (into which was inserted his *Last Paper*), and his much longer "Apology," which was actually his vindication. Sidney's manuscript of the "Apology" (no longer extant today) had been secreted by Sidney's servant Joseph Ducasse, himself a Huguenot refugee from France, until after the revolution, when he produced it for inspection by a committee of the House of Lords.[12] Its addition to the *Discourses* meant that, with the exception of his *Court Maxims,* all of Sidney's works were now available together. And Baron had put considerable scholarly work into this new edition of the *Discourses,* checking, expanding and correcting the marginal and footnote references.

But Baron's efforts were still further improved upon by Thomas Hollis's 1763 edition of Sidney's works. Hollis took over the Baron text of the *Discourses* and the "Apology," along with Baron's biography. He added a new portrait of Sidney; as compared with the romantic image of 1705, this was a severe Roman bust in profile, engraved by Cipriani after J. Basire. A flag over Sidney's shoulder identified his ruling passion as patriotism, while a famous anecdote beneath the portrait brought Lord Molesworth's testimony to ennoble his image. And opposite that image, on the title page, stands another motto taken from Milton's *Samson Agonistes,* "Or to the unjust tribunals under change of times" (l. 695) which pointed to Hollis's most substantial addition to the Sidney legend; not the letters to his father and Henry Savile, which were also now included, but the transcript of the trial itself, which had now been transformed, by its proximity to the *Apology,* from government propaganda into testimony for Sidney. As the *Discourses* had been defined by Jeffreys as the missing second witness for the prosecution, so the "Trial" was now transformed by Hollis into a witness for the defense.

Hollis's application of Milton's "unjust tribunals" to the trials of 1683, which showed a shrewd grasp of liberal historiography, had been prompted, surely, by his own careful reading of the *Discourses,* which evince an obsession with just and unjust tribunals that has so far escaped the notice of his modern commentators. Alan Houston focused on the great themes of freedom and slavery, virtue and corruption, constitutionalism and revolution, the ethico-political poles of Sidney's conceptual universe;[13] Jonathan Scott identified the *Discourses'* inconsistent mixture of natural law, ancient constitutionalism, and historical example, their "unqualified bellicosity" (p. 236), and their commitment to political relativism and the inevitability of change. But Sidney's concern with the legal *system* and its corruption under Charles II was more urgent than can be explained by any generalized theory of government according to law and resistance (as authorized by Grotius) toward magistrates who exceed its mandate.

Sidney's concern with unjust tribunals surfaces explicitly in his account of Restoration political culture:

> These men having neither will nor knowledge to do good, as soon as they come to be in power, justice is perverted, military discipline neglected, the public treasures exhausted, new projects invented to raise more; and the princes wants daily increasing, through their ignorance, negligence, or deceit, there is no end of their devices and tricks to gain supplies. To this end, swarms of spies, informers, and false witnesses, are sent out to circumvent the richest and most eminent men: *the tribunals are filled with court-parasites of profligate consciences, fortunes, and reputation, that no man may escape who is brought before them. If crimes are wanting, the diligence of well-chosen officers and prosecutors, with the favour of the judges, supply all defects; the law is made a snare.*[14]

Conversely, when Sidney encourages his reader to look back to the heroic era of the English commonwealth before Cromwell's ascendancy, he includes a praise of republican justice alongside that of the republic's military success:

> I could give yet more pregnant testimonies of the difference between men fighting for their own interests in the offices to which they had been advanced by the votes of numerous assemblies, and such as serve for pay, and get preferments by corruption and favor, if I were not unwilling to stir the spleen of some men by obliging them to reflect upon what has passed in our own age and country; to compare *the justice of our tribunals within the time of our memory,* and the integrity of those who* for a while managed the public

treasure; the discipline, valour, and strength, of our armies and fleets; the increase of our riches and trade; the success of our wars in Scotland, Ireland, and at sea, the glory and reputation not long since gained, with that condition into which we are of late fallen. (Chap. 2, section 28, p. 220; marginal note at asterisk: "The parliament of 1641"; italics added)

In a less polemical context not even Sidney would have been able to maintain so clear a distinction between Commonwealth justice and Restoration injustice. His own attitude during the Popish Plot trials presided over by his Whig allies goes unregistered here, but we have to suspect inconsistency, if not absolute hypocrisy. In his own trial, Sidney was to be caught by Jeffreys in that trap.

Indeed, one of the distinctions between Sidney's *Discourses* and Locke's *Two Treatises,* which have largely the same agenda, is their relative stress on law. Both begin with a devastating logical attack on Filmer's patriarchal theory on its own terms, largely those of scriptural citation. Both move to a reassertion of the theoretical bases of the English constitution; and both lead inexorably in the last sections to the conclusion that, since the constitution has been subverted by the present government, armed resistance to it is justified. In Sidney's case that move is not, as in Locke, through natural law contract theory, but through an increasingly broad definition of "law" as the English legal system, which includes constitutional law and history, and decrees, in Sidney's argument, that the king is subject to the law, not above it. Most of his third chapter is devoted to this theme, and his ancient constitutionalism and insistence on Parliament's sovereignty is only one aspect of the larger point. Filmer had conceded the standard position articulated by James I: "A king, governing in a settled kingdom, leaves to be a king, and degenerates into a tyrant, so soon as he ceases to rule according unto his laws"; but he had added a dangerous qualification: "yet where he sees them rigorous or doubtful, he may mitigate or interpret." This provocation inspired the eloquent statement with which we began and which caught John Adams's attention. Here it is in its original context:

Fortescue says plainly, the king cannot change any law: magna charta casts all upon the laws of the land, and customs of England: but to say, that the king can by his will make that to be a custom, or an antient law, which is not, or that not to be so, which is, is most absurd. He must therefore take the laws and customs, as he finds them, and can neither detract from nor add anything to them. The ways are prescribed as well as the end. Judgments are given by equals, "per pares." The judges, who may be assisting to those, are sworn to proceed according to law, and not to regard the king's letters or commands. The doubtful cases are reserved, and to be referred to the parliament, as in the statute of 35 [*sic*] Edw. III concerning treasons, but never to the king. The law intending that these parliaments should be annual, and leaving to the king a power of calling them more often, if occasion require, takes away all pretence of a necessity, that there should be any other power to interpret or mitigate laws. . . . That rule must always be uncertain, and subject to be distorted, which depends upon the fancy of such a man. He always fluctuates, and every passion that arises in his mind, or is infused by others, disorders him. The good of a people ought to be established upon a more solid foundation. For this reason, the law is established, which no passion can disturb. It is void of desire and fear, lust and anger. It is "mens sine affectu," written reason retaining some measure of the divine perfection. It does not injoin that which pleases a weak, frail man; but, without any regard to persons, commands that which is good, and punishes evil in all, whether rich or poor, high or low. It is deaf, inexorable, inflexible. (Chap. 3, section 15, pp. 315–16)

This passage is the intellectual center of Sidney's appeal to English law as the grounds of the constitutional contract, rather than merely a consequence of it. But other, equally farsighted explorations of legal theory appear in the *Discourses*. One is the proposal that the symbolic representation of an ideal of impersonal justice resides in the jury system, and that (a more radical proposal than even Lilburne made) "the law has put all judgments into the hands of the people. This power is executed by them in grand or petty juries, *and the judges are assistants to them,* in explaining the difficult points of the law. . . . The strength of every judgment consists in the verdict of these juries, which the judges do not give, but pronounce or declare" (chap. 3, section 26, p. 371; italics added).[15] For this assertion Sidney cited Bracton, who in chapter 3 competes with Grotius and Machiavelli as a primary authority.

Another legal issue was Filmer's claim that proclamations could replace laws, to whose refutation Sidney devotes the long late section 43, inserting into it one of his two clear indications[16] that this is, pace Scott, in part an Exclusion pamphlet:

Let proclamations obtain the power of laws, and the business is done. They may be so ingeniously contrived, that the antient laws, which we and our fathers have highly valued, shall be abolished, or made a snare to all those that dare remember they are Englishmen, and are guilty of the unpardonable crime of loving their country, or have the courage, conduct, and reputation required to defend it. This is the sum of Filmer's philosophy, and this is the legacy he has left to testify his affection to the nation; which having for a long time lain unregarded, has been lately brought into the light again, *as an introduction of a popish successor, who is to be established, as we ought to believe, for the security of the protestant religion, and our English liberties.* (Chap. 3, p. 448; italics added)

And then there is a little flurry of topical legal allusions in the last sections of the *Discourses,* allusions that substantially change its flavor, while completely undermining Sidney's claim in his defense that his answer to Filmer was pure theory, "not calculated to any particular government in the world" ("Trial," p. 134). Sidney engaged in a couple of topical ripostes directly at Charles II's expense. To demonstrate the limits of the king's power to pardon, he noted that "the waterman who had been pardoned by his majesty in the year 1680 for a murder he had committed, was condemned, and hanged, at the assizes upon an appeal" (p. 444). And still nearer to home, he turned to the example of Danby, languishing in the Tower since his impeachment in 1679 for complicity in the secret treaty of Dover:

> Nay, in cases of treason, which some men think relate most particularly to the person of the king, he cannot always do it [pardon]. Gaveston, the two Spencers, Tresilian, Empson, Dudley, and others, have been executed as traitors for things done by the king's command; and it is not doubted they would have been saved, if the king's power had extended so far. I might add the cases of the earls of Strafford and Danby; for, tho' the king [Charles I] signed a warrant for the execution of the first, no man doubts he would have saved him, if it had been in his power. *The other continues in prison, notwithstanding his pardon; and that will not be more to his satisfaction, unless he be found innocent, or something all out more to his advantage than his majesty's approbation of what he has done.*[17]

Seen through the lens of Sidney's obsession with law, then, it now appears that the structural goal of the *Discourses,* however prolix and unrevised they were, was remarkably clear. Sidney may have been following the structure of the *Patriarcha,* section by section, but his own thought was not dictated by it. His agenda was to move the reader gradually to understand that the only guarantor against partisan jurisprudence was *shared* jurisprudence. There was safety in numbers. "Two eyes see more than one, and human judgement is subject to errors" (chap. 3, section 46, p. 459). It was crucial to ensure that Parliament was the highest court in the land, with authority over the king. Not that Sidney was naive about parliament's integrity or institutional viability. Some of the most interesting passages late in the treatise register the influence of Andrew Marvell's *Account of the Growth of Popery and Arbitrary Government,* particularly in its lengthy account of how the long-lived Cavalier Parliament became so corrupted, in Marvell's words, that "by being so throughly acquainted, they understand their number and party, so that the use of so publick a counsel is frustrated, there is no place for deliberation, no perswading by reason, but they can see one another's votes through both throats and cravats before they hear them."[18] Sidney's version of this argument focuses

specifically on the way political corruption leads to the passing of bad statutes
—which means not that the parliamentary system is intrinsically bad, but only
that it is in need of a clean-up:

> Our kings had not wherewithal to corrupt many till these last twenty years,
> and the treachery of a few is not enough to pass a law. The union of many was
> not easily wrought, and there was nothing to tempt them to endeavour it; for
> they could make little advantage during the session, and were to be lost in the
> mass of the people, and prejudiced by their own laws, as soon as it was ended.
> They could not in a short time reconcile their various interests or passions, so
> as to combine together against the public; and the former kings never went
> about it. We are beholden to Hyde, Clifford and Danby, for all that has been
> done of that kind. They found a parliament full of lewd young men chosen by
> a furious people in spite to the puritans, whose severity had distasted them.
> The weakest of all ministers had wit enough to understand, that such as these
> might be easily deluded, corrupted, or bribed. Some were fond of their seats in
> parliament, and delighted to domineer over their neighbours by continuing in
> them: others preferred the cajoleries of the court before the honour of per-
> forming their duty to the country that employed them. Some sought to relieve
> their ruined fortunes, and were most forward to give the king a vast revenue,
> that from thence they might receive pensions: others were glad of a temporary
> protection against their creditors. Many knew not what they did when they
> annulled the triennial act; voted the militia to be in the king; gave him the ex-
> cise, customs, and chimney-money; made the act for corporations, by which
> the greatest part of the nation was brought under the power of the worst men
> in it; drunk or sober pass'd the five-mile act, and that for uniformity in the
> church. This embolden'd the court to think of making parliaments to be the
> instruments of our slavery, which had in all ages past been the firmest pillars
> of our liberty. (chap. 3, section 46, p. 456)

This was the penultimate section of the *Discourses,* and, as it closely
matches Marvell's analysis,[19] it also corresponds to the last chapter of Locke's
Second Treatise, which declares that the magistrate has broken his contract
with his subjects "when he either employs the force, treasure, and offices of the
society, to corrupt the representatives, and gain them to his purposes: or
openly pre-engages the electors, and prescribes to their choice, such, whom he
has by solicitations, threats, promises, or otherwise won to his designs; and
employs them to bring in such, who have promised beforehand, what to vote,
and what to enact."[20] Neither Marvell nor Locke faced the question of what to
do with a system vulnerable to such corruption. Sidney did. "But how great
soever the danger may be," he concluded, "'tis less than to put all into the
hazards of one man, and his ministers. . . . 'Tis better to depend upon those
who are under a possibility of being again corrupted, than upon one who

applies himself to corrupt them, because he cannot otherwise accomplish his designs." Parliament being, "under God, the best anchor we have, it deserves to be preserved with all care, till one of a more unquestionable strength be framed by the consent of the nation" (p. 457).

The Rhetoric of the Discourses

Despite his occasional appeals to God, Sidney's authorities and sanctions were largely secular, and a highly interesting, if predictable, collection they make: from the classical world, in descending order of importance, Tacitus, Livy, Lucan, Juvenal, Suetonius, Plutarch's *Lives* and Seneca's tragedies. Sidney's theme was, of course, the rise and fall of the Roman Republic, and the "literary" authority of Lucan and Juvenal is almost as important to him as the historical testimony of Tacitus and Suetonius. To cite just one example: when Sidney (in chapter 2, section 19) is refuting Filmer's claim that commonwealths are inevitably corrupt and monarchies inclined to integrity, one of his best negative examples is Julius Caesar:

> It is not easy to name a monarch that had so many good qualities as Julius Caesar, till they were extinguished by his ambition, which was inconsistent with them: he knew that his strength lay in the corruption of the people, and that he could not accomplish his designs without increasing it. He did not seek good men, but such as would be for him; and though none sufficiently addicted to his interests, but such as stuck at the performance of no wickedness that he commanded; he was a soldier according to Caesar's heart, who said,
>
> > Pectore si fratris gladium, juguloque parentis,
> > Condere me jubeas, gravidaeve in viscera partu
> > Conjugis, invita peragram tamen omnia dextra.
> > Lucan l.i.v.376.
> > [Tell me to plunge a sword into my brother's breast,
> > my father's throat, or the belly of my pregnant wife,]
> > I will nevertheless carry out all you command.]

That is, Sidney turns to the very *first* book of the *Pharsalia* for the account of how Caesar, having crossed the Rubicon, attempted to inspire his troops, and how he might have failed had not the centurion Laelius made this unnatural commitment. The prominence given to this brutal quotation in the text of the *Discourses* obscures the historical fact that Caesar is not *yet* the dictator he will become by the end of the first civil war.

The history of early modern Europe is equally inflected by Sidney's republican values. In addition to his use of Livy, a dozen times and prominently

Sidney cites Machiavelli, from whose *Discourses on Livy* the title of his own work was evidently taken. His reliance on Grotius has already been mentioned. Thuanus is another important figure; occasionally he invokes Calvin, Hotman, Buchanan, Boccalini. Biblical history, though often deployed, is outmatched by examples from recent history, and the early modern historians he draws on explicitly include Commynes, Guiccardini, Mariana, Davila, Las Casas.

Sidney's villains, on the other hand, are the absolutist theorists "Laud, Manwaring, Sibthorp, Hobbs, Filmer, and Heylin" (chap. 1, section 2, p. 8). The list, of which this is an obvious example, is one of his favorite rhetorical strategies; and sometimes this is deployed, to striking effect, in concert with the multiple historical analogy. Thus he inquires (at considerable length):

> whether they who desire no unjust advantage above their brethren, will not always desire that a people or senate constituted as that of Rome, from the expulsion of Tarquin to the setting up of Caesar, should rather judge of their merit, than Tarquin, Caesar, or his successors? Or whether the lewd or corrupted pretorian bands, with Macro, Sejanus, Tigellinus, and the like, commanding them, will not ever, like Brutus's sons, abhor the inexorable power of the laws, with the necessity of living only by their innocence, and favour the interest of princes like to those that advanced them? If this be not sufficient, they may be pleased a little to reflect upon the affairs of our own country, and seriously consider, whether Hide, Clifford, Falmouth, Arlington and Danby, could have pretended to the chief places, if the disposal of them, had been in a free and well-regulated parliament? Whether they did most resemble Brutus, Publicola, and the rest of the Valerii, the Fabii, Quintii, Cornelii, &c. or Narcissus, Pallas, Icetus, Laco, Vinnius, and the like? Whether all men, good or bad, do not favour that state of things, which favours them, and such as they are? Whether Cleaveland, Portsmouth, and others of the same trade, have attained to the riches and honours they enjoy by services done to the commonwealth? ... Whether the old arts of begging, stealing, and bawding, or the new ones of informing and trepanning, thrive best under one man who may be weak and vicious, and is always subject to be circumvented by flatterers, or under the severe scrutinies of a senate or people? (Chap. 2, section 25, p. 205)

Here are lists nested inside each other; list of heroes and villains from antiquity and the very recent past set side by side; lists of rhetorical questions leading to one last "severe scrutiny." The effect of these strategies is to divide the world, ancient and modern, into parties; to register the large numbers of men of integrity in early Rome (the Latin plurals, "Valerii," "Fabii," "Quintii," are quietly eloquent) and the absence of matching names in the present; and to denigrate Charles's chief ministers by paralleling them with the household slaves and favorites of the Roman emperors and their women.

As for "Cleaveland, Portsmouth, and others of the same trade," at this point Sidney's rhetoric unmistakably veers off in the direction of satire, a genre for which his frequent quotations from Juvenal establishes a predilection. "The services done to the commonwealth" to which he alludes with such heavy irony were the sexual services that Charles II's mistresses, Louise de Keroualle, duchess of Portsmouth, and Barbara Palmer, duchess of Cleveland, supplied, and for which they were so lavishly remunerated.[21]

Irony is one of Sidney's favorite devices; not merely for its own sake, though he clearly could have learned its effectiveness from Marvell's *Account of the Growth of Popery*, but also to demonstrate how ludicrous was Filmer's confidence in the rectitude of monarchical conduct and the lawlessness of popular assemblies.

Thus, in the long chapter in which he looked back to the just tribunals and the military successes of the Long Parliament, such that "all the states, kings, and potentates of Europe, most respectfully, not to say submissively, sought our friendship," Sidney added a final section whose misuse of the language of praise provides hilarious closure. His topic here is the disastrous Second Dutch War of 1665–68, which was also, of course, the subject of Marvell's most important political satire, the *Last Instructions to the Painter:* "These diseases [the Parliamentary successes], which proceed from popular corruption and irregularity, were certainly cured by the restitution of that integrity, good order and stability, that accompany divine monarchy. The justice of the war made against Holland in the year 1665, the probity of the gentleman, who, without partiality or bribery, chose the most part of the officers that carried it on; the wisdom, diligence, and valour, manifested in the conduct, and the glory with which it was ended, justifies all that our author can say in its commendation" (chap. 2, section 28, p. 222).[22]

These intrusions of zesty local polemic into the often repetitive discussion of law and constitutional theory make the *Discourses* a considerably better read. Though Sidney might define law in the abstract as "mens sine affectu," in the real world he knew that affect and effect must be conjoined in persuasion. But if Charles II had read any of these passages, it is not surprising that he should have decided that Sidney was unforgivable.

The Trial

For one who had thought so much about the *role* of law in maintaining the fences against arbitrary government, Sidney's grasp of its details was surprisingly inept. Of all the mistakes that Sidney made in his defense, and he made many, the most peculiar error was refusing to do sustained battle with Lord Chief Justice Jeffreys on his notorious new rule "Scribere est agere" ("Trial," p. 156). To do so, of course, would have been to own authorship of the *Discourses,* against his lawyers' advice. It was much too early in legal history to *win* that battle as an issue of free speech, though Sidney could have cited both Throckmorton's case and Lilburne's on whether words were indeed deeds. In fact, Sidney did refer to "Throgmorton's case" in relation to the distinction between talk, plans, and overt acts ("Trial," p. 147); but by this time he had lost his grip, his responses were incoherent, and half a sentence later he broke off with the pathetic appeal, "I should have somebody to speak for me, my lord." On the issue of authorship, Sidney prevaricated: "The attorney shews these papers to me, I do not know whether they are my own or no. . . . Look upon them, you see they are all old ink. These papers may be writ perhaps these twenty years, the ink is so old. But, my lord, it is a polemical discourse, it seems to be an answer to Filmer, which is not calculated for any particular government in the world" ("Trial," p. 134).

Meanwhile, Jeffreys in his summing-up had personified the *Discourses* in a skillful and devastating manner, turning them into precisely that speaking witness for whom they were made to substitute: "And though this book be not brought to that council to be perused, and there debated; yet it will be another, and more than two witnesses against the prisoner: for I would ask any man, suppose a man was in a room, and there were two men, and he talks with both apart. . . . And you have heard one witness prove it positively to you, that he consulted to rise in arms against the king, *and here is his own book says,* it is lawful for a man to rise in arms against the king, if he break his trust" ("Trial," p. 154; italics added).

By fudging the question of his authorship, Sidney gave up the high moral ground and was forced to rely on points of law that gave him no better foothold. One of his more embarrassing moves was to argue the need for two witnesses from the biblical case of Susanna and the Elders!

There *was* one interesting but extremely brief moment when Sidney appeared, without admitting to authorship, to be about to confront Jeffreys on the principle that writing, at least unpublished writing, is not a political act. "I think 'tis a right of mankind, and 'tis exercised by all studious men, that they write in their own closets what they please for their own memory, and no man can be answerable for it, unless they publish it." The statement was unusual, in that only here during the trial did Sidney use the term "right," and Jeffreys's ears caught it immediately: "Pray don't go away with that *right* of mankind, that it is lawful for me to write what I will in my own closet, unless I publish it.

I have been told, curse not the king, not in thy thoughts, not in thy bed-chamber, the birds of the air will carry it. I took it to be the *duty* of mankind, to observe that" ("Trial," p. 137; italics added).

Deprived of the defense on principle, Sidney wasted much of his day in court, and all of his witnesses, in trying to damage Lord Howard's already nonexistent credibility. Like Vane, he was constantly interrupted by Jeffreys, who in his own frightful way was extremely effective. Sidney made poor use of his legal prepa-ration. As Scott points out, he must have had an incomplete account of Russell's trial, for he did not know that one of the defenses he planned to make — that *conspiring* to levy war against the king was not treason under 25 Edw. III without some overt act — had already been rendered null by Sir Heneage Finch, solicitor general, on that occasion. Both Russell and Sidney were relying on Coke's opinion that the two branches of the statute, levying war and imagining the death of the king, were distinct, and could not be used as evidence of each other; but in Russell's case Finch, who had also been attorney general in Vane's trial, calmly decreed this "an error of my Lord Coke."[23] Even more calmly, in his summing up for the jury, and refuting Sidney's distinction between the two branches of 123 Edw. III, Finch remarked, "Gentlemen, I won't be long in citing authorities: it hath been settled lately by all the judges of England, in the case of my Lord Russel, who hath suffered for this conspiracy." The authority in this redefinition was Finch himself — and Finch's version of "reason": "And reason does plainly speak it to be so; for they that conspire to raise war against the king, can't be presumed to stop anywhere till they have dethroned or murdered the king" ("Trial," p. 148).

Indeed, whenever Sidney raised what he claimed was a point of law, Jeffreys simply told him he was mistaken. According to Burnet, in relation to Jeffreys's overruling Sidney's complaint that his jury was not composed of freeholders, Jeffreys "said on another occasion, why might they not make precedents to the succeeding times, as well as those who had gone before them had made prece-dents for them?"[24] Yet we should not merely shake our heads at Jeffreys's presumption; for making precedents for the future was precisely what Sidney himself was after, in hammering away at his right to see a copy of the indict-ment, producing the statute of 46 Edw. III, and attempting to hold off pleading guilty or otherwise until the indictment's validity had been tested. As Jeffreys remarked in the latter case, if they were to allow that procedure (which Lil-burne had used successfully), "all criminals would say in all cases, I doubt whether the bill be good or bad, and after I have thus considered of it, I will plead. . . . We must not introduce new methods or forms for anybody. The same case that is with you, may be with other people" ("Trial," pp. 109–10).

When Sidney wrote his "Apology," he attributed these failures of strategy to his lack of legal knowledge and the denial of counsel: "Being driven upon theis extremityes by the violence and fraude of the chief justice, whoe threatened, that judgement of treason should be immediately entered, if I did not come to the generall issue, I was forced to plead not guilty, and thearby lost the advantage, which was never to be recovered, unless the judges could have bin changed."[25]

In the "Apology," Sidney offered the world a critique of the trial he had received and a clear articulation of the principles by which it must be found unjust. During his trial, Sidney had been prevented from making a final address to the jury. "Nay, Mr. Sydney," said Jeffreys, "we must not have vying and revying . . . after the king's counsel have concluded, we never admit the prisoner to say anything" (p. 155). That "never" ignored the precedents of Throckmorton and Lilburne, who had both been permitted a final statement. In the "Apology," written as he awaited his execution, Sidney several times complained of the frequent interruptions he had suffered during the trial, and returned to the injustice of being denied counsel and a copy of the indictment, in language that made clear how broadly the issue was to be interpreted. This is a long passage, but by the same standards Sidney hoped for from his judges and jurors, it deserves our continued attention:

> Mr. Atturney [Sir Robert Sawyer, Knt.] had then so much confidence, and soe littell charity, as openly to avow, that I should not have councell, lest they should furnish or teach me the points of lawe that I might insist on. This appeared strange unto all thoes whoe have any knowledge of the lawes of God or man, and that are not equaly deprived of charity and humanity. *The obtaining of justice is the end of the lawe, and truth the rule of it: hereupon it is agreed by mankinde, that every man ought to know his accusation, that he may know to direct his deffence, or receave advice, if he be ignorant in it.* It is an absurd perversion of all lawe, to say, that I heard it read; when it was rendered soe long and intricate, that neither I, nor any other man, was, upon reading, able to comprehend it. One of the worst acts that were imputed unto Caligula, the worst and basest of men, was, that he caused edicts to be written in a hand, and set up in a place where no man could read them: hereby turned the lawe into a snare, and destroyed thoes whoe did not conforme themselves unto the rule they never knew. They fall under the same condemnation whoe make accusations obscure, and suffer them not to be examined, least they should be understood. To evade this, my prosecutors falsely pretend, that noe such privilege is allowed to prisoners in England. But, besides that naturall and universal rule of justice, which can be overruled by noe municipall law, I did produce the stat. of 46 Edw. III, which doth plainely enact, that all men, in all cases, wheather they be such as fall out against the king, or any others, shall have coppy of such records as are against them; and shewed, that the

parliament, whoes example all other courts ought to followe, had allowed unto the earl of Strafford, the earl of Danby, the lord Stafford, and the popisch lords now in the Tower, coppyes of their indictement: and, if it had bin pretended, that such a priviledge was allowed only unto peeres, I was ready to say, *that though I am not a peere, I am of the wood of which they are made, and doe not find, that our ancestors were lesse carefull of the lives of commoners, then of peeres, or that one lawe is made for them, and another for us.* (pp. 174–75; Hollis's italics)

Of course there are disingenuities here, not the least being Sidney's stress on his ignorance of the law, when he had spent at least three months studying it (however ineffectively). And to say, as he had at the opening of his arraignment, "I never was at a tryal in my life of any body, and never read a lawbook" (p. 108) was a bare-faced lie. But the point of this speech, which Sidney had *not* been "ready," or permitted, to deliver at his trial, was to broaden the argument rhetorically. In a single paragraph, which could be read only when the times had changed again, Sidney was able to articulate the old rule of legal intelligibility side by side with an as yet unheard-of principle of equality before the law; to merge the theory of natural law ("that naturall and universal rule of justice, which can be overruled by noe municipall law") with both statute law and ancient constitutionalism, the latter being implied in that appeal to "our ancestors." And all these supposedly different bases of political thought are further merged in that brilliant use of the first person plural where, given Sidney's arrogance, we might least expect it: "I doe not find . . . that one lawe is made for them, and another for *us.*"

Most important, however, Sidney was able to return in the "Apology" to the appalling dictum that "scribere est agere." Cut off as he was by Jeffreys when he attempted to cite the more reasonable policies of even the Spanish Inquisition, Sidney returned to this theme: "That noe tribunall did ever take notice of a man's private, crude, undigested thoughts: that, though the inquisition is the worst and most bloody tribunall that hath bin known in the world, I never feared to writte what I pleased against the religion there professed, when I lived under it" ("Apology," p. 179).

And in the *Last Paper* also, while maintaining the pretense that the *Discourses* were a treatise written decades earlier in merely theoretical response to Filmer, he made a simple claim for equivalent treatment: "If he might publish to the world his opinion . . . I know not why I might not have published my opinion to the contrary, without the breach of any law I have yet known. I might, *as freely as he, publicly have declared my thoughts, and the reasons upon which they are grounded.*"[26]

He then proceeded to summarize his republican principles.

Thus, by producing the *Last Paper* and the "Apology," and with the support of Joseph Ducasse, John Toland, Richard Baron, and Thomas Hollis, Sidney was eventually enabled to "publish" his political thought and its consequences to himself side by side.

Returned to court for his sentencing, Sidney had cried aloud (for once interrupting Jeffreys): "I must appeal to God and the world. I am not heard"; and Jeffreys had callously replied, "Appeal to whom you will" (p. 167). That the appeal was, in fact, successfully made, especially in the American colonies, has been well established;[27] not least by the tribute paid to Sidney by John Adams during his defense of Captain Preston.

Long after his retirement, when Adams had put politics behind him, he went back to reading Sidney's *Discourses*. Writing to Thomas Jefferson, his old political rival, from the perspective of their very old age and new philosophical friendship, he informed him on September 17, 1823, that he had been rereading "Algernon Sidney on Government," with, as it were, new eyes:

> There is a great difference in reading a book at four-and-twenty and at eighty-eight. As often as I have read it and fumbled it over, it now excites fresh admiration that this work has excited so little interest in the literary world. As splendid an edition of it as the art of printing can produce, as well for the intrinsic merits of the work, as for the proof it brings of the bitter sufferings of the advocates of liberty from that time to this, and to show the slow progress of moral, philosophical, political illumination in the world, ought to be now published in America. (10:410)

If Adams was correct in this judgment in the early nineteenth century, why not today?

Notes

1. I cite Adams from *The Works of John Adams,* ed. Charles Francis Adams, 10 vols. (Boston, 1851), 2:238 and 1:114; itals. added.

2. *A Complete Collection of State Trials,* ed. T. B. Howell, 21 vols. (London, 1816), 8:733–34; italics added.

3. *A Complete Collection of State Trials,* ed. Thomas Salmon, 4 vols. (London, 1719), 1:2. For an account of the various editions of *State Trials* and the agendas they served, see Donald Thomas, *State Trials,* 4 vols. (London and Boston, 1972), 1:4–8.

4. For a full account of this trial and its publication in the *Chronicles,* see my *Reading Holinshed's Chronicles* (Chicago, 1994), 154–83.

5. John Bradford, "Remarks on a Memorable Trial," from Emmanuel College Library, Cambridge, MS 2.2.15, no. 98; reprinted in *The Writings of John Bradford . . . Martyr, 1555,* ed. Aubrey Townsend, 2 vols. (Cambridge: Cambridge University Press, 1848), 1:405–7.

6. See Jonathan Scott, *Algernon Sidney and the Restoration Crisis, 1677–1683* (Cam-

bridge, 1991), pp. 303–16, for Sidney's letters to John Hampden describing his preparation for his defense.

7. For the publication of Lilburne's and Vane's trials, see my *Early Modern Liberalism* (Cambridge, 1997), 113–28.

8. Scott, *Algernon Sidney and the Restoration Crisis, 1677–1683*, pp. 340–41. This is the second of two monographs by Scott on Sidney, the first, *Algernon Sidney and the English Republic, 1623–1677* (Cambridge, 1988), being devoted to Sidney's earlier career.

9. Gilbert Burnet, *The History of My Own Time*, ed. Osmund Airy, 2 vols. (Oxford, 1907), 2:369.

10. *The Arraignment, Tryal & Condemnation of Algernon Sidney, Esq. for High-Treason. For Conspiring the Death of the King and Intending to raise a Rebellion in this Kingdom. Before the Right Honourable Sir George Jeffreys . . . at . . . King's Bench at Westminster, on the 7th, 12th, and 17th of November, 1683* (London: Benjamin Tooke, 1684).

11. See Scott, *Algernon Sidney and the Restoration Crisis*, pp. 311–12.

12. See *Journal of the House of Lords* (1689), p. 390.

13. Alan Craig Houston, *Algernon Sidney and the Republican Heritage in England and America* (Princeton, 1991).

14. Sidney, *Discourses concerning government*, ed. Thomas Hollis (London, 1763), p. 214; italics added (chap. 2, section 27). All subsequent quotations will be from this edition; but for the convenience of those using 1772 or other editions, chapter and section references are given.

15. Compare also chap. 3, section 22.

16. Compare chap. 2, section 27, p. 211: "If [the reader] be not convinced of this, he may soon see a man in the throne, who had rather be a tributary to France than a lawful king of England." Compare also chap. 3, section 43, where Sidney states that Filmer's argument in effect proposes that "we should waive the bill of exclusion, and not only admit [James] to reign as other kings have done, but resign the whole power into his hands," (p. 449).

17. *Discourses*, chap. 3, section 42, p. 444; italics added; Thomas Osborne, earl of Danby, imprisoned in April 1679, had been pardoned by Charles prior to a vote on the articles of impeachment by the Commons. Charles then prorogued the Parliament before the procedural impasse could be resolved. In August 1682 Danby sought a writ of habeas corpus in King's Bench, but his judges deferred to Parliament as the higher court. He was not granted bail until February 1684, when the credibility of Oates had failed, and Jeffreys had become lord chief justice. Sidney's statement that Danby "continues in prison" therefore provides another set of chronological boundaries for the composition of the *Discourses*. Compare the briefer discussion of the significance of these references for dating in Blair Worden, "The Commonwealth Kidney of Algernon Sidney," *Journal of British Studies* 24 (1985): pp. 38–39. It is possible that Sidney's mean-spirited reference to Danby, when the manuscript was close to completion, was motivated by that habeas corpus appeal in August 1682.

18. Andrew Marvell, *Complete Works*, ed. A. B. Grosart, 4 vols (A. B. Grosart (p.p. 1875), 4:331.

19. Compare Sidney's selection of the bad legislation with Marvell's stinging expla-

nation for "the three acts of Corporations, of Militia, and the Five Miles," *Account,* pp. 305–7, and his diagnosis of the makeup of the Cavalier parliament that made it susceptible to corruption (pp. 323–31). Of course, Sidney nowhere refers to Marvell's *Account* in the *Discourses.*

20. John Locke, *Two Treatises of Government,* ed. Mark Goldie (London, 1993), p. 227.

21. See, for instance, Marvell's letter "to a friend in Persia" of August 1671, in which he reported that the Parliament had "signed and sealed ten thousand Pounds a Year more to the Dutchess of Cleveland, who has likewise near ten thousand Pounds a Year out of the new Farm of the Country Excise of beer and Ale, five thousand Pounds a Year out of the Post Office, and, they say, the Reversion of all the King's Leases, the Reversion of all Places in the Custom House, the green Wax, and indeed, what not? All Promotions, spiritual and temporal, pass under her Cognizance." Marvell, *Poems and Letters,* ed. H. M. Margoliouth, rev. Pierre Legouis, 2 vols. (Oxford, 1971), 2:325.

22. It seems likely that Sidney is here parodying not only Filmer, but also John Dryden's preface to *Annus Mirabilis* (1667), in which he defined the second Dutch War as "a most just and necessary War" illustrating "the care, management and prudence of our King; the conduct and valour of a Royal Admiral, and of two incomparable Generals; the invincible courage of our Captains and Sea-men, and three glorious Victories, the result of all." See Dryden, *Poems, 1649–1680,* in *Works,* ed. E. N. Hooker and H. T. Swedenberg, Jr. (Berkeley, 1956–96), 1:50.

23. *Tryal of William Lord Russell,* in *State Trials,* 9:629.

24. Burnet, *History of My Own Time,* 2:401.

25. "The Apology of A. Sydney in the day of his death," in *Discourses* (1763), p. 174.

26. Cited from Hollis's edition, p. 38.

27. See Houston, *Algernon Sidney and the Republican Heritage in England and America,* pp. 223–78. Houston's point, that "to the colonists, the single most important fact about Sidney's life was the manner of his death," is well taken. But he also carefully documents the fluctuations in Sidney's reputation in America before 1760, during the Stamp Act crisis, during the Revolutionary and Constitutionalist periods, and during the slavery debates.

10

"The Duty to Love": Passion and Obligation in Early Modern Political Theory

VICTORIA KAHN

For that Law may bandy with nature, and traverse her sage motions, was an error in Callicles *the Rhetorician, whom* Socrates *from high principles confutes in Plato's* Gorgias.
— *Milton,* The Doctrine and Discipline of Divorce

It is a well-known topos of the history of political theory that during the seventeenth century a distinctively modern language of natural rights and social contract developed. In contrast to medieval and neo-Scholastic notions of obligation, theorists such as Grotius, Pufendorf, and Hobbes predicated their accounts of political association first and foremost on a secular idea of human nature, including the natural desire for self-preservation, rather than on divine law.[1] Some combination of the rational deduction of the laws of nature, the rational calculation of self-interest, and the natural right of self-preservation then dictated the social contract as the best way to guarantee life and long-term security. Once we rationally deliberate about the insecurity of the state of nature—so the argument ran—we will consent to set up a sovereign: we will consent, that is, to the political contract. Consent is what authorizes the sovereign and thus what distinguishes legitimate from illegitimate power, sovereignty from coercion.

Easily said. But here we confront the dilemma of early modern theories of contractual obligation: for, once individuals are imagined as the prepolitical matter of society or as — in Hobbes's metaphor — mushrooms sprung up out of the earth, with no ties of status or lineage — it becomes necessary to provide an account of the motives that induce them to join together.[2] Grotius posited a principle of natural human sociability, while Hobbes emphasized rational self-interest. Yet if these were sufficient — if individuals could already cooperate in the state of nature — the state of nature would already be one of society. For logical as well as empirical reasons, sociability and rational calculation are not enough — hence the necessity of a variety of supplementary motives, what one seventeenth-century critic of Hobbes called supplementary "laws of fear."[3]

The role of the passions in securing consent — whether in the form of political allegiance or legal conviction — was an important part of classical and early modern rhetorical theory. Aristotle devoted book 2 of the *Rhetoric* to this topic, and Cicero in book 2 of *De officiis* and elsewhere stressed the instrumentality of the passions in securing reputation and political influence. In England, Thomas Wilson's *Arte of Rhetoric* (1553), a manual for lawyers and poets, stressed the affective dimension of persuasion: "In moving affections, and stirring the judges to be grieved, the weight of the matter must be so set forth, as though they saw it plain before their eyes." In his *Arte of English Poesie* (1589) George Puttenham praised the power of the poet-legislator to "affectionately bend" the hearer's ear. From Plato's *Republic* on, political treatises have shown a similar concern with the rhetorical force of the passions. In the sixteenth century, fear and love were central to Machiavelli's analysis of the prince's virtù and his subversion of the classical rhetorical tradition. Hobbes, who wrote a "brief" of Aristotle's *Rhetoric,* drew on the Latin rhetorical tradition in his analysis of political obligation.[4]

Despite the continuing influence of classical rhetoric, however, the relation between rhetoric and the passions began to undergo a transformation in the late sixteenth and the seventeenth centuries. This transformation may be explained in part by the Ramist challenge to humanist conceptions of rhetoric, and by the challenge of the new science to older, humanist conceptions of virtue and motivation.[5] At the same time that the passions were beginning to be neglected in rhetoric manuals, we begin to see persuasion treated as a subset of the passions. Thomas Wright's treatise *The Passions of the Minde in General* (1604) is exemplary in this regard; other, contemporary treatises on ethics, psychology, or natural philosophy ignored the formal discipline of rhetoric altogether, while still addressing questions of passion, affect, and effect that were crucial to imagining a political subject who consents to obey the sovereign. The passions, in short, began to be conceived as a materialist rhetoric in their own right, with crucial effects in the social and political realm.[6]

In this chapter I argue that the full story of the subject of contract — the subject of rights — cannot be told without attending to the supplementary role of this materialist rhetoric of the passions in forging political obligation.[7] In so doing, I build on and revise three strains in the secondary literature on early modern theories of political contract. According to the first and most prominent, contract is more rationalistic and more voluntarist than in earlier accounts of obligation. In this first account the role of the passions is basically ignored.[8] The second acknowledges the role of the passions but has little to say about their role in *constituting* the subject of contract.[9] The third is that of Foucault, who sees the legalistic language of contract as continuous with earlier forms of sovereignty, as a form of law rather than of discipline, and thus as distinct from a normative conception of the passions.[10]

In contrast, I want to suggest, first, that contract is less a coherent rationalist or voluntarist account of obligation than a set of antinomies — involving coercion and consent; second, that in some seventeenth-century theories of contract, the passions have an important role in responding to and making sense of these antinomies; and third and consequently, that the passions function as a vehicle of Foucauldian discipline and thus complicate any purely legalistic conception of early modern contract. Moreover, in contrast to the usual focus on the canonical texts of political theory, I suggest that treatises on "domesticall duties" and gender relations in the decades leading up to and including the English civil war are as crucial to this narrative as are the canonical works of early modern political theorists.[11] In the work of Gouge and Milton, as well as in that of Hobbes, the constitution of the affective subject is central to early modern contract theory. Together, these texts help us to explore the early modern preoccupation with the necessity of producing certain passions — whether in relation to traditional obligations or to natural rights. More specifically, they allow us to trace the trajectory from the derivation of passion from obligation to the derivation of obligation from passion. In so doing, they help us understand the emergence of the argument that the production of the right passions constitutes the subject of rights.

Let me turn to the antinomies first. Seventeenth-century theories of contract were caught on the horns of a dilemma. Consent involves the will, and the will — as Patrick Riley has argued — has both a moral and a psychological meaning. The moral meaning assumes that the will is based on reasons; the psychological meaning assumes that it is based on causes. In the first case, the will involves rational choice, but it is unclear what motivates the will; in the second case, the will is already determined by antecedent factors, so it is unclear what the role of reason is. Contract or consent theory thus becomes the locus of a set of antinomies between rationalism and voluntarism, voluntarism and determinism.[12]

In their attempts to address these antinomies, some seventeenth-century theorists of contract turned to the passions. Particularly in materialist theories of human nature, the passions seemed to offer a new psychology of political obligation, and thus a solution to the antinomies of contract. According to this psychology, the passions are at once caused and volitional, but this fact is less of a problem than a virtue. For the passions so conceived become a way of imagining a consent that is also compelling, a coercion that is also willed. In short, the passions are no longer simply the object of Stoic or neo-Scholastic supervision. Instead, they are conceived of as the source of obligation. Rational consent is figured as consent to one's own passions; and the subjects of contract are imagined as binding themselves, rather than submitting to purely external coercion. The passions, in short, become a vehicle of Foucauldian discipline, a way of producing the subject of contract.[13]

As we will see, however, this psychology — the psychology of what we might call the modern affective subject — raised as many problems as it solved. In particular, gender emerged as a troubling element in early modern theories of political contract. This is not just because the marriage contract was a central seventeenth-century analogy for political contract, nor because political contract presupposed a prior sexual contract of subordination, but also because theories of political contract drew on a rhetoric of the passions that was both an asset and obstacle to the construction of a specifically male subject of rights.[14]

In the following pages I focus on three exemplary works: William Gouge's *Domesticall Duties* (1622), Milton's *Doctrine and Discipline of Divorce* (1644), and Hobbes's *Leviathan* (1651). Although the primary subject of the first two of these works is domestic relations, while the third treats political contract, all three take up the issue of the relation between the domestic and political.[15] To varying degrees, all three share a growing preoccupation with the passions as the vehicle of a kind of Foucauldian discipline, the means of forming a conscientious subject who consents to be bound, who consents to bind himself or herself. In addition, as we move from Gouge to Milton and Hobbes, we see a gradual but important transformation in the account of the passions. Although Gouge sees fear and love initially as obligations that follow on contract, he also begins to imagine passion as constitutive of the subject of obligation. He thus sets the stage for Milton and Hobbes, who treat love and fear, respectively, as sources of individual rights and thus as motives to contract. In so doing, Milton and Hobbes attempt, through passion, to make the antinomies of contract into their own solution: for them, the paradoxical coexistence in the passions of coercion and consent, rationalism and voluntarism, voluntarism and determinism, is not so much a logical weakness as a source of psychological strength. Finally, in both cases, this new affective subject is gendered male, yet in ways that trouble the original model of contract: Milton runs the risk of excluding women altogether from the marriage contract, while in Hobbes the male subject of political contract is conspicuously feminized.

I begin with Gouge because his work is representative of the enormous outpouring of manuals of "domesticall duties" in this period, and of their crucial role in arguments for political obligation. I also begin with Gouge because his ambivalent treatment of the passions makes the innovations of Hobbes and Milton more striking. Gouge's main argument is that duty should dictate passion rather than the other way around. Speaking of the gender-specific duties of husband and wife in marriage, Gouge observes that the duty of the husband is to love his wife, while the duty of the wife is to fear (show reverence to) and obey her husband. These affective duties follow upon and lighten other, more serious ones: "*Love* [is] as sugar to sweeten the duties of authoritie, which appertaine to an husband. *Feare* [is] as salt to season all the duties of subjection which appertaine to a wife."[16] The passions are thus marital obligations; at the same time, as we already begin to see in the lines just quoted, the passions have a gendered, asymmetrical role to play in producing the willing subject of the marriage contract.

For Gouge and his readers, this rhetoric of the passions had obvious political implications. The husband is explicitly compared not only to Christ but also to the magistrate (357), while the wife is cast as the representative political subject—"the first to whom subjection was injoyned" (25). In the rhetoric of *Domesticall Duties* and other such manuals, domestic order is the font of political order, and the passions that help constitute domestic order have a role to play in the political realm as well. Like the husband, the sovereign declares his love for his subjects; like the wife, the subject is expected to be fearful and obedient. In both cases, passion is part of the "conscionable performance" of one's duty (dedicatory epistle).

Yet—and here Gouge begins to anticipate Milton and Hobbes—passion is not simply the object of religious dictates, stoic mastery, or moral supervision but is itself productive of conscience. Gouge emphasizes that not all passions are duties, only those dictated to us by Scripture and natural law. Crucially, these passions are linked to consent. Thus, Gouge distinguishes between "slavish feare" and "filial feare": the former is a product of coercion, while the latter—with its experience of reverence and awe—helps produce the subject capable of consent. In other words, passion, correctly understood, is not only a duty; it is also what constitutes duty as duty rather than as coercion.

The distinction between coerced and consensual passion first emerges in a theological context. Slavish fear is what Adam felt "when after he had broken Gods commandment, he hid himselfe from the presence of God. This slavish feare is a plaine diabolicall feare (for *the devils* so feare as they *tremble:*) It maketh men wish there were no hell, no day *of Judgement,* no Judge, yea no God" (9). In contrast, filial fear of God combines garden-variety fear with awe; it mitigates the threat of punishment with grace: "after *Adams* fall, . . . God . . . fixed this affection of *feare* in mans heart, and thereby both re-straine[d] him from sinne, and also provoke[d] him unto every good dutie" (11). In this respect, filial fear (which Gouge elsewhere identifies with con-science) functions as a kind of Foucauldian discipline: it works not simply by negation or punishment but by inciting the subject willingly to perform cons-cionable acts, thereby constituting the individual as subject to conscience. Filial fear is now a source of obligation rather than a passion that follows on obligation. One might even argue that this divinely given passion constitutes us as active and thus as *capable* of consent. In appealing to the theological doctrine of grace as the enabling condition of filial fear and human agency, Gouge both exemplifies and resolves what will elsewhere in the treatise appear as the antinomies of the marriage contract: the paradoxical coexistence of coercion and consent, nature and right.

Gouge tries to effect a similar reconciliation of coercion and consent in his treatment of the wife's fear of and subjection to her husband. As in the case of Adam's willing subordination to God, the wife's consent is crucial to the dis-tinction between slavish and wifely fear, and thus between the husband's legit-imate and illegitimate power.[17] At the same time, what the wife consents to is, paradoxically, a kind of coercion — in this case, the coercion of nature. Gouge calls our attention to this paradox and attempts to resolve it grammatically in his remarks on *Ephesians* 5:22 ("Wives submit your selves unto your owne husbands, as unto the Lord"):

> The word by which the Apostle hath noted out the duties of wives, is of the middle voice, and may be translated passively as many have done, or actively as our English doth (*submit your selves*) and that most fitly: for there is a double subjection.
>
> 1. A *necessary* subjection: which is the subjection of *order.*
> 2. A *voluntary* subjection: which is the subjection of *duty.* (26)

Whereas the believer's filial fear leads him willingly to perform "every good dutie," the wife's filial fear leads her to consent to what is already naturally the case: her subjection to her husband. Why, then, is consent necessary? Because, Gouge replies, it turns a natural relationship of "order" into a moral relationship of "duty," thereby "mak[ing] a vertue of necessity" (26, 27). Of course, in calling attention to the necessity of consenting to nature, Gouge reveals the ideological operation according to which socially constituted relationships are represented as natural and necessary. He thus implies (as does every manual of moral instruction) that the natural order is not as fixed as that phrase might suggest. In fact, nature must be turned into a duty because "wives for the most part are most backward in yeelding subjection to their husbands" (25–26). Thus, for the natural order to be a moral order, it—or our response to it— must be mutable, though not too mutable. The discourse of passion is one locus of this divided imperative: it both naturalizes and moralizes, and thus legitimates, the relationship of husband and wife, sovereign and subject. Specifically, wifely fear is a natural passion to which wives (must) actively consent; as such, wifely fear contains or productively recasts the antinomies of determinism and voluntarism, nature and right.

A different version of this paradox of consensual passion, or active subjection, appears in Gouge's treatment of the husband's duty to love his wife. Gouge tells us that "self-love" is a "naturall affection," which extends to a man's "second selfe," his wife, "by reason of the bond of mariage, which maketh *one* of *two*" (81, 77). Commenting on Paul's command in *Ephesians,* Gouge writes, "*Husbands ought to love their wives.* So as this dutie is not a matter arbitrarie, left to the husbands will to doe it, or leave it undone: there is a necessitie laid upon him: he must love his wife. Woe therefore unto him if he doe it not" (76–77). By "arbitrary," Gouge means theologically indifferent— left to the discretion of the individual believer—while by "necessary" he means morally necessary and thus "voluntary" or a matter of "duty." Husbands don't need to be instructed to exercise dominion over their wives—for the desire for power is a truly natural desire; they do need to be instructed to love their wives. Significantly, the argument Gouge adduces to support this moral imperative is the natural desire for self-preservation, the psychological imperative of self-love (81–83). Although love of one's wife is presented as an obligation, self-love is stronger than the obligation of conscience or obedience to God's word (86). Hence the error of the "Stoicks" in condemning all passion, for passion is the means that God himself has devised for the "better preservation of man" (83).[18]

In his treatment of the passions, Gouge thus moves from the gendered marital duties of love and fear to passion as a source of obligation and consensual activity to passion as a right. In these last two cases, the passions simultaneously provide evidence of the fall and help solve the problem of obligation. They are the locus of rational consent and of compelling—even irresistible— psychological motivation. In helping to internalize the law, however, passion also threatens to subvert it. This instability of Gouge's calculus of the passions is particularly apparent in his treatment of the wife's love of her husband and of herself.

Although the wife's chief duty is to fear and obey, she is also supposed to love her husband.[19] And, as a creature like her husband, she is also naturally inclined to love herself, naturally possessed of the right of self-preservation. How then can one distinguish between the husband's love and that of the wife, between self-love and love of one's superior? How does one keep self-love from being an argument for mastery instead of subordination?[20] Gouge is acutely aware of this dilemma and of its domestic and political implications, which he tries to address by invoking the concept of equity: reciprocal duties are not necessarily identical ones; equity is not the same as equality (172–74). The relationship of husband and wife is like that of magistrate and subject (357). He also goes out of his way to condemn wives who confuse subordination with slavery, for Gouge knows that subjection will be yielded only by women who acknowledge men as superior. If, instead, wives think they have been unjustly enslaved by their equals, they will behave like defeated warriors in battle who hope to rise up against their conquerors (269–70). For Gouge, true consent implies *psychological* contentment (287): it implies the need for the internalization of the law in a discipline of the affections.

As we have seen, Gouge attempted to deal with this instability in part by distributing the passions along gender lines; in so doing, he attempted to psychologize and reproduce the gender hierarchy that is a mainstay of social and political order: love is the duty of the husband, fear of the wife. But in psychologizing consent (in making consent a consent to our very own passions) in an effort to provide a more secure foundation for marital obligation, Gouge ran the risk of turning externally imposed duties into a subjectively determined rights.[21] This collision of duty and right in turn had potentially subversive implications not only for the husband's duty to love but also for the wife's duty to fear and obey. What was a problem for Gouge — the conception of passion as a right rather than a duty, as discipline rather than law — would in Milton and Hobbes form the basis of a new approach to the problem of domestic and political obligation. But gender relations remained a thorn in the side of these early modern theorists of contract.

At first glance, Milton and Hobbes on contract, rights, and the passions would appear to be the exact opposite of each other. For Milton's emphasis on love, Hobbes substitutes fear. To Milton's revocable contract, Hobbes opposes an irrevocable one. The right of self-preservation in Milton leads to a radical argument for domestic and political divorce, while in Hobbes the right of self-preservation leads to political absolutism. Despite these differences, however, there are important similarities. In attempting to provide a new account of domestic or political association — one that does not take for granted older conceptions of natural law — each imagines a contract that is predicated on rational deliberation about one's passions, construed as the embodiment of natural right. At the same time, because reason alone is insufficient, each portrays the passions as the source of a kind of coercion as well as consent, of "resistless sway," in Milton's phrase, as well as free will. Each thus confronts and attempts to resolve, by way of the passions, the antinomies of contract: the paradoxical coexistence of determinism and voluntary action, nature and right. And in each case, gender has a crucial role to play in both constituting and destabilizing the male subject of contract.

With the exception of *Paradise Lost, The Doctrine and Discipline of Divorce* is probably the closest Milton ever came to writing a manual of "domesticall duties," and, like the authors of such manuals, Milton was acutely aware of the political resonance of his argument.[22] In *The Doctrine* Milton takes several steps away from conventional arguments based on divine or natural law and toward a discourse of rights; and, like Gouge, he does so by means of an argument about the passions. In contrast to Gouge, however, Milton claims that love is not a domestic obligation imposed on the husband but is itself the source of obligation.

As is well known, this argument about the husband's rights is played out as a drama of interpretation, specifically the interpretation of Christ's prohibition of divorce. If the husband does not love his wife, he is allowed — according to a charitable interpretation of Christ's prohibition — to divorce her. Milton thus makes the husband's affective disposition the psychological equivalent of the theological and hermeneutical principle of charity, which dictates the equitable interpretation of the law. In so doing, he complicates the Foucauldian distinction between (Old Testament) law and discipline by conflating the law with its own conscientious, equitable interpretation, which is itself based on the passions, "the resistless sway in love or hate" (347).

Milton's argument about the passions as both the object of law and the source of equity is modeled on the hermeneutical dilemmas he confronts regarding natural law and Scripture. In *The Doctrine* Milton illustrates the paradox of all appeals to natural law, or what he calls blameless nature — for if nature were truly a self-sufficient or self-evident criterion of judgment or action, there would be no need to discuss it, let alone instruct one's readers about it. But natural law is obscure and needs to be construed. Hence the necessary intervention of what we might call the "filial" labor of interpretation, which Milton distinguishes from the servile yoke of literalism (see, for example, 242, 342).

Accordingly, Milton emphasizes the labor of gathering scriptural passages — the difficulty of interpreting Christ's words — because the self-evident meaning of his pronouncements is against divorce. But, as in his glosses on natural law, Milton stresses that this interpretive labor is itself a function of equity or the hermeneutical principle of charity. In contrast with the effort-filled marriage of two unsuited partners, the labor of interpretation is a labor of love. *The Doctrine* is thus structured as a chiasmus, according to which laborious married love is a form of enslavement, whereas interpretive labor is a form of charity. In the first case, labor signals a kind of coercion: "grinding at the mill" (257); in the second case, labor is the means by which the law is assimilated to one's own disposition.[23]

In illustrating a tension between the labor of interpretation on the one hand and the "resistless sway" of one's passions on the other, between ethical (or interpretive) voluntarism and psychological determinism, *The Doctrine* captures and attempts to recast the dilemma of the new language of contract. On the one hand, contract — whether a marriage contract or a political contract — presupposes a rational act of consent. On the other hand, a theory of contractual obligation needs to explain not only that it is rational to form contracts but also why we might be moved to do so. In psychologizing charity, Milton both answers the question of motive and introduces an element of psychological determinism that is as important to his argument as the antithetical emphasis on free will.

Let us now look more closely at the two steps of Milton's argument, the equation of conscience with equity, and the link between equitable interpretation and the passions. First, Milton tells us that conscience is a function of the "Law not onely written by *Moses*, but character'd in us by nature . . . which Law is to force nothing against the faultles proprieties of nature" (237). Against the "letter-bound servility of the Canon Doctors" (342), conscience engages in equitable interpretation, which takes into account the intention of the lawgiver as well as the circumstances of the particular case. According to Milton, in permitting divorce in Deuteronomy 24:1, Moses "establish't a grave and prudent Law, full of moral equity" (306). This equation of the law with its equitable interpretation means that "every command giv'n with a reason, binds our obedience no otherwise then that reason holds" (308). Obedience that runs counter to reason would be "mis-obedience" (309); so the standard of conformity to the law is not the law but reason.

Second, in the process of such reasoning, conscience itself begins to look very different from the usual portrayals of it in Protestant theological treatises. In the Protestant casuist William Perkins's *Discourse of Conscience,* conscience functions as a surveyor, accountant, or judge of the erring individual; in *The Doctrine* conscience is much less a judge of sin than an agent of satisfaction.[24] Moses' law, Milton continues, is not only "full of moral equity" but also "full of due consideration towards nature, that cannot be resisted" (306). Because human nature is both irresistible and "blameless" (279, 355), the function of the law is not to constrain but to conform to our nature (310). Milton draws the obvious conclusion about bad marriages:

> There is no Christian duty that is not to be season'd and set off with cherfulness; which in a thousand outward and intermitting crosses may yet be done well, as in this vale of teares, but in such a bosom affliction as [a bad marriage], crushing the very foundations of his inmost nature, when he shall be forc't to love against a possibility, and to use dissimulation against his soul in the perpetuall and ceaseles duties of a husband, doubtles his whole duty of serving God must needs be blurr'd and tainted with a sad unpreparednesse and dejection of spirit, wherein God has no delight. Who sees not therefor how much more Christianly it would be to break by divorce that which is more brok'n by undue and forcible keeping. (259)

In this passage Milton articulates a traditional Christian view of patient suffering only to reject it. In matters of love, there can be no "duty," for duty implies putting up with "*outward* and intermitting crosses," whereas a bad marriage is "a bosom affliction" (my emphasis). In other words, love is both a passion over which we have no control — we cannot "be forc't to love against a possibility" — and part of our "inmost nature." We are a long way here from assuming, as do Perkins and Gouge, that husbands have "a duty to love" and that they need to be instructed in it. Instead of prescribing our duty, Milton condemns canon law for subjecting "that ancient and naturally domestick prerogative [which God from the beginning had entrusted to the husband] to an external & unbefitting judicature. For although differences in divorce about dowries, jointures, and the like, besides the punishing of adultery, ought not to passe without referring, if need be, to the Magistrate" (344), yet "to interpose a jurisdictive power upon the inward and irremediable disposition of man, to command love and *sympathy*, to forbid dislike against the guiltles instinct of nature, is not within the province of any law to reach" (346).

These passages are important if we are to understand the link between passion and right in *The Doctrine:* here we see Milton implicitly reject the notion of property in one's person in favor of a conception of the self still more inward.[25] Disputes about dowries, jointures, and other such transactions may be adjudicated by the magistrate, but love or hate are part one's disposition. Not alienable property but the irremediable and resistless passion is the source of — and model for — the husband's rights, including the right of political resistance to positive law.

As in his earlier remarks about equitable interpretation, the result of this argument is to identify nature and law, the compulsion of the natural order and rational consent: "For that Law may bandy with nature, and traverse her sage motions, was an error in *Callicles* the Rhetorician, whom *Socrates* from high principles confutes in Plato's *Gorgias*. If therfore divorce may be so natural, and that law and nature are not to goe contrary, then to forbid divorce compulsively, is not only against nature, but against law" (346). Just as Gouge distinguishes between servile and filial fear, so Milton invokes the possibility of illegitimate compulsion ("to forbid divorce compulsively") to define by contrast the legitimate compulsion of the husband's love. To have true freedom is to act in accordance with one's natural passions, to be compelled by them. And yet, this passage does more than identify resistless nature and law; it also engages the possibility that nature might very well be resisted, or compelled, however illegitimately. And, as we read further, we discover that this illegitimate coercion may be internal as well as external.

For, despite arguing for "the resistless sway in love," Milton does not take self-love for granted as Gouge does. Instead, he warns the reader against the "self-cruelty" — what Nietzsche would later call asceticism — that results from the misapplication of conscience or the misunderstanding of Scripture.[26] Although the husband cannot be coerced to love, he might coerce himself to remain within a loveless marriage. This in turn would amount to self-cruelty, self-hatred, or what we might call the coercion of despair. These are compelling passions but not ones to which we willingly consent.

In his efforts to distinguish between legitimate and illegitimate compulsion, Milton could be said to re-encounter — even as he tries to resolve — the antinomy between nature and law within the realm of the passions. Passion is the locus of consent but also of coercion — and not simply the beneficent coercion of self-love but also the coercion of self-hatred. Hence the necessity of distinguishing between two antithetical affective states — resistless love and self-cruelty — by aligning the first with nature and second with law, that is, with legalism and literalism.[27] It is not the case, Milton argues, that conscience must always be bad conscience, although the legacy of Catholicism and of Calvinism — which Milton calls the "tyranny of usurpt opinions" (343) — suggests as much. Instead, conscience should follow the dictates of blameless nature and resistless love; its discipline should be productive rather than coercive or restrictive, a matter of passion rather than legislation, love rather than the law. The problem is that this "should" reintroduces an element of obligation (the paradoxical obligation to be true to one's nature) that Milton's equitable interpretation of Scripture was designed to avoid.

This destabilization of Milton's argument occurs as well when we look closely at the gender dimension of *The Doctrine* — for Milton famously sees self-cruelty as a trap specifically for the husband. Although he differs from Gouge in describing love exclusively in terms of rights rather than obligation, like Gouge, he attempts to make the freedom of interpretation that love licenses specifically masculine. In other words, the standard of equitable interpretation is itself inequitably applied, since while the legitimate reason for divorce — "fornication" — is interpreted charitably to mean disobedience, disobedience is then ascribed inequitably to the wife alone (335–36). Like many of his contemporaries, Milton views contract — and equity — through a particular ideology of gender. This ideology, as a number of critics have argued, makes the wife into a dangerous supplement, at once necessary and superfluous, superfluous but still threatening to the status quo.[28]

This superfluity is particularly obvious when Milton articulates the hermeneutic "axiom" of the text — that no law "should bind against a prime and principall scope of its own institution." As we see in the following passage, the wife is first conspicuously absent from the marriage covenant and then conspicuously subordinate:[29]

> For all sense and reason and equity reclaimes that any Law or Cov'nant how solemn or strait soever, either between God and man or man and man, though of Gods joyning, should bind against a prime and principall scope of its own institution, and of both or either party cov'nanting: neither can it be of force to ingage a blameless creature to his own perpetuall sorrow, mistak'n for his expected solace, without suffering charity to step in and doe a confest good work of parting those whom nothing holds together, but this of Gods joyning, falsly suppos'd against the expresse end of his own ordinance. And what his chiefe end was of creating woman to be joynd with man, his own instituting words declare, and are infallible to informe us what is mariage and what is no mariage; unless we can think them set there to no purpose: *It is not good,* saith he, *that man should be alone. I will make a help meet for him.* (245)

Milton's failure explicitly to name "man and wife" in the first sentence describing the parties to a covenant is striking; it suggests that the marriage covenant is for Milton essentially a covenant between "man and God" or even (to borrow Carole Pateman's argument) a covenant between men.[30] This is not surprising when we remember that the model of covenant Milton invokes in the preface to the second edition *is* a covenant between men: the political covenant of male citizens. Hence Milton's focus on the specifically political consequences of enforced marriage: "If natures resistles sway in love or hate be once compell'd, it grows careless of it self, vitious, useles to friend, *unserviceable and spiritles to the commonwealth*" (347, my emphasis).

The seventeenth-century jurist Samuel Pufendorf noticed the homoerotic, or as I have suggested autoerotic, tendency of Milton's argument when he asked rhetorically, "And surely if a happy association had been the primary purpose of God, what need would there have been of different sexes?"[31] Different sexes were divinely created for the purpose of procreation; if companionship is what Milton wants, he should associate with other men — or commune with himself. At the very least, we can say that Milton's tendency to eclipse the wife — like his frequently remarked-upon tendency to eclipse the male body — is part of an effort to internalize contract — in the sense of making it a contract with oneself and thus a symbol of ethical and political self-determination rather than a matter of negotiation with or dependence upon another.[32] In contrast to Gouge, who analyzes the contractual and affective relationship of husband and wife, Milton is more concerned with the contractual and affective relationship to himself. As I have argued, this is a relationship not only between the husband's conscience and the moral law, but also between his conscience, conceived of as a principle of interpretation, and his passions. Together, these two articulate a new conception of right — both personal and political — that moves beyond traditional conceptions of natural law. The male subject of the marriage contract for Milton is crucially the autonomous political subject who, in the words of Terry Eagleton, "discovers the law in the depths of [his] own free identity, rather than in some oppressive external power. The liberated subject is the one who has appropriated the law as the very principle of [his] own autonomy, broken the forbidding tablets of stone on which that law was originally inscribed in order to rewrite it on the heart of flesh. To consent to the law is thus to consent to one's own inward being."[33] And at the center of this new conception is the paradoxical experience of the subject of contract, at once voluntary and involuntary, rational and passionate.[34]

As his contemporaries realized, Hobbes too aimed to move beyond traditional conceptions of natural law. Critics as diverse as the Cambridge Platonist Ralph Cudworth and the Whig James Tyrrell connected this move with the new prominence of the passions in Hobbes's account of political obligation. In particular, they recognized the link Hobbes was trying to establish between passion, right, and contract, and they were not convinced. Cudworth complained that Hobbes based his argument on "certain Counterfeit Laws of Nature, of [his] own devising, that are Nothing but meer Juggling Equivocation; they being but the Laws of Fear, or [his] own Timorous and Cowardly Complexion." And he condemned Hobbes's theory of contract as a "vain Attempt, by Art to Consociate, what Nature hath Dissociated, like tying Knots in the Wind or Water. Their Artificial Obligation, or Ligaments, by which the Members of their Leviathan are held together, [are] more slender then Cobwebs."[35]

Cudworth was alluding in part to chapter 14 of *Leviathan,* Hobbes's infamous description of the state of nature. According to Hobbes, men in the state of nature are characterized by a restless seeking after power and the desire for self-preservation, by vainglory and the fear of violent death. While vainglory prolongs our misery, fear of violent death is our springboard out of the state of nature. Although such fear will in the short run exacerbate distrust and conflict, once we reason about this fear, we recognize that rivalry and suspicion — what Hobbes called competition and diffidence — will in the long run only be self-defeating. In this way, our fundamental insecurity dictates the first law of nature, "to seek peace" through setting up a political contract.[36] Fear of violent death is thus the best possible motive for political contract. This is the case even though we may not all actually fear violent death at one and the same time; the important point, for Hobbes, is that we can rationally agree to act as though we did fear violent death because we recognize each other's *right* to self-preservation. Note that this is not simply an empirical argument about the coercive power of fear; it is an argument about the coincidence of passion and right.

Hobbes thus makes fear the locus of both compulsion and reason. That is to say, he makes fear the locus of legitimate compulsion — a compulsion to which we consent — and in so doing provides a motive for political contract. Just as Gouge and Milton distinguish between servile passion and consensual passion, so Hobbes distinguishes between slavery and contract: a legitimate contract must be entered into voluntarily, by consent. Thus Hobbes argues — improbably — that the parent's dominion over the child derives from "the Childs Consent, either expresse, or by other sufficient arguments declared" (20.139). In contrast, "a Captive, which is kept in prison, or bonds . . . [has] no obligation at all" (20.141). Hobbes's crude definition of compulsion as physical restraint (chains or bonds) or as an external impediment to action is crucial in allowing him to locate a legitimate, internal compulsion in the passions and thus to argue that consent is perfectly compatible with coercion. Accordingly, Hobbes argues that contracts made for reasons of fear are binding (20.138; 21.146–47). And he repeatedly tells us that mere verbal covenants and contracts "are too weak to bridle mens ambition, avarice, anger, and other Passions, without the feare of some coercive Power" (14.96).

The paradoxical coexistence of coercion and consent — the paradox of the consent to fear — is vividly illustrated by Hobbes's treatment of women in the state of nature and in the family. As J. P. Sommerville has pointed out, Hobbes treats the family "as virtually identical with a kingdom by conquest."[37] In the state of nature, mothers have dominion over their children; fathers acquire this dominion by subjugating mothers by force. According to Sommerville, because force is compatible with consent in Hobbes's account, "the point of the argument [about a mother's dominion over the child] was to show that the power of the *father* was derived from the consent of the mother" rather than by virtue of natural superiority, as patriarchalists thought (73, 72).[38] Hobbes's treatment of women thus follows from a rigorous application from his political principles, his belief that political relationships are conventional rather than natural.[39] And yet, as Carole Pateman has pointed out, it also reveals a logical inconsistency at the heart of Hobbesian political theory. For, given what Hobbes has said about the equality of men and women in the state of nature, and the unenforceability of contracts in this state, there is no reason women should consent to be coerced — should consent to fear — while still in the state of nature. Conversely, if women are capable of entering into contracts in the state of nature, why should they not also be capable of entering into the political contract to set up the commonwealth?[40]

The Hobbesian political subject is thus, irrationally, exclusively male; but, ironically, as a subject who is motivated by fear rather than vainglory, by desire for self-preservation rather than self-aggrandizement, the Hobbesian subject is also (in the traditional terms set out by Gouge and others) conspicuously feminized.[41] There is thus a submerged analogy between the marriage contract and the political contract in Hobbes, just not the one parliamentarians such as Milton wanted. Something like marriage has to exist in the state of nature prior to the establishment of matrimonial laws in society, just as something like political contract has to exist prior to its embodiment in the sovereign; in both cases, the crucial components are coercion and consent, summed up in the versatile emotion of fear.

Hobbes's claim about the compatibility of coercion and consent is buttressed by a crucial assumption regarding the passions: the Hobbesian subject can consent to be coerced by his own fear of the sovereign — can consent to fear — because the passions, in Hobbes's analysis, are voluntary and allied with the faculty of deliberation.[42] What this means in practice is that we may deliberate about our passions incorrectly and thus will to act in irrational ways; but we cannot conclude from this that the passions are the source of involuntary actions. The passions are thus the source not only of both coercion and consent but also of their compatibility.

By basing his argument for political contract on the fear of violent death and the right of self-preservation, Hobbes believed he had solved the problem of obligation: for the laws of nature, including the obligation to seek peace and keep our covenants, are deduced from the right of self-preservation. This is a natural desire — a natural interest — and thus the best possible basis for establishing government. At the same time, Hobbes acknowledged that —

practically speaking—the performance of one's obligations cannot be generated from right alone. In the state of nature, the laws of nature "oblige onely to a desire [that they should be observed]"; that is, we are not obliged actually to perform them, only to wish we could, because the conditions of security that would oblige absolutely do not exist. Such laws concerning what we *should* desire, Hobbes remarked with his usual caustic wit, "are easy to be observed" (15.110). For this reason, fear of violent death must become the specific fear of the sovereign's power of the sword. Only this fear of the sovereign, which alone grants us the security to perform our obligations without fear of others, saves us from the conflict of rights in the state of nature.

Once again, Hobbes's critics were not convinced. Cudworth commented, "Now this Previous Obligation to Civil Obedience, cannot be derived (as the aforementioned Writer [of] *De Cive,* and of the Leviathan, supposes) from mens Private Utility only, because every man being a Judge of this for himself, it would then be Lawful for any Subject, to Rebel against his Sovereign Prince, and to Poyson or Stab him, whensoever he could reasonably perswade himself, that it would tend to his own Advantage" (698).[43]

And Locke, in the *Essays on the Law of Nature,* was probably thinking of Hobbes when he wrote in a similar vein: "For if the source and obligation of all this law is the care and preservation of oneself, virtue would seem to be not so much man's duty as his convenience. . . . The observance of this law would be not so much our duty and obligation, to which we are bound by nature, as a privilege and advantage, to which we are led by expediency."[44]

In a sense, what Hobbes's critics were noticing was simply that Hobbes's argument was not purely prudential or, at least, could not be if it was to work. In so doing, they help us to see that, even more than Milton's, Hobbes's theory of contractual obligation dramatizes a conflict between a juridical concept of natural right and a naturalistic account of the passions.[45] As Leo Strauss remarked (in what is still, to my mind, the best account of Hobbes), "Consistent naturalism would have been the ruin of his political philosophy": it would have obliterated the distinction between might and right, and rendered Hobbes incapable of distinguishing between the good passion of fear of violent death and the bad passion of vanity.[46] Precisely this distinction between good and bad passion—between a passion that is a right and one that is not—informs Hobbes's political philosophy: the argument for political contract is based not on a naturalistic antithesis between animal appetite (the restless seeking after power) and the striving after self-preservation but on "the moral and humanist antithesis of fundamentally unjust vanity and fundamentally just fear of violent death" (27). As in Milton's account of the husband's resistless love of his wife, Hobbes's account of the passionate fear of violent death exemplifies the paradoxical coexistence of coercion and consent, nature and right, but only because it depends, paradoxically, on a prior distinction between the two.[47]

In both Milton and Hobbes, arguments for contract are predicated on a new conception of natural rights that is inextricably bound up with the motivating power of the passions. Like Milton, Hobbes aims to constitute the male subject of political rights. And, as with Milton, Hobbes's argument about political right is inseparable from his account of the passions as powerful motives, at once coercive and persuasive. In both cases the new discourse of the passions performed a crucial role in helping construct a subject who consents to be bound, who consents to bind himself. Both thus address and attempt to reconfigure through the passions the antinomies of determinism and voluntarism, coercion and consent.

Equally important, however, in articulating these antinomies Milton and Hobbes present two different constructions of the subject of rights. Milton's argument is in the service of a defense of the male individual conscience and individual satisfaction; his version of "male self-esteem" is closer to Hobbesian glory than to fear.[48] In contrast, Hobbes's argument involves a critique of the manly cult of glory, hence the crucial importance of fear of violent death. Thus, while Milton fears the effeminizing power of passion, Hobbes's goal is to use passion to effeminize the male political subject, to render him passive and subordinate like the wife in Gouge's *Domesticall Duties*.

Together, Milton and Hobbes might seem to anticipate the two poles of modern political rationality that Foucault analyzed in terms of pastoral care and state power. For Foucault, these two poles were mutually constitutive: despite his insistence that "there is no power without potential refusal or revolt," Foucault also argued that self-examination fostered total obedience, first to one's director of conscience and then to the state.[49] In fact, what Milton and Hobbes show is that there is no such unitary account of the politics of the affective subject. Crucially, although both subjects consent to be bound by their passions, such consent ideally empowers the revolutionary Miltonic subject, whereas the Hobbesian subject is, ideally, primarily constrained.

In moving from Gouge through Milton to Hobbes, I have traced a trajectory from "the duty to love" to love and fear as sources of rights. In so doing, I have tried to capture a shift in the role of the passions in early modern accounts of obligation. I have argued that Milton and Hobbes respond to the antinomies of contract by attempting to recast a logical contradiction as a dialectical and psychological solution. With the crisis of natural law in the seventeenth century, contract became a way of producing—and then imagining how to join together—autonomous, divided subjects. The rational subject of contract is the subject of rights, but rights alone did not seem to offer a compelling motive for political allegiance, without the supplement of the passions — the locus of nature and right, coercion and consent. And yet this solution, as I have only begun to suggest, posed as many problems as it solved.

Notes

1. The appeal to natural disposition is not necessarily incompatible with the argument from divine law, but they are analytically distinct. In the "Prolegomena" to *De jure belli ac pacis libri tres,* ed. James Brown Scott; trans. Francis W. Kelsey with Arthur E. R. Boak, Henry A. Sanders, Jesse S. Reeves, and Herbert F. Wright(1625; reprint, Indianapolis, 1925), Grotius famously divorced natural law and theology, claiming, "What we have been saying would have a degree of validity even if we should concede [*etiamsi daremus*] that which cannot be conceded without the utmost wickedness, that there is no God, or that the affairs of men are of no concern to him." On Grotius' distinctive use of the phrase "etiamsi daremus," which also appears in some of his scholastic predecessors, see Knud Haakonssen, "Hugo Grotius and the History of Political Thought," *Political Theory* 13 (1985): 239–65; and A. P. D'Entrèves, *Natural Law: An Introduction to Legal Philosophy,* 2nd ed. (London, 1970): "Grotius's aim was to construct a system of laws which would carry conviction in an age in which theological controversy was gradually losing the power to do so" (55).

2. See Hobbes, *On the Citizen,* ed. and trans. Richard Tuck and Michael Silverthorne (Cambridge, 1998), 102; and Robert Filmer, "Observations on Mr Hobbes' *Leviathan* or His Artificial Man a Commonwealth," in *Patriarcha and Other Writings,* ed. Johann Sommerville (Cambridge, 1991), 187. It is important to note here the differences between Grotius, Pufendorf, and Hobbes on the question of sociability: Grotius and to a lesser extent Pufendorf believed in a natural sociability in the state of nature, whereas Hobbes did not.

3. Ralph Cudworth, *The True Intellectual System of the Universe,* ed. René Wellek, 2 vols. (1678; reprint, New York, 1978), 2: "Contents," gloss on pp. 893, 895. For contrasting accounts of the originality of seventeenth-century theories of natural right, see Ian Shapiro, *The Evolution of Rights in Liberal Theory* (Cambridge, 1986), and Richard Tuck, *Philosophy and Government, 1572–1651* (Cambridge, 1993), who stress the innovations of seventeenth-century thinkers; and Brian Tierney, *The Idea of Natural Rights: Studies on Natural Rights, Natural Law and Church Law, 1150–1625* (Atlanta, 1997), who argues that modern theories of natural right developed in the twelfth century. I am more persuaded by the accounts of Shapiro and Tuck. For a good brief discussion of the differences between Grotius, Pufendorf, and Hobbes, see Richard Tuck, *Natural Rights Theories* (1979; reprint, Cambridge, 1987).

4. See Cicero *De officiis,* trans. Walter Miller, Loeb Classical Library (London, 1968), 2.7.23 (p. 191): "But, of all motives, none is better adapted to secure influence and hold it fast than love; nothing is more foreign to that end than fear. For Ennius says admirably: 'Whom they fear they hate [*Quem metuunt, oderunt*]. And whom one hates, one hopes to see him dead.'. . . For fear is but a poor safeguard of lasting power; while affection, on the other hand, may be trusted to keep it safe for ever"; Thomas Wilson, *Arte of Rhetoric*

(1552; reprint, Amsterdam, 1977), Tlv; George Puttenham, *The Arte of English Poesie,* ed. Baxter Hathaway (Kent, Ohio, 1970), 24. The Bible, of course, was also an important source of injunctions concerning the passions, and these injunctions in turn had political implications. Especially important, as we will see, was the emphasis on fear of God as the beginning of wisdom.

For an excellent analysis of the rhetorical implications of the passions in Plato's *Republic,* Aristotle's *Politics,* and Machiavelli's *Prince,* see Rebecca Bushnell, *Tragedies of Tyrants* (Ithaca, N.Y., 1990), esp. 26–28. On Hobbes's relation to the rhetorical tradition, see Leo Strauss, *The Political Philosophy of Hobbes* (1936; Chicago, 1963), chap. 3; Victoria Kahn, *Rhetoric, Prudence and Skepticism* (Ithaca, N.Y., 1985), chap. 6; Tom Sorell, "Hobbes's Un-Aristotelian Political Rhetoric," *Philosophy and Rhetoric* 23 (1990): 96–108; and Sorell, "Hobbes's Persuasive Civil Science," *Philosophical Quarterly* 40 (1990): 342–51; Quentin Skinner, *Reason and Rhetoric in the Philosophy of Hobbes* (Cambridge, 1996); Victoria Silver, "Hobbes on Rhetoric," *The Cambridge Companion to Hobbes,* ed. Tom Sorell (Cambridge, 1996), 329–45.

5. In his edition of Thomas Wright's *Passions of the Minde in Generall* (Urbana, Ill., 1971), Thomas O. Sloan argues that "seventeenth-century rhetoricians did not treat the passions extensively," owing to the influence of the Ramist narrowing of rhetoric to style and delivery (xxxii). Ramus, whose goal was to reform the teaching of rhetoric, argued that two of its traditional parts (invention and disposition) were the province of logic. Rhetoric, accordingly, would be primarily concerned with elocution—in the English tradition, "schemes and tropes"—and to a lesser extent with memory and action (delivery or performance). Ramist manuals of rhetoric, although they still mentioned the power of tropes to elicit the passions, showed much less concern with the civic or political function of rhetoric.

6. The idea that the passions were themselves a kind of rhetoric of the body was already present in faculty psychology, but it became more pronounced with the waning of humanist rhetoric. For a survey of sixteenth-century treatments of the passions in rhetoric manuals and treatises on faculty psychology, see William Rossky, "Imagination in the English Renaissance: Psychology and Poetic," *Studies in the Renaissance* 5 (1958): 49–73. In *Passion and Action: The Emotions in Seventeenth-Century Philosophy* (Oxford: Clarendon Press, 1997), Susan James argues that the passions became a topic of renewed philosophical importance in the seventeenth century because of the challenge to Aristotelianism by the new science and various materialist philosophies.

7. Although "passions" sometimes means violent emotions, and "affections" weaker or more constant ones, seventeenth-century English usage did not consistently distinguish between the two terms. Often "passions and affections" appears as a hendiadys for the realm of the emotions in general. See Susan James, *Passion and Action.*

8. J. W. Gough, *The Social Contract,* 2nd ed. (Oxford, 1957), for example, stresses the voluntaristic elements of contract; and D'Entrèves, chap. 4, and Ernst Cassirer, *The Myth of the State* (New Haven, 1946), chap. 13, stress the rationalist elements. For accounts that dwell on both the rationalism and voluntarism of early modern contract theory, see, for example, Otto Gierke, *Natural Law and Theory of Society,* 2 vols., ed. Ernest Barker (Cambridge, 1934); Ernest Barker, *Social Contract* (Oxford, 1948); and the works cited in n. 12.

9. See Albert Hirschman's *The Passions and the Interests* (Princeton, 1977); Leo Strauss, *The Political Philosophy of Hobbes;* and Stephen Holmes, *Passions and Constraint* (Chicago, 1995). I have learned from all these writers, particularly Strauss, to whom I return in the conclusion of his essay.

10. In "Two Lectures" (in *Power/Knowledge,* ed. Colin Gordon [New York, 1980]), Foucault distinguished between a "juridical-political model of sovereignty," in which power is conceived of as a commodity that can be alienated through contract, and "a new mechanism of power [which is] absolutely incompatible with the relations of sovereignty" (103–4), which involves the "continuous surveillance" and "disciplining" of the subject (104). He associated the former with "Hobbes's project in *Leviathan.*"

There is a slipperiness in Foucault's analysis of law and discipline that is illuminating for an understanding of the role of contract in the seventeenth century. According to Foucault, the Western notion of sovereignty, with its discourse of right and legitimacy, obscures the more fundamental relations of power in the sphere of politics (95); his goal, accordingly, is to "substitute the problem of domination and subjugation for that of sovereignty and obedience" (96). But this is in a sense to reinstate the coercive notion of power that discipline was designed to supplement and criticize. It is undoubtedly true that the twentieth-century language of contract—associated as it is with "rights" and "legitimacy"—can mask fundamentally inequitable relations of power, of domination and subordination, but as Foucault himself acknowledged, coercion is only one aspect of power and ultimately inadequate to explaining why people act the way they do. Equally important are those forms of discipline which help to constitute the political subject—which help, for example, to create the subject who is *willing* to consent to a contract that, in many cases, is *explicitly* inequitable. For many seventeenth-century authors, the problem of obligation—of voluntary obedience—was much more difficult to grapple with that of forcible domination and subjugation—and it was this that the rhetoric of contract and the new language of the passions—in both domestic and political treatises—were designed to address.

11. In suggesting that we draw on treatises of "domesticall duties" as well as canonical works of political theory in considering the seventeenth-century rhetoric of contract, I take issue with Foucault on contract but draw on Foucault and others who have characterized the early modern period as exhibiting a wide-ranging conception of government. See Foucault, "Governmentality," in *The Foucault Reader,* ed. Graham Burchell, Colin Gordon, and Peter Miller (Chicago, 1991): "Government as a general problem seems to me to explode in the sixteenth century, posed by discussions of quite diverse questions. . . . [These questions of government of souls, lives, children, and the state, lie] at the crossroads of two processes: the one which, shattering the structures of feudalism, leads to the establishment of the great territorial, administrative, and colonial states; and that totally different movement which, with the Reformation and the Counter-Reformation, raises the issue of how one must be spiritually ruled and led on this earth in order to achieve eternal salvation.

"There is a double movement, then, of state centralization on the one hand and of dispersion and religious dissidence on the other: it is, I believe, at the intersection of these two tendencies that the problem comes to pose itself with this peculiar intensity, of how to be ruled, how strictly, by whom, to what end, by what methods, etc. There is a problematic of government in general" (86–87). Foucault links these two tendencies in the early modern period to reason of state and casuistry, political rationality and pastoral care. See "Omnes et singulatim: Towards a Criticism of 'Political Reason,'" in *The Tanner Lectures on Human Values, 1981,* ed. Sterling M. McMurrin (Salt Lake City, 1981): 225–54. I return to this argument at the end of this chapter. For two discussions of early modern political theory that draw on Foucault's notion of governmentality, see James Tully, "Governing Conduct," in *Conscience and Casuistry in Early Modern Europe,* ed. Edmund Leites (Cambridge, 1988), and Richard Tuck, *Philosophy and Government.*

12. To the extent that these antinomies are recognized in the secondary literature, they are treated as an unintended logical weakness of seventeenth-century contract theory. See Patrick Riley, *Will and Political Legitimacy* (Cambridge, Mass., 1982), chap. 1; Michael Lessnoff, *Social Contract* (Houndsmill and London, 1986); and David Gauthier, "The Social Contract as Ideology," *Philosophy and Public Affairs* 6 (1977): 130–64. For an earlier discussion of the problems created by thinking of the will and intellect as autonomous faculties in seventeenth-century moral theory, see Anthony Levi, S. J., *French Moralists: The Theory of the Passions, 1585–1649* (Oxford, 1964), 27, 198–200, 316; much of this analysis is relevant to England as well. I suggest, in contrast to these works, that for some seventeenth-century writers these antinomies were reconceived as a source of strength. Although he does not relate it to contract, John Guillory offers a useful discussion of the tension between ethical voluntarism and psychological determinism in "Milton, Narcissism, Gender: On the Genealogy of Self-Esteem," in *Critical Essays on John Milton,* ed. Christopher Kendrick (New York, 1995), 225.

13. Although in "Two Lectures," Foucault sees contract — including Hobbes's — as the representative trope of juridical conceptions of sovereignty, in "Governmentality" he argues that seventeenth-century contract theory, including Hobbes's, was a kind of compromise formation between sovereignty and government (98). In his uncertain location of contract, Foucault seems implicitly to recognize that contract functioned as a point of stress in early modern relations of law and discipline. Moreover, despite the distinction between law and discipline, at moments Foucault acknowledges that law itself can be the vehicle of discipline: e.g., "Governmentality," 95, where he remarks on the possibility "of using laws themselves as tactics."

14. On the analogy between the marriage contract and political contract, see Mary Lyndon Shanley, "Marriage Contract and the Social Contract in Seventeenth-Century English Political Thought," *Western Political Quarterly* 32 (1979): 79–91. On the sexual contract as the precondition of political contract, see Carole Pateman, *The Sexual Contract* (Stanford, 1988).

15. Gouge does not explicitly compare the marriage contract to political contract, but he does make consent a condition of the marriage contract and he explicitly analogizes the relation of husband and wife to magistrate and subject; Milton distinguishes domestic and political relations but sees the husband's position in the marriage contract as formally similar to his role in political contract; and Hobbes discusses the political implications of gender relations, while ostentatiously eliding discussion of the marriage contract altogether.

16. William Gouge, *Domesticall Duties* (London, 1622), 128.

17. On consent, see Gouge, e.g., 112, 288, and 358: "As the soule therefore ruleth over the body, by a mutuall and loving consent and agreement, so must a man over his wife." For a useful discussion of the Foucauldian discipline of love in manuals of "domesticall duties," which came to my attention only after I had completed this essay, see Laura Lunger Knoppers, "Rewriting the Protestant Ethic: Discipline and Love in *Paradise Lost*," *English Literary History* 58 (1991): 545–59.

18. The whole passage reads: "What do they aime at, but to root that out of man, which God hath planted in him, and to take away the meanes which God hath used for the better preservation of man? That wise man whom they frame to themselves is worse then a brute beast: he is a very stocke and blocke" (Gouge, *Domesticall Duties*, 83).

19. Gouge represents the wife's love as not absolutely necessary for preservation of marriage, but as necessary for a good marriage. "In some respects *Love* is proper and peculiar to an husband," but wives are supposed to love as well, since "*love fulfilleth the law* (Rom. 13:10, Col. 3:14)" (*Domesticall Duties*, 224).

20. We see the same tension in language of general and specific calling, which Gouge uses on 130 and elsewhere. The general calling of Christian believer may conflict with the specific calling of wife. On the conflict between general and specific calling, see John Guillory, "The Father's House: *Samson Agonistes* in its Historical Moment," in *Milton*, ed. Annabel Patterson (London, 1992), 202–25.

21. By this I don't mean to suggest that rights are subjective, only that we may choose to exercise them or not.

22. I will be quoting from volume 2 of *Complete Prose Works of John Milton*, ed. Ernest Sirluck (New Haven, 1949). See Sirluck's introduction to this volume for the political context in which Milton worked out his argument for divorce.

23. Annabel Patterson has discussed the contradictory logic of *The Doctrine* in biographical terms, delineating a "grammar of self-division" in Milton's shifting portrayal of himself as both heroic warrior and abandoned husband, active and passive. See her "No Meer Amatorious Novel?" in *John Milton*, ed. Patterson (London, 1992), 95 and passim. But whereas Patterson emphasizes the plot of frustration in *The Doctrine* — "When we get what we thought we wanted we no longer want it. . . . *The Doctrine and Discipline of Divorce* is . . . a special case of the renunciative novel" (100) — I would like to stress the positive vision behind this renunciation or divorce. For a compatible positive interpretation of the labor of interpretation in *The Doctrine*, see also Dayton Haskin, *Milton's Burden of Interpretation* (Philadelphia, 1994), chap. 3. In commenting on the hermeneutics of *The Doctrine*, which inform *Samson Agonistes* as well, Haskin observes that Milton's reading of the New Testament challenges a "work-centered consciousness" (170).

24. William Perkins, *A Discourse of Conscience* in *William Perkins, 1558–1602*, ed. Thomas F. Merrill (Nieuwkoop, 1966), 8 (conscience as notary), 10 (as magistrate or jailer), 32 (as judge).

25. In *The Political Theory of Possessive Individualism* (Oxford, 1962), C. B. Macpherson argued that Hobbes's and Locke's contract theory presupposes a protocapitalist notion of property in one's person. See Janel M. Mueller, "On Genesis in Genre: Milton's Politicizing of the Sonnet in 'Captain or Colonel,'" in *Renaissance Genres*, ed. Barbara

Kiefer Lewalski (Cambridge, Mass., 1986), for a related argument regarding the "connection between liberty, political identity, and property [in] . . . Milton's political consciousness" (236).

26. Christ's command concerning marriage "can be no new command, for the Gospel enjoyns no new morality, save only the infinit enlargement of charity. . . . Those commands therfore, which compell us to self-cruelty above our strength, so hardly will help forward to perfection that they hinder & set backwards in all the common rudiments of Christianity" (330–31). See Guillory, "Milton, Narcissism, Gender," 220 ff., on "the problem of legitimizing self-love, of negotiating its discursive relations to 'pride' and 'glory,'" in Milton and in the period in general. On Nietzsche, see n. 34.

27. Leo Strauss makes a similar argument regarding Hobbes's distinction between the good passion of fear and the bad passion of vanity, as I shall discuss.

28. On the tie between contractualism and masculinism in the divorce tracts, see also Mary Nyquist, "The Genesis of Gendered Subjectivity in the Divorce Tracts and in *Paradise Lost*," in *Re-membering Milton*, ed. Mary Nyquist and Margaret W. Ferguson (New York, 1987), 99–127, esp. 114 and 124. For a helpful discussion of the concept of intention and the role of woman as dangerous supplements to Milton's argument in *The Doctrine,* see Stanley Fish, "Wanting a Supplement: The Question of Interpretation in Milton's Early Prose," in *Politics, Poetics and Hermeneutics in Milton's Prose,* ed. David Loewenstein and James Grantham Turner (Cambridge, 1990), 41–83. The gender dimension of contract — of consenting to the passions — is particularly obvious in *Paradise Lost.* When Eve turns away from her first sight of Adam, her hand is forcibly "seiz'd" by him; at this point, she consents to be his helpmeet; John Milton, *Paradise Lost,* ed. Alastair Fowler (Essex, Eng., 1971), 4.488–91. Adam, in contrast, is compelled by his desire for Eve: "Here passion first I felt" (8.530).

29. Ernest Sirluck calls this Milton's "axiom" in his introduction to *The Doctrine,* 147.

30. See *The Doctrine,* 276, for a similar ellipsis: "So every covnant between man and man, bound by oath, may be call'd the covnant of God, because God therin is attested. So of marriage he is the author and witnes." Milton's famous allegory of Eros and Anteros also suggests that the marriage contract is between men (254–55); on this passage, see Patterson, "No Meer Amatorious Novel," 97.

31. Samuel Pufendorf, *De jure naturae et gentium libri octo,* trans. C. H. Oldfather and W. A. Oldfather, 2 vols. (Oxford, 1934) 2:883.

32. See Guillory, "Milton, Narcissism, Gender," on the disappearance of the body in male self-esteem, which is analogous to the disappearance of sex — or the degrading of it in favor of intellectual activity of interpretation — in *The Doctrine;* and Annabel Patterson, "No Meer Amatorious Novel?" 97 and passim, on Milton's ambivalence about heterosexual sex in *The Doctrine.*

33. Terry Eagleton, *The Ideology of the Aesthetic* (Blackwell, 1990), 19. See G. W. F. Hegel, *The Philosophy of History,* trans. J. Sibree (New York, 1956), on the Reformation: "Man himself has a conscience; consequently the subjection required of him is a free allegiance" (423). Here we see that it is not the economic contract (see n. 25) that is central to Milton's conception of the husband's self-realization in marriage, but the theological covenant: whereas the former is based on alienable property in oneself, the latter is anticipates what Eagleton has called aesthetic ideology.

34. In *The Genealogy of Morals,* trans. Francis Golffing (New York, 1956), Nietzsche discusses identity as the product of a contract with oneself: the ability to keep one's promises presupposes a kind of internal contract which constitutes the conscientious and "calculable" ethical subject (189–92). Here too we see the paradoxical coexistence of coercion and consent: although the discourse of contract might appear to be antithetical to any notion of force or coercion, the contract with oneself that Nietzsche calls memory involves a kind of originary violence, a mnemotechnics predicated on pain and asceticism (192–93). As I have been arguing, Milton's struggle in *The Doctrine* is to locate that coercion in the passions rather than in self-cruelty.

35. Ralph Cudworth, *The True Intellectual System,* 2: "Contents," gloss on pp. 893, 895. See also 699 for criticism of Hobbes's conflation of right and force in *Leviathan;* and 890–91 on the new vocabulary of rights: "Jus and Lex, or Justitia, Right and Law or Justice in the Language of these Atheistick Politicians, are directly contrary to one another; their Right being a Belluine Liberty, not Made, or Left by Justice, but such as is Founded in a Supposition, of its [Justice's] Absolute Non-Existence." On Hobbes's inconsistent use of the term "right," see also James Tyrrell, *A Brief Disquisition of the Law of Nature . . . As also His Confutations of Mr. Hobb's Principles, put into another Method* (2nd ed., London, 1701), 281–97. Tyrrell specifically objects to the use of the term "right" to describe "Appetite or Passion"; a right is instead "a liberty left by the Law of Nature, of acting according to Reason" (292).

36. Thomas Hobbes, *Leviathan,* ed. Richard Tuck (Cambridge, 1991), chap. 14, p. 91. All further references will be to chapter and page number. See Otto Gierke, *Natural Law and the Theory of Society,* 1:79–84 on Hobbes as the culmination and destruction of earlier tradition of natural law. See also Johann P. Sommerville, *Thomas Hobbes: Political Ideas in Historical Context* (New York, 1992), who argues that Hobbes was not alone "in distinguishing between the law and right of nature," and cites Valla as a predecessor and Dudley Digges and Jeremy Taylor as contemporaries (38).

37. Sommerville, *Hobbes,* 71; see *Leviathan,* 20.138–39.

38. Sommerville, *Hobbes,* discusses conquest and consent as distinct in Hobbes's typology of ways man can gain dominion over woman; after saying that Hobbes reduces conquest to consent, Sommerville doesn't cite any supporting passages from *Leviathan* about woman's consent.

39. Hobbes could thus be said to invert the patriarchal argument for political authority, which analogizes the sovereign to the head of the family. Hobbes, in contrast, models the family on "the contractual relationship among men." I borrow this phrase from David Gauthier, "The Social Contract as Ideology," 135.

40. See Carole Pateman, *The Sexual Contract,* 44–54.

41. In constructing his fearful political subject, Hobbes is also, of course, drawing on the religious discourse that emphasizes the believer's righteous fear of God. My point is that this fear is marshaled to create a subordinate political subject, structurally closer to the wife in Gouge than to the autonomous male political subject of Milton's domestic and political thought. On the effeminacy of the Hobbesian subject, see also Strauss, *Political Philosophy of Hobbes,* who argues that Hobbes, like Plato, criticizes traditional equations of manliness with military valor (147–48); see also Stephen Holmes, *Passions and Constraint,* who mentions Hobbes's appreciation of the Church's "unmanning" of

subjects by inculcating Christian meekness (96). See also the analysis of the effeminacy of the Hobbesian subject by Harvey C. Mansfield, "Virilité et libéralisme," *Archives de philosophie du droit* 41 (1997): 25–42.

42. See *Leviathan* 6.38–45. Moreover, Hobbes makes deliberation itself a sequence of appetites (or passions), and defines the will as "the last appetite in Deliberating": the will is no longer a separate faculty that links cognition and action. Rather, every action motivated by appetite or passion is by definition voluntary.

43. Cudworth, *True Intellectual System,* 698. See also James Tyrrell, *Brief Disquisition,* 367, and 384–85 on the problems with Hobbes's assertion that every man judges for himself regarding self-preservation in the state of nature.

44. John Locke, *Essays on the Law of Nature* (Oxford: Clarendon Press, 1965), 180; cited in Susan Staves, *Players' Scepters* (Lincoln, Neb., 1979), 273.

45. Strauss, *Political Philosophy of Hobbes,* offers an excellent analysis of how Hobbes's account of the passions vacillates between mechanism and vitalism, between a view of human appetite as similar to animal appetite, but with reason at its service; and a view of human appetite as infinite in itself, rather than as the result of external impressions (9).

46. Strauss, *Political Philosophy of Hobbes,* 169. For a contemporary comment on Hobbes's inconsistent argument about reason and the passions, see James Tyrrell, *Brief Disquisition.* Hobbes argues that men are more inclined to conflict than animals because men are emulous and have the use of reason, which contributes to the desire to reform and innovate; Tyrrell comments, "I dare appeal to the Judgment of any indifferent Reader, whether the condition of Mankind is worse than that of Brutes, because it is rational; and whether Mr. *H* doth not judg [sic] very hardly of all Men, by making their Reason guilty of all these miseries, which in other places he imputes only to the Passions" (340).

47. In a longer essay, it would be necessary to address the problems with Hobbes's attempt to distinguish between good and bad fear. As I argue in the book of which this essay forms a part, this effort depends on a previous contract of mimesis: an agreement to limit the role of mimetic desire, to constrain the mimetic dimension of the passions, in the realm of politics.

48. See Guillory, "Milton, Narcissism, Gender," for a persuasive account of male self-esteem in relation to glory in Milton.

49. Foucault, "Omnes et singulatim," 253; see 238–39, 254.

Intellectual Property and the Adages of Erasmus: Coenobium v. Ercto non cito

KATHY EDEN

Arguably the single hottest literary property of the first quarter of the sixteenth century, Erasmus' *Adagiorum chiliades* helped to secure the fame and fortune of Europe's two most powerful printing houses during this time, those of Aldo Manuzio in Venice and of Johan Froben in Basel. The Aldine edition of the *Adages*, by Erasmus' own account the product of friendship and close collaboration, appeared under its new title in 1508, vastly expanding and revising the Paris *Collectanea* of 1500. Seven years later, the second edition, again revised and expanded, launched the longstanding friendship and commercial partnership between Erasmus and Froben, his most successful northern publisher.[1] These publication events belong to a larger picture of the rapidly changing intellectual and material landscape inhabited by sixteenth-century Europeans—changes that had an especially jolting impact on their experience as readers.

For the published *Adages* not only represents an artifact that many more people could own because of the new technology of printing, but it also, in ways that worried some of Erasmus' colleagues, made these many book owners at once proprietors of a classical heritage that had previously been the intellectual property of very few. Both the resolute mission of one author to divulge the wisdom of the ancients and the anxiety of the few about this divulgation are recorded in the *Adages* themselves. In "Festina lente"—"Make haste slowly"—Erasmus recalls the reluctance of one acquaintance to share his manuscripts in this effort on the grounds that "everything is now becoming public property from which scholars hitherto had been able to secure the admiration of the common people" (LB, II, 405EF; *CWE, 33,* 15).[2] Denied access to this colleague's private property, Erasmus outspokenly upholds the need to subordinate one's personal stake to a common enterprise designed to benefit an entire community of readers (*Herculei labores,* LB, II, 715E–716B). And his friend and first biographer Beatus Rhenanus corroborates Erasmus' commitment to this enterprise. "When he was about to publish the *Adages,*" Beatus remembers, "certain scholars said to him, 'Erasmus, you are divulging our secrets.' But he was desirous that these be accessible to all so that they might attain to complete scholarship."[3]

The publication of the *Adages,* in other words, reflects changing attitudes and practices regarding property. It is my contention in this chapter that these attitudes and practices were complex and that Erasmus not only understood their complexity but actually exploited it in the composition of this most popular sixteenth-century book. Although material changes unquestionably exerted their pressures on these events, moreover, it is rather the issues concerning intellectual property that preoccupied Erasmus.[4] And what better forum for such a preoccupation than a compendium of proverbs?

The proverb is, as the prolegomena to the 1508 edition argues, a literary form that by definition defies individual ownership. Passed down from generation to generation and around from place to place, proverbs or adages encode over time and space a collective wisdom that belongs equally to all members of a community. On just this feature of proverbial statement, Erasmus quotes Quintilian (LB, II, 7DE; *CWE, 31,* 16; cf. *Institutio Oratoria,* 5.11.37–42): "Popular sayings which command general assent will also be found not without value as supporting material. . . . Those things too which command general assent seem to be, as it were, common property from the fact that they have no certain author."[5] Precisely because they constitute a common store, then, adages or proverbs invite reflection on the nature of private property, especially private intellectual property. With the coming of age of printing, moreover, authors like Erasmus had more reason than ever to reflect.

Indeed, it is in Venice during the last years of the fifteenth century and first years of the sixteenth—the where and when of the first edition of the *Adages* —that laws regarding intellectual property, including copyright, began their slow but continual evolution toward the modern legal institutions that form so familiar a part of our own landscape.[6] In 1486 a Venetian author, Marcantonio Sabellico, requests from the Venetian Council the first copyright, termed a privilege (*privilegium*), for his history of Venice, the *Rerum Venetarum Libri*

XXXIII. Six years later, Pier Francesco da Ravenna, requesting a similar privilege for his *Foenix,* a study of artificial memory, is granted his copyright by the council on the grounds not only that the community is entitled to a work that serves the common good (*ad universalem commoditatem et utilitatem*) but also that its author is entitled to the fruits of his own labor (*fructus laborum et vigiliarum suarum*). In 1496, four years later, the council grants Aldo Manuzio, Erasmus' publisher, a patent for his ancient Greek type on the same grounds — entitlement to the fruits of time and money spent on an enterprise so beneficial to the community, the illustrious city of Venice.[7]

In the years following, Aldus continues to look to the council to protect his intellectual property through patents and copyrights in the form of privileges. In 1498 he applies for copyright for editions of several ancient Greek authors, including Demosthenes, Hermogenes, Plutarch, and Xenophon; in 1500, for the letters of Catherine of Siena. In 1501, he receives a patent for his italic type; and in 1502 his request for protection from infringements on this privilege earns him a ten-year patent on both Greek and italic types.[8]

By 1507, the year before he and Erasmus collaborate on bringing out the first edition of the *Adages,* Aldus has already been embroiled in at least two lawsuits over intellectual property and has in fact just prevailed in one of them — a major litigation with a competitor over the pirating of a number of Aldine texts. His adversary, Filippo Giunti, refrained (it seems) from further copyright infringement, avoiding Aldus' titles, but was less compliant on the issue of patent, continuing to copy the fashionable italic type.[9]

It is, then, to a Venice at once anointed with the commercial spirit of the young printing industry and exercised in the newly developing legal protocols of intellectual property that Erasmus comes in 1508 with the express intention of publishing his *Adages.* According to Beatus Rhenanus, "When work on the *Adagia* was completed, he wrote to Aldus Manutius to ask if he wished to undertake the printing of the book. The latter replied that he would do so with pleasure. Erasmus then moved to Venice . . . and he received him as his guest in the home of his father-in-law, Andrea Asolani. . . . Nor was his stay in Venice a brief one."[10] Thus begins the mutually profitable friendship that Erasmus commemorates in one of the longest and best known adages, "Festina lente." Indeed, Erasmus, in collaboration with his friend and publisher, rearranges and expands the earlier edition, the Paris *Collectanea* of 1500, with an eye to foregrounding not only *amicitia* or friendship but the relation between friendship and wealth, material and intellectual.[11] In doing so, as we shall see, Erasmus explores the claims of author, publisher, and reader as heir to the so-called classical tradition, the intellectual legacy of Greek and Roman antiquity.

Three adages in the rearranged and expanded edition take on special significance; all three take up the theme of property, especially intellectual property. The first is "Amicorum communia omnia" or "Between Friends All Is Common" (LB, II, 13F-14F; *CWE*, 31, 29–30). The ninety-fourth adage in the *Collectanea*, it is here moved to initial position, thereby introducing not only the first thousand or *chilias prima* but the entire collection of more than three thousand proverbs.[12] Relying in the *Collectanea* on only the briefest allusions to Terence and Plato, this introductory adage is here expanded both to include other Greek and Latin authors, including Euripides, Aristotle, Menander, Cicero, Martial, and Plutarch, and to feature Pythagoras. So critical is the testimony of Pythagoras as the reputed source of this saying that when Erasmus reworks the Aldine edition for publication by Froben in 1515, he further expands the witnesses to the ancient philosopher's authority.[13] To Cicero (*De legibus* 1.12.34) and Diogenes Laertius (8.10) he adds Aulus Gellius, who records in his *Noctes Atticae* (1.9.12) that (LB, II, 14F; *CWE*, 31, 30): "not only was Pythagoras the author of this saying, but he also instituted a kind of sharing [*communionem*] of life and property in this way, the very thing Christ wants to happen among Christians. For all those who were admitted by Pythagoras into that well-known band who followed his instruction would give to the common fund whatever money and family property [*pecuniae familiaeque*] they possessed. This is called in Latin, in a word which expresses the facts, *coenobium*, clearly from community of life and fortunes [*vitae fortunarumque societate*]." Pythagoras, in other words, is not only the father of this saying; he is also the first philosopher of common—in contrast to private—property; as such, Erasmus infers, he is arguably the father of *coenobium* or cenobitic monasticism.[14]

Although Erasmus' inference may be sound, his copy of Aulus Gellius is flawed, reading *coenobium* for the unfamiliar Roman legal formula *ercto non cito*. The faulty reading, however, is telling. For the second-century Roman lawyer, like the sixteenth-century theologian, is taking special notice of the ancient Italian philosopher's position on property. Regarding the Pythagorean initiates at Croton, Aulus Gellius records that "as soon as they had been admitted by Pythagoras into that band of disciples, [they] at once devoted to the common use whatever estate and property they had, and an inseparable fellowship [*societas inseparabilis*] was formed, like the old-time association which in Roman legal parlance was termed an 'undivided inheritance' [*ercto non cito*]" (1.9.12).[15]

Like the late antique biographical essay, then, the Erasmian adage draws attention to this remarkable custom, alien to both the late antique Roman and the sixteenth-century European, of holding property in common. Whereas the Roman lawyer compares Pythagorean communalism to a special legal disposition of an inherited estate, the Dutch theologian associates it with the religious common life, which, moreover, resembles the first community of Pythagoreans at Croton in holding not only material but also intellectual property in common. Diogenes Laertius, whose testimony concludes the 1508 version of the adage before the addition of Aulus Gellius in 1515, preserves in his biography of the ancient philosopher the common sayings or *symbola* that grounded the fellowship of all Pythagoreans (8.17–18). Pythagoras himself, this biographer notes, experienced a deep bond of friendship with anyone who shared (*kekoinōnēkota*) these proverbs (8.16). And Erasmus follows this ancient source in listing them.[16]

Indeed, "Amicorum communia omnia," the opening proverb, introduces not only the first thousand adages as well as the entire collection of more than three thousand but also the *Pythagorae symbola,* the precepts of Pythagoras, that constitute altogether the first thirty-nine adages of both the 1508 and all subsequent editions (LB, II, 14F–25E). Erasmus, in other words, begins his compendium of ancient wisdom by establishing the Pythagorean legacy of common property as at once material and intellectual. Friends in the Pythagorean sense share not only a common store of material goods but a common stock of proverbial sayings. And it is by no means incidental that this philosopher of friendship, as Pythagoras was often called, should choose the proverb as the pre-eminent discursive form. For like friendship as a social praxis, proverbial statement as a discursive praxis forges a unity out of the experience of the many.[17]

By moving the ninety-fourth proverb of the *Collectanea* to the initial position in the Aldine *Adagiorum chiliades,* Erasmus initiates a case for the reader of the newly published book as heir to the intellectual tradition of antiquity. In contrast, say, to the figure from Exodus (12:35–36) of the Israelites despoiling their enemies, the Egyptians that Erasmus appropriated for his earlier work, here the Pythagorean adage allows him to figure the tradition about to be divulged as the common treasury of intellectual wealth belonging equally to a like-minded community of friends.[18] Like the first initiates at Croton, moreover, this broadly European intellectual community not only does not through use deplete the common store but, through sound investment in the form of the members' own literary production, leaves it enriched for the next generation. Under the favorable auspices of the first adage (LB, II, 13F), Erasmus signals to the reader the rights and obligations implicit in sharing the intellectual wealth of antiquity.[19]

By beginning his collection with this particular proverb, Erasmus also demonstrates the enormous power of the editor-author to dispose or arrange inherited material. Not surprisingly, when he uses this strategy again, it is in comparable circumstances. Number 196 in the *Collectanea*, "Festina lente" is moved in the Aldine edition to introduce the second thousand, or *chilias secunda*. It is also greatly expanded, maturing, as it were, into one of the longest and most popular adages of the entire collection.[20] And it too, retrieving the theme that inaugurated the first thousand, presses forward on the issue of intellectual property. Like "amicorum communia omnia," moreover, "Festina lente" situates its reflections on property in the larger context of political philosophy.

Whereas the opening adage adds the authority of Plato and Aristotle to that of Pythagoras in establishing the community of friends as the paradigm for the republic or commonwealth, "Festina lente" begins with the consequences of undue haste and sloth in the political arena, in the actions of men of state. For in this arena, the decisions of the one affect the material well-being of the many. So fundamental is this common wisdom to sound government that two of the most praiseworthy men of state (and emperors no less), Octavius Augustus and Titus Vespasian, take it as their motto (LB, II, 399B; CWE, 33, 5). Vespasian even goes so far as to have it impressed on the coins of the realm (LB, II, 399EF; CWE, 33, 5):

> Vespasian's approval of our maxim can easily be inferred from very ancient coins issued by him, one of which I was allowed to inspect by Aldo Manuzio. . . . The design [*character*] of the coin was as follows. One side showed the head of Vespasian with an inscription, the other an anchor, the central shaft of which had a dolphin coiled round it. Now the only meaning conveyed by this symbol [*symboli*] is that favorite maxim of the emperor Augustus "Make haste slowly"; and this we learn from the ancient texts relating to hieroglyphs [*monimenta literarum hieroglyphicarum*].

Already recognizable to the reader of the Aldine *Adages* as the mark of its publisher, the symbol of anchor and dolphin is here introduced as an object of material wealth inscribed with political wisdom and handed down to this same publisher, Aldus Manutius. Inscribing this apparently straightforward description of an inscription within an essay about publishing as part of a larger collection of proverbs representing the common intellectual wealth of antiquity, Erasmus prepares his reader to appreciate in the remainder of the essay the complex interplay of a number of related transfers or *translationes*.

First is the transfer from visual to verbal or literary symbol, a *translatio* effected by the hieroglyph itself. For this ancient form of writing, Erasmus explains immediately following the description, is a kind of drawing or engraving [*figura* or *scalptura*] that resembles the proverb as characterized both in the prolegomena to the entire collection and in the opening of this same essay — an opening that recapitulates the general introduction (LB, II, 397CE and 399F-400A; see also 3B). Like hieroglyphs, proverbs are often enigmatic. And like proverbs, hieroglyphs condense a more copious ancient wisdom (LB, II, 6DE; *CWE*, 31, 14). Being at once enigmatic, hieroglyphic, and proverbial, the concentrated symbol of dolphin and anchor must be diluted for public consumption.

In the form of a detailed explanation of the various parts of the symbol — circle, dolphin, and anchor — this dilution entails a journey through mythology, natural history, geometry, and physics. Finally returning to politics, Erasmus reiterates that "this saying, Make haste slowly, arose in the heart of ancient philosophy; whence it was called into their service by two of the most highly esteemed of all Roman emperors, one of whom used it as a device [*adagionis*] the other as an emblem [*insignium*], so well did it agree with the character and disposition of both" (LB, II, 402BC; *CWE*, 33, 9). Once back in the political arena, however, Erasmus effectively works his own transition to the next crucial *translatio*. "And now," he continues, "it has passed to Aldo Manuzio, citizen of Rome, as a kind of heir in the third generation [*ceu tertium haeredem*]. . . . Nor do I think this symbol was more illustrious then, when it was stamped on the imperial coinage and suffered the wear and tear of circulation as it passed from one merchant to another, than it is now, when in every nation, even outside the limits of any Christian empire, it spreads and wins recognition, it is held fast and prized in company with books of all kinds in both the ancient languages, by all who are devoted to the cult of liberal studies."

Formerly the property of Augustus and Vespasian, the symbol now belongs to Aldus (407D); and with this inheritance comes the complementary passing or transfer from material to intellectual property — from mercantile negotiations made possible by such coins as the one of Vespasian now in Aldus' possession to the circulation of knowledge promoted by easier access to such printed books as the *Adages* itself. Proving himself a responsible heir, Aldus not only maintains but increases the value of his inheritance.

With this inheritance from Vespasian to Aldus, in other words, comes the passing of pre-eminence from politics to scholarship. In the course of this essay, that is, Erasmus skillfully reinvests the traditional complementarity between *translatio imperii* and its corollary, *translatio studii*. The transfer of political power from one culture to another — say, from Egypt to Greece or Greece to Rome — routinely involves the appropriation by the victors not only of the material wealth of the vanquished culture but also of its intellectual wealth, usually in the form of literary and artistic production. On this occasion, however, Erasmus invokes a different kind of *translatio*: namely, the transfer from *imperium* to *studium*.[21] For the achievements of an Aldus, Erasmus insists, surpass those of a Ptolemy. Statesmen like Ptolemy merely widen the material boundaries of their empires, whereas Aldus extends the intellectual community; and as for the imperial prerogative of building libraries, between Ptolemy and Aldus there is no competition (LB, II, 403A; *CWE,* 33, 10):

> However loudly you may sing the praises of those men who by their valour protect or even extend the boundaries of their country, they are active at best in worldly things and constrained within narrow limits. But he who restores a literature in ruins (almost a harder task than to create one) is engaged on a thing sacred and immortal, and works for the benefit not of one province but of all nations everywhere and of all succeeding ages. Last but not least, this was in old days the privilege of princes, among whom Ptolemy won special glory, although his library was contained within the narrow walls of his own palace. Aldus is building a library which knows no walls save those of the world itself.

Heir to the power and prestige of the political ruler, the scholar-publisher inherits as well an obligation to protect and even enlarge his estate for his own beneficiaries. According to Erasmus, Aldus takes on this obligation with unremitting zeal, working day and night to assure that his legacy to the growing community of like-minded students of antiquity survives intact. The estate itself Erasmus identifies as literary property or *supellex literaria* (LB, II, 402D); and Aldus' goal in regard to this property is nothing less than full restoration of past damage and loss. Aldus promises to hand down an ancient literary tradition that is once again complete, genuine, and uncorrupted (*& integra, & syncera, puraque*); or, as Erasmus adds, one so restored that none of its heirs any longer feels that any part of his literary heritage — again, his literary property or *supellex literaria* — is missing ("& plenum habeant & emendatum, nullamque jam literariae supellectilis partem quisquam desideret," 402E).[22]

The second thousand of the Aldine edition, then, is introduced by an adage featuring Aldus in the role of scholar-publisher — a role in which he figures not only as heir to the most valuable of properties, the literary tradition of antiquity, but also as trustee or guardian of this intellectual wealth on behalf of a larger community. The enterprise, Erasmus claims, is a labor worthy of Hercules — what he calls in this adage a *Herculanum mehercule facinus* (402F). With the introduction of the third thousand, however, Erasmus transfers this qualification from the efforts of the scholar-publisher to those of the scholarly editor-author, or, in other words, from Aldus to himself.

Our third case of strategic relocation involves the equally well-known "Herculei labores" — "The Labors of Hercules" — which, numbering thirteen in the

Collectanea and comprising a single sentence, Erasmus moves to initial position of the third thousand in the Aldine edition (LB, II, 707D–717B; *CWE,* 34, 167–82). Thus relocated, this adage acquires the status of companion piece to the two other introductory adages already discussed, "Amicorum communia omnia" and "Festina lente"; and as their companion, it joins the ongoing conversation about intellectual, especially literary, property — here, one special piece of literary property, the *Adages.* For the focus of this adage is significantly neither Aldus Manutius, who appears only long enough to supply Erasmus with one of the best libraries of ancient texts in the world, nor the restoration of the entire ancient literary tradition, but Erasmus' own labors in the service of compiling for his readers this common treasury of proverbial sayings that constitute no small part of the intellectual wealth of antiquity.

Setting this difference in relief, however, are some noteworthy commonalities. Like the other two adages, this one begins by applying the saying to the political arena — here, the ruler's often unappreciated labors in the interest of the ruled (LB, II, 709AB; *CWE,* 34, 169–70). To support this claim, Erasmus adduces both the biblical story of Joseph and the testimony of Philo Judaeus. As in the other adages, moreover, in this one *imperium* soon gives way to *studium,* where the cultural property at issue is once again literary. This time Erasmus effects the transfer (*translatio*) from politics to scholarship with the contention that "if any human toils deserve to be awarded the epithet 'Herculean,' it seems to belong in the highest degree to those at least who devote their efforts to restoring the monuments of ancient and true literature. Incomparable as are the labours they undertake on account of the incredible difficulty of the subject, they arouse none the less the greatest unpopularity among the common herd" (LB, II, 709DE; *CWE,* 34, 170). The many-headed Hydra that threatens such heroic service, however, is not, as we might be inclined to think, the recalcitrance of the subject matter; on the contrary, it is the *invidia* of the hypercritical reader. The writer's herculean battle, in other words, is with the monstrous ingratitude of his reading public.[23]

Understanding that in some circumstances the best offense is a good defense, Erasmus devotes the bulk of this essay to defending his own literary practices in composing the *Adages,* not, as he assures his audience, "to boast of my intelligence or advertize my own industry, but to make my reader more sympathetic [*aequiorem*]" (LB, II, 710C; *CWE,* 34, 171). In judging the *Adages,* the equitable or fair-minded reader — the *lector aequus* (cf. 715E) — will consider the particular, even peculiar, challenges facing the author of such a work — challenges that make unusual demands on his powers of invention, disposition, and elocution.[24]

Behind Erasmus' portrait of the judgmental reader, moreover, is the critic of the *Ars Poetica,* Horace's handbook for decorous reading as well as writing. Like Homeric epic in its large scale and common themes (*Ars Poetica,* 347–60), the *Adages* deserves pardon from its readers for any minor failings that result from the faults of a craftsmanship rendered fallible by the inherent imperfections of human nature (LB, II, 712CD; *CWE,* 34, 175). By contrast, the reader of the *Adages,* like that of the Homeric epics according to Horace, has every right to hold the writer responsible for the principles of his art. One such principle is literary economy (*oeconomia*), which entails both selecting the most appropriate details and arranging them for the maximum artistic effect.[25] Just as Homer does not rehearse the entire Trojan War from the first to the last episode, so Erasmus carefully culls and arranges the many available citations of a given adage. And here Erasmus defends his craftsmanship by giving just the right example to make his case. What, he asks, could be more absurd than "to start my explanation of the proverb An Iliad of troubles by proceeding to tell the whole history of the Trojan war, beginning (as Horace puts it) 'from that twin egg,' or to illustrate An invention worthy of Ulysses by unfolding the whole narrative of the *Odyssey?*" (LB, II, 713B; *CWE,* 34, 176; cf. *Ars Poetica* 147).

Erasmus even claims to be following decorum in avoiding the Horatian *callida iunctura,* the so-called clever connection or juxtaposition (*Ars Poetica* 47–48, 242). In a work such as the *Adages,* he argues, "it seemed to me somehow right and proper that there should be no order" (LB, II, 713DE; *CWE,* 34, 177). Not only would it weary the reader in so extended a work, but polishing it would have delayed publication the full Horatian nine years (LB, II, 713EF; *CWE,* 34, 177; *Ars Poetica* 388, and see also 291).

Then distancing himself one final step from the artistic enterprise theorized in the *Ars,* Erasmus proclaims a communal, in contrast to a private, agenda. For the Horatian poet who is truly accomplished effects the difficult task of making what is common his own private property ("Difficile est proprie communia dicere" [*Ars Poetica* 128]); or, as Horace continues, he wins private rights (*privatus ius*) to public property (*publica materies, Ars Poetica* 131). The author of the *Adages,* in contrast, welcomes (so he says) the prospect of both shared labor and shared credit (LB, II, 715E; *CWE,* 34, 180). What holds for the writer seeking glory for himself, in other words, does not hold for the one who aims at being useful to the community (LB, II, 715C; *CWE,* 34, 179–80).[26] So Erasmus concludes the 1508 version of this adage by upholding the "general advantage [*publicum negocium*] of all who wish to learn" over "my own private ends" (*privatim*): "But in my opinion at any rate, in rebuilding the republic of letters [*res literaria*] one must display the spirit of a second Hercules, and no fear or weariness at the prospect of your own loss should discourage you from serving the common good (LB, II, 716B; *CWE,* 34, 181)."

Advancing the theme of the initial adage of the first and second thousands, the opening adage of the third thousand features the *Adagiorum chiliades* as common intellectual property. In this more traditional sense, *res literaria* parallels *res publica;* the republic of letters—the common literary wealth—models itself on the political republic or commonwealth, whose paradigm, in turn, is the community of friends. On the other hand, in the context of Erasmus' defense of his herculean efforts on behalf of an invidious reading public, *res literaria* invokes the emerging legal sense of privately owned literary property, *supellex literaria*—the kind of private property just now coming under the protection of copyright in the form of political privilege.[27]

As we have seen, the very first of the more than three thousand adages—"Amicorum communia omnia"—sets in relief the intellectual communalism of the readers of the *Adages.* In the wake of its publication, all of them share equally the literary wealth of antiquity. As we have also seen, "Festina lente" opens the second thousand by featuring the scholar-publisher as heir to antiquity and thus responsible for handing down the fully restored legacy of its literary tradition. In company with these two adages, as it were, "Herculei labores" introduces the third and last thousand of the Aldine edition by foregrounding the community-mindedness of the author-editor. Fully expecting the collaboration of other author-editors on this project (LB, II, 715E; *CWE,* 34, 180), he succeeds in making the *Adages* not only a common treasury of the intellectual wealth of so-called classical antiquity but also, toying with the emerging legal sense, a commonly held literary property. Despite his protestations in this adage against Horatian law, then, Erasmus has carefully arranged his work, effecting a more subtly decorous callida iunctura: not, to be sure, adage by adage, but rather thousand by thousand. Each succeeding chilias of the *Adagiorum chiliades* is introduced by an adage that returns the readers' attention to the question of property: not so much to the newly published book they are reading as an article of material property but rather to the complex issues of ownership that attach to the intellectual property therein.

Notes

1. On the evolution of the *Adages* through its several editions see Margaret Mann Phillips, *The "Adages" of Erasmus* (Cambridge, 1964). On the importance of this publication event to the careers of both author and publisher, see Martin Lowry, *The World of Aldus Manutius: Business and Scholarship in Renaissance Venice* (Ithaca, N.Y., 1979),

151, 228, and 263. On the role of these publishing houses in Erasmus' career, see Peter G. Bietenholz, "Ethics and Early Printing: Erasmus' Rules for the Proper Conduct of Authors," *Humanities Association Review* 26 (1975): 180–95, Lisa Jardine, *Erasmus, Man of Letters: The Construction of Charisma in Print* (Princeton, 1993), and James D. Tracy, *Erasmus of the Low Countries* (Berkeley, Calif., 1996), 43–46.

2. For the Latin text of Erasmus, I have used *Desiderii Erasmi Roterodami Opera Omnia,* ed. J. LeClerc (Leiden, 1703–6), 10 vols., hereafter LB; for the English translation, *Collected Works of Erasmus* (Toronto, 1974–), hereafter *CWE.*

On book sharing as an element of friendship, see Martin Lowry, *Nicholas Jenson and the Rise of Venetian Publishing in Renaissance Europe* (Oxford, 1991), 31–35. On Erasmus' undertaking the project of the adages as an act of friendship, see "Herculei labores," LB, II, 715AB; *CWE,* 34, 179, and Letter to Botzheim, Ep. 1341A, *Opus Epistolarum Des. Erasmi Roterodami,* ed. P. S. Allen (Oxford, 1906; rpt. 1992), I, 16–17 (hereafter Allen); *CWE,* 9, 315–17.

3. "The Life of Erasmus by Beatus Rhenanus," in *Christian Humanism and the Reformation: Selected Writings,* ed. and trans. John C. Olin (New York, 1965), 47–48; for the Latin see Allen, I, 67. See also John F. D'Amico, *Theory and Practice in Renaissance Textual Criticism: Beatus Rhenanus Between Conjecture and History* (Berkeley, Calif., 1988), esp. 47–55.

4. For the impact of material changes on the history of the book see, for instance, Roger Chartier and Daniel Roche, "New Approaches to the History of the Book" in *Constructing the Past: Essays in Historical Methodology,* ed. Jacques Le Goff and Pierre Nora (Cambridge, 1985), 198–214, and Robert Darnton, "What is the History of Books?" and "First Steps Toward a History of Reading," in *The Kiss of Lamourette: Reflections in Cultural History* (New York, 1990), 107–35 and 154–87.

It is the commonly held view that the notions of literary property and its corollary, copyright, are the offspring of the printing press. Before Erasmus' day, as one scholar puts it, "the owner of a book also possessed legal rights to its contents. In other words, an author's rights passed to the owner of the book, which indicates that there was no distinction between physical and intellectual property rights" (Leonardus Vytautas Gerulaitis, *Printing and Publishing in Fifteenth-Century Venice* [Chicago, 1976], 32). For a slightly different formulation, see Rudolf Hirsch, *Printing, Selling and Reading, 1450–1550* (Wiesbaden, Germany, 1967), 8–9; for a conflicting view, see F. D. Prager, "The Early Growth and Influence of Intellectual Property," *Journal of the Patent Office Society,* 34 (1952): 106–40.

5. On this feature of the proverb, especially as it is treated in the Prolegomena, see my " 'Between Friends All Is Common': The Erasmian Adage and Tradition," *Journal of the History of Ideas* 59 (1998): 405–19.

6. On the early history of intellectual property, especially copyright, see John Feather, "From Rights in Copies to Copyright: The Recognition of Authors' Rights in English Law and Practice in the Sixteenth and Seventeenth Centuries," *Cardozo Arts and Entertainment Law Journal* 10 (1992): 455–73; Paul Goldstein, *Copyright's Highway: The Law and Lore of Copyright from Gutenberg to the Celestial Jukebox* (New York, 1994); F. D. Prager, "The Early Growth and Influence of Intellectual Property," 106–40; A. J. K. Robinson, "The Evolution of Copyright, 1476–1776," *The Cambrian Law Review* 22

(1991): 55–77; Mark Rose, *Authors and Owners: The Invention of Copyright* (Cambridge, Mass., 1993); Mladen Vukmir, "The Roots of Anglo-American Intellectual Property Law in Roman Law," *IDEA: The Journal of Law and Technology* 32 (1992): 123–54.

7. On the early privilege system, especially in Venice, during the last years of the fifteenth century and first years of the sixteenth, see Elizabeth Armstrong, *Before Copyright: The French Book-Privilege System, 1498–1526* (Cambridge, 1990), esp. 1–6; Carlo Castellani, *La Stampa in Venezia dalla sua origine alla morte di Aldo Manuzio Seniore* (Trieste, 1889; rpt. 1973); Ruth Chavasse, "The First Known Author's Copyright, September 1486, in the Context of a Humanist Career," *Bulletin of the John Rylands University Library of Manchester* 69 (1986): 11–37; R. Fulin, "Primi privilegi di stampa in Venezia," *Archivio Veneto*, 1 (1871): 160–64; Gerulaitis, *Printing and Publishing in Fifteenth-Century Venice*, 33–46; Hirsch, *Printing, Selling and Reading*, 78–103.

For the texts of these first *privilegia*, see R. Fulin, "Documenti per servire alla storia della tipografia veneziana," *Archivio Veneto* 23 (1882): 84–212, esp. 102 (to Sabellico and Pier Francesco da Ravenna), 120, and 136 (to Aldo Manuzio). See also Castellani, *La Stampa in Venezia*, 69–78, esp. 71–72.

8. For the texts of the *privilegia* see Castellani, *La Stampa in Venezia*, 75–77 and Fulin, "Documenti," 136, 141–42, 144–45, 149–50; for discussion see Castellani, *La Stampa in Venezia*, 35–60; Gerulaitis, *Printing and Publishing in Fifteenth-Century Venice*, 40–45; Lowry, *The World of Aldus Manutius*, 111–54; Robert Proctor, *The Printing of Greek in the Fifteenth Century* (Oxford, 1900; rpt. Hildesheim, 1966), 110–14 and N. G. Wilson, *From Byzantium to Italy: Greek Studies in the Italian Renaissance* (Baltimore, Md., 1992), 124–56.

On the overlapping early history of copyright and patent law see Prager, "Early Growth and Influence of Intellectual Property," 122–40, and Rose, *Authors and Owners*, 45. On the potential for conflict see Lowry, *The World of Aldus Manutius*, 89–90.

9. On these lawsuits see Lowry, *The World of Aldus Manutius*, 156–58, concluding, "Success in this case, which was presumably decided some time in the late autumn of 1507, must have given Aldus real encouragement as he prepared to resume operations. Planning appears to have been in hand for some time: [Johannes] Cuno reported before the end of December 1506, that preliminary work on the texts of Plato and Plutarch was being discussed, and when Erasmus made his famous approach to Aldus on 28 October of the following year, he never doubted that the company was in business though it had not produced an edition for nearly two years."

On Johannes Cuno of Nuremberg (1463–1513), see D'Amico, *Theory and Practice in Renaissance Textual Criticism*, 47–48, esp. n. 34, and Wilson, *From Byzantium to Italy*, 148.

10. Olin, *Christian Humanism and the Reformation*, 37–38; Allen, I, 60.

11. See my " 'Between Friends All Is Common': The Erasmian Adage and Tradition."

12. Although Margaret Mann Phillips notes the relocation of the other two — "Festina Lente" and "Herculei Labores" — she leaves this one out of the account; and though she observes that the second and third deal with the "compilation and publication of the *Adages* themselves," she does not touch on the theme of intellectual property (*Adages*, 70).

On the first adage, see also *Opera Omnia Desiderii Erasmi Roterodami* (Amsterdam, 1993), II–I, 84–87.

13. On the important role of the *Adages* in launching Erasmus' association with the Froben press, see Lowry, *The World of Aldus Manutius,* 273, and Margaret Mann Phillips, *Adages,* 96. For Beatus Rhenanus on this publishing event, see Olin, *Christian Humanism and the Reformation,* 41; Allen, I, 63.

14. Again, Margaret Mann Phillips notes the importance of Pythagoras' authority in the *Adages,* alongside Plato's and Aristotle's, but does not pursue the reasons for it (*Adages,* 94). See also S. K. Heninger, Jr., "*Pythagorean Symbola* in Erasmus' *Adagia,*" *Renaissance Quarterly* 21 (1968): 162–65, esp. 165, n. 15, where he cites the place of the *carmina aurea,* falsely attributed to Pythagoras, in Aldus' grammars.

On the Pythagorean origins of cenobitic monasticism, see my "*Koinonia* and the Friendship between Rhetoric and Religion," *Rhetoric and Religion in Our Time,* ed. W. Jost and W. Olmsted (New Haven, forthcoming).

Not incidentally, the Aldine press greatly contributed to the accessibility of Pythagoras' teaching, by publishing not only his sayings but also Iamblichus and Philostratus. See Castellani, *La Stampa in Venezia,* 41, and Lowry, *The World of Aldus Manutius,* 111, 119, and 148. Both Aulus Gellius and Diogenes Laertius were already available from Nicholas Jenson's press, the former in 1472, the latter in 1475. See Lowry, *Nicholas Jenson and the Rise of Venetian Publishing in Renaissance Europe,* 242, 244. The Aldine press also brought out Philostratus' *Life of Apollonius of Tyana* with a Latin translation by Alamanno Rinuccini (1501–1504). See Wilson, *From Byzantium to Italy,* 137: "The first book to be set up in type was not one of the most significant. It is difficult to know why Aldus interested himself in Philostratus' *Life of Apollonius of Tyana.* . . . Neither Aldus nor More could be expected to take much interest in an ascetic Pythagorean of the first century, who presents an intriguing figure for students of the history of religion in antiquity."

15. Aulus Gellius, *The Attic Nights,* trans. John C. Rolfe (Cambridge, Mass., 1927; rpt. 1984), 3 vols. See also *A. Gellii Noctes Atticae,* ed. P. K. Marshall (Oxford, 1968), 2 vols.

On the legal formula *ercto non cito,* see *De oratore* 1.56.237 and Servius, *Comm. Aen.* 8, 642. And see Alan Watson, *The Law of Property in the Later Roman Republic* (Oxford, 1968), 110, 121–24, and *Roman Private Law Around 200 b.c.* (Edinburgh, 1971), 140–43. See also Edwin L. Minar, Jr., "Pythagorean Communism," *TAPA* 75 (1944): 34–46.

16. Sources other than Diogenes Laertius (8.17–19) include Plutarch (*Moralia* 12DF) and Iamblichus (*On the Pythagorean Life,* trans. Gillian Clark [Liverpool, 1989], 103–5, 161–62). See also *Opera Omnia,* II-I, 87–89.

17. See my " 'Between Friends All Is Common': The Erasmian Adage and Tradition." For Pythagoras as the philosopher of friendship, see, for instance, Iamblichus, *On the Pythagorean Life,* 69–70, 229–30.

18. On Erasmus' use of the *spoliatio Aegyptiorum,* see *Antibarbari,* LB, X, 1732B–1733A; *CWE,* 23, 97–98; Charles Béné, *Erasme et Saint Augustin* (Geneva, 1969), 59–95; and Marjorie O'Rourke Boyle, *Christening Pagan Mysteries: Erasmus in Pursuit of Wisdom* (Toronto, 1981), 16–17 and 55–58.

19. As early as 1498 in a letter to Christian Northoff (Ep. 61, Allen, I, 183; *CWE,* I,

127), Erasmus writes about *bonae literae* that "solas illas esse proprias hominis opes, neque dari a fortuna neque eripi posse; usu augeri, non minui." See Tracy, *Erasmus of the Low Countries,* 28.

20. Called simply "Matura" in the *Collectanea,* this adage addresses the importance of *maturity* in the arenas not only of scholarship but also of politics. See LB, II, 399 and Margaret Mann Phillips, *Adages,* 174.

21. For the more customary parallel transfers of politics and literary culture see, for instance, *Antibarbari, CWE,* 23, 24, and 97. On the relation in Roman law between *translatio* and *traditio* see Fritz Schultz, *Classical Roman Law* (Oxford, 1951), 343–44.

22. Erasmus uses this same phrase that I am translating here as "literary property" in his discussion of the *spoliatio Aegyptiorum* of the *Antibarbari* (LB, X, 1732B–1733A; *CWE,* 23, 97): "I wish I could give you the exact words of what follows, a charming passage about the household goods [*supellectile*] of the Egyptians. . . . when the Hebrews were secretly preparing to fly under their leader Moses from their servitude in Egypt, each took from his obliging neighbor all sorts of household goods [*supellectilem*]. . . . To take away the wealth of Egypt is to transfer heathen literature [*litteras Ethnicarum*] to the adornment and use of our faith. . . . But if there is among them any gold of wisdom [*sapientiae aurum*], any silver of speech [*eloquentiae argentum*], any furniture of good learning [*bonarum litterarum supellex*], we should pack up all that baggage and turn it to our own use, never fearing to be accused of thieving, but rather venturing to hope for reward and praise for the finest deeds."

On *supellex,* see Watson, *Roman Private Law Around 200 B.C.,* 113–14, and Cicero, *Topica* 5.27. On Holland as famous for its *supellex domestica,* see "*Auris Batava,*" LB, II, 1084E.

Erasmus also uses the term *res literaria* (LB, II, 402F, 403B, 406A; *CWE,* 33, 10, and 15), here translated as "the cause of literature" but also fairly understood as "literary property" with the emphasis on property that has sustained damage.

23. The earliest form of this adage in the *Collectanea* reads, "Proverbio dicuntur, qui aliis quidem utiles, auctori preter invidiam nihil adferunt."

On the ungrateful reader, see Ep. 396, *CWE,* 3, 262–63, where Erasmus also refers to the task of editing Jerome as herculean. In this instance, however, the monstrosity of the task characterizes the material and not the reader (263): "And so I despised all the difficulties, and like a modern Hercules I set out on my most laborious but most glorious campaign, taking the field almost unaided against all the monsters of error. I cannot think that Hercules consumed as much energy in taming a few monsters as I did in abolishing so many blunders. And I conceive that not a little more advantage will accrue to the world from my work than from his labours which are on the lips of all men." Cf. Ep. 334, *CWE,* 3, 97, and Ep. 335, *CWE,* 3, 107.

On this adage see Jardine, *Erasmus, Man of Letters,* 41–45 and 67–73. Her final chapter touches on the issue of literary property. See 164–69, esp. the section entitled "Textual Theft: A Footnote on Ownership," 168–69.

24. On Erasmus' quest for the *lector aequus* see my *Hermeneutics and the Rhetorical Tradition: Chapters in the Ancient Legacy and Its Humanist Reception* (New Haven, 1997), 1–3, 70–78, 100.

During conversation, Annabel Patterson suggested that Erasmus' defensiveness here about his haste offers another point of correspondence between this adage opening the third thousand and "Festina lente," which opens the second.

25. On the Horatian principles, see Wesley Trimpi, "The Meaning of Horace's *Ut Pictura Poesis*," *Journal of the Warburg and Courtauld Institutes* 36 (1973): 1–34, and "Horace's 'Ut Pictura Poesis': The Argument for Stylistic Decorum," *Traditio* 34 (1978): 29–73.

On the principle of oeconomia, see my *Hermeneutics and the Rhetorical Tradition*, 27–31.

26. Although Horace imagines art [*ars*] and natural talent [*natura, ingenium*] sharing their wealth [*opes*] and property (*res*) in friendly — perhaps Pythagorean — style (410–11; cf. 167), he nevertheless expects the poet to make the *res* of literary tradition, also called the wealth, or *opes* (307), his own private property (128–52). See C. O. Brink, *Horace on Poetry* (Cambridge, 1971), 204–7, 208–10, 432–42, 486–90. On the "friendship" between the poet and the critic, see Brink, *Horace on Poetry*, 513–15.

Indeed, throughout the *Ars Poetica*, Horace, like Roman law itself, places the emphasis on res. On the tripartite division of Roman law into *res, persona*, and *actio*, with the greatest attention to matters of res, see W. W. Buckland, *A Text-book of Roman Law from Augustus to Justinian* (Cambridge, 1921), esp. 182–232.

27. In the 1516 letter to Archbishop Warham that serves as preface to the same *Hieronymi Epistolae* that we learn in the final version of this adage cost Erasmus such herculean labor, Erasmus refers to the epistolary Jerome as his own literary property (Ep. 396, Allen, III, 220; *CWE*, 3, 265): "Though why should it any longer look like something borrowed rather than my own? — real estate [*multae res soli*] often passes from one ownership to another [*in ius alienum*] by occupation or prescriptive right. In any case, in this line of business Jerome himself has laid down a principle [*legem*] for me in his preface to the books of Kings, repeatedly calling that work his, because anything that we have made our own by correcting, reading, constant devotion, we can fairly claim is ours [*id iure nobis vindicamus*]. On this principle why should not I myself claim a proprietary right in the works of Jerome ["Hac lege cur non et ipse mihi ius vindicem in Hieronymianis libris"]? For centuries they had been treated as abandoned goods; I entered upon them as something ownerless, and by incalculable efforts reclaimed them for all devotees of true theology." Cf. Ep. 1341A, *CWE*, 9, 356, and see Jardine, *Erasmus, Man of Letters*, 164. For the legal action of *vindicatio* in the Roman law of property, see Buckland, *A Text-book of Roman Law*, 198 and 668–75, and Watson, *The Law of Property in the Later Roman Republic*, 96–104.

It is worth noting that Erasmus' defense echoes the two arguments used to justify the granting of privileges: the fruits of an individual's labors and the interest of the community. For Erasmus on the dangers of private property, see *Enchiridion*, LB, V, 59F–61B.

12

"Race," Religion, and the Law: Rhetorics of Sameness and Difference in the Work of Hugo Grotius

JANE O. NEWMAN

Ita ubique similia peccantur.
— *Hugo Grotius to L. Camerarius (1635)*

(Re)Locating "Race" in Early Modern Legal Theory

Advocates of recent developments in legal theory such as critical legal studies, feminist legal studies, and critical race theory have argued for taking the racialized and gendered subject into account in analyses of the law. Patricia Williams claims in *The Alchemy of Race and Rights,* for example, that "subject position is everything"; the subtitle of her book, "Diary of a Law Professor," underscores — even as it strategically elides — the ways in which Williams's experience as a black, female subject both is defined by and illuminates a variety of legal institutions.[1] Her occupation of this position allows Williams to critique from a "local" perspective both the apparatus of legal education and a number of legal concepts, such as contract and the right to privacy, that have often been taken to be "objective," universally accessible, and thus race-neutral.

The privileging of the racialized and gendered individual as both the object and the subject of the law belongs to a more general critical move in late twentieth-century legal theory that offers particularized "counterstories" as a way of "comba[ting] the dominant stories" of "traditional legal scholarship." These stories, critics contend, with their interest in systematic legal theory and "legal transcendentals," in doctrine and the abstract logic of the law, efface the relations of power subtended by the discipline in both theory and practice.[2] The use of counterstories to underscore the "salience" of the category of race as a category of *difference,* or *dissimilarity,* in recent critical discussions of the law of course follows from and is in some sense unavoidable in societies "predisposed to develop modes of discourse which reflect historical realities" —in those modern Euro- and Anglo-American societies, in other words, in which the inequities of current political and social relations remind us of their historical involvement in systems of race-based exploitation and victimization.[3] In these contexts, discussions of jurisprudential theory that focus on systematic or rational legal method efface "the race question" when they fail to account for the difference that difference makes in access to or even ways of talking about the law.

In this chapter about European receptions of Ethiopia in the first half of the seventeenth century, I offer counterstories of a somewhat different sort. They are designed to open a window onto the complexity of "race relations" as they were not other than but, rather, intersected with systematic legal and political theory in the early modern period, and thereby to give both historical and generic depth to the critique discussed above. The Ethiopian connection provides a way to begin discussing, first, whether "race" was marked as an indicator of difference and oppositionality in the same ways then as it is today and, second, whether there is not in fact a place for the analysis of "race" in a set of early modern discursive contexts and genres of systematic legal theory that goes beyond those at which scholars have looked to date. For, parallel to the developments in legal study just reviewed, literary scholars and cultural historians of the period have mounted an assault on the only apparently race-neutral traditions of texts and events that they study by focusing on the objectifying treatment of Africans that, to be sure, did characterize the plays, novels, images, and artifacts of the period. Parker and Hendricks's anthology, together with the work of Kim Hall and others, have nevertheless not included analyses of the hierarchies of legal practice and jurisprudential theory in their critiques of the "racial" nature of early modern literature and culture, nor have they acknowledged the existence of alternative, less "othering" discourses about Africa at the time. In the several stories from across a variety of genres that I introduce here, Ethiopia was considered not within the framework of arguments about otherness and difference but, rather, as part of a complex logic of *sameness* that had its origins in the confessional-political conflicts of the time.

That is, even though it was in fact exemplary of resistance to Europe in one instance in particular, the literal geopolitical entity that was Ethiopia appears here not in the context of outlandish claims about barbarism and unknown worlds used (less precisely) in connection with the term *aethiops* to signify Europe's "dark Others," but rather associated with positions familiar within contemporary European debates about the possibility of confessional agreement in an era of religious war, on the one hand, and about the nature of the legal relationship between individual nation-states and "international society," on the other.[4] In both cases, moreover, "racial" arguments from sameness occur not just in the stories I relate in the second section, but also in texts concerned with "legal" and doctrinal "transcendentals." I analyze the role that the rhetoric of sameness and difference played across several genres of theological and legal debate as they are exemplified by the work of the great legal theorist, Hugo Grotius (1583–1645), in sections 3 and 4.[5] I conclude by returning to an example of early modern legal storytelling that deals with events in Ethiopia for the positions in early modern systematic jurisprudential and theological theory that its narrative organization encodes.[6] In this case, stories and theories about "race" coincide.

Grotius' interest in questions of theology and of the law was both theoretical and applied.[7] After finishing university studies begun at the astoundingly precocious age of eleven, Grotius followed the example of his father and uncle, the one a lawyer, the other a professor of law at Leiden, and was already *Advocaat fiscaal* (a kind of public prosecutor and legal adviser) of the States of Holland at twenty-four; by virtue of this position, he was active in several high-profile legal cases on international issues in the first decade of the seventeenth century. His subsequent appointment as the pensionary of Rotterdam by the Remonstrant leader Oldenbarnevelt involved Grotius in the complex and dangerously divisive confessional world of the early modern Dutch Reformed State Church. After the collapse of his political career in his homeland in 1618, precisely because of his association with the Remonstrant cause, and then three years of imprisonment, Grotius was exiled to France in 1621. Employed to what some have argued were rather ineffectual ends as the Swedish ambassador to France for much of the rest of his life, he went on to devote his energies to irenic causes and, as he writes, to "the philosophy of the law, which previously, in public service, I practiced with the utmost degree of probity of which I was capable."[8] The tensions in Grotius' work between "philosophy," or theory, and practical application, or pragmatism, figure in his discussions of the vexed relations between several versions of the sameness-difference divide, in his desire for universal religious accord in the face of the fractious realities of multiple confessions, on the one hand, and in his inventory of the universals of a natural law of reason that sat uneasily alongside the demands for sovereignty of local authorities, on the other.[9] In what follows, I read the rhetorics of sameness and difference as they emerge in Grotius' theology and legal theory for the light they shed on the issue of "race" and law in the early modern period.

"Race": The Ethiopian Connection, Part 1 — Africans in Paris and the New World

In August of 1635, Hugo Grotius makes mention in two letters of the presence of an African in Paris. According to Grotius, the young man, Zaga Christos, claimed that he was the "son of the king of the Abyssinians" (*imperatoris Abyssinorum filium*) of Ethiopia and had been robbed of his rightful place on the throne by his father's brother.[10] Buried at the end of a lengthy letter dated August 2 to Axel Oxenstierna, the imperial chancellor of Sweden, the very brevity of this first reference to Christos helps little in explaining why the great Grotius would have considered the case of the African (a potential impostor, according to some) worth mentioning.

The somewhat more detailed description of the tense political situation in Ethiopia that Grotius includes in his letter of August 9 to Ludwig Camerarius helps explain, if only indirectly, why a senior European diplomat would have taken any notice of an alleged offspring of this particular African royal house.[11] There, Grotius reports to his learned friend the details of his correspondence the previous year (in August 1634) with one Peter Holing (or Heyling) of Lübeck, who had been a member of Grotius' circle in Paris. Holing had left Europe for Africa in order to "spread the word of the teachings of the New Testament throughout the world" ("die Lehre des Evangelii in der Welt auszubreiten").[12] Grotius is more interested in relating Holing's testimony about matters Ethiopian than in giving that of the "native informant," Christos, who appears to be of interest here only because he is now "espousing the Roman religion" ("romanam religionem profitens"). The importance of Christos's conversion from his native Monophysitism becomes clear in Grotius' letter to Camerarius, in which, following Holing, he describes the recent decision of the Ethiopian government to require that everyone — Africans and Europeans alike — who had anything to do with the "foreign" (*externi*) Roman teachings depart from the country "within ten days," and the Abyssinians return to their "ancient customs" (*ad avitos mores*).[13] The reference here is to practices of the Abyssinian church that predated a series of bloody internal religious conflicts with origins reaching back at least into the mid-sixteenth century, when King John of Portugal requested Jesuit assistance in taking up contact with the

African Christians whose church had fallen from "the Catholick Faith in its Purity" after the Council of Chalcedon in 451;[14] the doctrinal decisions taken at Chalcedon had a mighty impact on Ethiopia's place in the international community of Christian nations, as we shall see. That Christos, whose Monophysite royal family had finally defeated the local, Jesuit-inspired opposition in Ethiopia in the early 1630s, was said to have converted to Catholicism was in all likelihood taken as a sign not merely of Rome's spiritual victory in an individual, but also of the possibility that Christos and eventual European supporters could ultimately return to the homeland to reassert Jesuit ways. In 1635, even only virtual, future successes of Catholicism in Africa could be used to propagandizing ends in Europe; it was surely in this respect that Grotius had felt it appropriate to warn Oxenstierna in his report to him the week before about the uses to which Christos's presence in Paris might be put.

In his letter to Camerarius, Grotius casts the relation between Ethiopia and Europe in terms not of difference but of similitude. Holing's report in particular offers proof of the underlying sameness (albeit of a negative sort) between Africa and the West. Grotius writes: "From these same letters I learn that the Christians, by not obeying the pope, the Greeks, by obeying too readily, and the Egyptians, by disputing as vehemently as in the West, disagree among themselves on questions about the natures of Christ and their properties. So everywhere similar sins are committed."[15]

The very same battles over questions of church authority and doctrine that were tearing Europe asunder at the time were thus consuming Europe's "Others" as well. Grotius' rhetorical move of juxtaposition here stands in marked contrast to gestures of "othering" that characterize the negative depictions of the "Moors" discussed by Eldred Jones, for example. Indeed, Grotius does not see these particular Africans as figures of alterity at all. Rather, they resemble the Europeans insofar as all appear to be fighting about the same things.[16]

After 1635, there is no further mention of Zaga Christos in Grotius' correspondence and thus little support for Debrunner's suggestion that they may have met personally.[17] But Grotius' interest in the Ethiopians as carriers of the marks of Christian similarity does not disappear. In an odd little pamphlet entitled *De origine gentium Americanarum dissertatio*, published in 1642, Grotius comments on "whence the people came who inhabited certain lands," in particular the people of the "continent . . . some of us have called America from Vespucius."[18] Using an eclectic selection of genres of evidence, among which protoanthropological observations about religious ritual dominate, Grotius argues that, while some of the "tribes" in America are of "Norse descent," others of German, and still others descend from the "Chinese," the tribes that "possess Yucatan" found their origins in "the transplantation of the colony from Aethiopia into these lands." Grotius mentions that he has "read several of the Spanish, French, British, and Dutch writers who have been in those lands" and names Peter Martyr and the Spaniard Alverez as his sources for his argument about the Ethiopian connection. By publishing his little treatise, Grotius hopes to stir "up others who may possess a greater knowledge of these events . . . either to confirm my conclusions, or to refute them by valid reasoning."

And indeed, Grotius' *De origine* became the subject of a small squall of debate between its author and another Dutchman, Johan De Laet, in later years. In his *Notae ad dissertationem Hugonis Grotii de origine gentium Americanarum, et observationes aliquot ad meliorem indaginem difficillimae illius Quaestionis* (1643), De Laet delivered a polite but firm scholarly trouncing to his famous countryman on nearly every point. Grotius clearly felt obliged to defend his honor and responded with a peevish counterattack in his *De origine gentium Americanarum dissertatio altera,* published that same year. In light of De Laet's accusations, we must consider the significance of Grotius' admission in the 1643 *Dissertatio altera* that he actually had not read "such a quantity of books [on the topic] as [his] detractor"; rather, he admits, he relied on what he calls conjectures (*coniecturas*) to make his claims.[19] These "conjectures" about the Ethiopian connection in America again create a story about an essential sameness between the Ethiopians and this particular New World "race" to complement the one told in the letters in which Grotius mentions Zaga Christos.[20]

The evidence Grotius adduces in his construction of an Ethiopian lineage for the Yucatan peoples suggests that the category of *external* similitude was the primary analytic engine driving his conjecture. Dwelling at length on the practice of circumcision, for example, which had led other scholars to believe that the inhabitants of the Yucatan were originally Jewish, Grotius counters that the Ethiopian practice of circumcision was in fact much more ancient, indeed, "an old practice of the Aethiopians, as Herodotus, before others, has testified . . . [n]or did those of the Aethiopians who became Christians abandon the old practice of their race, as Alverez and others inform us." Grotius' "discovery" (conjecture) of the Ethiopian origins of the Yucatan tribes thus consists in making a claim for a genealogical link on the basis of similar ritual customs, like circumcision, currently practiced by both "races." He continues that the "Aethiopians who came there were Christians," and demonstrates this by means of a lengthy inventory of other religious rituals common to both the Ethiopian and Yucatan peoples, including baptism, the "confession of sins in sickness," extreme unction, and "a firm belief in rewards and punishments after this life."[21] All of these parallels contribute to a story that would prove common "racial" origins primarily by means of the schematic juxtaposition of ritual practices and traditions rather than as a matter of biology or phenotype.[22]

When taken together, Grotius' correspondence with Oxenstierna and Camerarius on Zaga Christos's presence in Paris and the Dutch author's deployment of the topos of the Ethiopians in his *De origine* to construct arguments about similarities between Europe, Africa, and the New World, suggest that these particular Africans, whose "Ethiopian" identity was actual rather than figurative, belonged to a somewhat different category than that of the "dark Others" on which scholarship to date has focused. Used by Grotius in both cases to indicate a logic of continuity rather than one of discontinuity, reference to the Abyssinians of Ethiopia on these several occasions calls attention to his commitment to conjecturing a narrative of sameness out of the fragmentary evidence of shared customs. It is reasonable to suppose that he conceived of the narrative about the common Christianity of disparate peoples as a potentially useful way to counteract the material realities of religious dissent that had both disrupted his life and torn Europe apart for nearly a hundred years. Grotius' commitment to the project of "inventing" ways to mediate conflict by appealing to a logic of sameness of practice is also visible in his theological writings, in which the Ethiopians are, again, present in both overt and "subterranean" ways.[23]

Religion: Sameness and Difference in Grotius' Theological Writings — Dogma, Ritual, and the "Primitive Christians"

Grotius' conjectures about the relationship of the tribes of the Yucatan to Ethiopia are based on shaping evidence of common ritual practices into a narrative of shared genealogies. His brief treatise on the origins of the American peoples belongs to an elaborate set of similar discourses about Ethiopia circulating in Europe, discourses in which the logic that conflated "race" and tradition in his *De origine* supported the assumption that religion could function as a sign of kinship between Christian peoples, including, in this case, Europeans and their African brethren.[24] Since at least the mid-sixteenth century, the story had been told of a return to the ancient origins of the Christian Church and to the pristine religious institutions and rites of "primitive Christianity" as a way of creating a *pax ecclesiastica* out of the ruins of contemporary controversy. The ability of the Ethiopian church in particular to testify to the *consensus quinquesaecularis,* the agreement of the first five centuries of Christianity, was crucial to this narrative about a moment and model of religious unity that could heal the wounds of a suffering "Christian commonwealth" in the here and now of contemporary Europe by recalling the shared

ways of the single "ancient Church" in apostolic times.[25] The Ethiopian Christians thus provided an important link in the creation of a narrative of sameness
both about the ancient *unitas Ecclesiae* and within the early modern Christian
world.[26]

Grotius' commitment to the humanist irenicism of Erasmus, Franciscus
Junius, Georg Calixt, and Isaac Casaubon and his linking of the Ethiopians in
particular with their projects for first inter-Protestant and then potentially also
Protestant-Catholic union are clear in a letter of April 21, 1637, to the Lutheran
missionary Holing. Grotius' first response to Holing's correspondence three
years earlier had consisted primarily of a kind of generic high praise of the
young man for the "magnitudinem" of his soul in undergoing so many "difficulties," or hardships (*incommoda*) in order "to know the status of by far the
most remote of Christian peoples" in Africa;[27] in his second letter to Holing in
1637, however, Grotius is less shy about the dimensions of his project. He
requests that Holing see if he can "scrape together" (*corradere*) as much material as possible connected with the "Christian churches of the East," "old
versions of the Old and New Testaments, liturgies, the decisions of the councils,
both national and international (universal), and declarations of faith," as well
as and especially anything that might serve as the "most ancient signs of
Christianity among the Abyssinians" ("quaenam sint antiquissima chris-
tianismi apud Abyssinos indicia"), from the time of Constantine or even before.
Indeed, if Holing "stumbles upon" them, Grotius would appreciate his sending
him any examples of their "rules, ordinations, titles, and last, [whatever] per-
tains to the entire governance of their church."[28] In this same month, Grotius
corresponds, moreover, several times with N. C. Fabry de Peiresc concerning a
manuscript "en langue Aethiopienne" reputed to be a copy of the Book of
Enoch that had belonged to the Old Testament canon of the ancient Ethiopian
church.[29]

Grotius thus seems to have become interested in the Ethiopians and their
texts insofar as they could provide models for uniformity in religious practice.
This same principle subtended most of his theological writings; if sameness of
belief was not present in the here and now, it could be discursively produced in
texts that used evidence of common practices to create a narrative of shared
first principles. We find such a narrative at the center of Grotius' theological
writings in one of his least-read but most important texts, *Meletius sive de iis
quae inter Christianos conveniunt epistola,* which was composed in approximately 1611.[30] The argument from sameness lies at the very heart of this
"letter on the points of agreement between Christians"; its purpose is to describe those principles which transcend the less essential points of discord
whose particularities were fueling the dangerous contentions not only be-

tween Catholics and Protestants, but in and among the various Reformed churches as well.[31] The desire to identify the "fundamental" and "necessary" essentials of religious agreement contends in *Meletius* with the need to admit difference into the very heart of the economy of unanimity it is designed to construct. Ironically, this difference must be allowed to exist at the level of external practices, the very level at which Grotius would later argue he found evidence of religious kinship among the peoples of the Yucatan. The principle of difference to which Grotius refers in his *Meletius* calls up the example of the original union between diverse Christian "sects," the existence of which the case of the ancient Ethiopian church proves.[32] It is the Ethiopians who can heal the wounds introduced by diversity; in this capacity, they play a key role in the logic of confessional sameness once again.

The poetic conceit of *Meletius* (1611) is that of a conversation between Grotius and an unnamed scholar about the wise thoughts of the learned Greek scholar Meletius Pegas (1549–1601), patriarch of Constantinople after 1590.[33] Grotius describes Meletius as a man who "loved peace among Christians so much that he could not refrain from tears when execrating our dissensions," and claims that his short, systematic text contains a summary of Meletius' understanding of "the points of consensus between the Christians" that might function as a way of doing away with the fierceness with which Christians had come to "contemplate one another" in recent years."[34] "From the moment that the Christian name had become widespread," the "disease" of disagreement, factionalism, and rivalry had infected so many that even "wars [had been] started under no other pretext than that of the very religion whose purpose is peace." The most important goal is to "remember our almost forgotten *kinship*" (emphasis added). Grotius defines this kinship earlier in the text as that which unites us (*coniungit*), the things that are, in other words, the same "among the Christians" (*ta tois christianois homologoumena*). Grotius' much later argument about the more literal kinship between the Ethiopians and some of the inhabitants of the New World "racializes" the origins of the homologies cited as part of a systematic theological logic here.

Grotius' "report" on Meletius' explanation of basic similarities among Christians is an example of what James Boyd White has called constitutive rhetoric.[35] Grotius moves rapidly out of the narrative frame story of the text into its systematic substance; the treatise is designed to create, rather than merely report, the "points of agreement" and contractual logic necessary for guaranteeing a harmonious community in an age of blatant confessional discord. Following Seneca, who followed Cicero, Grotius distinguishes at the outset between the "dogmas" and "ethical precepts," *decreta* and *praecepta,* the "principles and rules" of the Christian religion.[36] The treatise is divided nearly evenly between the two; the ways in which Grotius negotiates the relation between the abstract principles on which all Christians agree, on the one hand, and the practical tensions between differing religious groups, on the other, reveals the ways in which he will subsequently develop his theories of a kind of supranational natural law within the context of a world of multiple, autonomous states.[37] The inventory of decreta includes such principles as that there is "only one God," that "God is most simple, infinite, and best," that man "has the faculty of free choice," yet can also "deviate from God's law," and that there is "remission and reparation of sins." When Grotius moves on to the rules (*praecepta*), he describes what he characterizes as "*external* commands pertaining" (emphasis added) to the "cult of God," to religious gatherings and services, and to men's *officia* vis-à-vis other men. At the outset, Grotius suggests a certain degree of continuity between decreta and praecepta. Theory leads, providing, it would seem, the uniform basis of subsequent practice; "in every practical science," he writes, "the principles . . . should either incite to action or to some extent make clear what must be done and how it must be done."[38] The unity created through adherence to dogma, or decreta, is based on their universal truth, the guarantors of which are Scripture in its unity, antiquity, and simplicity as well as the "perfect example set by Christ"; the Holy Spirit in turn "incit[es]" men to respect these truths. "Rules," or praecepta, also participate in a "homologic" of unity, but their guarantor is the consensus ("omnium gentium . . . consensus") associated with them; they are thus authorized by the fact that they are common practices that can be observed "among Christians" (*apud Christianos*). If there is conformity in theory, there will be unity in practice as well.

And yet, as Grotius points out in the final section of *Meletius,* again in the voice of the "venerable Patriarch," the theory and practice of Christianity rely on different methods of achieving unity. In the end, this difference shifts the relation between decreta and praecepta to one in which practice rather than theory leads. The reversal suggests links to the pragmatic ways in which "kinship" is created in the *De origine gentium Americanarum.* Most controversy between Christians occurs over issues of dogma (*decreta*), Grotius writes; the "remedy for this disease" is to limit "the number of necessary articles of faith to those few that are the most self evident."[39] Wolf and others have identified Grotius' commitment to the well-known debate concerning the essentials and inessentials, the "dogmata ad salutem necessaria" and the "dogmata . . . non necessaria," of Christianity as the backbone of his irenic project; in the first part of *Meletius* he clearly understands part of his task to be the production of this remedy in a "minimalist" cataloguing of the decreta.[40] As far as the realm of praecepta is concerned, however, Grotius continues, difference is managed in a different and, in the end, more effective way. To be sure, he attempts to articulate universal "Christian laws" on celebration of the Sabbath, behavior in war, matrimony, and keeping one's word.[41] But if there is a "fight over praecepta," Grotius suggests, "a short cut to concord is to leave every man to his own discretion" (*suo arbitrio*); in such matters, everybody "establishes [precepts] for himself for the sake of preserving order."[42] The freedom that Grotius gives individuals here to arrange their practice as they see fit, provided that intersubjective, social "order" is preserved, suggests a model of numerous local inflections of a single principle, a model of fundamental sameness built on the toleration of second-order difference. The only way to guarantee harmony among Christians in matters of doctrine, it would seem, would be to rely on the strategies for *concordia* that work so well in the case of praecepta. And indeed, the text of *Meletius* carries out this solution to the problem of religious dispute.

In a crucial passage in the epilogue to *Meletius,* in which Grotius summarizes his views of Christian decreta and praecepta, of dogma and ethics, the mechanisms for achieving "concord" in the case of praecepta are effortlessly absorbed into the logic of decreta. The abstract logic of universal agreement can be guaranteed only by the toleration of local custom and difference. The passage is worth quoting in full:

> Now, when there is a fight over precepts, it hardly ever involves ethics — for these have definite and unequivocal rules — but deals with those matters which everybody establishes for himself for the sake of preserving order, and in which a short cut to accord is to leave every man to his discretion. What could be more foolish than the Spartans and the Athenians waging war against Greek city-states, the former to impose their government by aristocracy, the latter to yield everything into the hands of the people. Among the Christians, there are similar occurrences. For how often did not at some time in the past dissensions arise from the fact that Easter was celebrated on different days by different people? Irenaeus sensibly wrote to the Roman bishop Victor: "What? Can we not live in concord even though they perform their rites while we do ours? Some fast on the fortieth day, others for the period of two days, some for four, or ten, or fifteen, or twenty, or forty days, and concord is preserved notwithstanding." *Many controversies over dogmas [decreta] are merely due to words which must be avoided for consensus to appear.* With any further quarrels we have to check whether they concern matters which it is necessary to know.[43]

The paragraph begins by addressing the category and details of praecepta. Here, as noted above, the toleration of difference is the "shortcut to accord." Grotius nevertheless go on to conclude the argument very clearly on the level of dogma. The technical term *decreta* is used, and the suggestion is that here too, consensus can be achieved here also only by "leav[ing] every man to his own discretion," indeed, to his own language, or "words." That theory should follow practice here represents a major reversal from Grotius' claim at the beginning of the text that "principles . . . should either incite to action or to some extent make clear what must be done." That this new sequence, based on a balance between universal agreement and diversity, could provide a more reasonable alternative, is demonstrated by the example to which Grotius' words about the "avoidance of controversy" implicitly refer, namely, a moment in the history of Christianity when a point of common agreement had been impossible to translate — literally and figuratively — into local usage. Had local practice been tolerated at the time, unity in doctrine could have been achieved. To understand how this moment offers proof of Grotius' shortcut solution in his time and place, it is necessary to excavate the *Meletius* text at the point where it refers to controversial words.

Throughout the fifth century, debates about the human and divine attributes of Christ were fiercely waged; these disputes were finally settled at the Council of Chalcedon in 451, and universal doctrine was declared by Bishop Leo I of Rome. His articulation of the identity of Christ as consisting "of two natures" (*en duo physeis*) that existed "asynchytos, atreptos adiairetos, and achoristos" in "one person" (*prosopon*) was nevertheless one with which many, including members of the Abyssinian church in Ethiopia, could not agree.[44] The basis of this disagreement was, nevertheless, not a case of theory being unable to regulate external actions but rather precisely the opposite — namely, a case in which local (linguistic) custom had not been allowed to exist alongside, or even produce, universal doctrinal accord. Johann Michaelis, the eighteenth-century biographer of Holing, explains the re-emergence of this "ancient" controversy in the early modern period in this way: in their discussions of a possible rapprochement with Rome in the 1630s, Ethiopian church authorities recalled the disagreement over Christ's nature at Chalcedon that had caused their original exclusion from the Church and argued at meetings that they would have to "demur as far as the much disputed and severely misunderstood word 'nature' [*physis*] was concerned. For," according to Michaelis, the Abyssinians "take [this word, *nature*] to mean 'person' and thus think that, if they were to profess that there were two 'natures' in Christ, there would also be two 'persons' or Christs." According to Abyssinian belief, however, Christ is "entirely divine and entirely and truly man" ("vollkommen Gott und vollkommen oder wahrer Mensch") in one nature, hence "monophysite."[45] Thus the claims made at Chalcedon, if translated into their language, would be heretical, even in Leo's own terms; many in the eastern Church in Egypt and Syria agreed and characterized the Chalcedonians as heretics. Thereafter followed the split which Grotius sought to undo.

Under the conditions that prevailed at Chalcedon, then, the only way to have preserved doctrinal purity and Christian kinship would have been to admit linguistic difference and local systems of meaning, as Grotius suggests, looking away from "words" entirely to recapture the intention of doctrine as it had been agreed on in "ancient," pre-Chalcedon times. His recommendation in *Meletius* that "words . . . be avoided for consensus to appear" thus conjures up the very case in which a nontoleration of local linguistic difference had meant the collapse of what had originally been "universal" religious accord. The argument for sameness collides with the necessity for difference here and has the effect of reversing the sequence of theory and practice, of decreta and praecepta, articulated at the outset. Were pragmatic *externa* to have taken precedence at Chalcedon, the logic of the passage suggests, and dogma to have followed, the unity of theory and practice in ancient times would have been preserved. As it is, this unity has to be reconstructed in the here and now in the conjectured system of agreement created by the "minimalist" rhetoric of *Meletius,* repairing the rift in the Christian network and rejoining the Rome and the East, the European and the African churches.

In *Meletius* as well as in other important irenicist theological theory, Grotius makes it clear that he is aware of the dangers that the toleration of difference introduces into an argument for universal accord; precisely the existence of multiple subgroups, each with its own set of beliefs and practices, could be said to account for the religious strife most characteristic of the political and military events of the age.[46] The text of *Meletius* was designed to navigate these dangerous waters by providing a systematized "story" of religious accord. The consensus-building work that Grotius' theological writings perform displays parallels with those of his legal writings that concern the relationship between natural law, the *jus gentium,* and local jurisdiction, texts in which he addresses precisely the issue of how to institute uniform international interaction, or contact between different powers and states, in an era when such contact consisted primarily, if not exclusively, in acts of war.[47] In turning now to an examination in his most famous legal text, *On the Law of War and Peace* (*De jure belli ac pacis,* 1625), of similar tensions between abstract principles of sameness and the realities of difference, my purpose is to show how these two discourses, theology and the law, were part of a single project for Grotius. The case of Ethiopia, "racialized" in my account so far as an indicator of an original and potentially also future Christian sameness (rather than as Europe's Other), falls away, or, perhaps better, goes underground and resurfaces in the guise of the principle of local political and legal autonomy that is everywhere present in Grotius' legal theory. The pressure that this principle ultimately brings to bear on Grotius' system of natural law will allow me to conclude with a closer examination of events in Ethiopia from precisely this point of view—as an example, that is, of a country enacting its right to sovereign statehood within the international community of nations. Ethiopia's ability to enact this right—and to be recognized as doing so legitimately—indicates not its difference from similarly autonomous European polities but rather its "racial" identity with them.

Law: (Global) Sociability Versus (Local) Sovereignty— Natural Law, the Jus Gentium, and Municipal Law

Like many before him, Grotius distinguishes in *De jure belli ac pacis* between *jus ad bellum* and *jus in bello,* between the law as it concerns the justice of reasons for going to war and the law as it concerns wartime behavior. These two issues were, it is safe to say, among the main concerns of international legal proceedings at the time.[48] Hedley Bull has nevertheless claimed that, in spite of his attempt to distinguish them from one another in a systematic way in *De jure,* Grotius considered the link between these two kinds of legal reasoning to be crucial, for the legitimacy of behavior in war could also be attested to through reference to the justness of the reasons for which the war had been declared in the first place. This kind of tension between, yet ultimate resolution of, competing levels and definitions of justice runs throughout Grotius' famous book, and it is nowhere more in evidence than in the dialectic between global and local forms of legality that he explores. Scholars have argued that the tension between the authority of general versus particular legal systems in Grotius' work is the result of his attempt to reconcile two different forms of the law and levels of "international relations," the one an "idealist" "law of nature," theorists of which aimed at articulating those fundamental principles, such as sociability (the *appetitus societatis*), which derive from the universal reason, unite mankind, and can be abstracted into a kind of "rational jurisprudence," and the other, the "realist" "law of nations" (*jus gentium*), which, complexly defined in terms of both unwritten custom and the human will behind local traditions of positive law, in general concerned "the locus of human social experience."[49] While a necessary precondition for the possibility of international cooperation and understanding, the latter is of course premised on the existence of multiple sovereign states, each with its own needs.[50] Yet, precisely because of the realities of rampant international strife legitimated by ideologies of religious and political state sovereignty, Grotius and his generation understood that "the welfare of mankind" required the construction of a minimum of common first principles by which all would agree to abide.[51] The construction of a legal system of "objective" and even "scientific" dimensions equally applicable to all may thus be understood as part of a politics that sought to navigate between the global and local levels and ideologies of political identity in conflict at the time.[52]

The role of local legal autonomy, or difference, is initially somewhat elusive in *De jure belli ac pacis,* for it appears at the outset that Grotius deliberately defines it as inappropriate to the theoretical and rhetorical task at hand. The Prolegomena, for example, contains Grotius' definitions of the origins and dimensions of the two legal systems, natural law and the jus gentium, respectively, in which he claims to be most interested. He uses the illustration of the current "lack of restraint in relation to war" to distinguish between these forms of the law, which are "concerned with the mutual relations among states," and local "municipal law"; the latter is self-interested and, for that reason, legitimately permissive of "unjust" war. His treatise will address, he asserts, the prerogatives of the former, which he claims must be guided by a naturally present "impelling desire for society" on the part of human beings that guarantees the safety of both the other and the self.[53]

Grotius claims, then, that he seeks in *De jure belli ac pacis* always to "distinguish" between the *jus naturae* and the jus gentium, on the one hand, and municipal law, on the other; the study of "true justice . . . treats the parts of natural and unchangeable philosophy of law" that, "since they are always the same, can easily be brought into a systematic form."[54] The congeniality of these first two to a systematic presentation marks the treatise as a matter, again, of "constitutive rhetoric" in this respect, namely that it is a legal narrative told as system rather than as story. Indeed, because the elements of "positive" or applied law and legal decisions "undergo change and are different in different places," each of which would have to be narrated in turn, Grotius writes that they are "outside the domain" of those forms of law capable of "rational" presentation in textual form. He must thus look away from all local inflections of conflict or law, all "controversies of our own times, either those that have arisen or those which can be foreseen as likely to arise," for, "just as mathematicians treat their figures as abstracted from bodies, so in treating law," he will withdraw his "mind from every particular fact."[55] Yet, in the very terms in which Grotius invokes "geometrical" theory, we can discern the important place of local bodies in his text.[56]

Early on in his defense of the innovation that his treatise represents, for example, Grotius claims that all previous theorists of the law not only have not "dealt with the subject-matter as a whole" but also have "done their work without system."[57] His "system" will be that, again, of an experimental scientist: "I have made it my concern to refer the proofs of things touching the law of nature to certain fundamental conceptions which are beyond question. . . . For the principles of that law . . . are in themselves manifest and clear, almost as evident as are those things which we perceive by the external senses; and the senses do not err if the organs of perception are properly formed and if the other conditions requisite to perception are present" (23, Prolegomena). The will to a scientific method is everywhere apparent here; yet, the "proof" of the existence of this "law of nature" will have to be derived, he claims, from the *materia externa* that allow the legal "scientist" to conjecture a principle inherent in them that is the fundamental law.[58] Here, the *externa* are not the materials of empirical observation, however, but, as he writes, "the testimony of philosophers, historians, poets, finally, also of orators" (Prolegomena, 23). The "matter" of history thus constitutes the ground of Grotius' scientific system, thereby endowing the local with a certain priority in the construction of his global system.

The elaborate inventory of sources used in the Prolegomena and the plethora of marginal references and notes throughout *De jure belli ac pacis* indicate the encyclopedic origins of Grotius' "universals" in positive ancient and early modern legal practice and events. Myriad references to legal decisions by the Romans jostle up against invocations of the example of the ancient Hebrews, Athenians, Egyptians, and Persians; more than once the phrase "and histories everywhere teach"[59] dislodges (or, perhaps better, refines) the logic of natural necessity. Indeed, even as he writes — and revises — his text, new "historical" evidence of the fundamental principles of law is accruing: "While I am writing these words, a judgement to that effect was rendered in the higher chamber at Paris, under the presidency of Nicholas of Verdun," Grotius inserts at one point.[60] The diversity of his sources and the textual simultaneity of diverse cultures, systems, and times that Grotius uses in constructing his system are converted into a sign of "universal" sameness, to be sure: "When many at different times, and in different places, affirm the same thing as certain, that ought to be referred to as a universal cause; and this cause, in the lines of inquiry which we are following, must be either a correct conclusion drawn from the principles of nature, or common consent. The former points to the law of nature; the latter, to the law of nations."[61] But his breadth of research and the extent of his learning also reveal Grotius' awareness of the realities of legal localism and force him to recognize a counter-point to his universalist claims in positive law. This localism and its principles consistently interrupt the "story" of natural law and the jus gentium that scholars have claimed is told by this famously "rational" nine-hundred-page treatise.[62]

An ongoing battle between statements of the abstract principles of international relations derived from natural law and the jus gentium, on the one hand, and an acquiescence to the priority of the prerogatives of local government and municipal law, on the other, rages throughout the massive *De jure belli ac pacis.*[63] Grotius' much-attacked articulation of the inviolable rights of sovereigns, for example, constitutes not only one of the most obvious instances of the logic of localism in *De jure belli ac pacis* but also one of its very cornerstones. The better part of book 1 is devoted to the discussion of questions of local sovereignty and the maintenance of relations of power within single states — that is, among those "who associate themselves together . . . to form a civil society."[64] Yet even in international affairs such as war, it is the role of the sovereign that takes center stage: "In order that a war may be formal . . . on both sides it [must] be waged under the authority of the one who holds the sovereign power in the state."[65] Some critics cite Grotius' claim about the sovereign's absolute right to declare war as evidence of a contradiction in his system; a bad prince may declare war unjustly. In admitting that "sovereign power is a righteous thing even though it is held by a wicked man," however, Grotius places sovereignty above justice in this regard.[66] "We are to look upon public authorities as if they had been established by God himself," he writes.[67]

The transcendent logic of the local forces itself onto the stage of Grotius' "objective" and "rational" legal theory everywhere in the text. There are numerous instances in his elaborate investigation of both jus ad bellum and jus in bello in which, for example, in the face of a conflict between either the universal law of nature or the law of nations, on the one hand, and local jurisdiction, on the other, priority is awarded to the principle and power of municipal law. "According to the law of nature," he writes on the topic of "things that belong to men in common, "a man is free to hunt [wild] animals": "When, however, municipal law has laid down a different rule, the law of nature itself prescribes that this must be obeyed. . . . Thus, through exercise of the power which belongs to it, municipal law can by anticipation prevent an acquisition of ownership which by the law of nature might have been permitted."[68]

Similarly, "the right to acquire movable things [that exists, in fact, by permission of the law of nature] can be prevented by municipal law," and "so far as the law of nations is concerned, the right of killing . . . slaves, that is, captives taken in war, is not precluded at any time, although it is restricted, now more, now less, by the laws of states."[69] Indeed, the only fundamental (natural) principle articulated here appears to be that, where there are "special effects of municipal law" that have "nothing in common with the law of nature or the law of nations," it is "natural that they should be observed in the places where they are in force."[70] Grotius clearly did not intend to provide a catalogue of the "statutes of [individual] states, for that would be an endless task."[71] Rather, it is the first principle of recognizing the constraints placed on the "legal transcendentals" of nature by the "diversity" and "variation in pacts, laws, and customs" in human civil society that slowly comes to light in his text.[72] Recognizing such diversity of practice is of course the inevitable outcome of a practice of encyclopedic research such as the one on which Grotius' text relies; along with the inquiry into the sameness of "sociable" principles comes evidence of the variety of social practice.

Grotius does attempt in book 3 of *De jure belli ac pacis* to reintroduce a kind of leveling, moral law that would transcend the particularisms that dominate the legal economies of his book.[73] The series of chapters on moderation of behavior in war, for example, states explicitly that, although sacking, devastation, and destruction are permitted as acts of war by the law of nations, it is an "obligation of humaneness not to make the fullest use of one's right."[74] Moreover, although "according to the strict law of nations a hostage can be put to death, . . . [it] is not in accord with moral justice" to do so.[75] The high moral tone of these chapters and Grotius' attempt to recuperate a law and set of principles that unite mankind by standing above the local are nevertheless unmasked when he points out that it is in a sense a matter of self-interest and "prudence" to engage in such "act[s] of humanity."[76] If there is a choice to be made between following theory as dictated by an ethics consonant with the law of nature, and practice as legitimated by local needs, customs, and pragmatic concerns, Grotius' system appears to guarantee that the latter will in most instances prevail; or, if that is too strong, the priority of local jurisdiction in matters of international conflict will at least be acceptable within the system that he offers in his book.

The competition in *De jure belli ac pacis* between Grotius' desire to establish a form of law that had its origins in the permanencies of reason or nature, and his need to acknowledge that the rule of law respected at the time was for the most part the one enacted at the level of the individual nation, kingdom, or state, has confronted many scholars of his work and its legacy with a dilemma based on a set of false choices. How can we understand the coexistence of the toleration of difference within a coherent system of "objective" principles to be applied and accepted uniformly by all? Indeed, which interpretation more accurately reflects the Grotian agenda, that he favored a theory of international relations that would work categorically against the possibility of war, which he clearly hated so much, by developing suprastate principles on which nations in conflict could agree, or that he helped construct an "objective" definition of "just war" that recognized, and even permitted, war and the cruelty and destruction that accompanied it, on the basis of positive local exigencies and law? Indeed, could acknowledgment of the legitimacy of local rights peacefully coexist with the mandate to heed supra- and international law when the two were in conflict, and if so, at what level and in what way, either for Grotius or for the theorists of international law who followed him?

The example of early modern Ethiopia is once again useful by way of conclusion, for it illustrates how the apparent contradiction between two ideas was understood at the time: on the one hand, the notion that all nations and parties must conform to a single set of principles and laws and, on the other, the principle that demands for local autonomy and respect for diverse traditions must be acknowledged.

Revisiting "Race": The Ethiopian Connection, Part 2

Even though we know from his letter to Camerarius of 1635 that Grotius was familiar with contemporary Ethiopia, he does not appear to have written any specific commentary on the legal principles undergirding the arguments used by the Ethiopians in the early 1630s to address the tensions between their own government and the agents of a foreign government and institution, namely the Portuguese and the Jesuit order. Yet these arguments find a comfortable berth in a logic of international relations that would allow — indeed, rely upon — recognizing state sovereignty as a way of providing the conditions for the resolution of conflict, a logic that seems very familiar after reading *De jure belli ac pacis* for the subtext of localism. The arguments the Ethiopians used to expel the Jesuits from their country can be said to have had their origins in an idea of local sovereignty of the kind that Grotius felt should be permitted to compete with universalist and internationalist claims (in this case, those of the Catholic Church), and indeed to take precedence over them. The Africans, in this case, were thus resolutely and unmistakably opposed to "European" expectations — but opposed on the basis of European theories of local sovereignty, which scholars of race during the early modern period have not touched on to date. Indeed, at least one early modern account characterized the Ethiopians as adopting a rhetoric of political legitimacy. The author of that account, the Pietist theologian and Orientalist Johann Michaelis (1668–1738), describes the essential principles on which the Ethiopians insisted as including both the privilege of local custom and, not surprisingly, the inheritance by the Ethiopian church of the mantle of "primitive Christianity." No contradiction lay, then, in the argument that international conflict might be solved by giving precedence to local authority and traditions, especially when that localism appeared to exemplify an original, universal religious accord.

In his book *The Remarkable Life of Mr. Peter Heyling of Lübeck, and His Travels to Ethiopia (Sonderbarer Lebens-Lauff Herrn Peter Heylings, Aus Lübec, und dessen Reise nach Ethiopien,* 1714), Michaelis tells the story of the travels to Africa by Peter Holing, whom we will remember as one of Grotius' correspondents. Less a travelogue than a biography formulated as politico-religious history and commentary, the text relies on much the same logic of sameness in its discussion of Ethiopia as did Grotius' letter to Camerarius. At the very outset of his book, for example, Michaelis calls attention to the parallels between the "bloody wars" (*blutige Kriege*) "not only here at home in Germany between Catholics and Protestants, but also in Abyssinia between the Roman Catholics and the Ethiopian Christians." Although the text does include a detailed account of Holing's background and the various stations of his education and life, his biography takes a clear backseat to Michaelis's rendering of the background and conditions of the current political conflicts in Ethiopia, beginning with an account of its history as an "ancient Christian nation" (*uhralte Christliche Nation*) in the fourth century and ending with the political battles fought there with the Portuguese Catholics in the first half of the seventeenth century. The story of Peter Holing's life in fact begins only after eighty dense pages of historical detail. The two parts of the text tell the same story from two different perspectives, however, a story about what we may identify as Grotian principles at work in early modern international relations as they informed contemporary politico-theological disputes.

In the first part of his text, Michaelis describes the controversies of the early seventeenth century between the Ethiopian Monophysites and the Jesuits (*Patres Societatis*) as a matter of conflict between foreign infiltrators and a local people who, "following the ancient custom of the primitive Christians" ("nach uhralter Gewohnheit der ersten Christen"), had, until the advent of the Jesuits, organized their local practices (including circumcision, now practically a topos in discussions of Ethiopia) and religious observance "according to local custom" (*aus LandesGewohnheit*). The conflation of current Ethiopian practices with the uncorrupted ways of the ancient Church places Michaelis's text well within the tradition of stories about this African nation.[77] Michaelis pays great attention to the debates between the Monophysite nobility and clergy and one Prince Susneus (called Susnejos in other accounts), who came to power in 1607 after a dynastic struggle with his nephew, Jacob, for the throne of Ethiopia; Susneus was initially an ally of the Jesuits and the Portuguese. The Monophysite camp, with the support of the Ethiopian people, opposed the radical and sometimes violent measures — including the banning of the Ethiopian liturgy in church services and the suppression of the use of the "old Ethiopian Bible" — that had been taken by Susneus' government to efface the old ways. "It would be better," Michaelis reports that the nobles argued, "in those matters in which the substance of religion (*die Substanz der religion*) was not threatened, to allow the old ways and customs (*die alten Gebräuche*) to stand."[78] Otherwise, mass unrest and revolution against the government and its foreign supporters might occur.

In these words, we hear echoes of Grotius' argument in *Meletius* for the tolerance of difference at the level of *praecepta* as the "shortest way to peace." Michaelis characterizes Susneus' ultimate capitulation to the demands of his people and of the Monophysite church as the attainment of a "freedom of religion" that not only permits them to return to their "old customs" but allows their government to function autonomously, free of the pressure to conform to imperial expectations and European codes.[79] When Susneus died in 1632, his son, Basilides, inherited the throne and immediately ordered all Jesuits to leave the country. This is the action Grotius reported to Camerarius. Local sovereignty, established by both the expulsion of foreign nationals and the granting of permission to reassume traditional ways, triumphs in a practical sense here. The principles are familiar ones to readers of Grotius, and the African nation occupies not a position of otherness but rather one of concurrence with the legal logic that the Dutchman devised.

Michaelis goes on to relate the contents of a lengthy letter by the new king, Basilides, that explains why the Ethiopians have resisted the Jesuits and their ways; again, his logic recapitulates that of Grotius in his *Meletius* of nearly twenty years earlier. It was not so much a matter of disagreement on the doctrine of the two natures of Christ, the king maintains; on this, all Christians fundamentally agree. Rather, at issue was the way in which the Europeans had sought to force change in the *externa*, in performance of church ceremonies, the church calendar, and even the "rules of the monastic orders" — for example, in the Ethiopian church.[80] In these actions, the Jesuits had followed what proved to be a false — and foolish — logic of sameness; similar practices neither indicated nor sufficed to produce a fundamental kinship or underlying unity of belief. In a reversal of both the traditional argument and historical record, Michaelis reports that Basilides claimed that his people had never fundamentally opposed the stance that Christ was both divine and mortal; rather, they resented the imposition of Catholic ways on their local practices; expelling the Jesuits was the only way to have their traditional practices and "old ways" restored. Michaelis informs his readers that violence continued in Ethiopia from 1632 through approximately 1645, as the Jesuits resisted the local government's determination to readopt local custom by any means necessary.[81] Even though he describes the execution of one Jesuit sympathizer in detail, in general Michaelis appears to have preferred not to elaborate (*nicht umständlich erzehlen*) about those intervening years.[82] He chooses instead to move directly on to the account of Holing's life. The author may have decided to place the historico-political account before the biography to provide some background for the situation that appears to have drawn Holing, a young idealist, to travel throughout the Holy Lands and into Ethiopia in the 1630s.

But given the way he tells the story of Holing's role in the events that followed the expulsion of the Jesuits there, it may well be that Michaelis also had in mind to underscore his point about the power of local custom with a more personal tale.

In the second part of his text, Michaelis relates Holing's background, his association with the circle around Grotius in Paris, and his decision to "spread the teachings of the New Testament throughout the world" as part of a plan to introduce Protestantism to Christians outside of Europe.[83] Michaelis refers to another text that gives a detailed account of the Lutheran's activities in Ethiopia, *A Brief Account of the Rebellions and Bloudshed Occasioned by the Anti-Christian Practices of the Jesuits and other Popish Emissaries in the Empire of Ethiopia* (1678), attributed to Johann Michael Wansleben. This account and Michaelis's reliance on it tell us somewhat more about why it was important for Michaelis to include Holing's individualized story in his account of the general political and theological principles at work in the disputes in Ethiopia at the time. According to the Wansleben text, and Michaelis seconds it, Holing traveled throughout the Near East, where he learned Hebrew, Arabic, and Greek. He settled for a time in Cairo, where he was perfectly positioned to accompany the new Ethiopian metropolitan, Arminius, appointed by the patriarch of Alexandria, to take over the leadership of the Abyssinian church after the expulsion of the Jesuits in 1637. Once in Ethiopia, Holing became a great favorite of the court, opened a school for the sons of the nobility, and proved his integrity by initially refusing the riches with which the king would have rewarded him. Once accepted by the Ethiopians, however, the Lutheran apparently began to set his plan into action, by convincing the king that "all of those deplorable troubles wherein his Dominions had been so often involved . . . were solely occasioned by the Jesuits and Popish Emissaries"; thus, he (Holing) would advise that a "Penal Law" be established "against all people of Europe . . . forebidding any person bearing the native distinction of a white Complexion to enter his Territories upon pain of death." The irony of the situation — that this law against European intervention in Ethiopia was established by Basilides's council at the behest of a European — is of course apparent. The account of Holing's intervention in local politics nevertheless simply underscores his reputation for attempting to manipulate Ethiopian affairs even as he is being praised for attempting to spread the (Protestant) Word.[84]

Holing is subsequently accused of overstepping precisely the boundaries that would guarantee local political sovereignty in Grotius' system when Holing declares "divers Abissina Customes . . . as repugnant to true Religion and the Holy Scriptures"[85] and forbids his students to practice certain customary religious rites.[86] Although there appears to have been considerable debate about what Holing actually said and did, Michaelis and Wansleben agree that he rapidly fell into disfavor and was subsequently expelled or asked to leave the king's "Dominions." Wansleben reports he was killed by greedy "Turkish pasha" as soon as he left Ethiopia; Michaelis claims, however, that Holing's fate is unknown and that he may have lived quite a bit longer in other parts of the East. It is nevertheless clear from both accounts of the end of Holing's tenure at the Ethiopian court that it was precisely his dismissal of local custom and his failure to acknowledge Basilides' sovereignty that provoked the local authorities to order his departure. Even though Michaelis appears unwilling to condemn Holing outright for his acts, the point of telling his story — and including references to the much more detailed Wansleben account — is that for hostilities to be avoided, it would have been necessary for both the Jesuits and Holing to show respect for differences in local Ethiopian practices. Local powers will step in — and, in this case, did — to guarantee such respect and to defend local sovereignty. The organization of Michaelis's text makes it clear that the Ethiopians and their church provided an example not of an "inferior race" subject to "Eurocentric" hierarchies of aesthetic, political, or ideological value but rather of the legitimacy — at the level of both principle and story — of defending one's own customs, institutions, and political identity against intrusions by foreign states, individuals, and "causes," Catholic and Protestant alike.

Both Michaelis's and Wansleben's accounts of Holing's sojourn in Ethiopia and his interaction with the local governmental and church powers may seem like little more than exotic reports from the far reaches of early modern European political and legal culture. Yet precisely as stories, they effectively recreate the positions developed in more systematic form in Grotius' treatises on theology and the law. These several varieties of early modern legal story telling offer a somewhat different picture of the way Europe's African Others were represented in the early modern period than do those which have been most visible in scholarship to date. In a variety of genres and texts, the Ethiopians function as defenders of Christian unity and agents of international legal maturity as they fight to preserve their religious traditions. A rhetoric of sameness rather than a rhetoric of difference appears to characterize these particular "racialized" subjects within the complex legal and theological cultures of the early modern world.

Notes

1. Williams, *Alchemy*, 3.

2. On "counterstories," see Farber and Sherry, "Legal Storytelling," 47 and 37. The term "legal transcendentals" is Kelley's in *Human Measure*, 212.

3. Ratcliffe, "Conceptualizing," 8–9.

4. On the distinction between the idea of an "international system" exemplified by the empire and the Church, for example, and the new concept of an "international society" of nation-states that was emerging at the time, see Bull, "Importance of Grotius," 75.

5. Bull, "Importance of Grotius," 65, cites Martin Wight's description of the "baroque thickets" of Grotius' work, "where profound and potent principles lurk in the shade of forgotten arguments, and obsolete examples lie like violets beneath gigantic overgrown rhododendrons." Given the immensity and complexity of his writings, I have selected several of Grotius' texts as exemplary of the arguments I make here.

6. I am particularly interested in the case of Ethiopia because of its actual location in Africa and its figurative association with the cultural construction of "otherness" that has been so widely discussed by the mentioned scholars of race in the Renaissance. I want to make clear, however, that the analyses I provide here are not designed as a polemic against the studies of the politics and poetics of "race" in the early modern period that have been undertaken to date.

7. For useful overviews of Grotius' biography, see Bull, "Importance of Grotius," 67–70; Roelofsen, "Grotius"; and Tuck, *Philosophy and Government,* 154–201.

8. See Grotius, *De jure,* 21.

9. The tension between the competing methods of abstract forms of legal reasoning and the historical, more "humanistic" textual strategies and historical knowledge that he deployed in the composition of his best-known legal text, the *De jure belli ac pacis* (1625) deserves a separate, systematic analysis of its own. The consistent oscillation of Grotius' legal rhetoric between the articulation of universal principles and citation of particular, historical examples or contexts nevertheless prompts the question: When can one appropriately generalize (appeal to sameness), and where must one always specify (acknowledge difference and attend to historical example) in legal theory? Grotius' tendency is to deploy different modes of legal argumentation and rhetoric, elements of both the *mores italicus* and the *mores gallicus,* the Italian and the French methods of law, in his texts. He seeks to systematize, yet also to specify. For an analysis of these different modes of legal reasoning, see Kelley, "Civil Science in the Renaissance: Jurisprudence in the French Manner" and "Civil Science in the Renaissance: Jurisprudence in the Italian Style," and Maclean, *Interpretation,* 15–19.

10. See Grotius, *Briefwisseling* (1969), 132–33.

11. After all, Grotius had been a student of Scaliger at the University of Leiden. Subsequently dubbed the "miracle of Holland" by Henry IV of France for his youthful learnedness, Grotius had become well known enough in government circles by 1604 to be asked by the hugely influential Dutch East India Company to compose a brief, *De jure praedae* (The law of prize), defending the legality of the company's seizure of a Portuguese carrack and the selling off of its contents in a highly contested auction. See Bull, "Importance of Grotius," 70. In 1613, he became one of the key supporters of Oldenbarnevelt, one of the founders of the Dutch East India Company, Advocate of Holland, and the leader of the Remonstrant cause. Named the pensionary of Rotterdam, Grotius was sent to London as the Dutch legal expert in the negotiations on Asian trade; while there, he also tried to convince James I, as self-appointed "Protestant Pope," of the king's important role in the theological controversies that had been disrupting the Dutch Reformed State Church

since 1610 between the so-called Counter-Remonstrants, who held strictly to the Calvinist doctrine of predestination, and the Remonstrants, or Arminians (to whom both Oldenbarnevelt and Grotius were known to be sympathetic), who argued for a greater degree of human free will in rejecting or accepting divine grace. See Roelofsen, "Grotius," 112–14. The Stadtholder, Prince Maurice, leader of the Counter-Remonstrants, arrested both Oldenbarnevelt and Grotius in a power play in August of 1618. Oldenbarnevelt's execution in May of 1619 marked the beginning of a new regime in the Dutch Republic; Grotius, merely imprisoned for life in Loevestein Castle, escaped to France in 1621, hidden, as every Dutch schoolchild knows, in a trunk of books his wife had had delivered to his cell. He became the Swedish ambassador to France in 1634.

Zaga Christos, on the other hand, has practically vanished from the pages of history. His story is told in only barely suppressed tones of racist condescension and amusement by Saint-Aymour, in "Un Prince," and Mathorez, in *Les Etrangères*. He is branded an impostor by both Mathorez and da Leonessa in "Santo Stefano." For all their latter-day disdain, however, both Saint-Aymour and Mathorez describe in detail how the Coptic community in Cairo received Christos "comme prince et fils de Negous" (negus, or king), as Saint Aymour put it ("Un Prince," 37). Both report that the pope, having heard that the "prince" had converted to Catholicism in Jerusalem, sent for him; Christos stayed in Rome for two years. In 1634, "Monsieur le duc de Créqui," French ambassador to the Vatican, persuaded the African to come to Paris. Mathorez reports with certainty only that Christos died in Rueil in 1638; the fact that he passed away "dans la résidence du cardinal de Richelieu" (Mathorez, *Les Etrangères*, 391) seems an indication that he had moved in lofty political circles.

12. Holing's story is told in Michaelis, *Sonderbarer Lebens-Lauff*. The quote here is from 98–99. I shall return to Michaelis's account of Holing's travels and work in Ethiopia.

13. Grotius, *Briefwisseling* (1969), 143.

14. For a seventeenth-century version of the history of the Ethiopian church, see Wansleben, *Brief Account*, 4. The specific contest within the early Church had been a christological one involving the so-called monophysite contention that Christ was of a single "nature," both divine and human, rather than of two "natures" — "undivided" (*atreptos*) — combined, the stance advocated and in fact demanded by the leadership in Rome. See Ritter, *Alte Kirche*, 220–21.

15. Grotius, *Briefwisseling* (1967), 143. The Latin reads: "Ex iisdem literis disco Christianos pontifici non parentes, Graecos nimirum et Aegyptios, graviter inter se dissidere ob quaestiones de naturis Christi earumque proprietatibus, plane ut in occidente protestantes. Ita ubique similia peccantur."

16. Both the editor of Wansleben's Preface in *Brief Account* and Michaelis, *Sonderbarer Lebens-Lauff*, 10, comment at length on the parallels between the Catholic-Protestant conflicts in Europe and the Jesuit-Monophysite conflicts in Ethiopia, which I shall discuss. On negative stereotypes of Africans during this period, especially in literature, see Jones, *Othello's Countrymen*.

17. See Debrunner, *Presence and Prestige*, 53.

18. Grotius, *Native Races*, 7–8. The following quotes may be found on pp. 10, 13, 17–20, 13, 16, and 8, respectively of this text.

19. Grotius, *Dissertatio altera*, 6–7.

20. Jed, *Chaste Thinking,* and Kenney, *Classical Text,* have discussed the significance of the technical term "conjecture," in the philological practices of early modern European humanists; from the sixteenth up through the mid-seventeenth century and beyond, text editors and critics engaged in projects of "textual improvement" of works of profane as well as sacred literature by resorting to forms of *emendatio* of existing editions that relied on informed interpolation, on supplying links of both linguistic and thematic dimensions in order to construct a coherent and continuous narrative and text. Grotius was himself no stranger to the philological enterprise, having studied philosophy and the classics under Scaliger and produced numerous editions of his own. When he defends his reading of a somewhat limited selection of texts on the American tribes by describing his claims about the origins of the Yucatan peoples as "conjecturas," it is clear that he considers his interpolation of an Ethiopian origin for them an accurate solution to the challenge of producing a coherent narrative about Christian unity out of scattered evidence and in view of the dispersion of people through Europe, Asia, Africa, and the New World.

21. Grotius, *Dissertatio altera,* 13, 16.

22. See Ratcliffe, " 'Race' in Britain," 109–15, on contemporary definitions of "race" and "ethnicity" that measure a wide variety of indicators of "group membership," including "symbolic elements," such as religion, "which define the group's identity" (115).

23. For this use of the term "subterranean," see Greene, "Humanist Hermeneutic," 206.

24. This claim for kinship among diverse Christians (including true Ethiopians) was of course obviously made in the face of the religious heterogeneity of the early modern world, including the Jews and Turks, to whom more figurative Ethiopians were sometimes assimilated. See Boose, "Racial Discourse," for examples. It is worth noting, however, that in the early modern period the religious diversity within Christianity was at least as rich as the religious diversity between and among the various forms of Christianity and other religious systems represented in Europe and on the greater Eurasian continent at the time.

25. See Meyjes, "Hugo Grotius as Irenicist," 48, on the *consensus quinquesaecularis.* Wolf, *Irenik,* 14–16 and 24, has written compellingly about Grotius' use of the topos of the "primitive Church" as a genealogical reference point and guarantor of a recuperative religious harmony, but does not mention his interest in the Ethiopian church. The concept of the "primitive Church" was common throughout the early modern period; for specific examples, see Duffy, "Primitive Christianity," Greenslade, "Authority," and Neveu, "L'Erudition."

26. Meyjes, "Hugo Grotius as Irenicist," 49, calls attention to the fact that Grotius never referred to the consensus quinquesaecularis but rather referred to the consensus "trium optimorum saeculorum," of "the [first] three best centuries." In the texts with which I am concerned here, Grotius is far less precise about the exact centuries that he means.

27. Grotius, *Briefwisseling* (1967), 119.

28. Grotius, *Briefwisseling* (1971), 235.

29. Grotius, *Briefwisseling* (1971), 225 and 200–201.

30. The *Meletius* appears to have circulated widely at the time but was not published until more than 350 years after it was written. See Grotius, *Meletius,* and Meyjes, Introduction, for the publication history and context.

31. The rhetoric of consensus that permeates this brief text has been explained by reference not only to Grotius' loyalty to the Christian humanist tradition but also to his adoption of the ethical code of the Stoics, familiar to him from his early exposure to the classics. See Meyjes, Introduction, 61.

32. Grotius, *True Religion,* 192, refers to the various forms of Christianity in dispute as "sects."

33. Meyjes, Introduction, 15–22, identifies the unnamed interlocutor as the humanist Johannes Boreel (1577–1629).

34. Grotius, *Meletius,* 105. The following quotes are from pp. 103–104 and 75–76 of this text.

35. See White, *Heracles' Bow,* 28.

36. Grotius, *Meletius,* 109.

37. On the distinction between *decreta* and *praecepta,* see Meyjes, Introduction, 33–35.

38. Grotius, *Meletius,* 109–127.

39. Ibid., 133.

40. See Wolf, *Irenik,* 14, and Tuck, *Philosophy and Government,* 174 and 18.

41. Grotius, *Meletius,* 124, 126, 127–128, and 131.

42. Ibid., 133; the Latin text of this passage may be found on 101.

43. Ibid., 133. Emphasis added.

44. See Ritter, *Alte Kirche,* 223.

45. See Michaelis, *Sonderbarer Lebens-Lauff,* 18.

46. The implicit argument about the "fundamental principles common to all Christians" that Grotius makes in *Meletius,* namely that sameness could be achieved only through the admission of difference, received a somewhat more dogmatic, indeed polemical codification and elaboration nearly a decade later in his much lengthier *True Religion Explained* (*De veritate religionis christianae*). The religious orthodoxy that Grotius would orchestrate in *De veritate* relies less on any necessary logic of divinely inspired origins for doctrine and first principles, however, and more on invoking the authority of the early tradition of local receptions of Scripture in various countries and tongues, itself a model of the kind of unity-in-diversity to which Grotius aspires. The early translation of Scripture into Ethiopian serves in this argument as a guarantor of and witness to this unity. See Grotius, *True Religion,* 191.

47. Tuck, *Philosophy and Government,* 187–88, argues that Grotius' theory of natural law actually changed because of the arguments that he developed in *Meletius* as well as in other texts concerning religious tolerance. The sequencing implied in Tuck's argument seems purely heuristic, given that most of these ideas were developed in close chronological proximity to one another. Yet I agree that there were fundamental structural similarities in the arguments he developed in both areas.

48. Barnes, "Just War," deals primarily with jus ad bellum; for the distinction between jus ad bellum and jus in bello, also see Bull, "Grotian Conception," 58.

49. See, in particular, Kelley, *Human Measure,* 214–18.

50. Kelley, ibid., argues that the notion that the jus gentium was a "product of the human will" was one espoused by *opponents* of Grotius such as Samuel Rachel and J. W. Textor. I find it a more viable option to conclude that for Grotius, as for Rachel and Textor, the power of human volition was one that always exerted pressure on his system

beneath the surface of his text and was associated most often with local, municipal law rather than with the jus gentium.

51. Grotius, *De jure,* 9 (Prolegomena).

52. Grotius' identity as a "jus-naturalist" and his formulation of this kind of "quasi-geometrical" system of jurisprudence, which would be capable of producing universal consent, have been much discussed by scholars. See Kelley, *Human Measure,* 213–16; the term "quasi-geometrical" is used by Kelley to refer to the axioms of the Digest, but it does capture nicely and even echo Grotius' desire to be "mathematical" in his treatise. See Grotius, *De jure,* 30 (Prolegomena). The "thoroughly organized" and "scientific" nature of his master text has thus been assimilated into a characterization of his legacy as one of "order built on rational intercourse" (Der Derian, "Introduction," 4–5) that associates him with what late twentieth-century critical legal scholars have dismissed as the "older tradition" of the law as a "set of commands" (White, *Heracles' Bow,* 29). Such accusations of methodolatry in *De jure belli ac pacis* are usefully countered by scholarship that embeds his valorization of a system of natural law over "divine positive law" in the local, historical controversies between church and state in early modern Holland (see Dufour, "Grotius," for example), and by analyses that chart the development in Grotius' legal theory away from his early reliance on scholastic predecessors in texts like *De jure praedae* and toward a "positive system of international law" as it is articulated in *De jure belli ac pacis* (see Finch, Preface, xxii).

53. Grotius, *De jure,* 20, 9, and 11 (Prolegomena).

54. Ibid., 14, 19, 24, and 21 (Prolegomena). In this "parsing" of the law, divine law is more or less bracketed out; see p. 13 (Prolegomena). Dufour, "Grotius," 36, points out the importance of Grotius' substitution of Aristotelian for Suárezian distinctions that eliminate the "Loi eternelle."

55. Ibid., 29–30 (Prolegomena).

56. Cf. also ibid., 507 (II, XX, xliii), for Grotius' use of the analogy between the law of nature and mathematics. See Kelley, *Human Measure,* 213, for linkages between this rhetoric of "naturall Philosophy" and contemporary legal and theological movements influenced by the "mathematical" philosophy of the seventeenth century; other major influences, according to Kelley, were a Spanish "second scholasticism," as well as Ramism and Protestant neo-Aristotelianism." For Spanish influences on Grotius, see Feenstra, "Quelques Remarques."

57. Grotius, *De jure,* 22 (Prolegomena).

58. Ibid., 42 (II, I, xii, 1) on a priori versus a posteriori proof of the existence of the law of nature.

59. Ibid., 502; see also 584, 604, 616, and 658.

60. Ibid., 715.

61. Ibid., 23–24 (Prolegomena).

62. Haggenmacher, "Genèse," 46, has argued on the basis of an analysis of the early tract *De jure praedae commentarius* (Commentary on the law of prize, after 1603) that it was Grotius' concept of the law of nations, the jus gentium, in particular that first introduced nuances with the potential to challenge his claims about the transcendental nature of the universal first principles of natural law. In *De jure praedae,* what Grotius describes as the *jus gentium primarium* is more like natural law; "l'expression du consen-

tement universel des humains en tant qu'êtres rationnels." The *jus gentium secundarium,* however, Haggenmacher argues, is more like a tacitly understood positive "droit civil," but among states rather than within them. Indeed, Grotius goes on to distinguish this "true" jus gentium secundarium, "qui lie au contraire les Etats à la manière d'un accord," from its impersonator, the accord between states that is based on "simples coutumes qui, hasard ou imitation, se ressemblent d'un Etat à l'autre" (47). He thus introduces an element of contract that "binds" states together after the manner of a treaty and as an act of positive law; Finch, Preface, has explained this turn as the fundamental point that distinguishes Grotius' later work.

63. Knight, "Introduction," 18, is among the few who note that it was one of Grotius' most "striking and important achievement[s]" in *De jure* to have associated "in one system . . . the practical with the merely theoretical"; in opposition to Grotius' own claims that he will exclude questions of "laws of particular states" (19, Prolegomena) and devote himself to "treating of the law of nature" (227 – II, IV, x), the part of the lengthy treatise devoted to "general theory" is in itself a small one, and that the bulk of the remainder is given over to a "discussion of municipal law, public and private." Draper, "Grotius' Place," argues, however, that Grotius rejects the reason of state (199–201); my remarks here are partly to counter the general acceptance of Grotius' claims in the Prolegomena that he is leaving the question of the expediency, indeed, even legitimacy of state-based conduct in international relations behind.

64. See Grotius, *De jure,* 149 (II, IV, vii).

65. Ibid., 97 (I, III, iv).

66. Ibid., 65 (I, II, vii).

67. Ibid., 141 (I, IV, iv). Other important moments in book 2 concern the bounds of the sovereign's and the state's power over their subjects: ibid., 227–30 (II, IV, xi–xv); 253–54 (II, V, xxiv), and ibid., 260–66 (II, VI, passim).

68. Ibid., 192 (II, II, v).

69. Ibid., 207 (II, III, v) and 649 (III, IV, ix).

70. Ibid., 332 (II, XI, v).

71. Ibid., 267 (II, VII, i).

72. Ibid., 278 (II, VII, xi). On the topics of promises and contracts, Grotius is especially clear that "civil law" is binding (ibid., 335, II, XI and XII) – e.g., that even the law of nature as regards losses experienced in association with rental land "can be changed both by laws and by agreement," 35 – II, XII, xviii), and, in the case of the delineation of punishments in chapter XX, in which it seems that one can appeal only to the law of nature, Grotius concludes: "Nevertheless, within the state these things must be interpreted with reference to its laws" (47 – II, XX, ix).

73. See Draper, "Grotius' Place," 198–99 and 207, on Grotius' so-called *temperamenta belli.*

74. Grotius, *De jure,* 751 (III, XII, v) and 759 (III, XIII, iv).

75. Ibid., 828 (III, XX, liii).

76. Ibid., 773 (III, XV, vii).

77. Michaelis, *Sonderbaren Lebens-Lauff,* 18, 21, and 44.

78. Ibid., 29–30 and 44.

79. Ibid., 56–58.

80. Ibid., 61–63.
81. Ibid., 78–87.
82. Ibid., 81–83 and 80.
83. Ibid., 99.
84. See Wansleben, *Brief Account,* 28–30.
85. Ibid., 32.
86. See Michaelis, *Sonderbarer Lebens-Lauff,* 188.

Works Cited

Barnes, Jonathan. "The Just War." In *The Cambridge History of Later Medieval Philosophy,* ed. Norman Kretzmann, Anthony Kenny, and Jan Pinborg, 771–784. Cambridge, 1982.

Boose, Lynda E. " 'The Getting of a Lawful Race': Racial Discourse in Early Modern England and the Unrepresentable Black Woman." In *Women, "Race," and Writing in the Early Modern Period,* ed. Margo Hendricks and Patricia Parker, 35–54. London, 1994.

Bots, Hans, and Pierre Leroy. "Grotius et la réunion des Chrétiens." *XVIIe Siècle* 4 (1983): 451–469.

Bull, Hedley. "The Grotian Conception of International Society." In *Diplomatic Investigations: Essays in the Theory of International Politics,* ed. Herbert Butterfield and Martin Wight, 51–73. London, 1966.

——. "The Importance of Grotius in the Study of International Relations." In *Hugo Grotius and International Relations,* ed. Hedley Bull, Benedict Kingsbury, and Adam Roberts, 65–93. Oxford, 1990.

Debrunner, Hans Werner. *Presence and Prestige: Africans in Europe. A History of Africans in Europe before 1918.* Basel, 1979.

Der Derian, James. "Introduction: Critical Evaluations." In *International Theory: Critical Investigations,* ed. James Der Derian, 1–11. London, 1995.

Draper, G. I. A. D. "Grotius' Place in the Development of Legal Ideas About War." In *Hugo Grotius and International Relations,* ed. Hedley Bull, Benedict Kingsbury, and Adam Roberts, 177–207. Oxford, 1990.

Duffy, Eamon. "Primitive Christianity Revived: Religious Revival in Augustan England." In *Renaissance and Renewal in Christian History,* ed. Derek Baker, 287–300. Oxford, 1977.

Dufour, A. "Grotius et le droit naturel du dix-septième siècle." In *The World of Hugo Grotius, 1583–1645,* ed. R. Feenstra, 15–42. Amsterdam, 1984.

Farber, Daniel A., and Suzanna Sherry. "Legal Storytelling and Constitutional Law: The Medium and the Message." In *Law's Stories: Narrative and Rhetoric in the Law,* ed. Peter Brooks and Paul Gewirtz, 37–53. New Haven, Conn., 1996.

Feenstra, R. "Quelques remarques sur les sources utilisées par Grotius dans ses travaux de droit naturel." In *The World of Hugo Grotius, 1583–1645,* ed. R. Feenstra, 65–82. Amsterdam, 1984.

Ferguson, Robert A. "Untold Stories in the Law." In *Law's Stories: Narrative and Rhetoric in the Law,* ed. Peter Brooks and Paul Gewirtz, 84–98. New Haven, Conn., 1996.

Finch, George A. Preface. In Hugo Grotius, *De jure praedae commentarius,* 2 vols., ed. James Brown Scott and trans. G. L. Williams, ix–xxvi. Oxford, 1950.

Gellinek, Christian. *Hugo Grotius.* Boston, 1983.

Ginzburg, Carlo. "Morelli, Freud, and Sherlock Holmes: Clues and Scientific Method." In *History Workshop* 9 (1980): 5–36.

Greene, Thomas M. "Petrarch and the Humanist Hermeneutic." In *Italian Literature: Roots and Branches,* ed. Giose Rimanelli and Kenneth John Atchity, 201–224. New Haven, Conn., 1976.

Greenslade, Stanley L. "The Authority of the Early Church in Early Anglican Thought." In *Oecumenica* (1971/72): 9–31.

Grotius, Hugo. *Briefwisseling,* ed. P. C. Molhuysen et al. 15 vols. The Hague, 1928–96.

———. *De jure belli ac pacis libri tres.* 2 vols. Trans. Francis W. Kelsey. New York, 1964.

———. *De origine gentium Americanarum dissertatio altera, adversus obtrectatorem, paca quem bonum facit barba.* Paris, 1643.

———. *Meletius sive de iis quae inter Christianos conveniunt epistola.* Trans. and ed. Guillaume H. M. Posthumus Meyjes. Leiden, 1988.

———. *On the Origin of the Native Races of America: A Dissertation by Hugo Grotius* [1642]. Trans. Edmund Goldsmid. Edinburgh, 1884.

———. *True Religion Explained and Defended against Archenemies Thereof in These Times, In Six Bookes.* London, 1632.

Haggenmacher, Peter. "Genèse et signification du concept de 'ius gentium' chez Grotius." *Grotiana.* New Series 2 (1981): 44–102.

Hall, Kim F. *Things of Darkness: Economies of Race and Gender in Early Modern England.* Ithaca, N.Y., 1995.

Jed, Stephanie. *Chaste Thinking: The Rape of Lucretia and the Birth of Humanism.* Bloomington, Ind., 1989.

Jones, Eldred. *Othello's Countrymen.* London, 1965.

Kelley, Donald R. "Civil Science in the Renaissance: Jurisprudence in the French Manner." In *History of European Ideas* 2 (1981): 261–276.

———. "Civil Science in the Renaissance: Jurisprudence Italian Style." In *The Historical Journal* 22 (1979): 777–794.

———. *The Human Measure: Social Thought in the Western Legal Tradition.* Cambridge, Mass., 1990.

Kenney, E. J. *The Classical Text: Aspects of Editing in the Age of the Printed Book.* Berkeley, Calif., 1974.

Kingsbury, Benedict, and Adam Roberts, "Introduction: Grotian Thought in International Relations." In *Hugo Grotius and International Relations,* ed. Hedley Bull, Benedict Kingsbury, and Adam Roberts, 1–64. Oxford, 1990.

Knight, W. S. M. "Introduction" to Hugo Grotius, *Selections from De jure belli ac pacis.* In *Peace Projects of the Seventeenth Century,* ed. J. Jacob and M. C. Jacob, 5–23. New York, 1972.

Krogh-Conning, K. *Hugo Grotius und die religiösen Bewegungen im Protestantismus seiner Zeit.* Cologne, 1904.

Da Leonessa, Mauro. *Santo Stefano degli Abissine e le relazione Romano-Etiopiche.* Vatican City, 1929.

Maclean, Ian. *Interpretation and Meaning in the Renaissance: The Case of Law*. Cambridge, 1992.

Mathorez, J. *Les Etrangères en France sous l'Ancien Régime*. Paris, 1919.

Meyjes, G. H. M. "Hugo Grotius as an Irenicist." In *The World of Hugo Grotius, 1583–1645*, ed. R. Feenstra, 43–64. Amsterdam, 1984.

———. Introduction. In Hugo Grotius, *Meletius sive de iis quae inter Christianos conveniunt epistola*, 1–71. Leiden, 1988

Michaelis, Johann H. *Sonderbarer Lebens-Lauff Herrn Peter Heylings, Aus Lübec, und dessen Reise nach Ethiopien*. Halle, 1714.

Neveu, Bruno. "L'Erudition ecclésiastique du XVIIe siècle et la nostalgie de l'antiquité chrétienne." In *Religion and Humanism*, ed. Keith Robbins, 195–225. Oxford, 1981.

Parker, Patricia, and Margo Hendricks, ed. *Women, "Race," and Writing in the Early Modern Period*. London, 1994.

Pietri, Charles, and Luce et al., eds. *Die Geschichte des Christentums: Religion-Politik-Kultur*, vol. 2: *Das Entstehen der einen Christenheit (250–430)*. Freiburg, 1996.

Ratcliffe, Peter. "Conceptualizing "Race," Ethnicity, and Nation: Towards a Comparative Perspective." In *"Race," Ethnicity, and Nation: International Perspectives on Social Conflict*, ed. Peter Ratcliffe, 2–25. London, 1994.

———. "'Race' in Britain: Theory, Methods, and Substance." In *"Race," Ethnicity, and Nation: International Perspectives on Social Conflict*, ed. Peter Ratcliffe, 108–132. London, 1994.

Ritter, Adolf Martin. *Alte Kirche*. vol. 1 of *Kirchen- und Theologiegeschichte in Quellen*, ed. Heiko A. Oberman, Adolf Martin Ritter, and Hans Kromwiede. Neukirchen-Vluyn, Germany, 1994.

Roelofsen, C. G. "Grotius and the International Politics of the Seventeenth Century." In *Hugo Grotius and International Relations*, ed. Hedley Bull, Benedict Kingsbury, and Adam Roberts, 95–131. Oxford, 1990.

Saint-Aymour, Amédée Caix de. "Un Prince Ethiopien à la Cour de France, 1634–1638." In Saint-Aymour, *La France en Ethiopie: Histoire des relations de la France avec l'Abyssinie chrétienne*, 27–64. Paris, 1886.

Tuck, Richard. *Philosophy and Government, 1572–1651*. Cambridge, 1993.

Uhlig, Siegbert. *Hiob Ludolfs "Theologia Aethiopica."* 2 vols. Wiesbaden, 1983.

Wansleben, Johann Michael. *A Brief Account of the Rebellions and Bloudshed Occasioned by the Anti-Christian Practices of the Jesuits and other Popish Emissaries in the Empire of Ethiopia*. London, 1678.

Weisberg, Robert. "Proclaiming Trials as Narratives: Premises and Pretenses." In *Law's Stories: Narrative and Rhetoric in the Law*, ed. Peter Brooks and Paul Gewirtz, 61–83. New Haven, Conn., 1996.

White, James Boyd. *Heracles' Bow: Essays on the Rhetoric and Poetics of the Law*. Madison, 1985.

Wight, Martin. "Why Is There No International Theory?" In *International Theory: Critical Investigations*. ed. James Der Derian, 15–35. London, 1995.

Williams, Patricia. *The Alchemy of Race and Rights: Diary of a Law Professor*. Cambridge, Mass., 1991.

Wolf, Dieter. *Die Irenik des Hugo Grotius nach ihren Prinzipien und biographisch-geistesgeschichtlichen Perspektiven.* Marburg, 1969.

Wright, Herbert F. "Some Less Known Works of Hugo Grotius: The Controversy of Hugo Grotius with Johann de Laet on the Origin of the American Aborigines." In *Bibliotheca Visseriana* 7 (1928): 211–228.

13

Selden, Grotius, and the Seventeenth-Century Intellectual Revolution in Moral and Political Theory

JOHANN P. SOMMERVILLE

It is often said that there was an intellectual revolution in seventeenth-century Europe, and that it affected not just scientific thinking but also attitudes toward law and morality. Quite a number of scholars argue that old Scholastic and Aristotelian ideas about ethical and political matters decayed and were replaced by a new and distinctively modern theory of natural law. This "modern" school of natural law, so the argument runs, was founded by the great Dutch thinker Hugo Grotius, whose insights were later developed by John Selden, Thomas Hobbes, and Samuel Pufendorf.[1] Although these thinkers adopted startlingly innovative views on politics and morals, the case proceeds, they expressed their ideas in very traditional terms. In other words, there was a remarkable and profound disjunction between the language which Grotius and the rest employed, and the substance of what they said. As Richard Tuck notes, Grotius and the others used "the language of natural law and natural rights" which had been characteristic of "scholastic writers from the thirteenth century onwards." Indeed, he observes, the "use by the seventeenth-century writers of this vocabulary led many people during the last hundred

I would like to thank the Huntington Library, and the Graduate School of the University of Wisconsin, Madison, for funding which made possible the research on which this chapter is based.

years to suppose that it was a great mistake to posit some great divide between the Middle Ages and modernity."[2] But though the "medieval roots" of the moral language of thinkers like Grotius or Selden are undoubted, their theories were radically different from those of the Scholastics, from whom they were "poles apart."[3]

In recent years, it has become fashionable to talk about the languages or discourses of politics, rather than about political theories. It is not always clear that much is gained by this, and often the languages in question (say, civic humanism, or classical republicanism) are defined only very vaguely, leaving readers in doubt about exactly what they were. But one merit of analyzing past ethical or political thinking as discourse is to call attention to the links between rhetoric or language on the one hand and ideas or theories on the other. Shifts in ideas are commonly accompanied by linguistic change. New catch phrases grow into vogue, and old ones drop out of use. If there was indeed a revolution in moral thinking during the seventeenth century, we might expect that it would have been accompanied by major changes in language, as innovative terms were developed for describing new ideas, and as slogans were adopted for making the novel theories quickly and easily comprehensible. Yet Grotius and the other theorists of the "modern" natural law, we are told, were deeply conservative in their linguistic practices, and they couched their revolutionary claims in medieval terminology that had been designed to communicate antiquated Scholastic ideas. The purpose of this essay is to examine why it was that they did this. Why is it that the natural-law discourse we find in Grotius, Selden, or Pufendorf seems so similar to that of Aquinas, Suárez, or Molina?

One possible answer is that the members of the modern school of natural law were keen to disguise from their contemporaries just how original their thinking really was. Perhaps they were worried that their readers would be shocked by the breathtaking novelty of their ideas, and therefore wrapped them up in traditional-sounding language. By seeming rather staid and conservative, they hoped (we could argue) to persuade people to accept ideas that were in fact highly innovative. Or perhaps they did not fully appreciate their own originality and used an antiquated vocabulary because they overestimated their debt to the Scholastic past, and their links to medieval thinking. There are grave difficulties with both of these approaches. Some, at least, of the new theorists strongly believed that their ideas were highly original, and took pleasure in telling the world how innovative they were. The great English philosopher Thomas Hobbes famously declared that "civil philosophy" is "no older than my own book *De Cive*,"[4] interestingly failing to appreciate whatever role Grotius and Selden had played in the intellectual revolution. Hobbes was a combative and opinionated thinker who was happy to boast of how little he owed to his predecessors, and in particular to the medieval Scholastics. Equally hostile to Scholasticism was the German Samuel Pufendorf. In his *De jure naturae et gentium* of 1672, he dismissed the Scholastics as logic-chopping triflers who paid more attention to authority than to reason and were not worth quoting. He saw Grotius as his own most important predecessor, with Selden and Hobbes as intermediary figures of some significance.[5] Neither Pufendorf nor Hobbes seems to have had the slightest compunction about informing the world about his own originality, and neither acknowledged any great debt to the medieval Scholastics. Grotius and Selden were happier to quote medieval authors, and less boastful about their own achievements, but there seems to be no evidence that they underestimated their own originality or felt any need to use conservative language to avoid offending readers. So we need some other explanation of why the language of Grotius and the others is so strikingly reminiscent of medieval Scholasticism.

Another possibility is that their language sounds like that of earlier writers because there *was* no radical break between medieval and early modern notions of natural law. This is the view that I advance in this chapter. My purpose is to solve the paradox of a revolution in ideas that left no mark on language by showing that there was no revolution in ideas. This is not to suggest that Grotius and the others said nothing new. Hobbes, in particular, had many highly original ideas, and Pufendorf was also convinced of his own originality, though with rather less justification. But the thinking of the "modern" school of natural law as a whole was not novel enough to constitute a revolution. Indeed, it is unclear that there was any "modern" school of natural law at all, and that for several reasons. First, though Pufendorf looked back on Hobbes, Selden, and Grotius as his predecessors, there is little reason to suppose that Selden and Grotius saw themselves as constituting a school, and much to suggest that Hobbes would have disagreed profoundly with any claim that he belonged to the school of Grotius. Hobbes nowhere mentions the Dutchman, and he made it abundantly clear that he saw himself as a wholly original thinker who belonged to no one's school. Selden vigorously attacked Grotius' advocacy of freedom of the seas, and though the two elsewhere praised each other, nowhere in their writings does the suggestion appear that they saw themselves as part of one school. Grotius strongly rejected some of Hobbes's key political ideas.[6] Apparently no member of Grotius' "'modern' school" ever hinted that he belonged to the same school as any other member until the time of Pufendorf, and even he talked about the rest not as a school, but just as individuals, each of whom had said something sensible on natural law but none of whom had given a wholly adequate account of it—thus leaving it open for Samuel himself to do so. Perhaps, though, they were indeed a school, though they did not mention the fact. Maybe they were embarrassed about it, or had reasons to keep it secret, or even were unaware of it. It is odd, though, that the members of a revolutionary new school never mentioned that this was what they were. It is odd, too, that none of them wrote to any of the others, though Grotius lived far away from Selden and Hobbes for most of his career and though he wrote to a great many people. Grotius' correspondence fills many stout volumes, but not a single letter passed between him and Hobbes or Selden.[7] And it is odd that so few contemporaries of Grotius and the rest seem to have spotted that a revolution had taken place in moral thinking, and that a new school had been established. These various oddities are suggestive. But they do not demonstrate that there was no revolution. To do that we need first to examine what the "modern" school of natural law is said to have been.

So the first part of this chapter will discuss the various principles or doctrines of which the "modern" theory supposedly consisted. We will see what recent scholars say about the main elements in this kind of thinking, and why they contend that it was revolutionary. In the second section of the chapter I shall look at the ideas of the founding father of the "modern" school of natural law — Grotius. In the third we shall examine the ideas of John Selden. These two sections will argue that on many crucial points Grotius and Selden did not hold the principles said to be characteristic of the "modern" school. It follows that there was no "modern" school of natural law, or at least that Grotius and Selden were not members of it — raising the question of whether it had any members at all.

The "Modern" School of Natural Law

Scholars who argue that a "modern" school of natural law was established in the seventeenth century claim that the new style of theorizing was secular, rational, individualistic, radical, minimalist, intended to combat skepticism, and fundamentally centered on the principle of self-preservation. According to A. P. D'Entrèves, the conception of natural law of Grotius and his successors was "entirely 'secular.'" Though they did occasionally "pay homage to some remote notion of God," the deity had ceased to matter in their account of morality.[8] Grotius himself famously commented that natural law would have some sort of validity "even if we grant what cannot be granted without the greatest wickedness, that there is no God."[9] The Grotians, says J. B. Schneewind, were concerned neither with "cosmic harmonies" nor with "the highest good" but simply wanted to investigate "how rational beings . . . can live together." Though Hobbes "carried the Grotian sidelining of religion to an extreme," it was a key characteristic of the school as a whole to reduce religion to virtual irrelevance in moral matters.[10] In the Middle Ages, moral thinking was deeply religious. But Grotius' "separation of natural law from the Christian religion" (as Knud Haakonssen puts it) dramatically secularized moral theorizing.[11]

The natural law about which Grotius and his followers talked, says D'Entrèves, was "a purely rational construction." They no longer sought to discover moral truths by investigating the actual practices of different nations, for they recognized that customs could become corrupted and that peoples could radically depart from natural law. The fact that the majority of human societies act in a particular way was therefore no guide to how they ought to act, or to what the law of nature required. Grotius and his followers saw this law (the argument goes) as depending not "on experience, but on definitions, not on facts, but on logical deductions."[12] Neither history nor authority—and especially not the authority of the discredited Scholastics and Aristotelians— but deductive reasoning from first principles, on the model of mathematics and especially geometry, was to provide the basis for the new science of morals.[13] Again, it is said, the Grotian thinkers placed unprecedented stress on *individuals,* and in particular upon their rights.[14] Whereas earlier theorists had been interested in duties rather than rights, and communities rather than individuals, the Dutchman and his successors placed individuals and their rights at the center of their system. Another claim is that the new theory of natural law was *radical:* it was a "vindication of rights" that became "a theory of revolution" in eighteenth-century France and America, when people like Jefferson came to argue that any regime which undermined inalienable rights ought to be "altered or abolished."[15]

A central feature of the Grotian account of natural law, it has been suggested, is that it was *minimalist.* In other words, Grotius and the other members of his school believed that the actual contents of the law of nature were rather slender, leaving people largely and excitingly free to shape their own ethical lives. In particular, they reduced morality to just two basic principles— preserve yourself, but do not wantonly harm others.[16] This contention that the modern theory of natural law was minimalist connects up to a further idea about it, namely that it was intended to refute skepticism. Around 1600, so the case goes, European intellectuals were racked by doubts resulting from the discovery in distant places of people with strange and surprising customs, but especially from the skeptical writings of Montaigne and later Charron, who had revived the ideas of the ancient Greek Sextus Empiricus. The skeptics doubted pretty much everything that could be doubted—the argument proceeds—but there were limits beyond which they did not go, for they admitted that we do have some fundamental aims on which we can build an ethical code of sorts — since people desire to advance their self-interests and, above all, they seek self-preservation. "For Montaigne," Tuck informs us, "the fundamental desire in men was for *self-preservation*."[17] Grotius' "main intention" in his most famous work, the *De jure belli ac pacis* (On the law of war and peace, 1625), was "to answer the sceptic," and he did this brilliantly by taking the very principle which the skeptics accepted as valid — the principle of self-preservation — and then building a moral science upon it.[18] Scholastic moral philosophy, Haakonssen tells us, was "an obvious target" for the "moral scepticism" of Montaigne and Charron, and it was "Grotius's stated objective in *De iure*" "to overcome such scepticism."[19] In his *De iure naturali & gentium, iuxta disciplinam Ebraeorum, libri septem* (Seven books on the law of nature and nations, according to the teaching of the Hebrews, 1640), Tuck affirms, the great English scholar John Selden similarly "clearly signalled that his intention was to answer the sceptic by finding a minimal set of moral beliefs which as a matter of fact all societies and philosophers could agree on — precisely the same enterprise upon which Grotius had embarked."[20]

To sum up, the standard argument on the new school of natural law runs much like this — though individual scholars vary in their emphases. The members of the new school of natural law scorned the authority of earlier writers, and especially of Scholastics and Aristotelians. Unlike their predecessors, they kept religious dogma out of moral theorizing, separating Christianity from ethical theory and basing their conclusions on rational deductions from first principles. They claimed that the fundamental tenets of morality were very few in number, and they stressed above all the principle of self-preservation. In basing their new moral theory on self-preservation, they aimed to refute the skepticism of Montaigne and Charron, and their arguments were peculiarly effective at achieving this goal, for the skeptics themselves had admitted that our greatest desire is to preserve ourselves. Earlier thinkers had based their moral conclusions on authority, religious dogma, and the practice of nations, or at least of the most civilized nations. The skeptics had challenged authority and dogma. Moreover, they had shown that nations often do horrendous things, and that it is not at all clear which nations are the most civilized, for the notion that the peoples of western Europe are superior to others is largely prideful self-deception. The Grotians agreed with the skeptics in rejecting the substance of Scholastic thinking. But they retained the vocabulary of the Schoolmen, though they now employed it to express highly innovative secular, rational, and minimalist ideas. We are now in a position to turn to the thinking of Grotius himself, and to investigate the extent to which he was a Grotian, by the standard definition.

Grotius

In 1625 Grotius published his most famous work, *De jure belli ac pacis*. As we have seen, a fashionable modern view is that the primary purpose of this book was to refute the skepticism of writers like Montaigne and Charron. At first glance, this looks a little odd. One might be tempted to suppose that someone who wanted to write a treatise against skepticism would call his work something like *Against Skepticism* or, at least, would mention skepticism somewhere in the title. But of course authors do not always get to choose the titles of their books, and perhaps Grotius' publisher thought the book would sell better under a rather misleading name. If we delve into the book itself, however, we find that it is in fact about the law of war and peace, and that its title is therefore not deceptive at all. The book says remarkably little about skepticism. The idea that it is an attack on Montaigne and Charron is based on on a couple of brief passages in the Prolegomena (or Introduction) to the book, where Grotius dismisses the ideas of the ancient philosopher Carneades, who had claimed that there is no such thing as justice and that people simply do what they deem expedient.[21] Arguably, Grotius' target here is Machiavelli and later ideas on reason of state, rather than Montaigne and skepticism.[22] When Grotius came to say why he wrote the book, he was wholly silent on skepticism. There were, he declared, "many and grave" reasons which led him to take up the pen, and he went on to describe them. "I saw," he asserted, "such lawlessness in making war throughout the Christian world, that barbarian nations would be ashamed of it: people rush to arms for little or no cause, and having taken them up lose all regard for divine and human law."[23] Some thinkers, he continued — naming Erasmus, and the sixteenth-century German Johann Wild — had been so disgusted by the horrors of war that they had claimed it was altogether illegal. But this, he said, was going too far, and he argued that adopting such an overstated position often had the opposite of the intended effect. In discussing when war was lawful, and what could licitly be done in it, he himself intended to steer a middle course between allowing everything and allowing nothing.[24] Since he was writing during the Thirty Years' War, when much of Europe was involved in a long and extremely destructive series of conflicts, the times were peculiarly appropriate for a project such as this. He also said that he intended to contribute to jurisprudence by giving a systematic account of it, which earlier writers had sometimes attempted, but never successfully carried through, since they did not adequately distinguish natural from human laws.[25] In stating why he wrote the book, Grotius said nothing whatever about the skepticism of Montaigne or Charron.

Grotius did not mention Montaigne or Charron, but it has been suggested that in referring to Carneades, he "did signal quite clearly"[26] that he really intended to answer the two French skeptics. Yet his book offered little or no argument against their central contentions. A fundamental claim of skeptics like them was that our senses are unreliable. Montaigne noted that "sick people lend a bitter taste to sweet things" and asserted that we should doubt whatever our senses seem to tell us.[27] Sickness, age, and other factors change the way things appear to us. But how can we ever know what things are actually like, if the way they seem depends on a multitude of such variables? The French philosopher Pierre Gassendi — who accepted much of the skeptical case — argued that honey may seem sweet to us but that we cannot know what it is like in itself, since appearances may be deceptive.[28] To support his views, he observed how various are the customs of different peoples, and in the manner of Montaigne he intimated that few if any practices are common to all nations. So, observing the customs of nations is no way to discover natural law. How did Grotius cope with these skeptical arguments? If he had aimed to refute skepticism, we would expect him to have dealt at some length with points of this kind. In fact, he brushed them aside dismissively. Skeptics said that we cannot deduce natural law from the consent of nations, for they do not in fact consent. Grotius asserted that we can and they do — or at least all the more civilized nations do. Natural law, he declared, could be discovered by two methods — either a priori by deduction from first principles, or a posteriori, by observation of the customs of nations. There was "a high degree of probability" that "what all nations, or all the more civilized" took to be the law of nature was such indeed, "for a universal effect requires a universal cause."[29] True, some depraved peoples might have unnatural customs, but (in Grotius' view) we ought simply to ignore them. Honey, he said, is in fact sweet, and if sick people think otherwise, we ought to take no notice of their opinion.[30] For the rest of the work, he proceeded to use information about the customs of different nations as a reliable guide to the law of nature, paying no more attention to skeptical quibbles.

So there are problems with the thesis that Grotius' primary aim in *De jure belli ac pacis* was to refute the ideas of Montaigne and Charron. He did not mention them, and he simply ignored the central arguments which underlay their thinking. He referred to Carneades' cynical views on justice but said little about skepticism. There are further difficulties with the idea that he brilliantly undermined the skepticism of Montaigne and Charron by seizing on their admission that we overridingly strive for self-preservation and then using this same principle of self-preservation as the central plank on which he erected his new and revolutionary moral theory. The main problems here are that he did not ground his system on self-preservation and that they did not claim that self-preservation is the fundamental human desire. According to Richard Tuck, Montaigne held that "the fundamental desire in men was for *self-preservation*," and he and his associates argued that "the only secure basis for conduct was an acceptance of the force of *self-interest* or *self-preservation*."[31] But Montaigne and others who were influenced by ancient Stoic attitudes often said that scorn of death is praiseworthy, and that it is only foolish and corrupt people who set store by self-preservation. Arguing that the cannibals of Brazil were less barbarous than Europeans, Montaigne claimed that their warfare was "entirely noble and magnanimous." If they captured prisoners in war, they asked only "that they should admit and acknowledge their defeat — yet there is not one prisoner in a hundred years who does not prefer to die rather than to derogate from the greatness of an invincible mind by look or by word."[32] In another passage Montaigne praised the American natives who had so bravely resisted the Spanish conquistadors. He described in the most laudatory terms how they risked all "in defence of their gods and freedom" and how they had been willing to suffer "any hardship including death" rather than submit to Spanish domination.[33] In the opinion of Charron, death is something to be not feared or avoided but embraced with equanimity. It was, he declared, "the inconsiderate vulgar sort" who thought of death as "a very great evil," whereas "wisdom itself teacheth us, that it is a freedom from all evils."[34] Only the "vulgar unlearned sot," he declared, accounts life "a sovereign good, and preferreth it above all things," while wise people do not concern themselves with delaying death but quietly accept it when it comes along. The "fear of grief and pain is natural," he said, "but not of death."[35] So skeptics like Montaigne and Charron thought that sensible people should not bother themselves much about self-preservation. The thesis that Grotius cleverly built his system on the one principle which the skeptics endorsed — the principle of self-preservation — fails, for they did not endorse it.

A second problem with the idea that Grotius aimed to refute skepticism by grounding his system on the single principle of self-preservation is that he did not ground his system on self-preservation alone. He thought that self-preservation was just one of a number of basic moral principles, agreeing in this with old-style natural-law thinkers like the Spanish Jesuit Francisco Suárez and the medieval Dominican St. Thomas Aquinas. Aquinas argued that reason and nature teach us many moral truths. Of these, some are concerned with our most fundamental tendencies. Like all other substances, said Aquinas, people strive to preserve themselves. But they also have slightly more sophisticated instincts, which they share not with all substances but only with other animals. For example, they have sex, reproduce, and bring up children. Finally, people have some inclinations which are peculiar to them alone. Unlike other animals, humans have a *rational* nature, and seek to fulfill it. Aquinas held that natural law supplies us with moral precepts linked to each of these three kinds of inclination. The most elementary principle of natural law concerned self-preservation, while others were about propagating the species, and some dealt with what was "good according to the nature of reason, which is proper to man." This last sort of natural law included precepts about society and also some religious principles, for reason (in Aquinas' view, as in that of Grotius) gives us basic information about God.[36] Suárez likewise argued that different laws of nature correspond to three different types of human inclination—toward preservation, toward procreation, and last but not least toward more refined social and spiritual goods.[37] Grotius' discussion was not significantly different. Talking about how we can discover what the law of nature commands, he argued that we can either read its injunctions off from the practice of civilized nations or deduce it from what accords with the "rational and social nature."[38] Rational and social nature did much more than tell us that we should preserve ourselves. Grotius admitted that people, like other animals, strive for self-preservation, but he claimed that many laws of nature had nothing to do with preserving our bodies. Natural laws were dictates of reason, and reason was superior to the body and its instincts. "Honesty," he said, "consists in conformity to reason," which ought to have much more weight than the things to which mere instinct leads us.[39]

So Grotius thought that nature and reason tell us a great many things that have little to do with preserving ourselves. They also prompt us to take care of our lives, and, at least normally, to prefer our own preservation to that of other people. This doctrine that we should rank our lives ahead of those of other people was perfectly conventional among old-style thinkers in the natural-law tradition. Suárez said that the right of preserving your life is the greatest of rights. Aquinas argued that every person is normally "obliged to take care for his own life rather than the lives of other people."[40] Again, there was nothing especially novel about the weight Grotius placed on the idea that people may use violence in self-defense. His discussion of this point drew heavily on traditional Catholic thinking, and he favorably cited not only Aquinas himself but also a host of more recent Thomists, including Cajetan, Soto, and Valentia.[41] Later, Hobbes *did* try to ground a moral and political theory on self-preservation. He claimed that we can never forgo the right to defend ourselves against attack, even by the sovereign of the state we live in. Grotius, on the other hand, held that individuals have no right whatever to defend themselves against the superior authority of sovereigns.[42] So the theory that Grotius revolutionized thinking about natural law by basing his views on rigorous deductions from self-preservation lacks support.

As we saw, Grotius is famous for having declared that "even if we grant" ("etiamsi daremus") that there is no God, natural law would still retain some sort of force. It is often suggested that this principle encapsulates the secular spirit of the modern theory of natural law. There are two main difficulties with this thesis. First, the idea was clearly expressed by medieval Scholastics, including the fourteenth-century thinker Gregory of Rimini.[43] There was little revolutionary or secular about a thesis that was held by Catholic Scholastic theologians. Indeed, it has been claimed that Grotius probably drew his views and his terminology on this issue from Suárez.[44] Second, not all modern theorists of natural law did in fact accept Grotius' opinion. Pufendorf, in particular, went out of his way to attack Grotius' view in the most trenchant terms, styling it "an impious and idiotic theory," and insisting that natural law was law only because God had decreed it. The idea that morality preceded God's will, he remarked, was "a horrible absurdity."[45] It is difficult to see how Grotius' doctrine can lie at the heart of the secularism of the modern school of natural law, given that it was so vigorously rejected by Pufendorf—one of the main members of that school. Pufendorf adopted a voluntaristic theory of law, arguing that strictly it was the will of a lawgiver and not conformity to some abstract standard of reason that gave law its binding force. Hobbes and Selden were also legal voluntarists.

Despite the "etiamsi daremus," Grotius himself also had a great deal to say about God, in the *De jure belli ac pacis* and elsewhere. Of course, it is possible to mention God and still to uphold views that are in some respects essentially secular. One notion about Grotius is that he boldly broke the connection between revealed religion and natural law by minimizing the relevance of the Bible to universal moral duties. According to this approach, he held that the Ten Commandments did not impose universal obligations, because they "had been given only to the Jews," and he argued that Christ had not legislated at all, but merely offered people good advice.[46] The Bible, then, added nothing whatever to what pure unaided reason could tell us about our moral obligations. Grotius, in short, cut the links with the religious and superstitious medieval past by insisting that reason alone was the basis of morality.

A major problem with this argument is that thinkers like Suárez and Aquinas also held that the law of nature consisted of the dictates of right reason, and not of any nonrational or supernatural precepts that God had revealed to Jews or Christians in Scripture.[47] Grotius' emphasis on the usefulness of reason in religious as well as moral matters led his contemporaries to suspect that he was a secret Socinian or a Catholic, not that he was a secular revolutionary. While some Protestants argued that reason was so corrupt that we could not rely on it much in moral questions, and that we should therefore turn to the

Bible for information about our ethical duties, many held that reason can tell us a great deal about natural law. Indeed, the standard view among both Catholics and Protestants was that even pagans, who know nothing whatever about Christian revelation, can find out a great deal about morals through the light of nature. St. Paul himself had remarked that the Gentiles had a law "written in their hearts" which told them what was right and wrong (Romans 2:15). Grotius' claim that the law of nature was grounded on reason, not revelation, was nothing novel, for that is precisely what the natural-law theorists of the old school had been saying for centuries. Many Protestants shared Grotius' views on the role of reason in morals. Nathaniel Culverwell's treatise on natural law was published in England under the Puritan regime of the Rump Parliament and with the imprimatur of the noted Calvinist theologian Edmund Calamy. Far from taking Grotius to task for his revolutionary secularism, Culverwell repeatedly and approvingly cited him on the law of nature along with such Catholic stalwarts of Scholasticism as Aquinas, Suárez, and Vasquez, and Protestants like Zanchius and Vossius.[48] He thought that Grotius was engaged in much the same enterprise as Thomists like Suárez and Aquinas himself. Culverwell was perfectly happy with their use of reason to elucidate morals. What worried him was the overemphasis on reason in religious matters of the Socinians, and he attacked Socinianism and Arminianism.[49] Grotius, of course, sided with the Arminians in Holland, and his rationalistic religious views led some Calvinists to suspect that he was a Socinian or a Catholic.

So there was nothing much new about Grotius' thesis that the law of nature is the law of reason, not revelation. Earlier natural-law thinkers argued that though reason tells us what is right and wrong, the Bible is a very useful supplement to its teachings, for it contains the written word of God, who is supremely rational. God says and does nothing contrary to reason, and all His acts and assertions recorded in Scripture must therefore be compatible with natural law. If God gave the Jews some particular law, for example, then it was certainly congruent with reason, though it no longer necessarily obliged modern Christians—for times change, and the law might not suit current circumstances. Some of the laws God had given the Old Testament Jews, said the old-style natural-law theorists, were restatements of unalterable natural law, while others were compatible with it, though they could be changed by later governments if this became prudent. Again, in the New Testament, Christ set down a number of laws, some of which applied only to Christians, while others were reissues of natural law. The latter included the Golden Rule ("All things whatsoever ye would that men should do to you, do ye even so to them," Matthew 7:12), which was seen as a summary of the law of nature by medieval canonists and by many later theorists, both Catholic and Protestant.[50] To sum up, the usual view of old-style natural-law thinkers was that though the law of nature is grounded on reason — as Grotius, too, grounded it — the Bible also contains important information on our duties, including reassertions of natural-law precepts, and declarations of our specifically Christian (as opposed to natural) duties.

Now, as we have seen, it has been suggested that Grotius boldly rejected such ideas, by claiming that the precepts God gave to the Jews in the Old Testament did not apply universally and that Christ did not make laws at all but only gave people advice. "In the *De iure belli ac pacis*," so the case goes, "Grotius clearly stated that neither the Decalogue nor the teachings of Christ obliged all mankind — the former had been given only to the Jews, while the latter consisted largely of advice as to how to aim at 'the highest Perfection' rather than commands which must be obeyed (Prolegomena 51; see also 1.2.9)."[51] These are very striking claims, worth considering in a little detail.

If the precepts of the Decalogue, or Ten Commandments, oblige only Jews, then it is open to Christians, Mohammedans, and others to murder, commit adultery, steal, and so on — for those are activities the Commandments prohibit. Had Grotius in fact argued that we are free to do these things, his moral theory would undoubtedly have differed in a quite revolutionary way from the ideas of his contemporaries — though whether it would have been much more modern than theirs is questionable, since it does not seem that murder and theft are generally endorsed by modern moral thinkers, and there is debate even about adultery. But insurmountable textual problems arise with the thesis that Grotius said that only the Jews were under an obligation to obey the Decalogue, and similar problems with the notion that he believed Christ only gave advice and made no laws. Firstly, the passages cited to confirm these claims do no such thing. One (Prolegomena 51)[52] is about ecclesiastical canons and seems irrelevant to the points at issue. The other (1:2:9) is on whether it is ever lawful to wage war, and, in particular, on the pacifist views of some early Christians. It says that in those ancient times some Christians were so keen to achieve the highest excellence that they "often treated divine counsels as commands."[53] Christ had made some pacifist-sounding remarks about turning the other cheek, and overenthusiastic Christians had taken his words to involve a rigid prohibition of warfare. Grotius thought that in this particular case they had misconstrued his advice as law. But that does not, of course, at all imply that Grotius thought Christ had made no laws whatever.

Still, if there were no other relevant passages in the *De jure belli ac pacis,* or elsewhere in Grotius' writings, it might not be unreasonable to suspect that he believed Christ had only advised and never legislated. The problem is that he frequently spelled out in the most explicit terms that this was *not* his belief. Just before discussing canon law in the preface (or Prolegomena) to the *De jure belli,* he talked about the ways in which he intended to use the New Testament in his analysis of the laws of war and peace, remarking that those books of the Bible showed what was lawful for Christians. Some people, he declared, thought that Christians were bound only by the law of nature, like everyone else. But he insisted that they were under an obligation to achieve higher standards than non-Christians and stressed that it was certain that "in the most sacred law" of the New Testament "greater purity of moral conduct is imposed upon us than is required of us by the law of nature alone."[54] Christ, then, *legislated* for Christians in the New Testament. Indeed, Grotius argued that Christ made laws that applied not just to Christians but to everyone. Discussing the various kinds of law near the beginning of *De jure belli ac pacis,* he distinguished natural law from voluntary divine law. Natural law could be discovered by right reason, but divine voluntary law consisted of additional commands that God had given either to one particular people (namely the Jews) or "to the human race." He asserted that such "law was given by God to the human race three times: immediately after the creation of people, again in the restoration of the human race after the Flood, and lastly in that higher restoration that took place through Christ."[55] So Christ made new laws that imposed obligations not only on Christians but also on everyone else. Scholastics like Aquinas and Suárez, and many later authors, had argued that only natural law obliges the whole human race. God's positive laws, they said, applied only to the Old Testament Jews and (in the case of Christ's legislation) to Christians. As the great theorist of the early German Enlightenment Christian Thomasius noted, Grotius seems to have been the first writer to claim that Christ's laws bound not just Christians, but everyone.[56] Thomasius did not find anything particularly secular in Grotius' notion that anyone who hears of Christ's decrees has a duty to obey them. Grotius firmly rejected the claim that "we are no further bound by the laws of Christ" than by natural law and emphasized that "Christian law" forbids such things as concubinage, divorce, and polygamy, which natural law had permitted.[57]

Grotius did *not* say that the Ten Commandments laid obligations only on Jews. Like earlier natural-law thinkers, he argued that the laws of the Old Testament are fully compatible with natural law.[58] And like them, he claimed that much of what they said was a restatement of natural law, which applied not just to the Jews but to all peoples in all times and places. He argued, for instance, that the first four of the Ten Commandments — on our duties to God (Exodus 20:3–10) — provide a summary of the "true religion which is common to all ages."[59] So four of the Ten Commandments applied universally.

Elsewhere, he insisted that the rest of the commandments were also precepts of natural law. "Thou shalt not kill," "Thou shalt not steal" and the rest, he asserted, "were not *only* declarations of natural law," but also added a new obligation to the old natural duty.[60] Jews who disobeyed these decrees after God Himself had promulgated them through Moses were guilty not just of acting wickedly (by doing something against the law of nature) but also of disobeying a specific divine prohibition. It has been argued, on the strength of this passage, that Grotius believed that the Ten Commandments were *not* natural laws (applying to everyone) but merely instructions which God had given to the Jews alone.[61] But Grotius was at pains to spell out here that they *were* natural laws. Misreadings of his position on the relation between Christ's laws — he *did* think Christ legislated — or the Ten Commandments, and natural law do not serve to show that he was a revolutionary secularist.

The modern theory of natural law — as opposed to more traditional theories — is sometimes said to have been minimalist as well as secularist. In other words, modern thinkers like Grotius not only approached the law of nature in a daringly secular way but also boldly reduced its precepts to a very few obligations. Rejecting the notion that the Ten Commandments were statements of natural law, so the case goes, Grotius painted "an extremely minimal picture of the natural moral life" that excitingly liberated people "from a weight of moral and juridical dogmas."[62] At the center of his moral vision, the argument proceeds, was the principle that "it had to be literally inconceivable that things could be otherwise for an action to be properly part of the natural law."[63] If Grotius really had adopted this principle, he certainly would have revolutionized moral theory. All sorts of practices are conceivable and so, according to this interpretation of Grotius, are not condemned by natural law. Subjecting husbands to wives, and fighting unjust wars, for example, are both perfectly conceivable. Therefore, if this account of his theory were correct, he could not have argued that husbands hold power over their wives by the law of nature. But he did.[64] Again, Grotius claimed that we should fight only just wars, and he spent much of *De jure belli ac pacis* discussing what the just grounds of warfare are and what may justly be done in the course of the fighting. The third book, for instance, begins with a chapter on "general rules from the law of nature on what is lawful in war, in which trickery and lying are discussed."[65] But it is manifest that unjust wars are conceivable, as are trickery and lying in warfare. Indeed, they are not just conceivable; they regularly happen. Clearly, then, Grotius did *not* hold that the law of nature can give us information only on that tiny category of practices whose negatives are "literally inconceivable." As we have seen, he argued that we can deduce natural law from the practices of civilized nations and ignore the deviance of depraved peoples. But patently, what the corrupt nations do *is* conceivable, and so cannot be a breach of natural law — if that law really is composed only of things that cannot conceivably be otherwise. In fact, what Grotius argued was that natural law consists of precepts that follow *necessarily* from human nature, and not of principles which it might merely be useful or convenient for us to adopt in some circumstances.[66] This was a perfectly conventional position, and no traditional natural-law thinker appears to have supposed anything else. Suárez, for example, talked of natural laws as obvious first principles of nature and reason, and precepts drawn from them by "evident necessity."[67] Like Suárez and others, Grotius held that the laws of nature were deducible from a few principles, but he did not argue that the conclusions which could be drawn from those principles were minimal in number, and (as we have seen) he accepted the traditional view that most of the Decalogue summarized natural laws. True, he thought that polygamy and divorce were permitted by natural law. But there was nothing particularly original about this. For instance, St. Ambrose and the medieval Scholastic Durandus of St.-Pourçain had argued that polygamy is not contrary to nature, and the leading German reformers Philip Melanchthon and Martin Bucer adopted the same position.[68] Nor did Grotius intend to promote sexual freedom; indeed, he insisted that Christ had ended earlier liberties in such matters: polygamy and divorce were now wrong, and experimentation in these areas was no longer an option.[69] If we are looking for an early modern apostle of minimalist morality, Rabelais — with his Abbey of Thélème and its single rule, "Do what you want" ("Fay ce que vouldras"),[70] fits the bill much better than the rather staid Grotius, and his massive *De jure belli ac pacis,* which is packed full of rules.

The modern theory of natural law, it is sometimes suggested, was also individualistic. Grotius, who did talk about the rights of individuals and groups, often preferred to investigate moral questions in terms of rights rather than duties. It is not clear that this involved much significant change to the substance of earlier discussions, for commonly it does not greatly matter whether we view things in terms of your duty or my right. For instance, whether we analyze my right to be told the truth by you, or your duty to tell me it, we will be examining largely one and the same problem. Rights, Pufendorf later asserted, imply correlative duties on the part of others.[71] Though Grotius had much to say about the rights of individuals under natural law, he spelled out that they are subordinate to the public good. In a case of the greatest necessity, one individual could take what belonged to another. But governments had the additional right of taking the individual's property where "public utility" required such a course.[72] Public rights trumped private ones in Grotius' system.

A final claim commonly made about the modern theory of natural law is that it was radical. But Grotius was careful to reject radical political ideas, insisting rather that we must abide by old constitutional arrangements. If a people had set up a government on terms that were highly disadvantageous to itself, he insisted, they were nevertheless obliged to obey it. In the late sixteenth century some old-style Calvinist and Catholic thinkers had argued that sovereignty resides in the people and that if a king rules in a way that conflicts with the public good, he may be violently resisted. The author of the famous Calvinist pamphlet *Vindiciae contra tyrannos* (1579) argued that if a king misruled, he could be disciplined by "inferior magistrates"—nobles and officeholders—acting on the people's behalf. Some other Calvinists agreed. Grotius went out of his way to reject their claims and denied that "inferior magistrates" had any such power. He stressed that kings may not be resisted even if they act against the public good, and he permitted resistance only in the most extreme circumstances.[73] In 1644 Grotius' conservatism led Samuel Rutherford—an old-style Calvinist, who defended resistance to Charles I—to class Grotius among royal absolutists—or, as he put it, "anti-magistratical royalists" (that is to say, royalists who denied that lesser magistrates held any power independently from the king).[74] His conservatism likewise caused the radical Jean-Jacques Rousseau to class him with Hobbes as an apologist for tyranny.[75]

So Grotius was neither a radical nor an individualist. His ideas on natural law were no more secularist, rationalist, or minimalist than those of earlier writers. Nor was his main aim to refute the thinking of skeptics like Montaigne. But, we are told, the members of the modern school of natural law were antiskeptical, secularist, individualist, minimalist radicals. It follows that Grotius cannot have been a member of that school, let alone its founder. If its members were Grotians, Grotius was no Grotian. So who *was* the first Grotian? The answer might seem to be John Selden, for his main work on natural law was published in 1640, before the political writings of other candidates, like Hobbes, were printed.

Selden

Selden's *De iure naturali & gentium, iuxta disciplinam Ebraeorum, libri septem* (Seven books on the law of nature and nations according to the teaching of the Hebrews) was licensed for the press by Archbishop Laud's chaplain in 1639 and printed the following year. In 1631 Selden had published *De successionibus ad leges Ebraeorum in bona defunctorum* (On inheritance of the goods of the dead, according to the laws of the Hebrews), which was reissued with a dedication to Laud in 1636 and 1638. In 1646 his *Uxor*

Ebraica: seu, De nuptiis & divortiis ex jure civili, id est divino & Talmudico veterum Ebraeorum, libri tres (The Hebrew wife; or, three books on marriage and divorce according to the civil law, that is, divine and Talmudic law, of the ancient Hebrews). Between 1650 and 1655, the three volumes of Selden's *De synedriis & praefecturis juridicis veterum Ebraeorum* (On the Sanhedrins and juridical offices of the ancient Hebrews) were published. At first glance, this list suggests that Selden was interested in ancient Hebrew institutions and attitudes, and wrote a number of books about them. The *De iure naturali & gentium*, we might suppose, was one of a series of works intended to cast light on Judaism. That does, indeed, seem to be how the work was read by contemporaries. The book was frequently cited on ancient Jewish traditions. No one, however, seems to have recognized that its purpose was to refute the skepticism of Montaigne and Charron. Nor does anyone appear to have observed that it introduced a revolutionary new theory of morality. Indeed, Pufendorf himself read the book as an account of ancient Jewish ideas. Discussing the writings of his predecessors in the field of natural law, he remarked that Selden "might possibly have held a position second to none, if he had set himself to apply the law of nature to all mankind with the same akribeia [precision] as he did to the traditions of the Hebrews; or if the decisions of a single nation could have been regarded a sufficient proclamation of a law that would obligate all nations."[76] Pufendorf and the rest can easily be forgiven for supposing that Selden's massive and learned tome was intended to describe Jewish tradition. The book's title suggests as much, and individual chapters confirm the suspicion, discussing such things as slavery among the Jews, Jewish attitudes toward the Samaritans, Jewish marriage rites, Jewish coinage (illustrated with woodcuts), the Herodian dynasty (with a family tree), and a vast number of other things closely linked to Jewish antiquities but perfectly irrelevant to expounding a stunningly modern, secular, and minimalist theory of natural law.[77] The text is larded with many extensive Hebrew quotations and reads very much like a work of Hebraic scholarship. Yet it has recently been suggested that the purpose of the book was to refute skepticism and continue the Grotian revolution in moral theorizing.

According to Richard Tuck, Selden in *De iure naturali* "clearly signalled that his intention was to answer the sceptic by finding a minimal set of moral beliefs which as a matter of fact all societies and philosophers would agree on—precisely the same enterprise upon which Grotius had embarked. The late seventeenth-century view that Selden was the first major follower of Grotius was absolutely correct."[78] These claims are open to several objections. First, it is not clear that anyone in the late seventeenth century saw Selden as a follower of Grotius. Although Tuck talks of "late seventeenth-century historiographers" who adopted this view, he does not name any of them except Pufendorf. He informs us that Pufendorf saw Selden and Hobbes as the "principal followers of Grotius."[79] But although Pufendorf did indeed regard the two Englishmen as thinkers who had said important things about natural law, he did *not* claim that they were disciples of Grotius.[80] Nor did he read Selden's work as an attack on skepticism or an attempt to base a new moral theory on a minimal set of principles that all peoples could endorse. Indeed, he criticized Selden precisely for *failing* to construct any such basis for natural law. "Selden," he asserted, "does not deduce natural law from any principle or hypothesis for which the evidence is acknowledged by all nations, or which they could be brought to acknowledge by arguments drawn from the light of reason." Instead of outlining any such principles, he continued, Selden merely documented what Jewish tradition had to say about the seven precepts of the sons of Noah (or humans in general), which Jews regarded as the fundamental rules of morality. Selden, he remarked, only "expounds what Hebrew scholars thought; he does not sufficiently examine whether their opinion accords with sound reason."[81] If Tuck's account is correct, Pufendorf deeply misconstrued the nature of Selden's enterprise.

In fact, Pufendorf was quite right to regard Selden's book as primarily a description of Jewish attitudes. But Selden did occasionally compare Jewish with Christian ideas on natural law, and at one point he discussed some skeptical views about morality. According to the Jews, he said, the law of nature cannot reliably be derived from the actual practice of nations, nor does it simply consist of precepts deduced by pure, unaided human reason.[82] Selden argued that Jewish tradition on both these points was well grounded. In order to support the claim that the customs of nations are not a reliable guide to natural law, he quoted Carneades' remark that people arrange things according to their own convenience and that it is foolish to act otherwise, since if you follow some abstract notion of justice instead of your own interests, you will harm yourself and benefit others. Selden declared that people commonly call things that are advantageous to them good and just, though they are not in fact so. The practices that nations have described as just are therefore no guide to what justice actually is. Moreover, many nations have plainly flouted natural justice even on such central matters as incest and homicide.[83] Selden considered the idea that we can read off natural law from the customs of the more civilized nations, if not of absolutely all nations. He rejected it on the grounds that it is impossible to establish which peoples are the more civilized. Furthermore, philosophers of even the greatest nations had favored quite exotic practices. Plato supported communism, for instance, and Zeno permitted a man to have intercourse with his mother. Selden concluded that Jewish tradition was correct in rejecting the notion that the customs of nations tell us what natural law is.[84] Although he did not mention Grotius in this section of his book, Selden's case is evidently diametrically opposed to that of the Dutchman, who claimed that the activities of the nations, or at least of the more civilized of them (both he and Selden used exactly the same term for these: "gentes moratiores"), *could* inform us what the law of nature was.

Grotius argued that even if there were no God, human reason would be sufficient to enlighten us on our natural duties. Selden observed that Jewish tradition had viewed unaided reason as fallible, and he endorsed this position, noting that different philosophical schools reached widely differing conclusions, though all employed reason.[85] Moreover, reason alone could not create a genuine law. Laws imposed obligations on those to whom they applied, but reason only "persuades and demonstrates; it does not command, nor does it oblige anyone to carry out a duty, unless it is accompanied by the authority of someone who is superior to the person being commanded."[86] In the case of natural law, he claimed, this superior was God, and he noted that the Hebrews, the Fathers of the Christian Church, and many Roman lawyers agreed in regarding the laws of nature as divine commandments.[87] Moreover, he observed, precisely the same view was to be found in the works of more recent theologians. As evidence for the point, he quoted approvingly from the writings of the Jesuit Luís de Molina and cited Aquinas, Suárez, and other Scholastics.[88] Our obligation to obey natural law, argued Selden, derives not from the law's rationality, but from the fact that God has commanded it. This looks very much as though it flatly contradicts the notion that natural law would oblige even if we grant—*etiamsi daremus*—that there is no God. It is also difficult to see what is specifically modern and secular about a principle that Aquinas and other Scholastics endorsed. Though Selden was mainly concerned to elucidate Jewish traditions, he did deviate a little from that task in order to criticize some of Grotius' central claims, not to follow them.

Having established that Jewish tradition derived natural law from God's command rather than from unaided reason, Selden went on to investigate Jewish ideas on how the Deity had in fact communicated the contents of the law to humans. The Jews claimed that God had given people the fundamental principles of morality—the seven precepts of the sons of Noah—at the creation, and again after the Flood. This, said Selden, could be understood in two different ways. First, it could mean that God provided them with the information on those occasions, and that they then passed it on to their descendants by word of mouth. Second, it could signify that God had constructed the human soul in such a way that people, provided that they did not fall into corrupt ways, would naturally recognize moral truths.[89] In ancient and medieval philosophy, he noted, God was said to have communicated moral knowledge to people by means of the *intellectus agens* or "agent intellect." The Hebrews had regarded the agent intellect not as a part or faculty of the human soul but as a divine emanation, which flowed into us from God Himself. Early Christians adopted the same view, but from the thirteenth century onward the alternative attitude began to prevail among Christian writers. Thinkers like Albertus Magnus, Aquinas, Alexander of Hales, and Bonaventure claimed that the active intellect *was* part of the soul. However, proceeded Selden, even these authors agreed that God continually helped and informed the active intellect; thus both the Christian and the Jewish traditions endorsed the fundamental principle that God is the source of our moral knowledge.[90] According to Richard Tuck, Selden thought that the agent intellect was not a faculty of the soul but "a god or angel, capable of giving illumination to the human mind."[91] The textual warrant for this is obscure, and it seems strange that the archbishop's chaplain would have licensed a polytheistic book, which posited as many gods as there are humans. Moreover, it looks odd that one of the founding fathers of a startlingly modern, minimalist, and secular moral theory should populate the world with so many invisible gods and angels.

Selden, claims Tuck, said that it "was the posterity of Noah through Shem who were particularly open to the operation of this divine light, and it was therefore in their doctrines that other peoples would find the clearest and most accurate account of what God had decreed so long ago."[92] This Judaizing doctrine would be strange in a book by a purported Christian, were it present. But all Selden actually says is that the Jews maintained this view, citing the twelfth-century Rabbi Judah Halevi to prove the point.[93] The thesis that Selden was a moral minimalist is open to a similar objection. He did, indeed, confine his discussion to just seven main moral principles. But that is because the Jewish tradition did precisely the same thing. His book is about the seven precepts of the sons of Noah because the Jews thought those precepts were natural law. He learnedly describes their attitudes, telling us what they thought about the prohibition on eating limbs taken from live animals (the seventh precept), for example, and giving us information on their attitudes toward eating blood, and strangled animals.[94] Nowhere did he hint that he wanted contemporary Europeans to adopt Jewish practices on such matters, or that he thought a modern, secular, minimalist universal morality could somehow be deduced from them.

It is no easier, then, to find the key doctrines of the modern school of natural law in Selden's book about Jewish traditions than in Grotius' work on the laws of war and peace. But we can quite easily find large traces of the older, Scholastic approach to natural law in both writers. Grotius not only adopted Scholastic terminology in talking about the law of nature but also cited Scholastics frequently and favorably. At the very beginning of his discussion of law in *De jure praedae,* he drew on Aquinas to confirm the idea that *"what God has shown to be His Will, that is law,"*[95] and he cited St. Thomas and other Schoolmen repeatedly in the pages that followed. If he wrote the *De jure praedae* in order to start an anti-Scholastic revolution in moral theory, he was strangely silent about the fact and seems to have disguised it from himself as well as his contemporaries. In the *De jure belli ac pacis* he again drew extensively on Scholastics, and in the course of surveying the various kinds of writing that were useful in understanding moral theory, he turned specifically to medieval Schoolmen, arguing that there were "many things to be praised" in them. Given the dark times in which they had lived, he said, it was not surprising if they sometimes made mistakes, "but where they consent on questions of morals they scarcely ever err."[96] This does not look like a particularly revolutionary attitude, and it contrasts strongly with the views of someone like Hobbes, who thought that Scholastic thinking was thoroughly flawed. It is rather similar, though, to the approach of Selden. In the *De iure naturali* he displayed an extensive knowledge of Scholastic writings on natural law, favorably citing such recent Jesuits as Adam Contzen, Juan Azor, Francisco Suárez, and Robert Bellarmine, as well as a host of earlier authors.[97] He nowhere hinted that there had been a Grotian moral revolution to which he had contributed. But he did remark that "Popish Bookes teach and informe what wee knowe; we know much [out] of them; ye ffathers; Church story, Schoolmen; all may passe for popish Bookes and If you take away them: what learning will you leave?" "Without schoole Divinity," he said, "a Divine knowes nothing Logically, nor will bee able to satisfye a rationall man out of the pulpit." "The Jesuites," he declared, "& the Lawyers of ffrance & the Low Country men have engrossed all learning, the rest of the world make nothing but Homilies."[98]

Grotius and Selden seem to have approved rather than disapproved of Scholasticism. They used Scholastic vocabulary in talking about natural law. What they said about it disqualifies them for membership in the modern school of natural law. But on many points they held views that were close to, or the same as, those of the old school. They used old-style language about natural law, not to disguise the startlingly innovatory nature of their ideas about it but because the ideas were mostly old-style too. If we want to find the founder of the modern school, we must look to others than Grotius and Selden. Or perhaps there was no such school.

Notes

1. Richard Tuck, "The 'Modern' School of Natural Law," in Anthony Pagden, ed., *The Languages of Political Theory in Early-Modern Europe* (Cambridge: Cambridge University Press, 1987), 99–119.

2. Tuck, *Philosophy and Government, 1572–1651* (Cambridge: Cambridge University Press, 1993), xiv–xv.

3. Ibid., xv.

4. Thomas Hobbes, *Elements of Philosophy. The first section, concerning body,* in *The English Works of Thomas Hobbes,* ed. Sir William Molesworth, 11 vols. (1839–45), 1:ix; cf. *Thomae Hobbes . . . Opera philosophica quae Latine scripsit omnia,* 5 vols. (1839–45), 1:cv.

5. Samuel Pufendorf, *De jure naturae et gentium libri octo,* 2 vols. (Oxford: Clarendon Press, 1934); vol. 1: Latin text of 1688 edition; vol. 2: English translation by C. H. and W. A. Oldfather, 2:viii, v–vi.

6. Grotius read Hobbes's *De cive* in 1643 and reported to his brother that "what he says in favor of kings pleases me. But I cannot approve of the foundations on which he has built his judgments. He thinks that by nature there is war between all men, and he says some other things which do not accord with my views. For he thinks that it is the duty of every private individual to follow the religion approved in his country, if not by assent at least by obedience. And there are some other things which I cannot approve. I do not think that the book is for sale, but I will inquire. I will be glad if the king's cause is defended as it ought to be, and have written some things pertaining to that matter to D. Reigersbergius." ("Placent quae pro Regibus dicit. Fundamenta tamen quibus suas sententias superstruit, probare non possum. Putat inter homines a natura esse bellum & alia quaedam habet nostris non congruentia. Nam & privati cujusque officium putat sequi Religionem in patria sua probatam, si non assensu, at obsequio. Sunt & alia quaedam quae probare non possum. Librum non puto venalem esse, sed inquiram. Gaudebo si causa Regis ita ut oportet defendatur: quam ad rem pertinentia quaedam scripsi ad D. Reigersbergium.") Hugo Grotius, *Epistolae quotquot reperiri potuerunt* (Amsterdam, 1687), 951–52. Richard Tuck, *Philosophy and Government,* 200, construes the last sentence as meaning, "'I will be glad if the King's cause can be defended in this way,'" which suggests that Grotius thought Hobbes's arguments might work, though he was uncertain about this. But "ita ut oportet" means "as it ought to be," and Grotius is here saying that Hobbes has not adequately defended kings and expressing the hope that someone else will do so.

7. So far, fifteen volumes have come out in the collected correspondence of Grotius: Hugo Grotius, *Briefwisseling,* ed. P. C. Molhuysen et al., 15 vols. (The Hague, 1928–96).

8. A. P. D'Entrèves, *Natural Law: An Introduction to Legal Philosophy* (New Brunswick, N.J.: Transaction Publishers, 1994; originally published in 1951), 55.

9. Grotius, *De jure belli ac pacis* (Amsterdam, 1689), viii; Prolegomena 11: "etiamsi daremus, quod sine summo scelere dari nequit, non esse Deum."

10. J. B. Schneewind, "Locke's Moral Philosophy," in Vere Chappell, ed., *The Cambridge Companion to Locke* (Cambridge: Cambridge University Press, 1994), 199–225, at 209, 210–11.

11. Knud Haakonssen, *Natural Law and Moral Philosophy from Grotius to the Scottish Enlightenment* (Cambridge: Cambridge University Press, 1996), 29.

12. D'Entrèves, *Natural Law,* 55. However, Schneewind in "Locke's moral philosophy," 212, adopts what may be a different stance, claiming that "the whole Grotian project" was to derive "a natural law morality from propositions capable of being defended on empirical grounds."

13. D'Entrèves, *Natural Law,* 56.

14. Ibid., 57–62.

15. Ibid., 60.

16. Tuck, *Philosophy and Government,* 175–76.

17. Ibid., 51.

18. Tuck, "The 'Modern' School of Natural Law," 109; *Philosophy and Government,* 173, 304.

19. Haakonssen, *Natural Law and Moral Philosophy,* 24–25.

20. Tuck, *Philosophy and Government,* 214–15.

21. Grotius, *De jure belli ac pacis,* iv, xi–xii; Prolegomena 5, 16–18; a similar passage appears in Grotius, *De jure praedae commentarius: Commentary on the Law of Prize and Booty,* trans. Gwladys L. Williams with the collaboration of Walter H. Zeydel, 2 vols. (Oxford: Clarendon Press, 1950), 1:9–13. Grotius wrote the *De jure praedae* at the request of the Dutch East India Company between 1604 and 1606. It was first published in 1868.

22. G. I. A. D. Draper, "Grotius' place in the development of legal ideas about war," in Hedley Bull, Benedict Kingsbury, and Adam Roberts, eds., *Hugo Grotius and International Relations* (Oxford: Clarendon Press, 1990), 177–207, at 200.

23. Grotius, *De jure belli ac pacis,* xvii–xviii; Prolegomena 28: "Cur de eo instituerem scriptionem causas habui multas ac graves. Videbam per Christianum orbem vel barbaris gentibus pudendam bellandi licentiam: levibus aut nullis de causis ad arma procurri, quibus semel sumtis nullam jam divini, nullam humani juris reverentia."

24. Ibid., xviii; Prolegomena 29.

25. Ibid., xviii; Prolegomena 30.

26. Tuck, "The 'Modern' School of Natural Law," 109.

27. Michel de Montaigne, *The Essays,* translated and edited by M. A. Screech (London: Allen Lane/New York: Penguin Press, 1991), 676, n. 458; from *Essays* 2:12, "An Apology for Raymond Sebond," the classic statement of Montaigne's skepticism.

28. Pierre Gassendi, *Dissertations en forme de paradoxes contre les Aristotéliciens (Exercitationes Paradoxiae Adversus Aristoteleos), Livres I et II,* edited and translated by Bernard Rochot (Paris: Vrin), 1963, 436–37. Gassendi's work was first published in 1624.

29. Grotius, *De jure belli ac pacis,* 14; 1:12:1: "Certe probabiliter admodum, juris naturalis esse colligitur id, quod apud omnes gentes, aut moratiores omnes tales esse creditur. Nam universalis effectus universalem requirit causam."

30. Ibid., 15–16; 1:1:12:2.

31. Tuck, *Philosophy and Government,* 51, 62.

32. Montaigne, *Essays,* ed. Screech, 236–37; this is from 1:31, "On the Cannibals."

33. Ibid., 1030; from 3:6, "On Coaches."

34. Pierre Charron, *Of wisdome. Three bookes* (London, c. 1612), 330.

35. Ibid., 114, 336.

36. St. Thomas Aquinas, *Summa Theologica,* ed. J.-P. Migne, 4 vols. (Paris: Garnier, 1872–82), 2:722–23; 1a2ae, q. 94, art. 2, resp. "Tertio modo inest homini inclinatio ad bonum secundum naturam rationis, quae est sibi propria." Grotius set out his views on what reason tells us about religion in his *De veritate religionis Christianae* of 1627, arguing that Christianity is more rational than other religions. Aquinas mounted a similar case in *Summa contra gentiles.*

37. Francisco Suárez, *Tractatus de legibus ac Deo legislatore* (Naples: Typis Fibrenianis, 1872), 1:108; 2:8:1. This book was first published at Coimbra in 1612.

38. Grotius, *De jure belli ac pacis,* 14; 1:1:12:1. "Cum natura rationali ac sociali."

39. Ibid., 26; 1:2:1:2. "At post haec cognita sequi notionem convenientiae rerum cum ipsa ratione, quae corpore est potior, atque eam convenientiam, in qua honestum sit propositum, pluris faciendam, quam ad quae sola primum animi appetitio ferebatur."

40. Suárez, *De iuramento fidelitatis,* ed. L. Pereña, V. Abril, and C. Baciero, with A. Garcia and C. Villanueva (Madrid, 1978, 75). This book is chapter 6 of *Defensio fidei catholicae,* which was first published in 1613; the passage is at 4:5). Aquinas, *Summa Theologica,* 2:511; 2a2ae, q. 64, art. 7, resp.: "Plus tenetur homo vitae suae providere quam vitae alienae."

41. Grotius, *De jure belli ac pacis,* 164; 2:1:3–4.

42. Grotius, *De imperio summarum potestatum circa sacra. Commentarius posthumus* (Paris 1647), 45.

43. The medieval background to Grotius' "etiamsi daremus" is discussed in J. St. Leger, *The "Etiamsi Daremus" of Hugo Grotius* (Rome, 1962).

44. W. von Leyden in his edition of John Locke's *Essays on the Law of Nature* (Oxford: Clarendon Press, 1954), 53–54, n. 2.

45. Pufendorf, *De jure naturae et gentium libri octo,* 2:215; 2:3:19; *Eris Scandica, qua adversus libros de jure naturali et gentium objecta diluuntur,* (Frankfurt-am-Main, 1686), 31: "horribile absurdum."

46. Tuck, *Philosophy and Government,* 194; "The Civil Religion of Thomas Hobbes," in Nicholas Phillipson and Quentin Skinner, eds., *Political Discourse in Early Modern Britain* (Cambridge: Cambridge University Press, 1993), 120–38, at 130.

47. Aquinas, 1a2ae, q. 94. Suárez, *De legibus,* 1:96; 2:5:10.

48. Nathaniel Culverwell, *An elegant and learned discourse of the light of nature* (London, 1652), e.g., 14, 15, 20–21, 39, 48, 127, 202.

49. Ibid., 2, 6–7.

50. John Laird, *Hobbes* (London, 1934), 179–80, n. 4.

51. Tuck, *Philosophy and Government,* 194.

52. Grotius, *De jure belli ac pacis,* xxx–xxxi.

53. Ibid., 59–62: "Saepe consilia divina pro praeceptis amplecterentur."

54. Ibid., xxx; Prolegomena, 50: "Pro certo habens in illa sanctissima lege majorem nobis sanctimoniam praecipi, quam solum per se jus naturae exigat."

55. Ibid., 1:1:15:2, "humano generi": "Humano generi ter jus datum a Deo reperimus: statim post hominem conditum, iterum in reparatione humani generis post diluvium, postremo in sublimiori reparatione per Christum."

56. Christian Thomasius, *Dissertationum Academicarum varii inprimis iuridici argumenti, tomus primus* (Halle, 1773), 289.

57. Ibid., 37; 1:2:6:2, "Christiana lex": "Sed non ulterius nos obligari legibus Christi quam ad ea quae jus naturae per se obligat, cur concedam, non video."

58. Ibid., 23; 1:1:17:2.

59. Ibid., 542–43; 2:20:45:1–2: "Religionem veram, quae omnium aetatum communis est, quatuor praecipue pronunciatis niti. . . . Haec quatuor totidem decalogi praeceptis explicantur."

60. Grotius, *Opera Theologica*, 3 vols. (Amsterdam, 1678), 3:212. "Nam lex Divina Decalogi dicens Iudaeo *non occides, non furaberis* & quae sequuntur, non solum declaravit quid juris esset naturalis, sed ipso praecepto obligationem novam priori addidit, ita ut Iudaeus contra faciens non eo tantum peccaret, quod actum commiteret vitiosum, sed etiam quod vetitum." In his *Explicatio decalogi ut Graece exstat* (Amsterdam, 1640), 75, Grotius argued that the Ten Commandments consisted of the most basic precepts forbidding activities that undermined piety and human society; only the prohibition against working on the seventh day was given to the Hebrews rather than to all people (ibid., 60).

61. Tuck, *Philosophy and Government*, 188.

62. Ibid., 176, 174.

63. Ibid., 190.

64. Ibid., 237–38; 2:5:8:1–2.

65. Ibid., 637; 3:1: "Quantum in bello liceat, regulae generales ex jure naturae: ubi & de dolis & mendacio."

66. Grotius, *Opera Theologica*, 3:311.

67. Suárez, *De legibus*, 93; 2:5:2, "evidenti necessitate."

68. M. R. Sommerville, *Sex and Subjection: Attitudes Towards Women in Early Modern Society* (London: Edward Arnold, 1995), 163.

69. Grotius, *De jure belli ac pacis*, 37; 1:2:6:2.

70. François Rabelais, *Oeuvres*, ed. Jacques Boulanger and Lucien Scheler (Paris: Pléiade, 1955), 159 (*Gargantua*, chap. 57).

71. Pufendorf, *De jure naturae et gentium libri octo*, 2:125; 1:7:13.

72. Grotius, *De jure belli ac pacis*, 853; 3:20:7:1; cf. 82; 1:3:6:2; 406; 2:14:7, "publicam utilitatem."

73. Ibid., 83–98 (1:3:8), 137–50 (1:4:6–7).

74. Samuel Rutherford, *Lex rex. The law and the prince: a dispute for the just prerogative of king and people* (London 1644). The title page, asserts that the book is written against "the ruinous grounds of W. Barclay, H. Grotius, H. Arnisoeus, Ant. de Domi P. Bishop of Spalata, and of other late anti-magistratical royalists."

75. Jean-Jacques Rousseau, *The Social Contract*, bk. 1, chap. 2, in *The Social Contract and Discourses*, trans. and ed. G. D. H. Cole, J. H. Brumfitt, and John C. Hall (London, J. M. Dent and Sons, 1973), 166–67.

76. Pufendorf, *De jure naturae et gentium libri octo*, vi (Preface); cf. *Eris Scandica*, 200–201.

77. John Selden, *De iure naturali & gentium, iuxta disciplinam Ebraeorum* (London 1640), 171–84, 197, 558–60, 641.

78. Tuck, *Philosophy and Government,* 214–15.

79. Tuck, "The 'Modern' School of Natural Law," 106.

80. Pufendorf, *De jure naturae et gentium libri octo,* vi (Preface); *Eris Scandica,* 200–206.

81. Pufendorf, *Eris Scandica,* 201: "Deinde *Seldenus* legem naturalem non deducit ex tali aliquo principio aut hypothesi, cujus evidentiam omnes nationes agnoscant, aut ad quam agnsocendam argumentis ex rationes lumine petitis adduci queant. Nam fundamenti loco substernit septem illa praecepta Noachidarum, quorum autoritas apud Judaeos antiqua traditione nitebatur." "Denique & illud tantum agit *Seldenus,* ut quid Doctores Ebraeorum senserint, exponat; quam accurate autem istorum sententia cum sana ratione congruat, parum examinet."

82. Selden, *De iure naturali & gentium,* 83, 88.

83. Ibid., 80–82.

84. Ibid., 82–90.

85. Ibid., 88, 91–92.

86. Ibid., 92–93: "Quin Ratio, quatenus talis solum & simplex, suadet & demonstrat, non jubet aut ad officium, nisi superioris eo qui jubetur accedat autoritas, obligat."

87. Ibid., 95.

88. Ibid., 102.

89. Ibid., 109.

90. Ibid., 115–16.

91. Tuck, *Philosophy and Government,* 216.

92. Ibid.

93. Selden, *De iure naturali & gentium,* 117: "Praesentiam illam divinam, seu Juris naturalis Lumen Sethianis in posteris Adae & Semianis in posteris Noachis prae aliis maxime volunt affulsisse." He says nothing to hint that he endorses this opinion.

94. Ibid., 783–91.

95. Grotius, *De jure praedae commentarius,* 1:8.

96. Grotius, *De jure belli ac pacis,* xxxi; Prolegomena 52: "multa laudanda." "Tamen ubi in re morum consentiunt, vix est ut errent."

97. Selden, *De iure naturali & gentium,* at 108, e.g.

98. Selden, *Table Talk,* ed. Sir Frederick Pollock (London: Quaritch, 1927), 23, 80, 71.

Index

354   *Index*